KINGDOM COME™

Dedicated to
CHRISTOPHER REEVE
*who makes us believe
that a man can fly.*

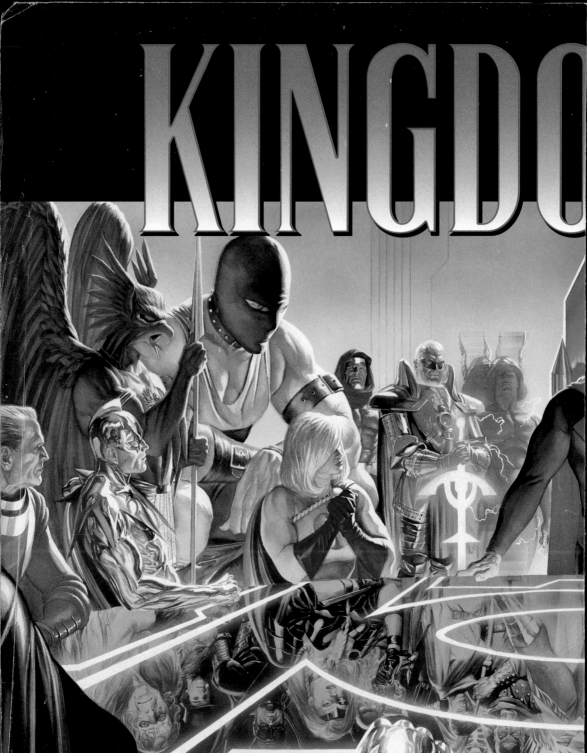

KINGDO

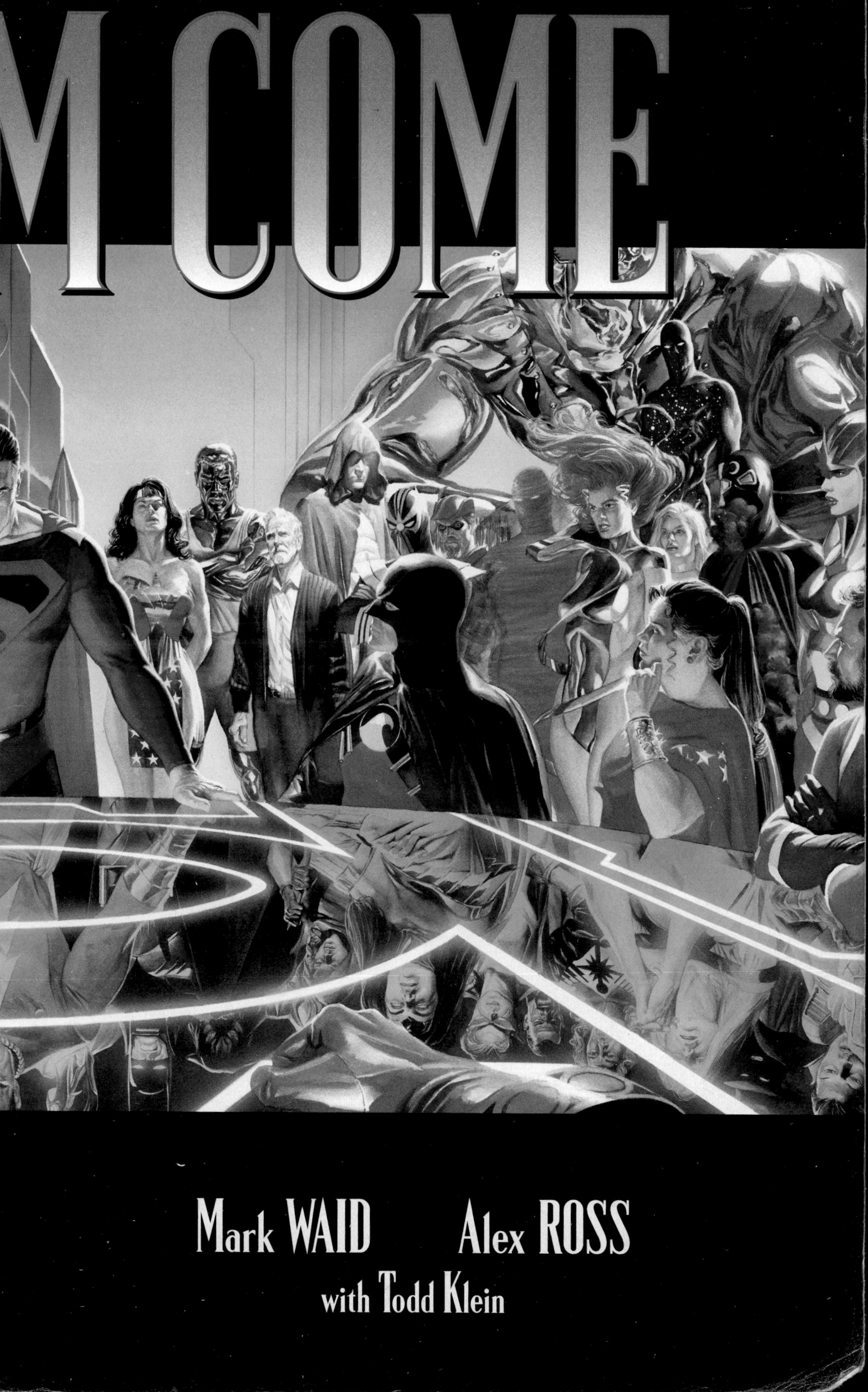
M COME

Mark WAID Alex ROSS
with Todd Klein

TABLE OF CONTENTS

Dan Raspler
Editor – Original Series

Peter J. Tomasi
Assistant Editor – Original Series

Bob Kahan
Editor

Jim Spivey
Associate Editor

Robbin Brosterman
Design Director – Books

Graphitti Designs/J. Beatman
Publication Design

Bob Harras
Senior VP – Editor-in-Chief,
DC Comics

Diane Nelson
President

Dan DiDio and **Jim Lee**
Co-Publishers

Geoff Johns
Chief Creative Officer

John Rood
Executive VP – Sales, Marketing
& Business Development

Amy Genkins
Senior VP – Business
& Legal Affairs

Nairi Gardiner
Senior VP – Finance

Jeff Boison
VP – Publishing Planning

Mark Chiarello
VP – Art Direction & Design

John Cunningham
VP – Marketing

Terri Cunningham
VP – Editorial Administration

Alison Gill
Senior VP – Manufacturing
& Operations

Hank Kanalz
Senior VP – Vertigo &
Integrated Publishing

Jay Kogan
VP – Business &
Legal Affairs, Publishing

Jack Mahan
VP – Business Affairs, Talent

Nick Napolitano
VP – Manufacturing Administration

Sue Pohja
VP – Book Sales

Courtney Simmons
Senior VP – Publicity

Bob Wayne
Senior VP – Sales

KINGDOM COME

Published by DC Comics. Cover, introduction and additional
material Copyright © 2008 DC Comics. All Rights Reserved.

Originally published in single magazine form as KINGDOM COME
1-4. Copyright © 1996 DC Comics. All Rights Reserved.
All characters, the distinctive likenesses thereof and related elements
featured in this publication are trademarks of DC Comics.
The stories, characters and incidents featured in this publication
are entirely fictional. DC Comics does not read or accept
unsolicited submissions of ideas, stories or artwork.

DC Comics, 1700 Broadway, New York, NY 10019
A Warner Bros. Entertainment Company.

Printed by RR Donnelley, Owensville, MO. 10/23/13.
Sixth Printing. ISBN: 978-1-4012-2034-1

Cover painting by Alex Ross.
Kingdom Come font created by
Alex Ross & Todd Klein.

Library of Congress Cataloging-in-Publication Data

Waid, Mark, 1962-
  Kingdom come / Mark Waid, Alex Ross.
     p. cm.
  "Originally published in single magazine form in Kingdom Come
#1-4."
  ISBN 978-1-4012-2034-1
  1. Graphic novels. 2. Superhero comic books, strips, etc. I. Ross,
Alex, 1970- II. Title.
  PN6727.W26K56 2012
  741.5'973–dc23
                                                    2012040863

CHAPTER ONE

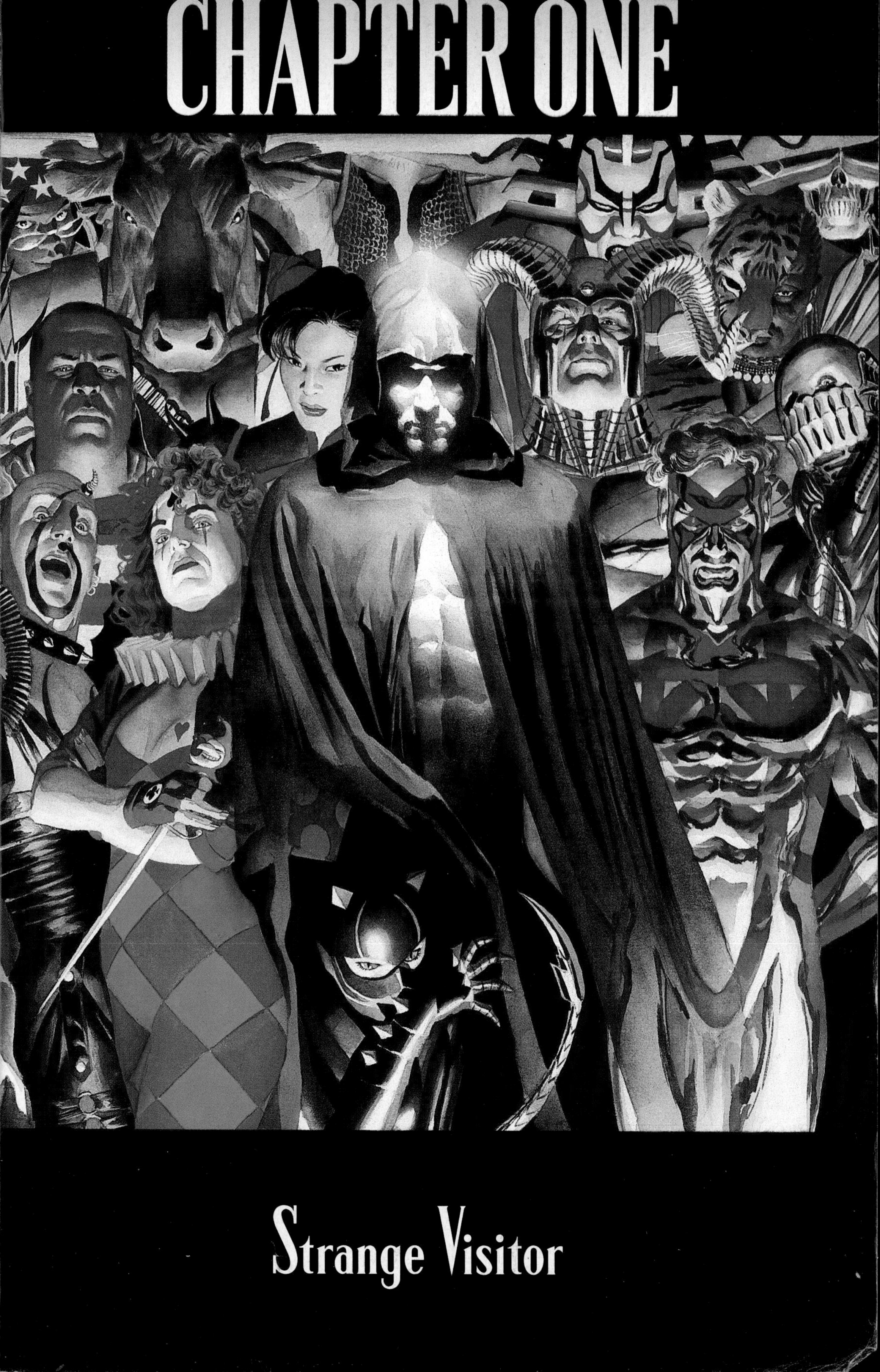

Strange Visitor

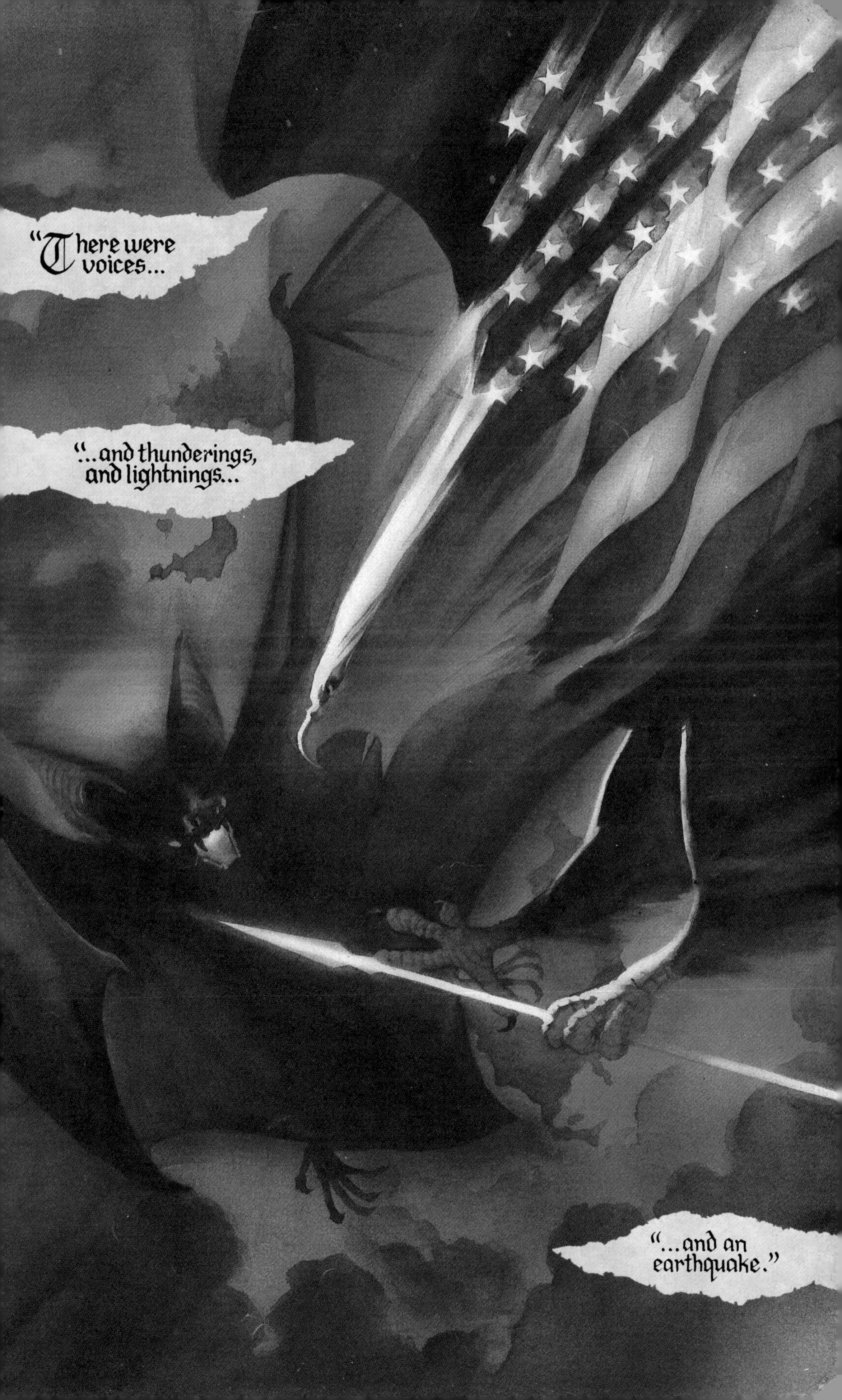
"There were voices...
"...and thunderings, and lightnings...
"...and an earthquake."

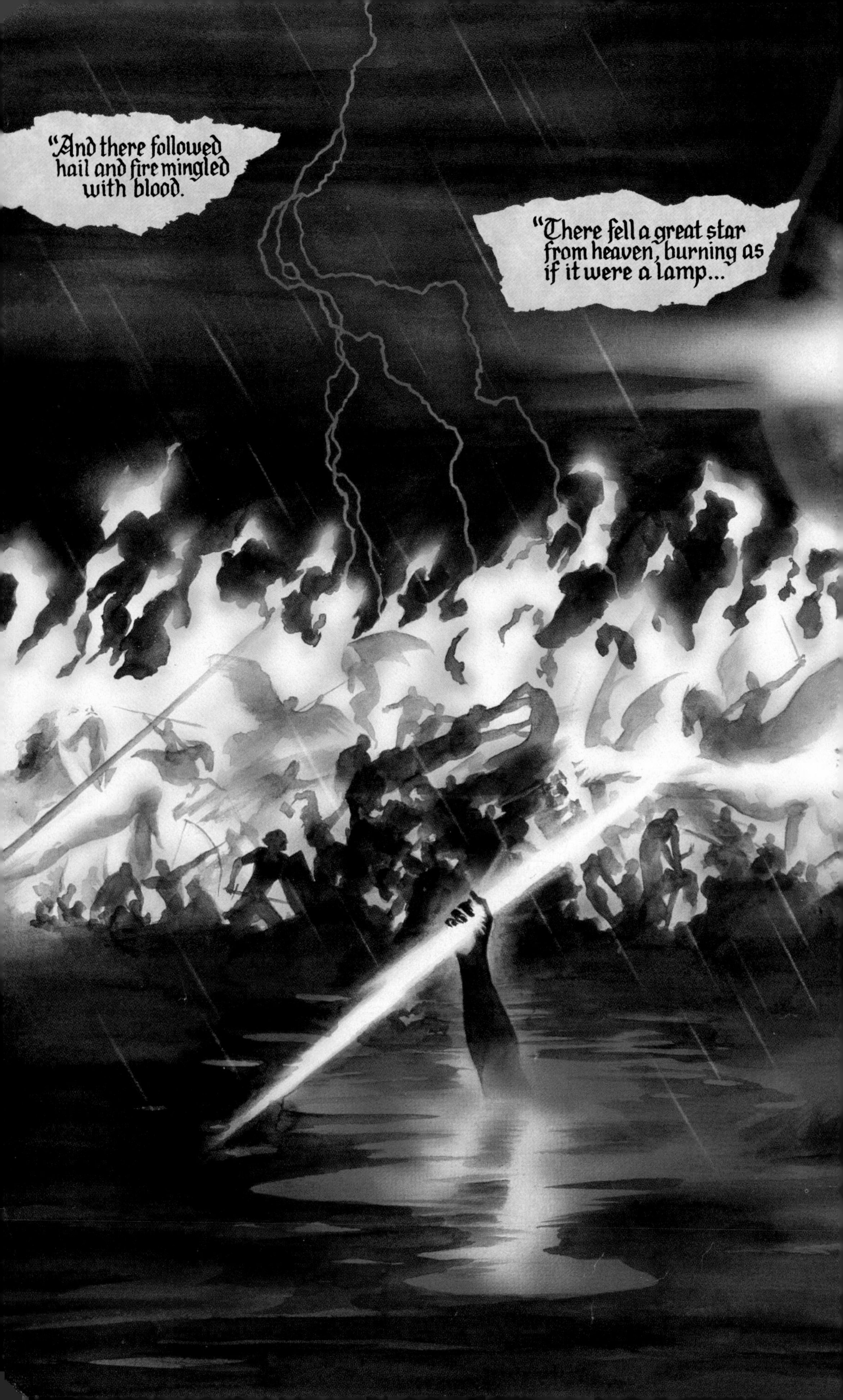
"And there followed hail and fire mingled with blood.
"There fell a great star from heaven, burning as if it were a lamp...

"...and I beheld, and heard an Angel...
"...saying with a loud voice...
"...woe, woe, WOE to the inhabiters of the Earth."

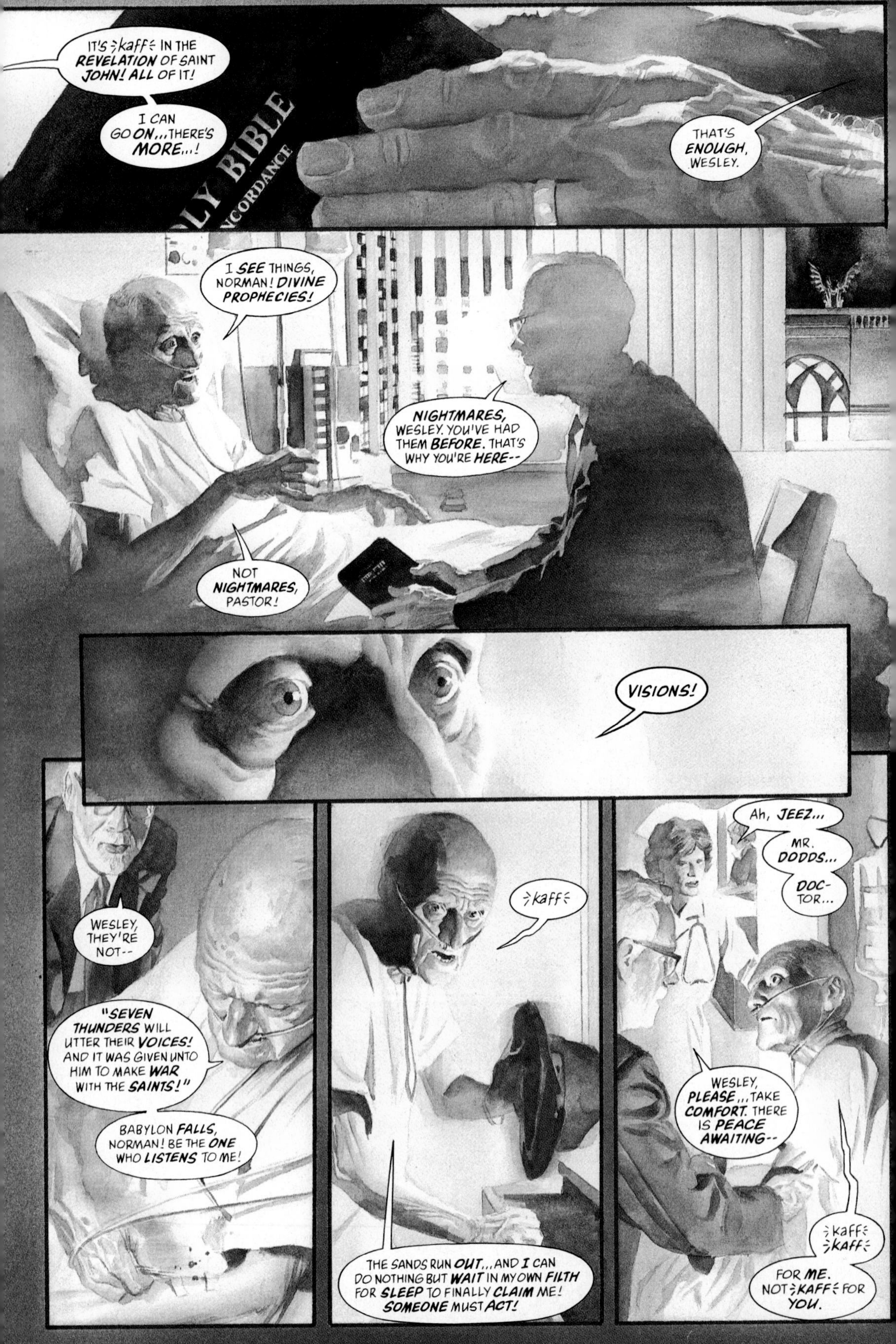

IT'S ≑kaff≑ IN THE REVELATION OF SAINT JOHN! ALL OF IT!
I CAN GO ON... THERE'S MORE...!
HOLY BIBLE
CONCORDANCE
THAT'S ENOUGH, WESLEY.
I SEE THINGS, NORMAN! DIVINE PROPHECIES!
NIGHTMARES, WESLEY. YOU'VE HAD THEM BEFORE. THAT'S WHY YOU'RE HERE--
NOT NIGHTMARES, PASTOR!
VISIONS!
WESLEY, THEY'RE NOT--
"SEVEN THUNDERS WILL UTTER THEIR VOICES! AND IT WAS GIVEN UNTO HIM TO MAKE WAR WITH THE SAINTS!"
BABYLON FALLS, NORMAN! BE THE ONE WHO LISTENS TO ME!
≑kaff≑
THE SANDS RUN OUT... AND I CAN DO NOTHING BUT WAIT IN MY OWN FILTH FOR SLEEP TO FINALLY CLAIM ME! SOMEONE MUST ACT!
Ah, JEEZ...
MR. DODDS...
DOC-TOR...
WESLEY, PLEASE... TAKE COMFORT. THERE IS PEACE AWAITING--
≑kaff≑ ≑kaff≑
FOR ME. NOT ≑kaff≑ FOR YOU.

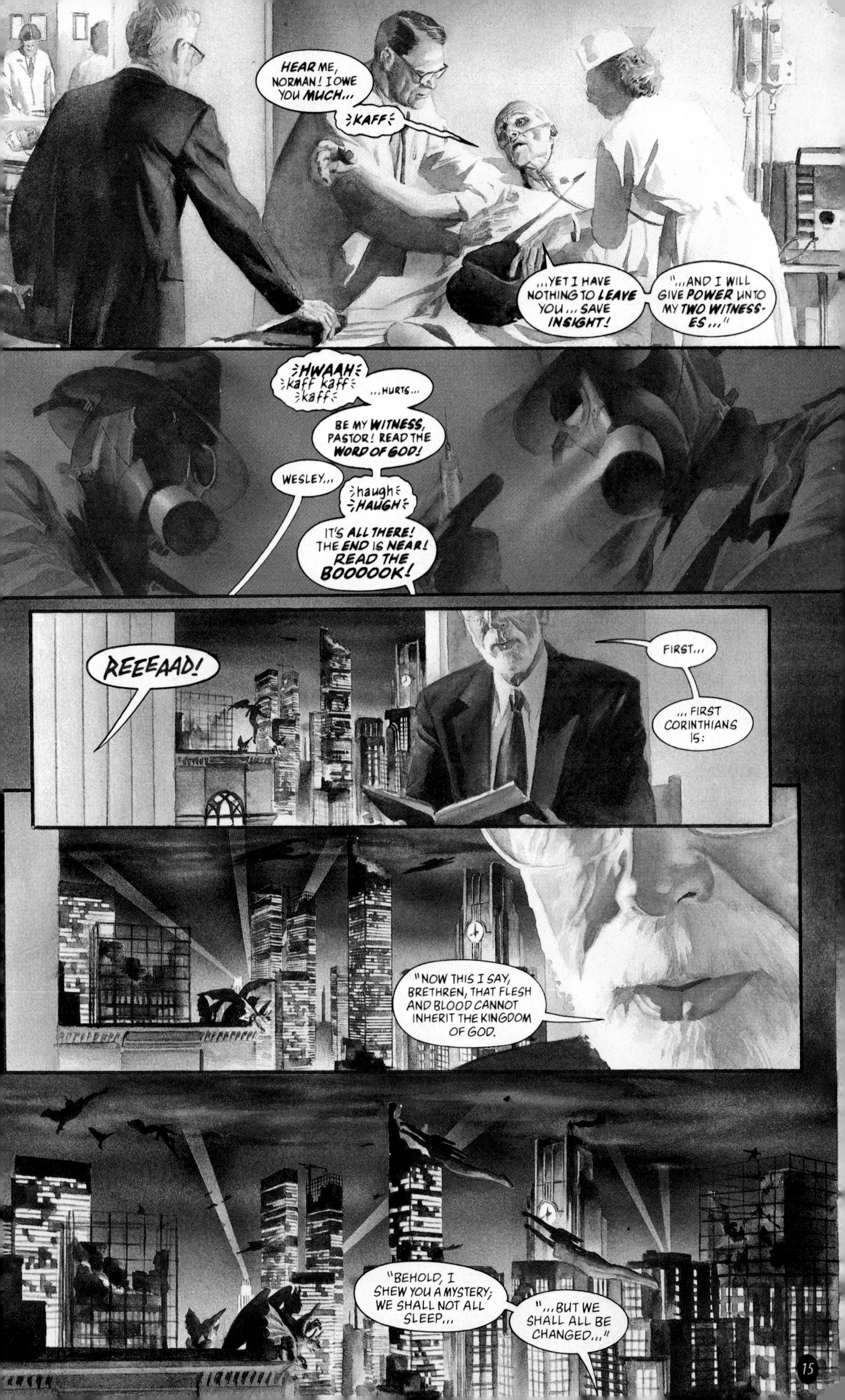

HEAR ME, NORMAN! I OWE YOU MUCH...
KAFF
...YET I HAVE NOTHING TO LEAVE YOU... SAVE INSIGHT!
"...AND I WILL GIVE POWER UNTO MY TWO WITNESS-ES..."
HWAAH kaff kaff kaff
...HURTS...
BE MY WITNESS, PASTOR! READ THE WORD OF GOD!
WESLEY...
haugh HAUGH
IT'S ALL THERE! THE END IS NEAR! READ THE BOOOOOK!
REEEAAD!
FIRST...
...FIRST CORINTHIANS 15:
"NOW THIS I SAY, BRETHREN, THAT FLESH AND BLOOD CANNOT INHERIT THE KINGDOM OF GOD.
"BEHOLD, I SHEW YOU A MYSTERY; WE SHALL NOT ALL SLEEP...
"...BUT WE SHALL ALL BE CHANGED..."

There was **more**, but Wesley never **heard** it.

In the **end**, he was listening to **another** voice...from Lord knows where.

My service was **brief**... his mourners, **few**. My **wife** and I met Wesley in his **twilight**...and had been the **last** of his **friends**.

He came to our **church** questioning what there was to **believe** in these days. I wish **now** I'd had better **answers**.

The **three** of us shared **many** a **dinner** in this apartment. Ellen, God rest her soul, would in **one** moment tease Wesley **mercilessly** about living in the past...

...and in the **next**, beg him to spin another tale of his... how did she put it?...his **glory days**.

Sometimes, I wish I'd made more time to listen **with** her. Wes's **stories** were melodies of **wonder**. Back **then**, it seemed, his dreams were of **yesterdays**, not **tomorrows**...of of times **bright**, not **barbaric**.

Once upon a time, he said, he'd called himself the **Sandman**.

DAILY PLANET

U.N. Enacts More Metahuman Censures

Will Censures Curb Metahuman Violence?

91% NO
7% YES
2% UNDECIDED

He was a **super-hero**.

KLIK

...man Censu...

YES
2% UNDECIDED

You'll excuse the **expression**.

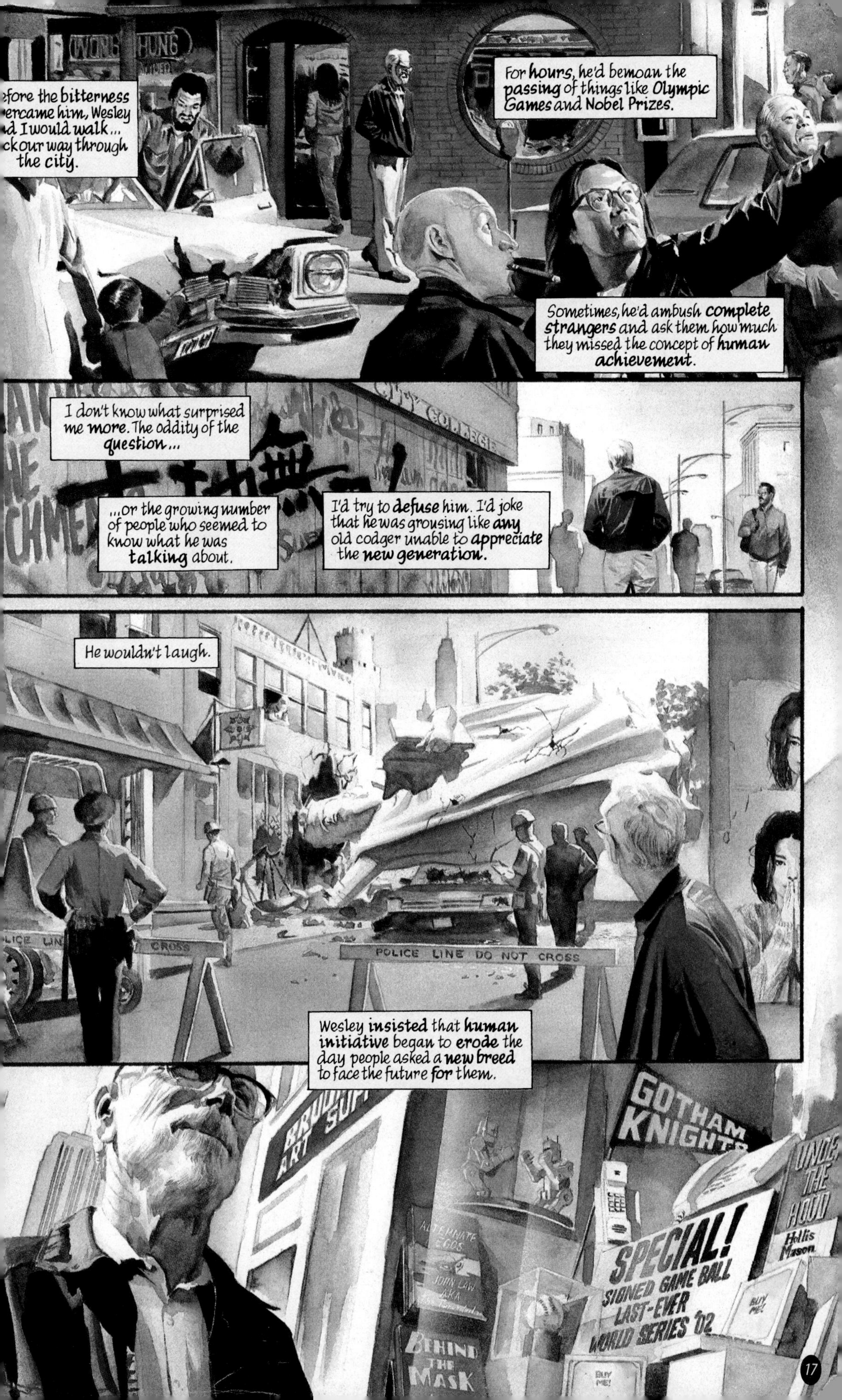

efore the bitterness
ercame him, Wesley
d I would walk...
ck our way through
the city.
For hours, he'd bemoan the passing of things like Olympic Games and Nobel Prizes.
Sometimes, he'd ambush complete strangers and ask them how much they missed the concept of human achievement.
I don't know what surprised me more. The oddity of the question...
...or the growing number of people who seemed to know what he was talking about.
I'd try to defuse him. I'd joke that he was grousing like any old codger unable to appreciate the new generation.
He wouldn't laugh.
POLICE LINE DO NOT CROSS
Wesley insisted that human initiative began to erode the day people asked a new breed to face the future for them.
GOTHAM KNIGHTS
SPECIAL! SIGNED GAME BALL LAST-EVER WORLD SERIES '02
Hollis Mason
BEHIND THE MASK
BUY ME!

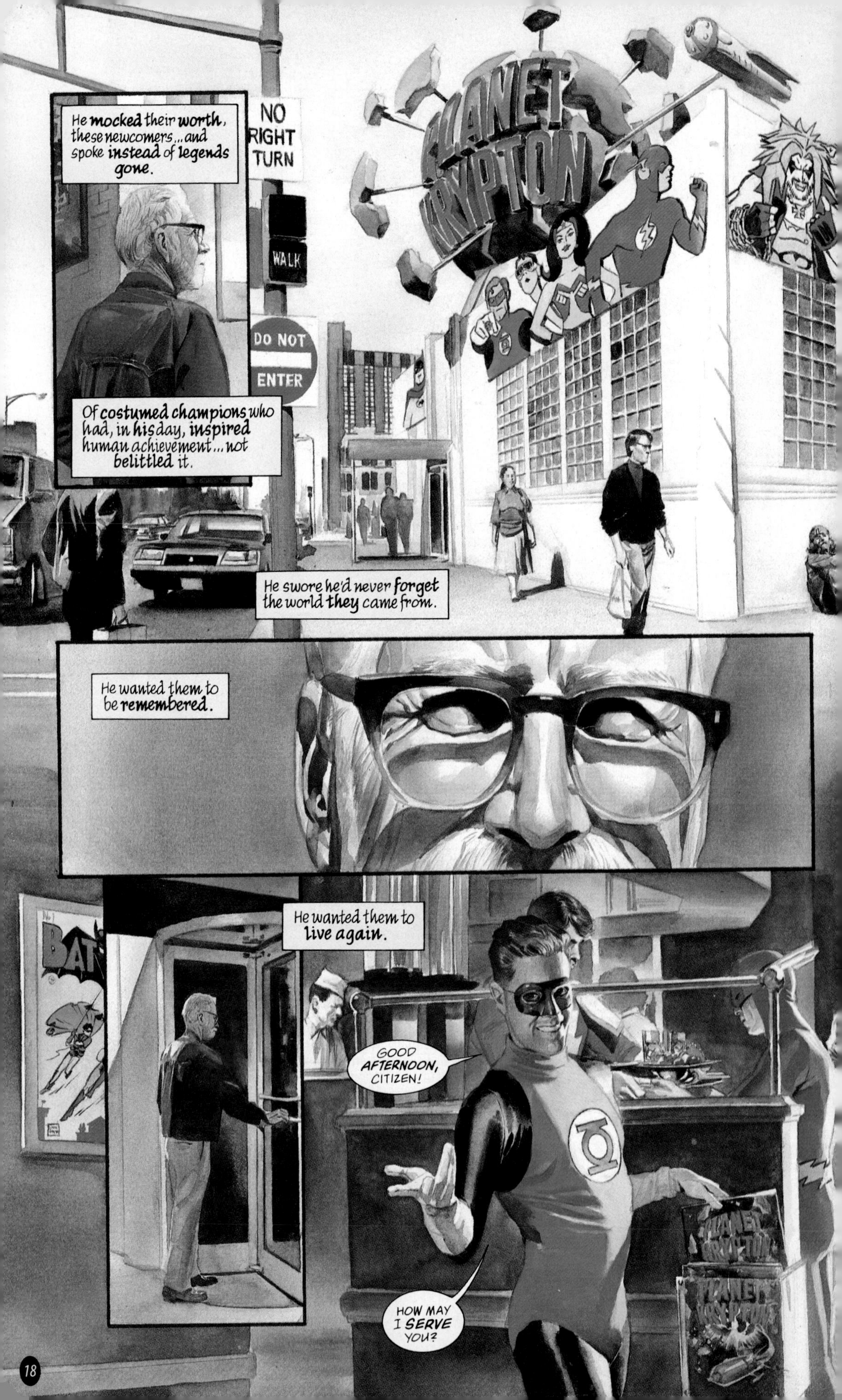

He mocked their worth, these newcomers,...and spoke instead of legends gone.
NO RIGHT TURN
WALK
DO NOT ENTER
PLANET KRYPTON
Of costumed champions who had, in his day, inspired human achievement... not belittled it.
He swore he'd never forget the world they came from.
He wanted them to be remembered.
He wanted them to live again.
GOOD AFTERNOON, CITIZEN!
HOW MAY I SERVE YOU?

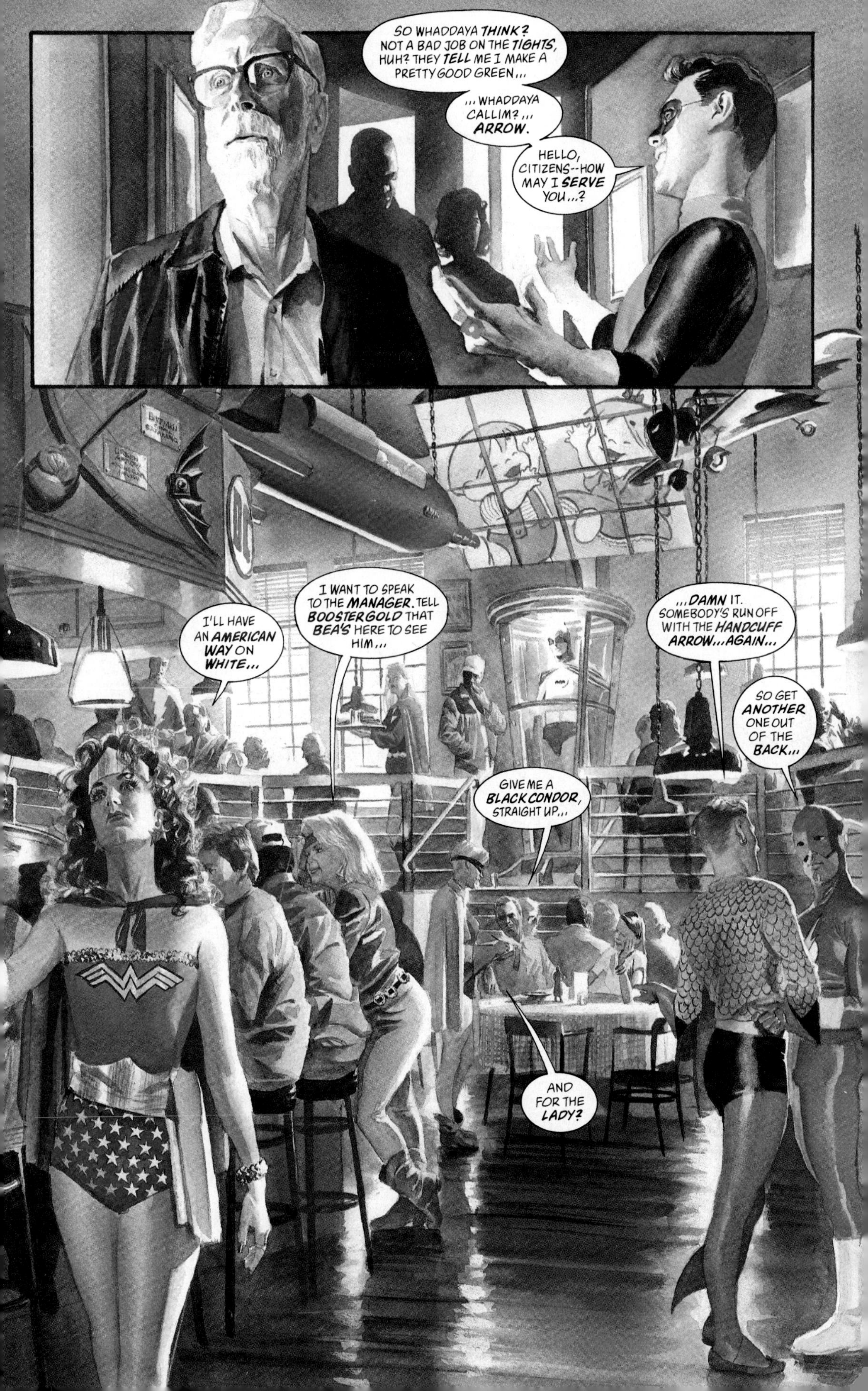
SO WHADDAYA THINK? NOT A BAD JOB ON THE TIGHTS, HUH? THEY TELL ME I MAKE A PRETTY GOOD GREEN,,,
,,, WHADDAYA CALLIM? ,,, ARROW.
HELLO, CITIZENS--HOW MAY I SERVE YOU,,,?
I'LL HAVE AN AMERICAN WAY ON WHITE...
I WANT TO SPEAK TO THE MANAGER. TELL BOOSTER GOLD THAT BEA'S HERE TO SEE HIM,,,
,,,DAMN IT. SOMEBODY'S RUN OFF WITH THE HANDCUFF ARROW...AGAIN...
SO GET ANOTHER ONE OUT OF THE BACK...
GIVE ME A BLACK CONDOR, STRAIGHT UP,,,
AND FOR THE LADY?

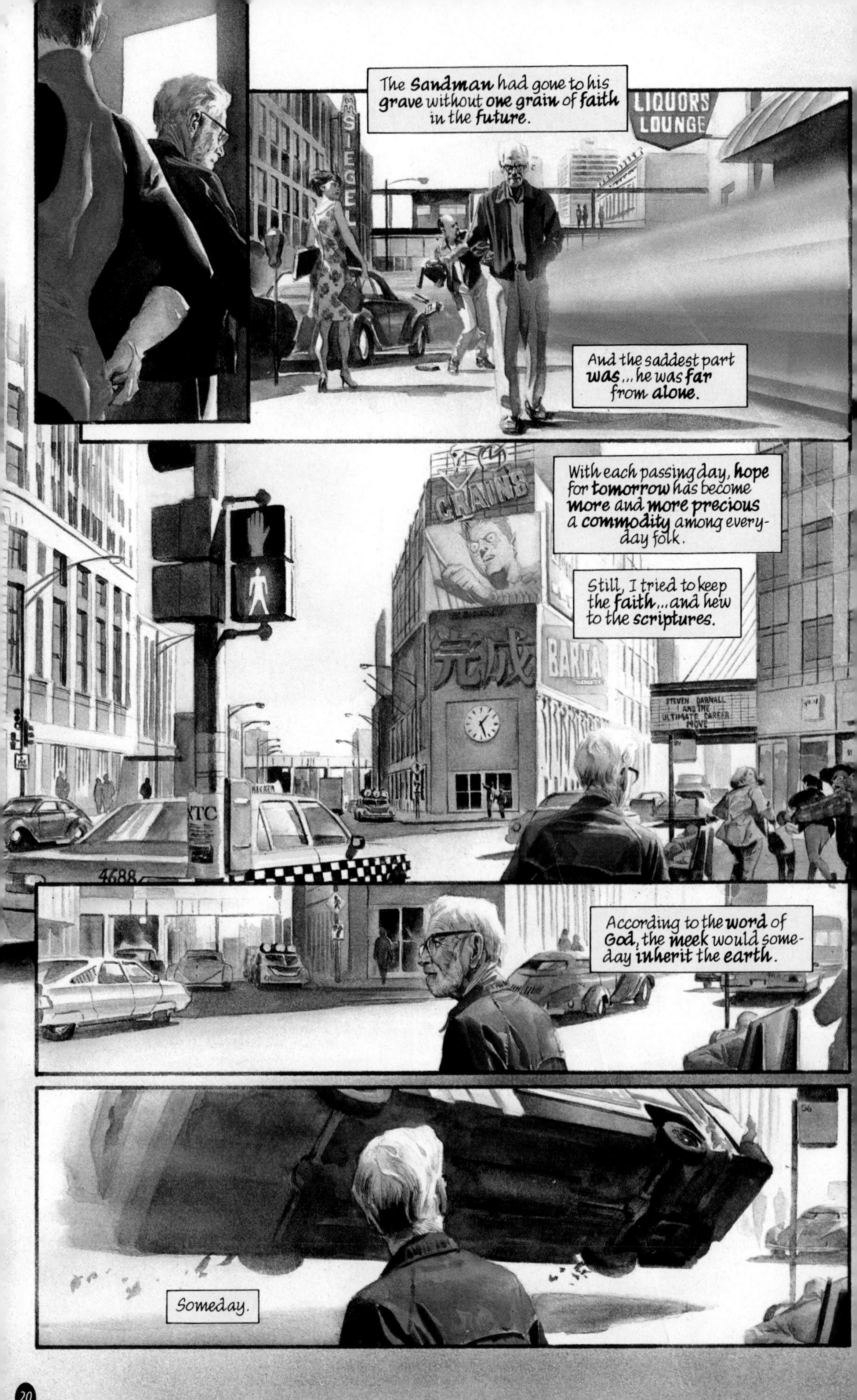

The Sandman had gone to his grave without one grain of faith in the future.
SIEGEL
LIQUORS
LOUNGE
And the saddest part was... he was far from alone.
With each passing day, hope for tomorrow has become more and more precious a commodity among every-day folk.
CRAINS
Still, I tried to keep the faith... and hew to the scriptures.
完成
BARTA
STEVEN DARNALL AND THE ULTIMATE CAREER MOVE
XTC
4688
According to the word of God, the meek would some-day inherit the earth.
Someday.

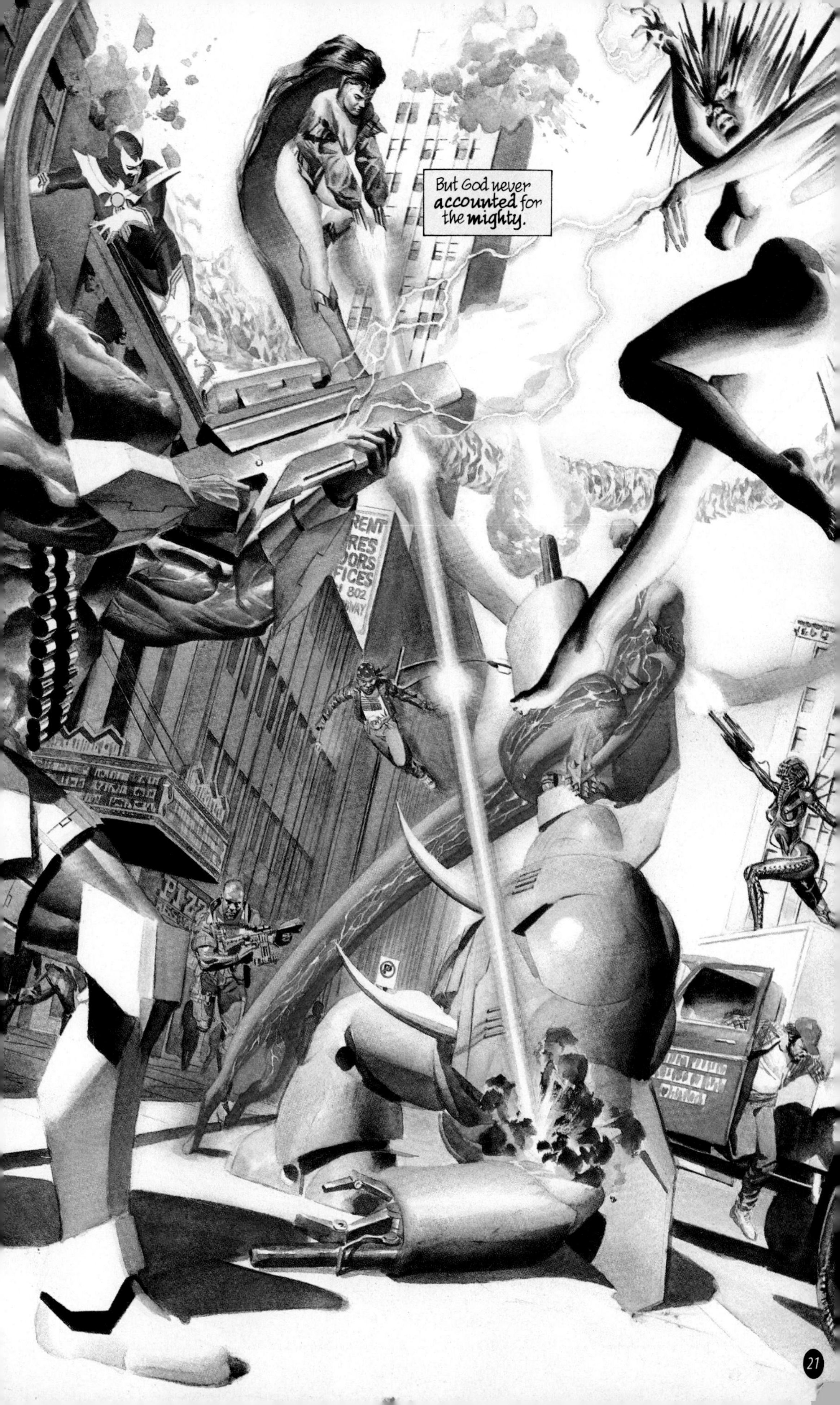
But God never accounted for the mighty.

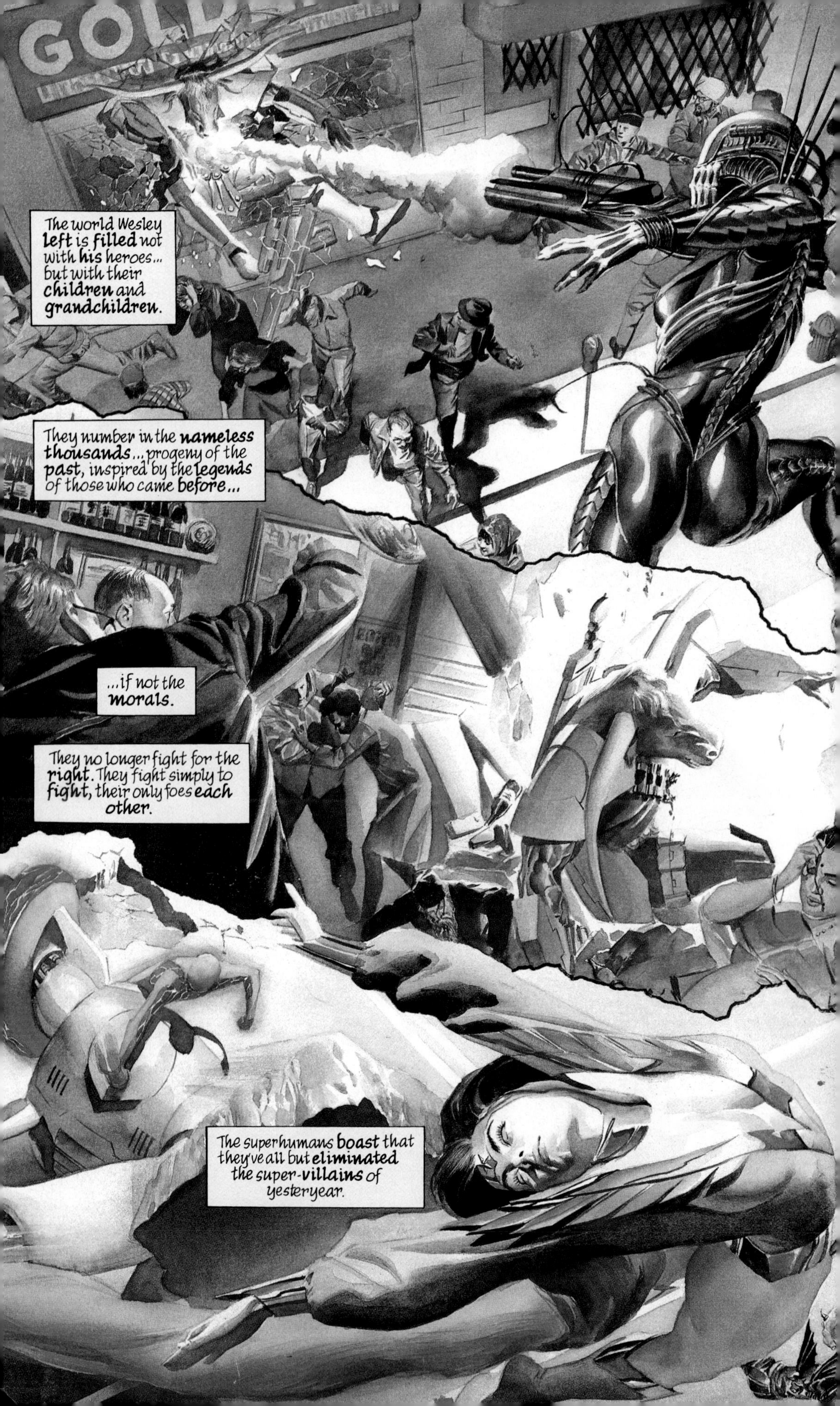
GOLD
The world Wesley **left** is **filled** not with **his** heroes... but with their **children** and **grandchildren**.
They number in the **nameless thousands**... progeny of the **past**, inspired by the **legends** of those who came **before**...
...if not the **morals**.
They no longer fight for the **right**. They fight simply to **fight**, their only foes **each other**.
The superhumans **boast** that they've all but **eliminated** the super-**villains** of yesteryear.

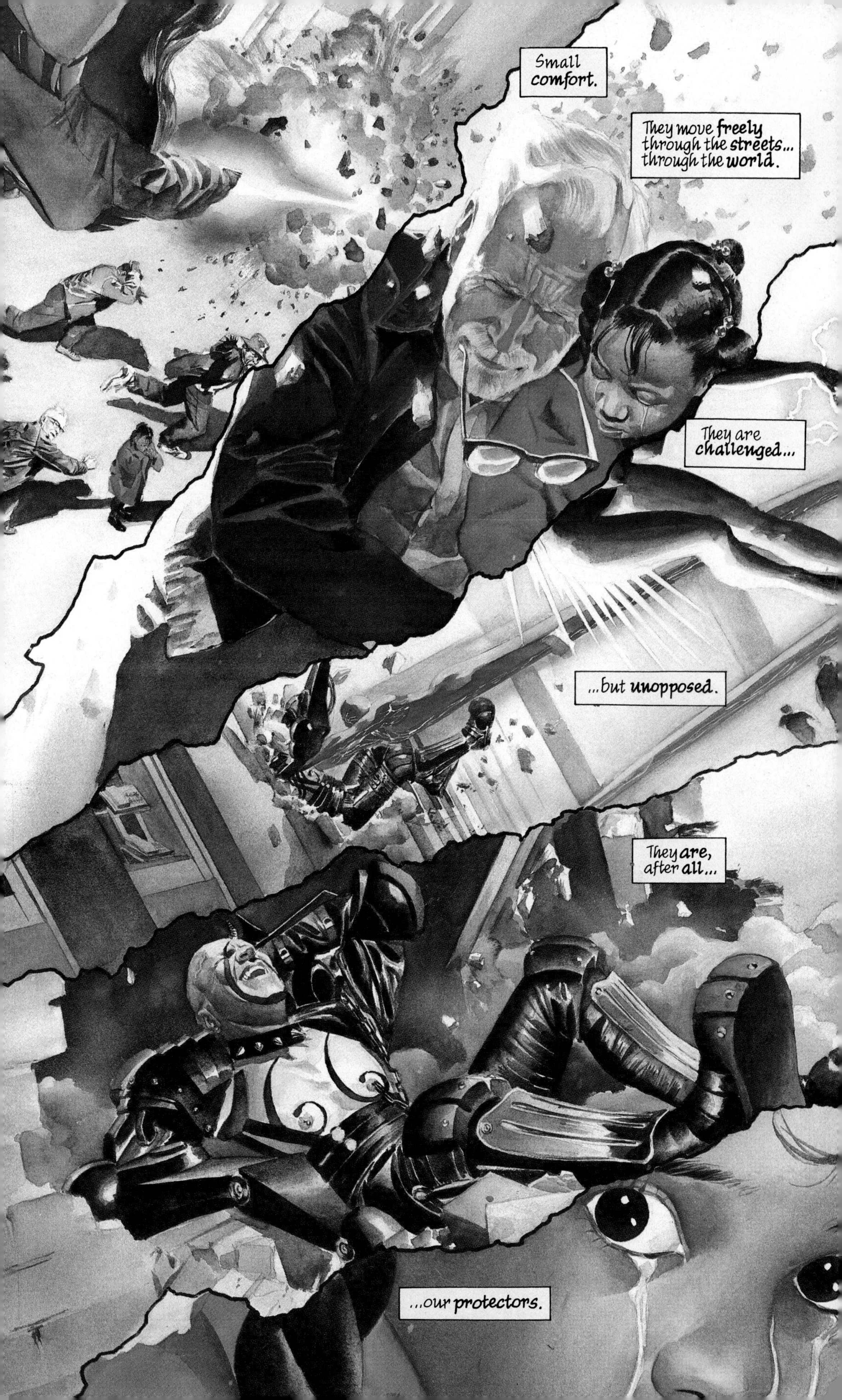
Small comfort.
They move freely through the streets... through the world.
They are challenged...
...but unopposed.
They are, after all...
...our protectors.

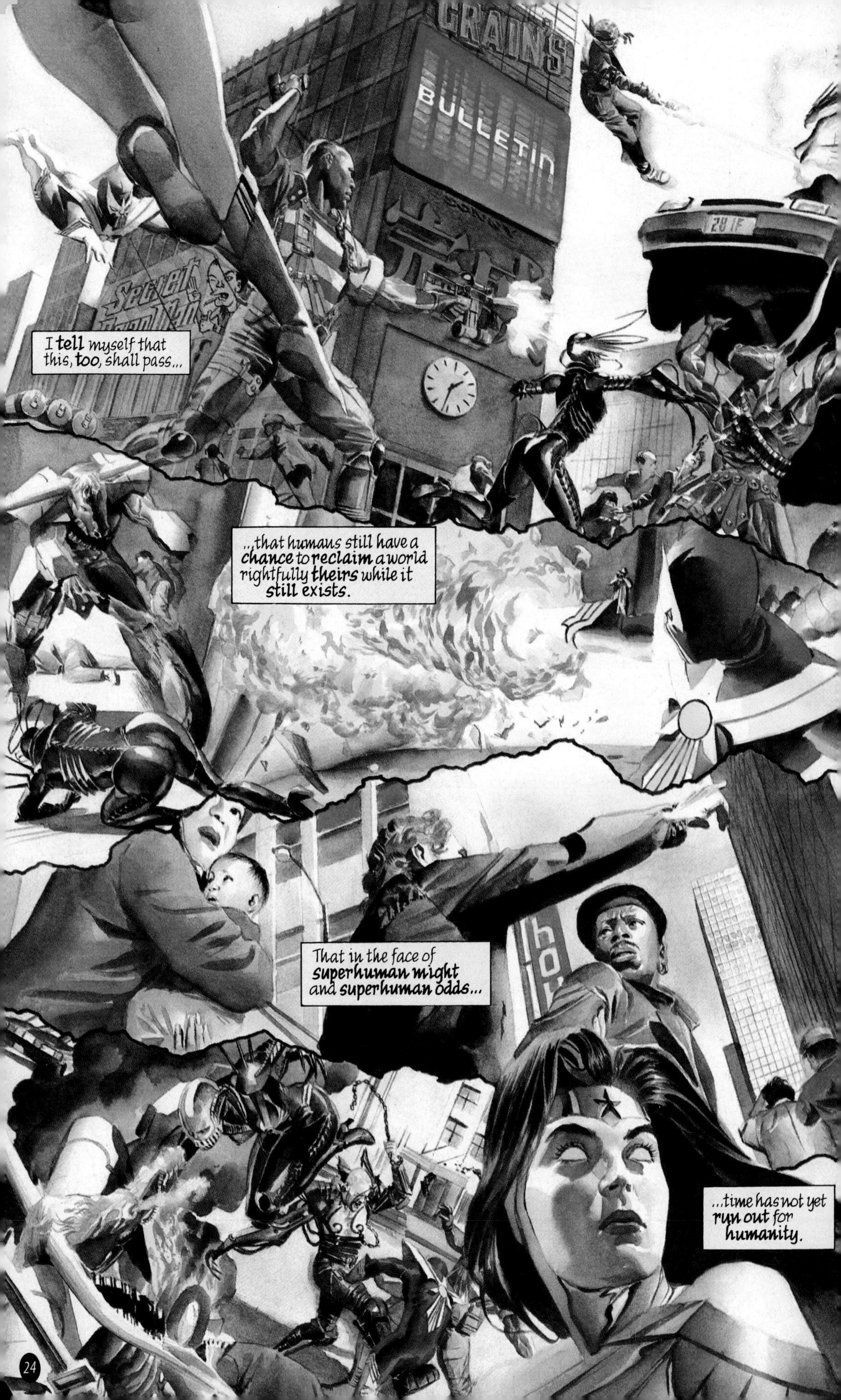
GRAIN'S
BULLETIN
I tell myself that this, too, shall pass...
...that humans still have a chance to reclaim a world rightfully theirs while it still exists.
That in the face of superhuman might and superhuman odds...
...time has not yet run out for humanity.

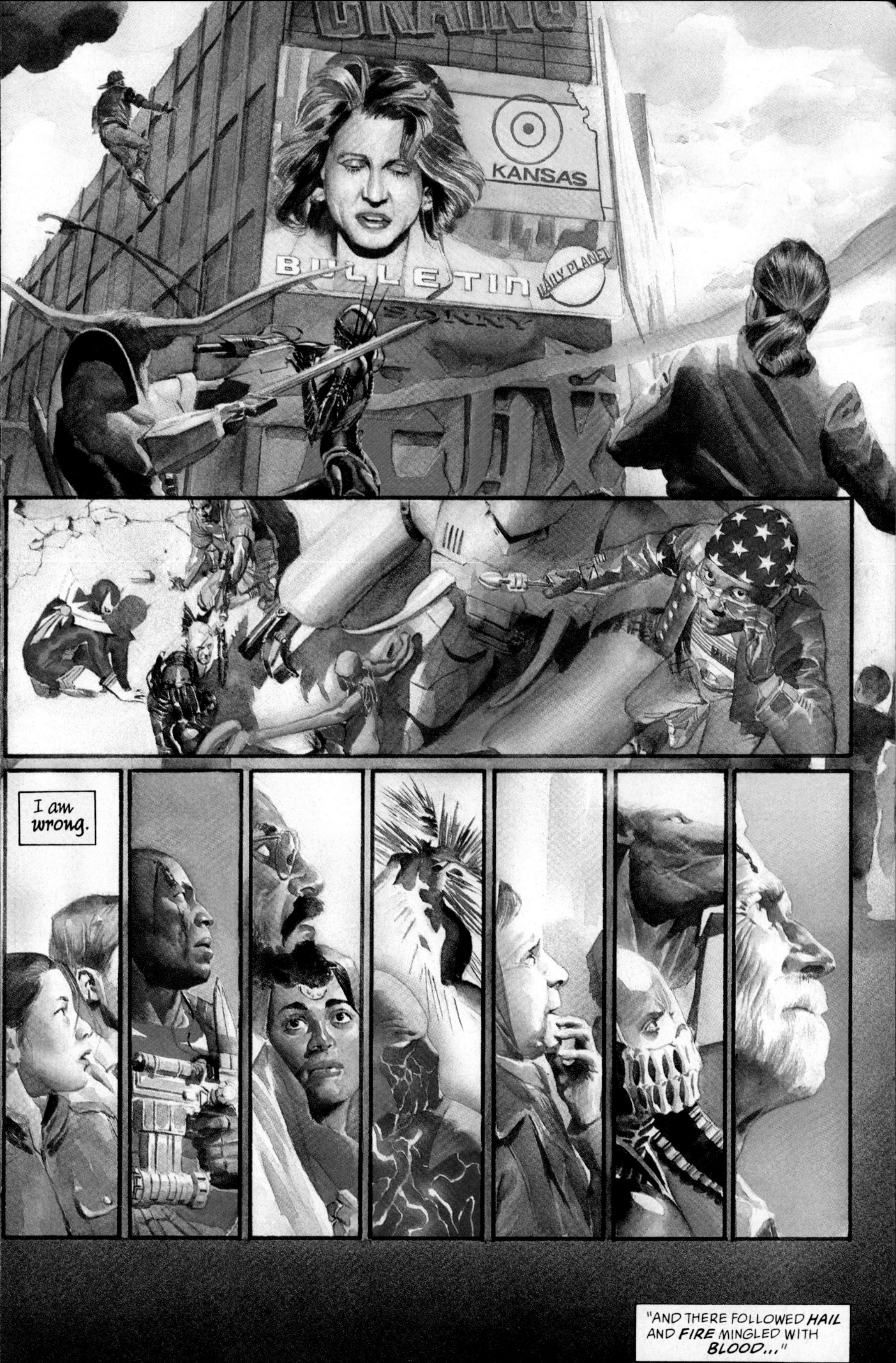
KANSAS
BULLETIN
DAILY PLANET
I am wrong.
"AND THERE FOLLOWED HAIL AND FIRE MINGLED WITH BLOOD..."

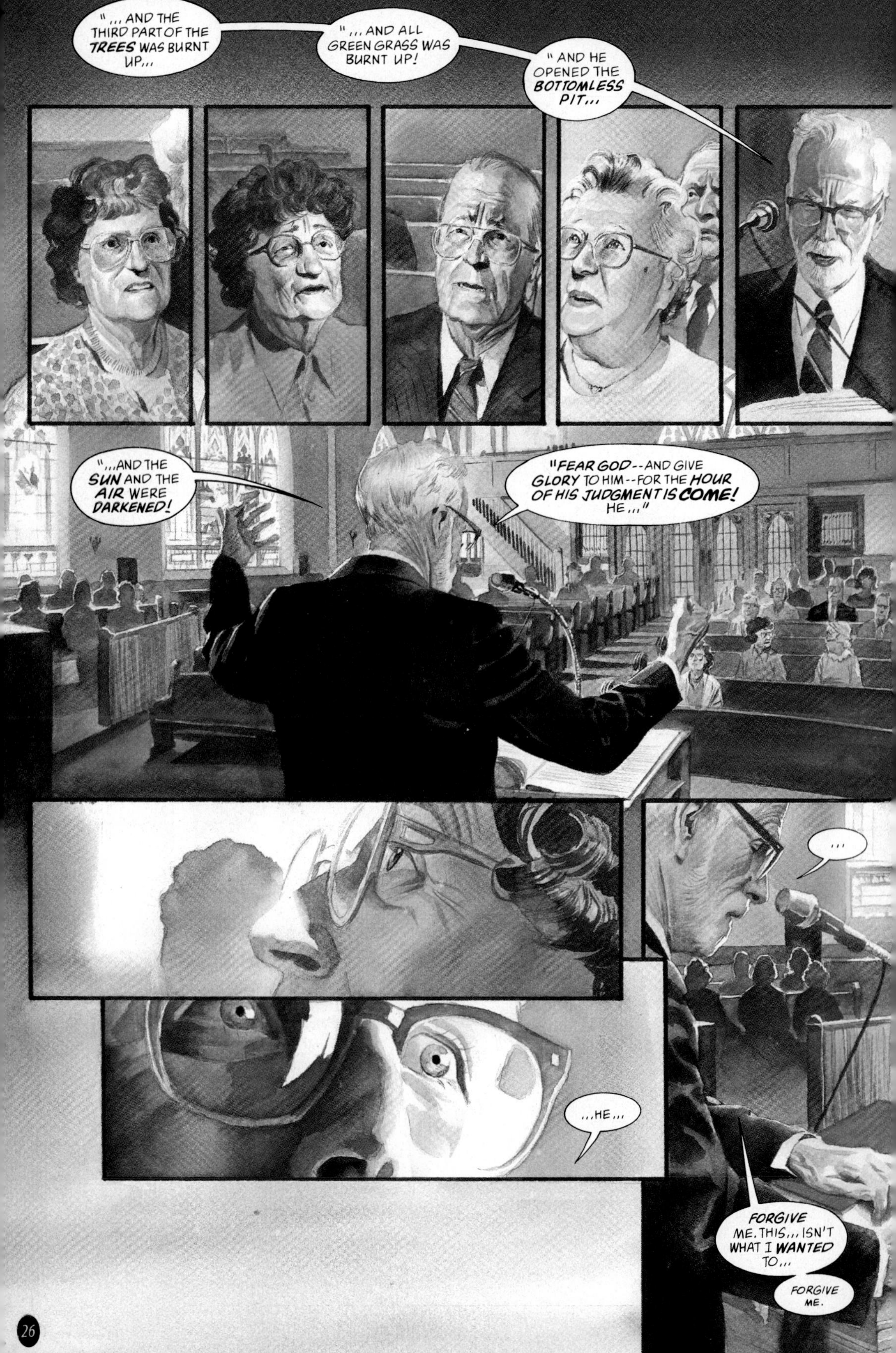
"...AND THE THIRD PART OF THE TREES WAS BURNT UP...
"...AND ALL GREEN GRASS WAS BURNT UP!
"AND HE OPENED THE BOTTOMLESS PIT...
"...AND THE SUN AND THE AIR WERE DARKENED!
"FEAR GOD--AND GIVE GLORY TO HIM--FOR THE HOUR OF HIS JUDGMENT IS COME! HE..."
...
...HE...
FORGIVE ME. THIS... ISN'T WHAT I WANTED TO...
FORGIVE ME.

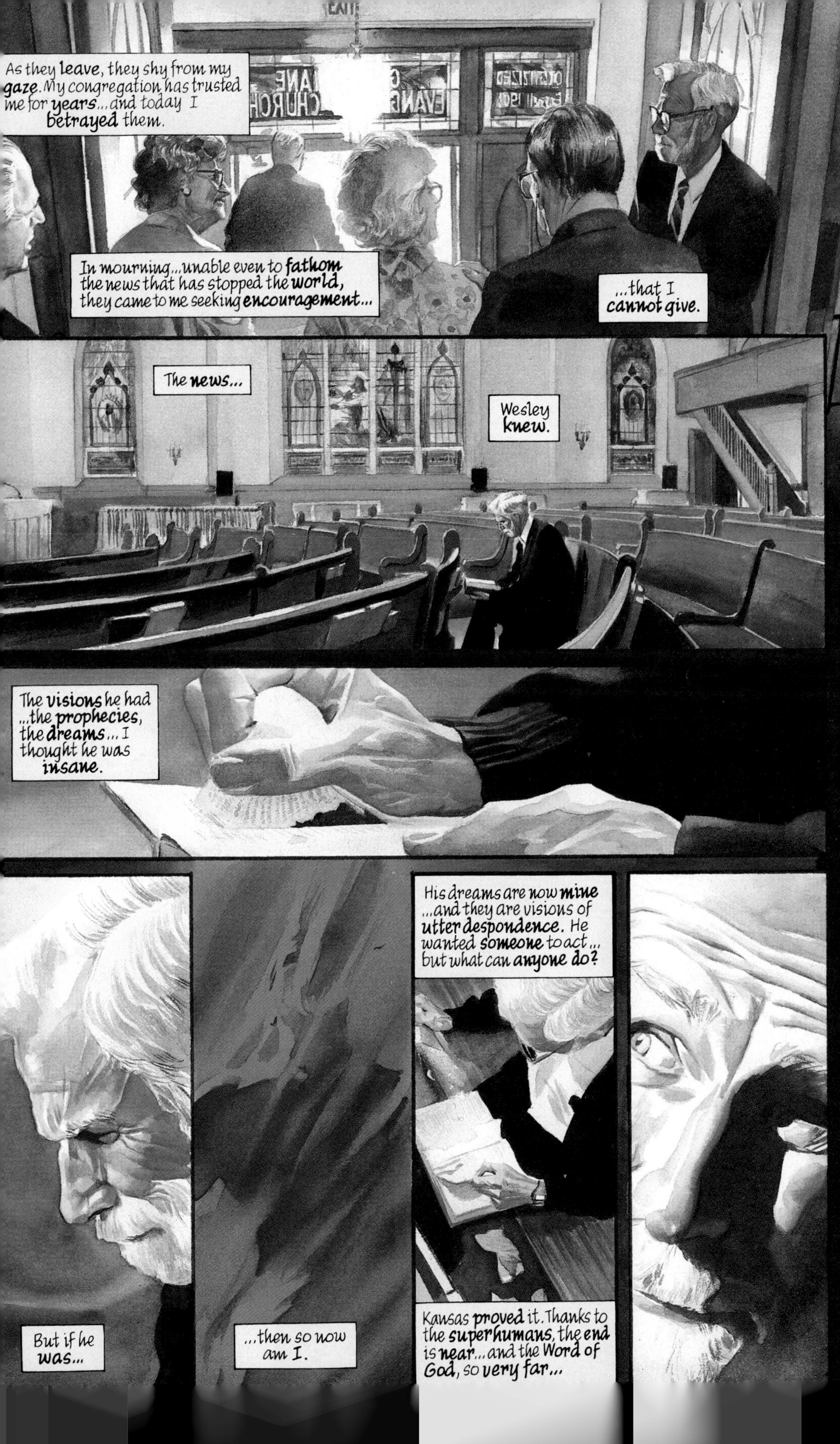

As they leave, they shy from my gaze. My congregation has trusted me for years... and today I betrayed them.
In mourning... unable even to fathom the news that has stopped the world, they came to me seeking encouragement...
...that I cannot give.
The news...
Wesley knew.
The visions he had ...the prophecies, the dreams... I thought he was insane.
But if he was...
...then so now am I.
His dreams are now mine ...and they are visions of utter despondence. He wanted someone to act... but what can anyone do?
Kansas proved it. Thanks to the superhumans, the end is near... and the Word of God, so very far...

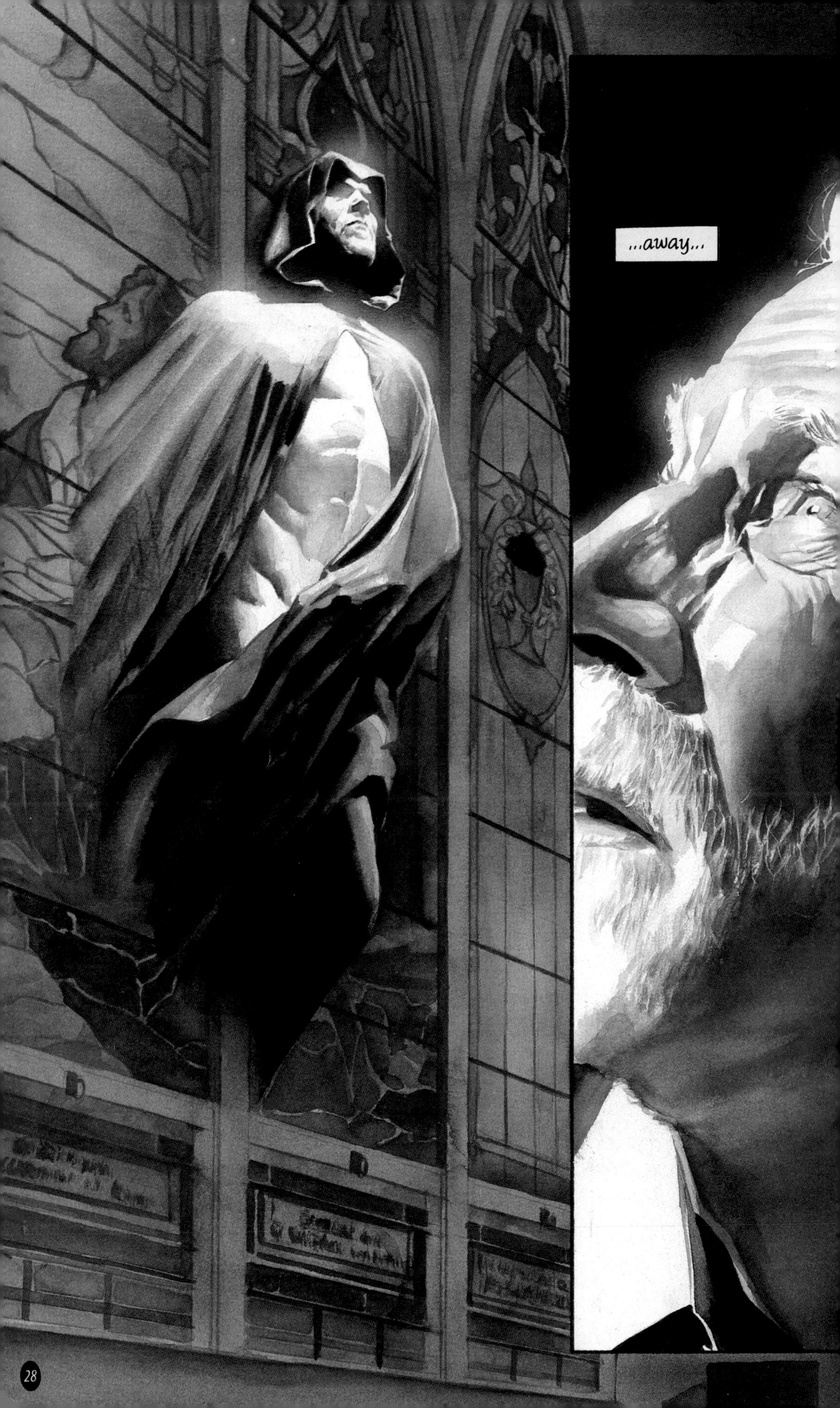
...away...

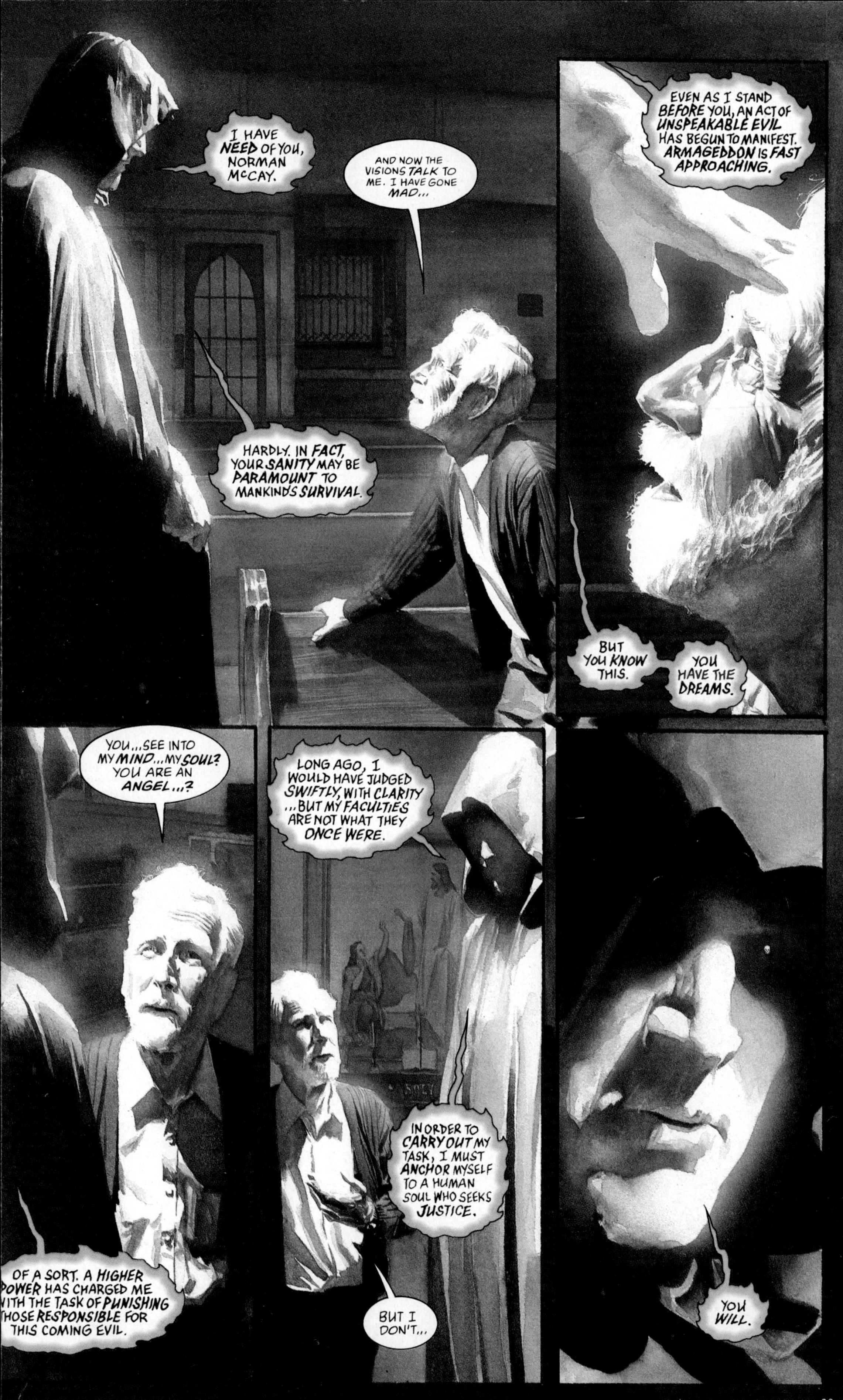

I HAVE NEED OF YOU, NORMAN McCAY.
AND NOW THE VISIONS TALK TO ME. I HAVE GONE MAD...
HARDLY. IN FACT, YOUR SANITY MAY BE PARAMOUNT TO MANKIND'S SURVIVAL.
EVEN AS I STAND BEFORE YOU, AN ACT OF UNSPEAKABLE EVIL HAS BEGUN TO MANIFEST. ARMAGEDDON IS FAST APPROACHING.
BUT YOU KNOW THIS.
YOU HAVE THE DREAMS.
YOU...SEE INTO MY MIND...MY SOUL? YOU ARE AN ANGEL...?
OF A SORT. A HIGHER POWER HAS CHARGED ME WITH THE TASK OF PUNISHING THOSE RESPONSIBLE FOR THIS COMING EVIL.
LONG AGO, I WOULD HAVE JUDGED SWIFTLY, WITH CLARITY ...BUT MY FACULTIES ARE NOT WHAT THEY ONCE WERE.
IN ORDER TO CARRY OUT MY TASK, I MUST ANCHOR MYSELF TO A HUMAN SOUL WHO SEEKS JUSTICE.
BUT I DON'T...
YOU WILL.

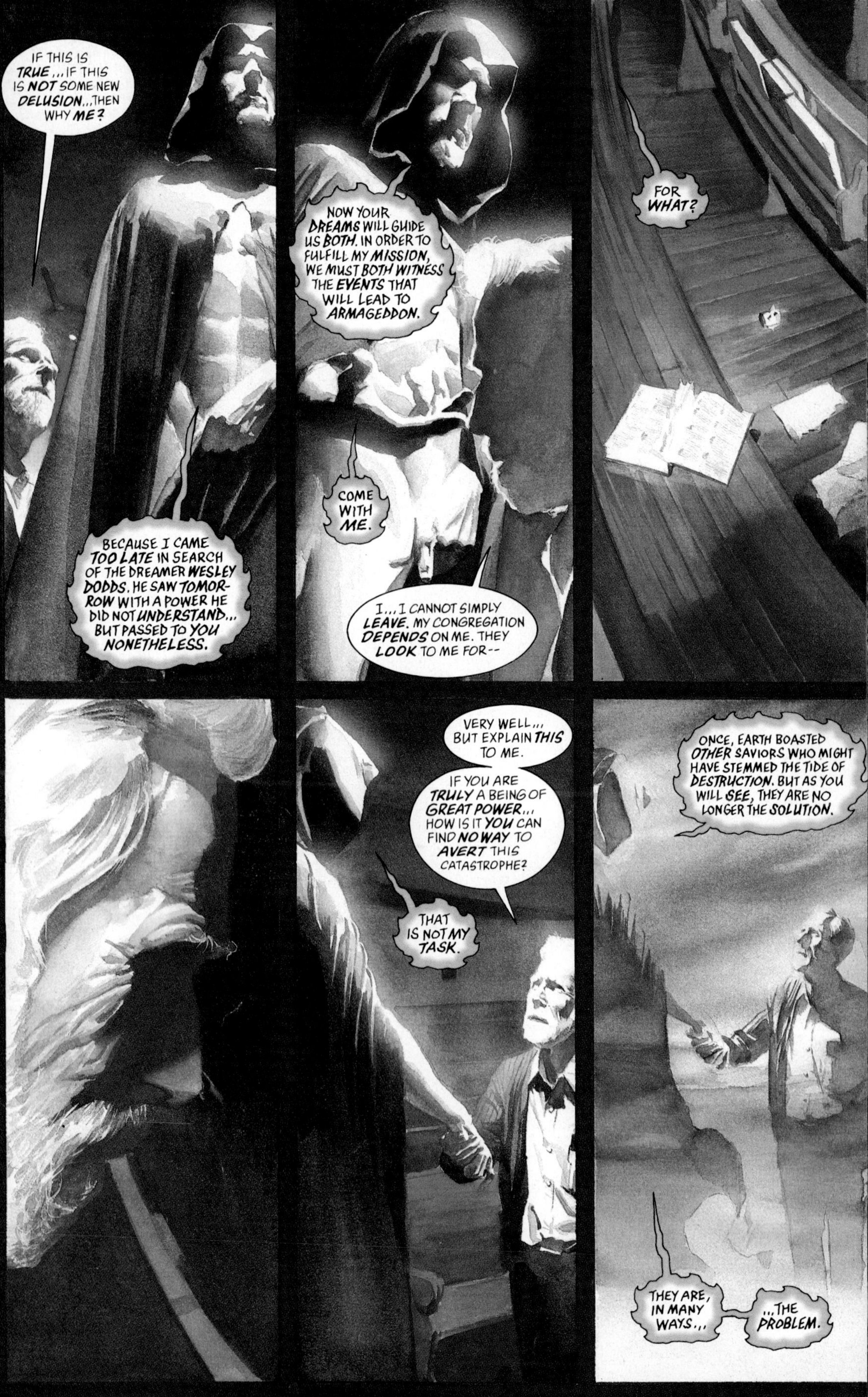
IF THIS IS TRUE... IF THIS IS NOT SOME NEW DELUSION... THEN WHY ME?
BECAUSE I CAME TOO LATE IN SEARCH OF THE DREAMER WESLEY DODDS. HE SAW TOMORROW WITH A POWER HE DID NOT UNDERSTAND... BUT PASSED TO YOU NONETHELESS.
NOW YOUR DREAMS WILL GUIDE US BOTH. IN ORDER TO FULFILL MY MISSION, WE MUST BOTH WITNESS THE EVENTS THAT WILL LEAD TO ARMAGEDDON.
COME WITH ME.
I... I CANNOT SIMPLY LEAVE. MY CONGREGATION DEPENDS ON ME. THEY LOOK TO ME FOR--
FOR WHAT?
VERY WELL... BUT EXPLAIN THIS TO ME.
IF YOU ARE TRULY A BEING OF GREAT POWER... HOW IS IT YOU CAN FIND NO WAY TO AVERT THIS CATASTROPHE?
THAT IS NOT MY TASK.
ONCE, EARTH BOASTED OTHER SAVIORS WHO MIGHT HAVE STEMMED THE TIDE OF DESTRUCTION. BUT AS YOU WILL SEE, THEY ARE NO LONGER THE SOLUTION.
THEY ARE, IN MANY WAYS...
...THE PROBLEM.

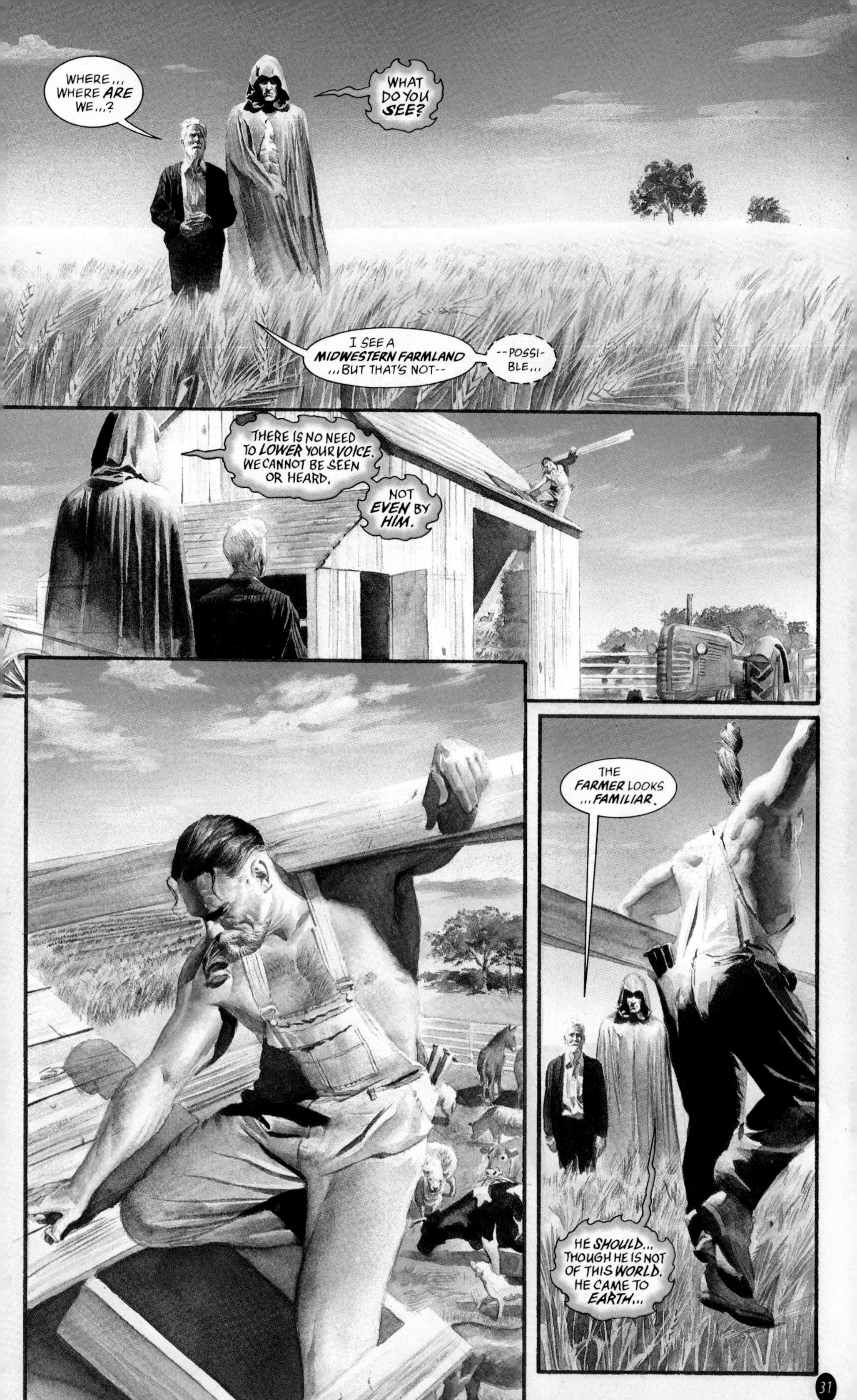
WHERE... WHERE ARE WE...?
WHAT DO YOU SEE?
I SEE A MIDWESTERN FARMLAND ...BUT THAT'S NOT--
--POSSI-BLE...
THERE IS NO NEED TO LOWER YOUR VOICE. WE CANNOT BE SEEN OR HEARD.
NOT EVEN BY HIM.
THE FARMER LOOKS ...FAMILIAR.
HE SHOULD... THOUGH HE IS NOT OF THIS WORLD. HE CAME TO EARTH...

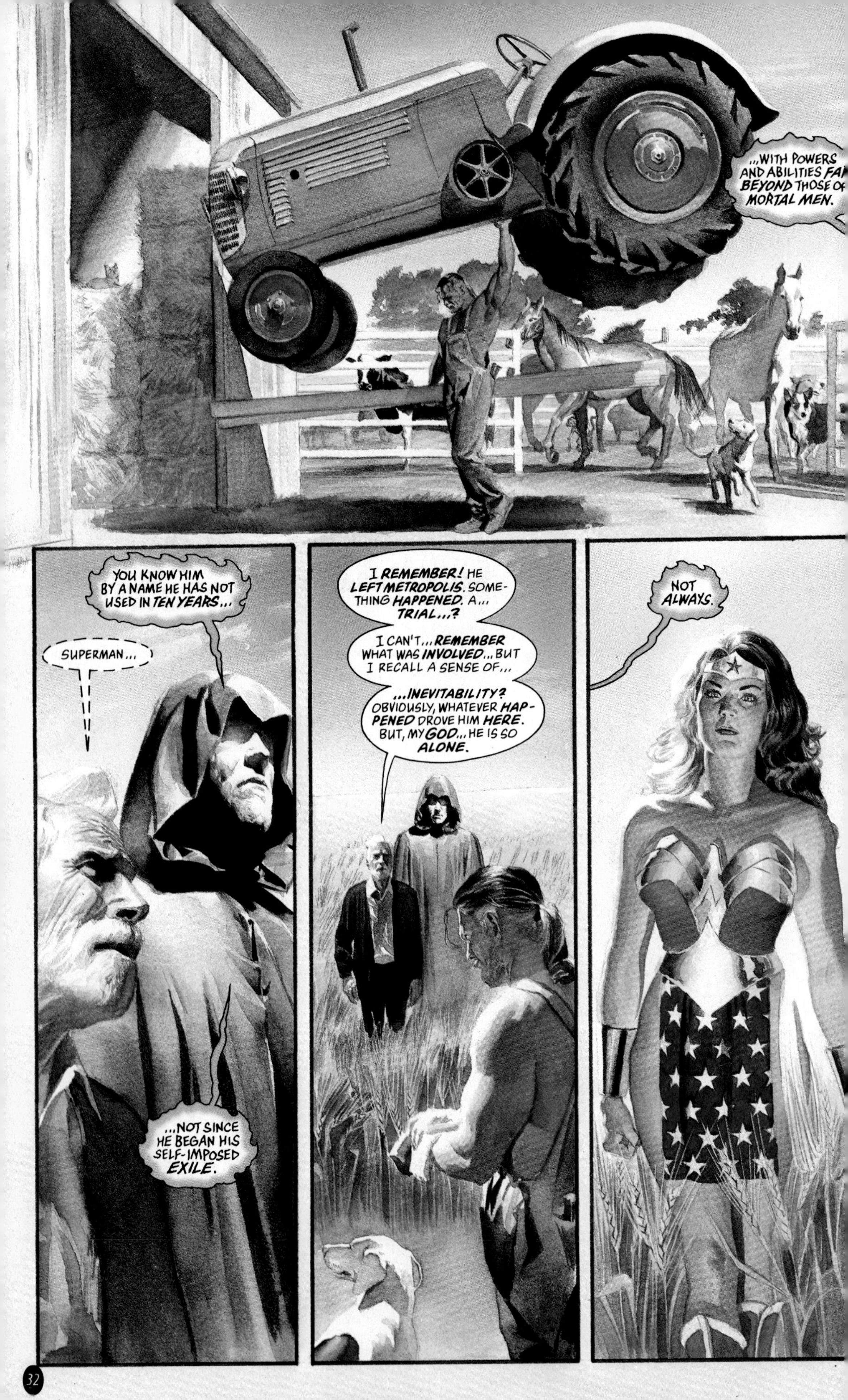
...WITH POWERS AND ABILITIES FAR BEYOND THOSE OF MORTAL MEN.
YOU KNOW HIM BY A NAME HE HAS NOT USED IN TEN YEARS...
SUPERMAN...
...NOT SINCE HE BEGAN HIS SELF-IMPOSED EXILE.
I REMEMBER! HE LEFT METROPOLIS. SOMETHING HAPPENED. A... TRIAL...?
I CAN'T... REMEMBER WHAT WAS INVOLVED... BUT I RECALL A SENSE OF...
...INEVITABILITY? OBVIOUSLY, WHATEVER HAPPENED DROVE HIM HERE. BUT, MY GOD... HE IS SO ALONE.
NOT ALWAYS.

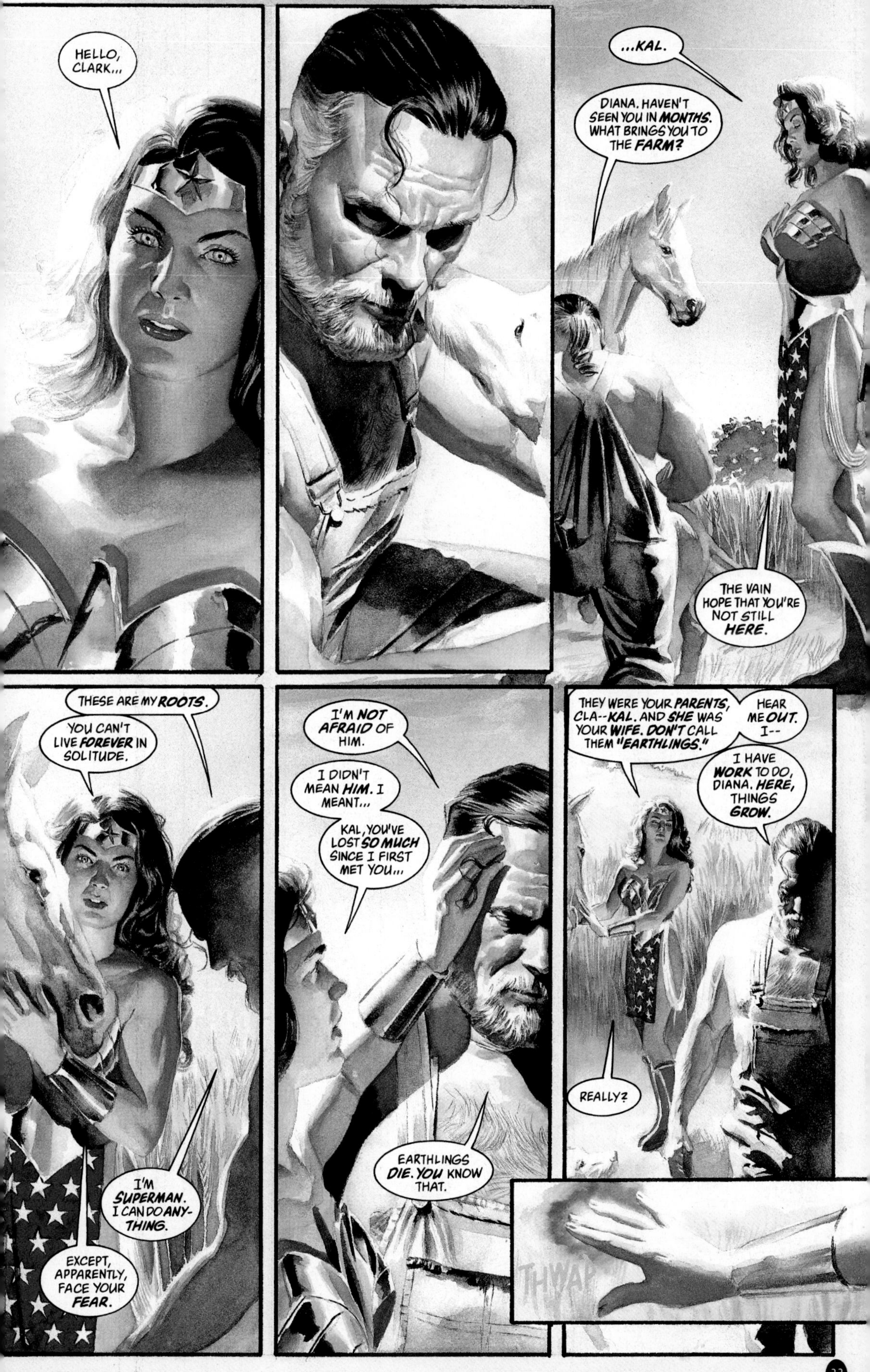
HELLO, CLARK...
...KAL.
DIANA. HAVEN'T SEEN YOU IN MONTHS. WHAT BRINGS YOU TO THE FARM?
THE VAIN HOPE THAT YOU'RE NOT STILL HERE.
THESE ARE MY ROOTS.
YOU CAN'T LIVE FOREVER IN SOLITUDE.
I'M SUPERMAN. I CAN DO ANY-THING.
EXCEPT, APPARENTLY, FACE YOUR FEAR.
I'M NOT AFRAID OF HIM.
I DIDN'T MEAN HIM. I MEANT...
KAL, YOU'VE LOST SO MUCH SINCE I FIRST MET YOU...
EARTHLINGS DIE. YOU KNOW THAT.
THEY WERE YOUR PARENTS, CLA--KAL. AND SHE WAS YOUR WIFE. DON'T CALL THEM "EARTHLINGS."
HEAR ME OUT. I--
I HAVE WORK TO DO, DIANA. HERE, THINGS GROW.
REALLY?
THWAP

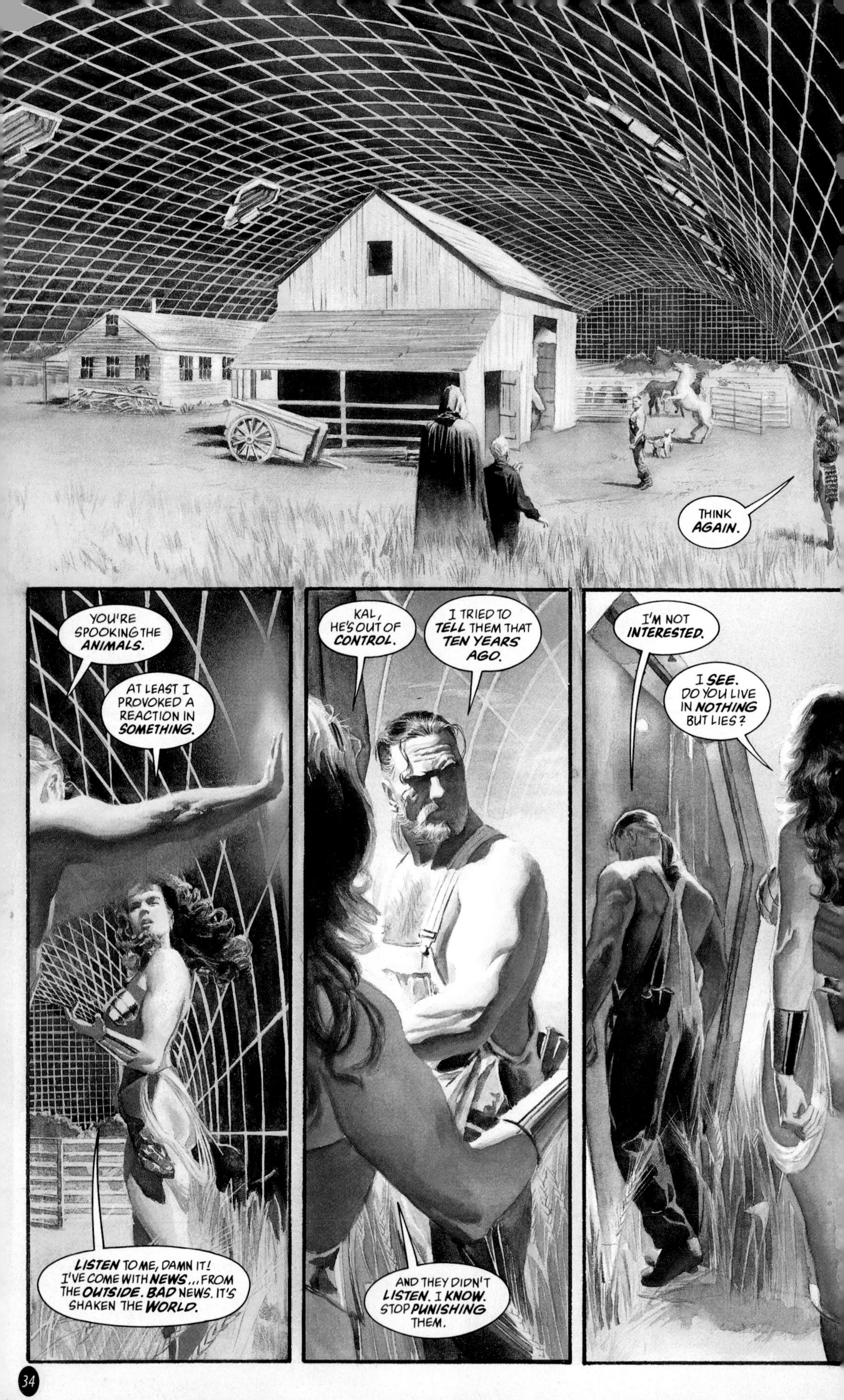
THINK AGAIN.
YOU'RE SPOOKING THE ANIMALS.
AT LEAST I PROVOKED A REACTION IN SOMETHING.
LISTEN TO ME, DAMN IT! I'VE COME WITH NEWS... FROM THE OUTSIDE. BAD NEWS. IT'S SHAKEN THE WORLD.
KAL, HE'S OUT OF CONTROL.
I TRIED TO TELL THEM THAT TEN YEARS AGO.
AND THEY DIDN'T LISTEN. I KNOW. STOP PUNISHING THEM.
I'M NOT INTERESTED.
I SEE. DO YOU LIVE IN NOTHING BUT LIES?

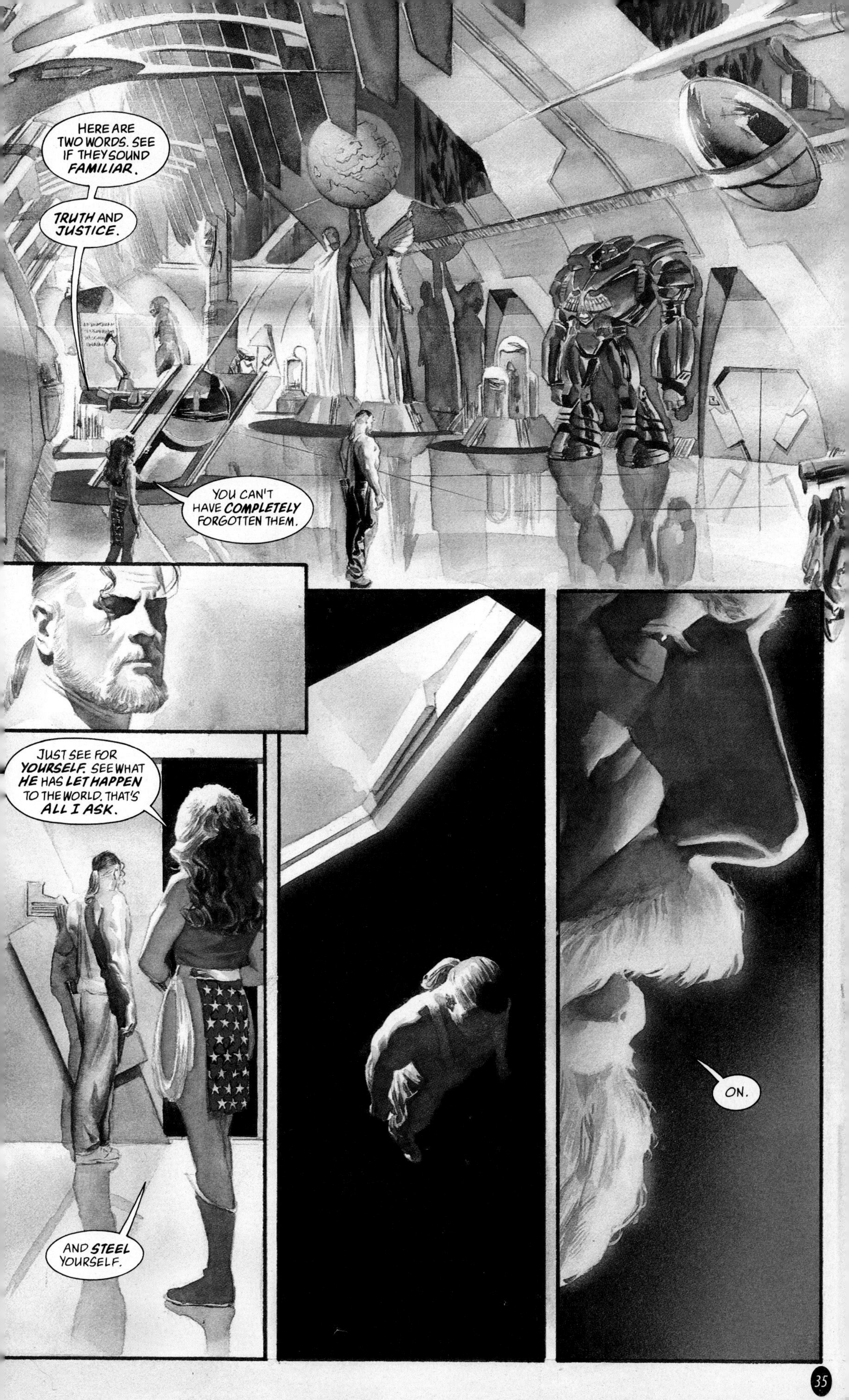
HERE ARE TWO WORDS. SEE IF THEY SOUND FAMILIAR.
TRUTH AND JUSTICE.
YOU CAN'T HAVE COMPLETELY FORGOTTEN THEM.
JUST SEE FOR YOURSELF. SEE WHAT HE HAS LET HAPPEN TO THE WORLD. THAT'S ALL I ASK.
AND STEEL YOURSELF.
ON.

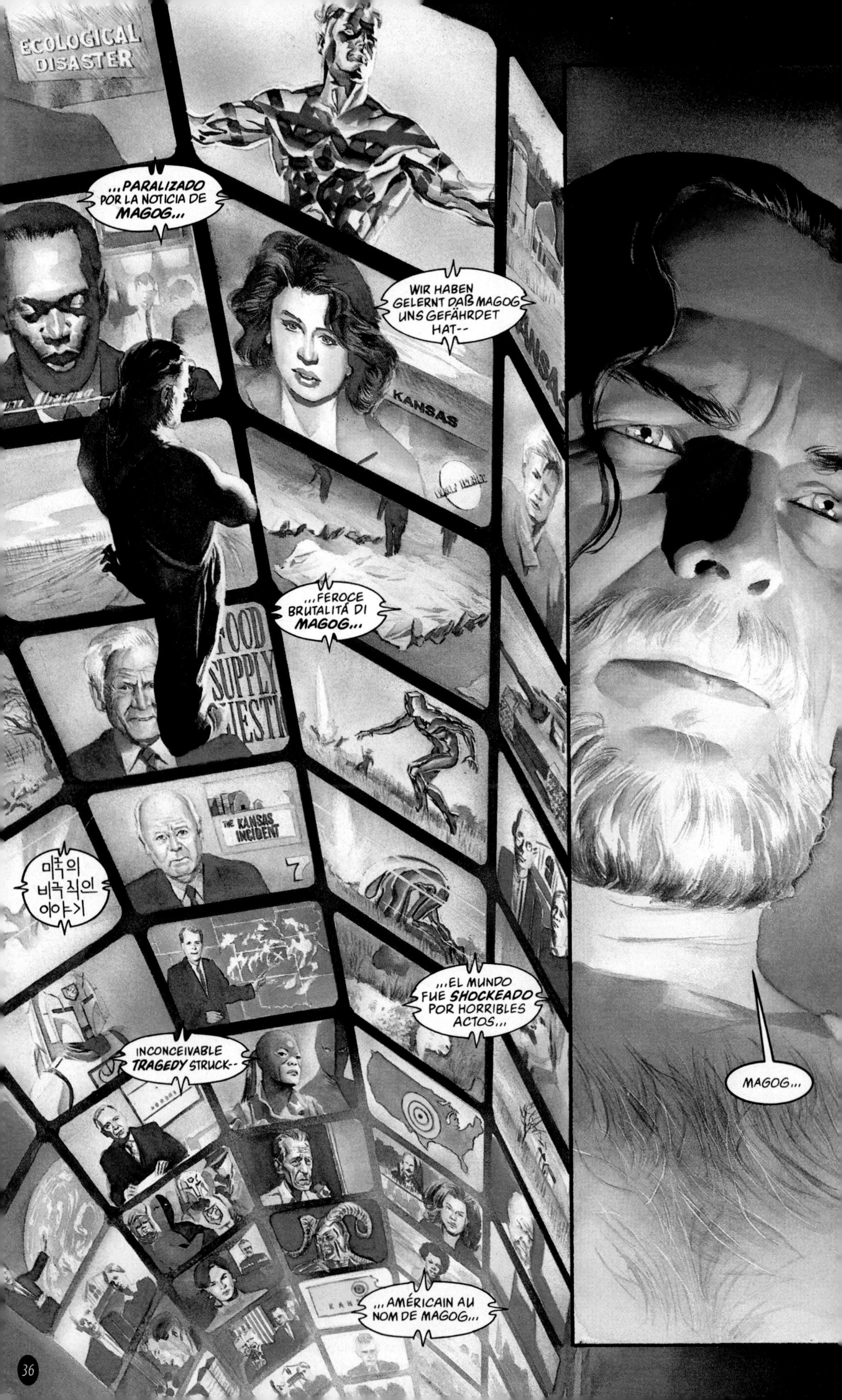
ECOLOGICAL DISASTER
...PARALIZADO POR LA NOTICIA DE MAGOG...
WIR HABEN GELERNT DAß MAGOG UNS GEFÄHRDET HAT--
KANSAS
...FEROCE BRUTALITÀ DI MAGOG...
FOOD SUPPLY
THE KANSAS INCIDENT
미국의 비극적인 이야기
...EL MUNDO FUE SHOCKEADO POR HORRIBLES ACTOS...
INCONCEIVABLE TRAGEDY STRUCK--
...AMÉRICAIN AU NOM DE MAGOG...
MAGOG...

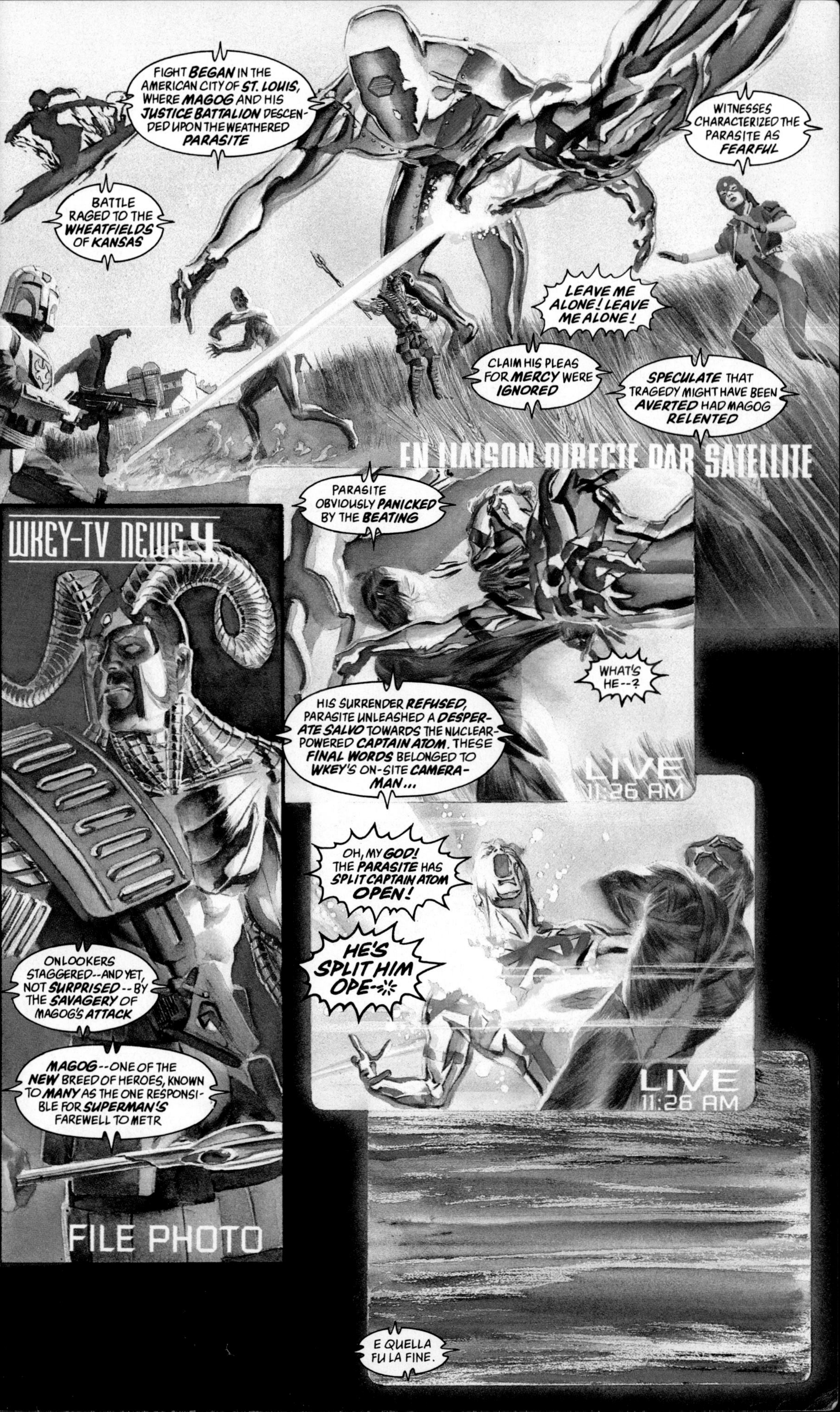
FIGHT BEGAN IN THE AMERICAN CITY OF ST. LOUIS, WHERE MAGOG AND HIS JUSTICE BATTALION DESCENDED UPON THE WEATHERED PARASITE
WITNESSES CHARACTERIZED THE PARASITE AS FEARFUL
BATTLE RAGED TO THE WHEATFIELDS OF KANSAS
LEAVE ME ALONE! LEAVE ME ALONE!
CLAIM HIS PLEAS FOR MERCY WERE IGNORED
SPECULATE THAT TRAGEDY MIGHT HAVE BEEN AVERTED HAD MAGOG RELENTED
EN LIAISON DIRECTE PAR SATELLITE
WKEY-TV NEWS 4
PARASITE OBVIOUSLY PANICKED BY THE BEATING
WHAT'S HE--?
HIS SURRENDER REFUSED, PARASITE UNLEASHED A DESPERATE SALVO TOWARDS THE NUCLEAR-POWERED CAPTAIN ATOM. THESE FINAL WORDS BELONGED TO WKEY'S ON-SITE CAMERAMAN...
LIVE
11:26 AM
OH, MY GOD! THE PARASITE HAS SPLIT CAPTAIN ATOM OPEN!
HE'S SPLIT HIM OPE--
ONLOOKERS STAGGERED--AND YET, NOT SURPRISED--BY THE SAVAGERY OF MAGOG'S ATTACK
MAGOG--ONE OF THE NEW BREED OF HEROES, KNOWN TO MANY AS THE ONE RESPONSIBLE FOR SUPERMAN'S FAREWELL TO METR
LIVE
11:26 AM
FILE PHOTO
E QUELLA FU LA FINE.

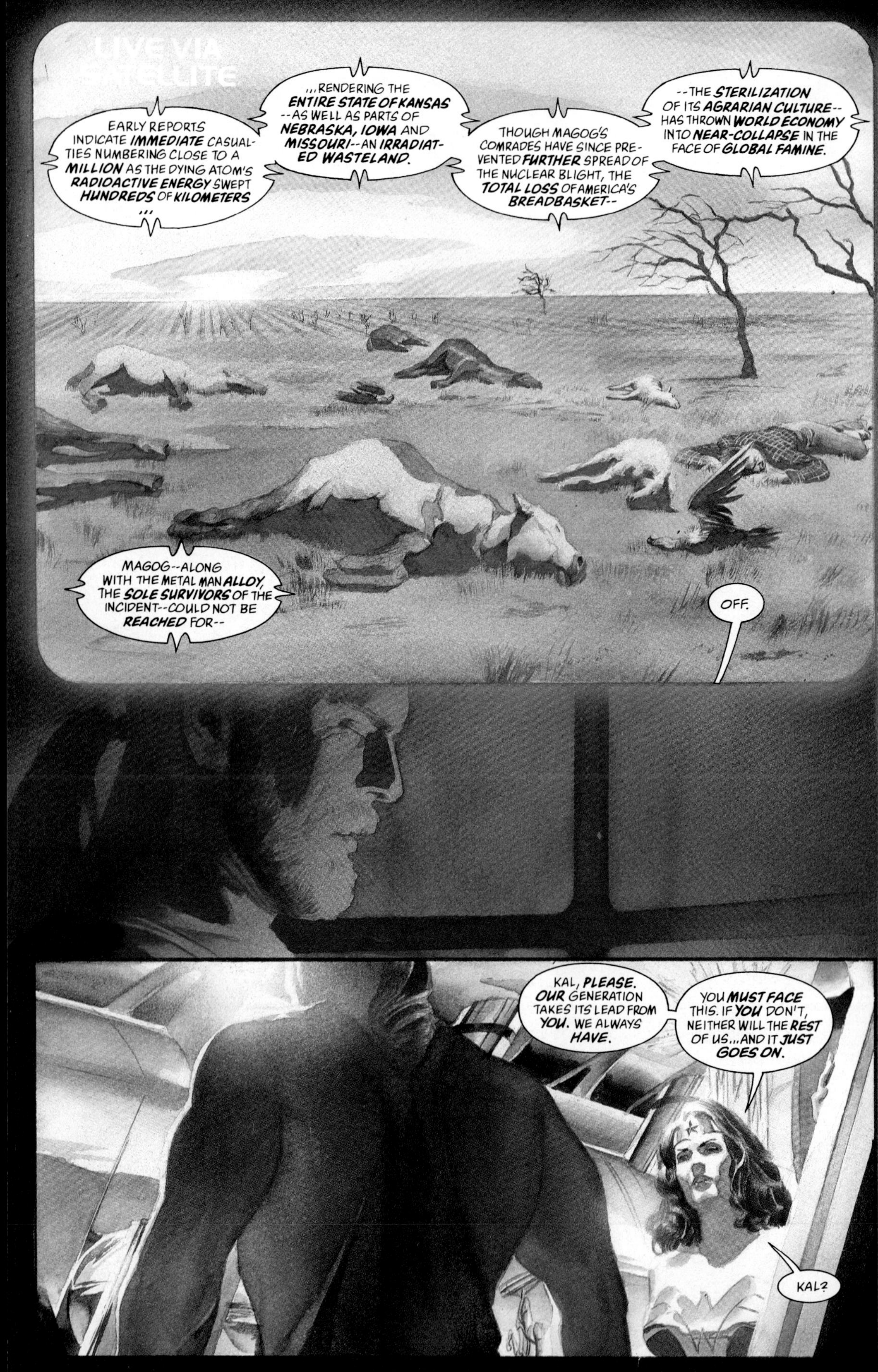
LIVE VIA SATELLITE
EARLY REPORTS INDICATE IMMEDIATE CASUALTIES NUMBERING CLOSE TO A MILLION AS THE DYING ATOM'S RADIOACTIVE ENERGY SWEPT HUNDREDS OF KILOMETERS ...
...RENDERING THE ENTIRE STATE OF KANSAS --AS WELL AS PARTS OF NEBRASKA, IOWA AND MISSOURI--AN IRRADIATED WASTELAND.
THOUGH MAGOG'S COMRADES HAVE SINCE PREVENTED FURTHER SPREAD OF THE NUCLEAR BLIGHT, THE TOTAL LOSS OF AMERICA'S BREADBASKET--
--THE STERILIZATION OF ITS AGRARIAN CULTURE--HAS THROWN WORLD ECONOMY INTO NEAR-COLLAPSE IN THE FACE OF GLOBAL FAMINE.
MAGOG--ALONG WITH THE METAL MAN ALLOY, THE SOLE SURVIVORS OF THE INCIDENT--COULD NOT BE REACHED FOR--
OFF.
KAL, PLEASE. OUR GENERATION TAKES ITS LEAD FROM YOU. WE ALWAYS HAVE.
YOU MUST FACE THIS. IF YOU DON'T, NEITHER WILL THE REST OF US...AND IT JUST GOES ON.
KAL?

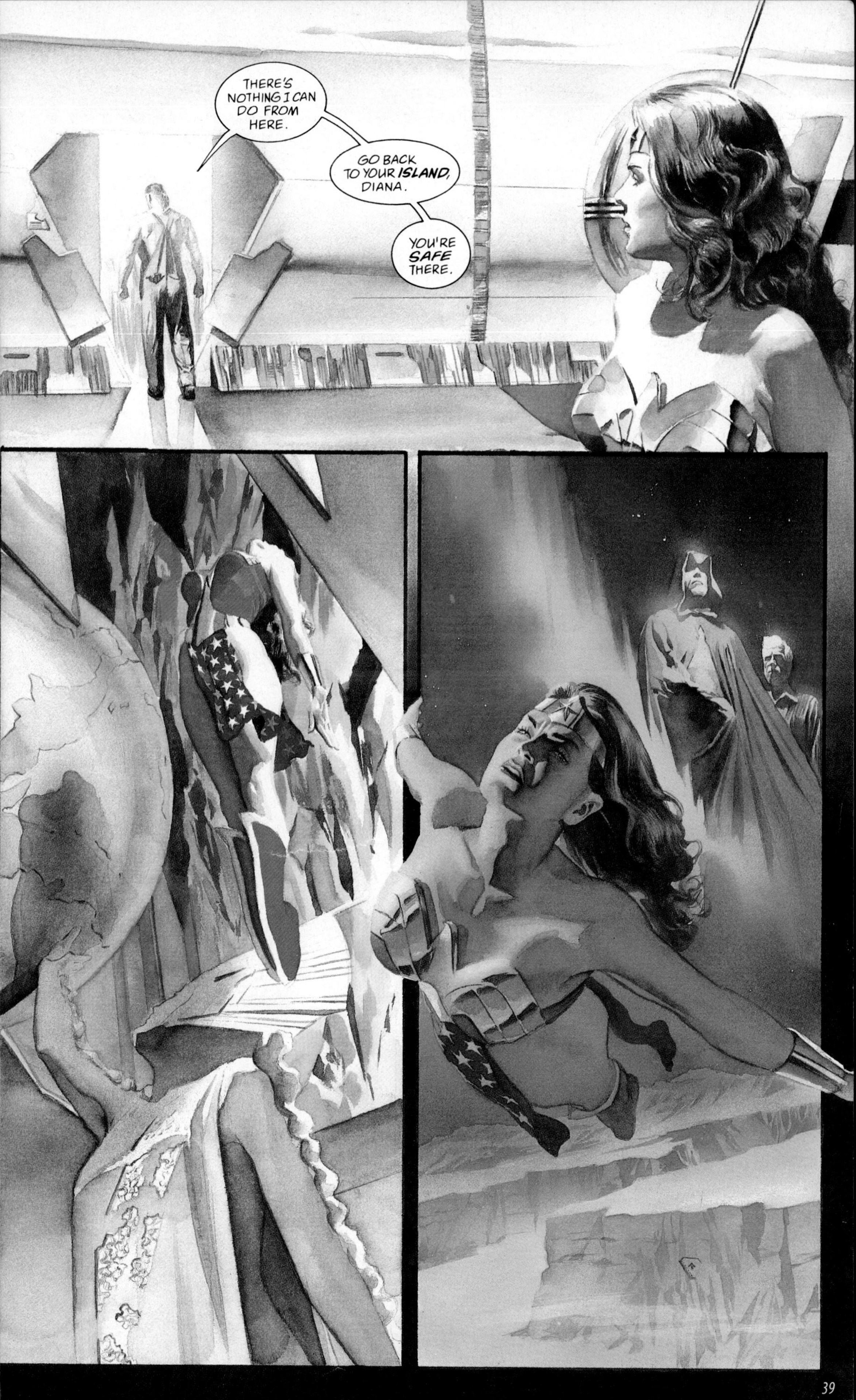
THERE'S NOTHING I CAN DO FROM HERE.
GO BACK TO YOUR **ISLAND**, DIANA.
YOU'RE **SAFE** THERE.

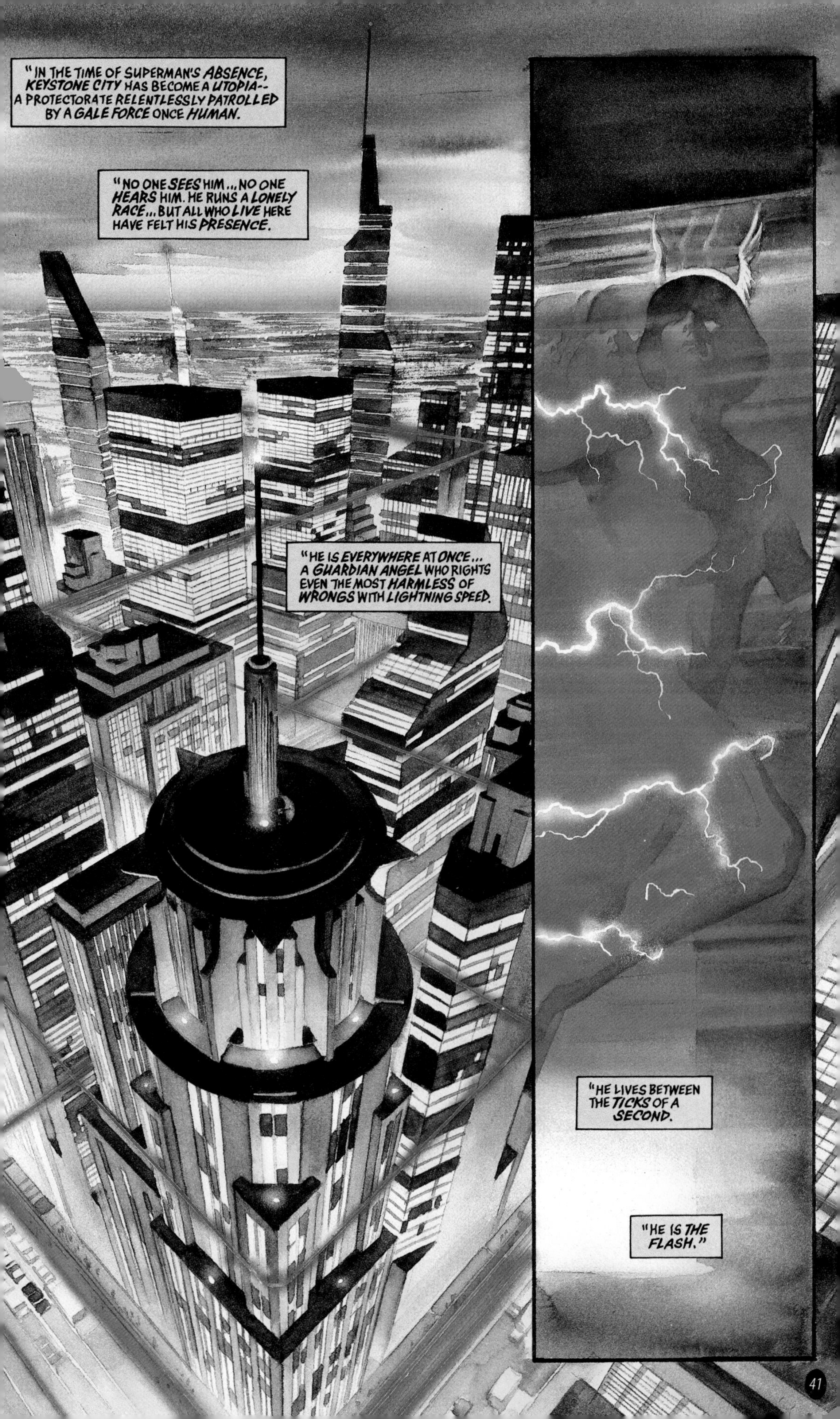
"IN THE TIME OF SUPERMAN'S ABSENCE, KEYSTONE CITY HAS BECOME A UTOPIA-- A PROTECTORATE RELENTLESSLY PATROLLED BY A GALE FORCE ONCE HUMAN.
"NO ONE SEES HIM... NO ONE HEARS HIM. HE RUNS A LONELY RACE... BUT ALL WHO LIVE HERE HAVE FELT HIS PRESENCE.
"HE IS EVERYWHERE AT ONCE... A GUARDIAN ANGEL WHO RIGHTS EVEN THE MOST HARMLESS OF WRONGS WITH LIGHTNING SPEED.
"HE LIVES BETWEEN THE TICKS OF A SECOND.
"HE IS THE FLASH."

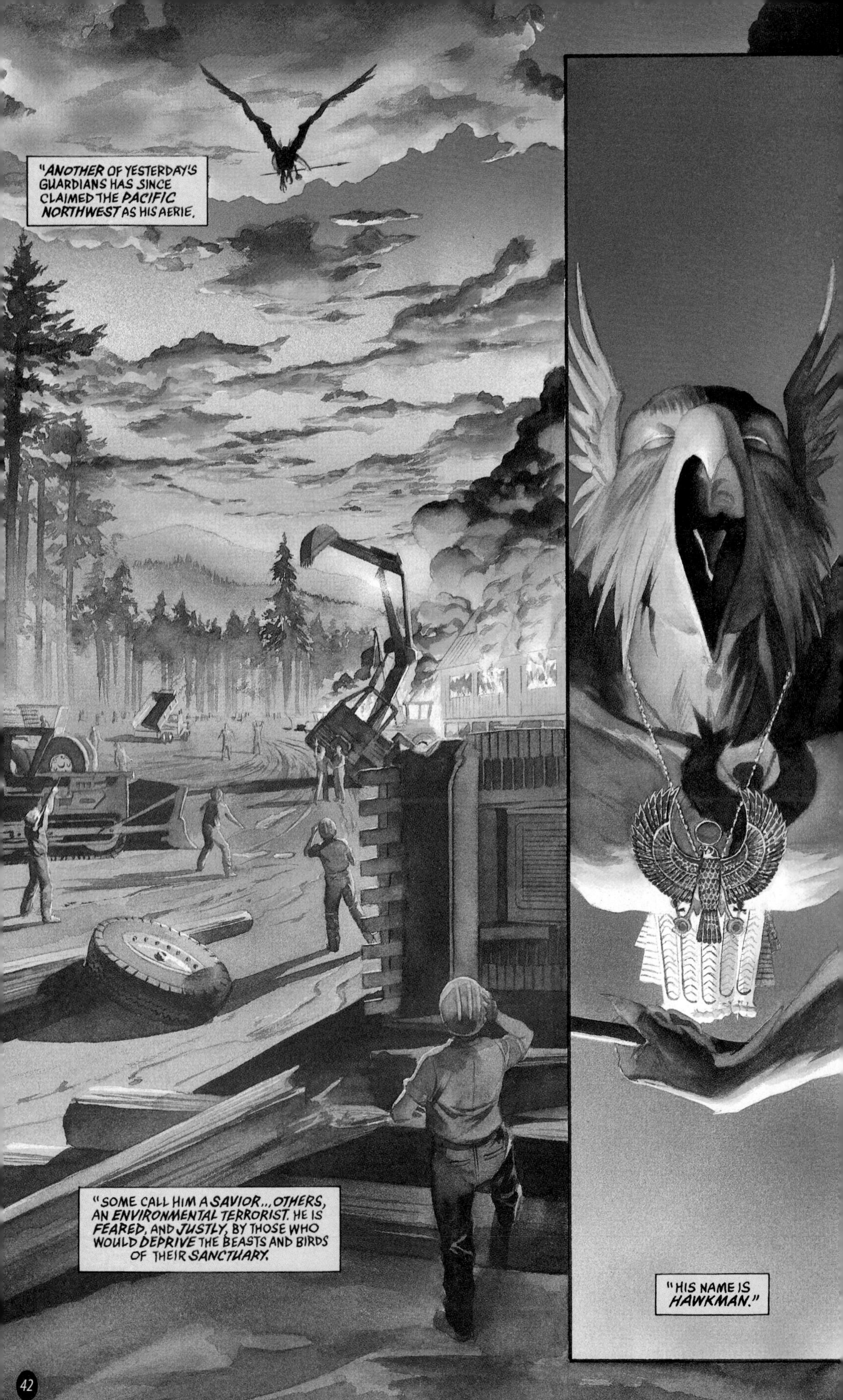
"ANOTHER OF YESTERDAY'S GUARDIANS HAS SINCE CLAIMED THE PACIFIC NORTHWEST AS HIS AERIE.
"SOME CALL HIM A SAVIOR... OTHERS, AN ENVIRONMENTAL TERRORIST. HE IS FEARED, AND JUSTLY, BY THOSE WHO WOULD DEPRIVE THE BEASTS AND BIRDS OF THEIR SANCTUARY.
"HIS NAME IS HAWKMAN."

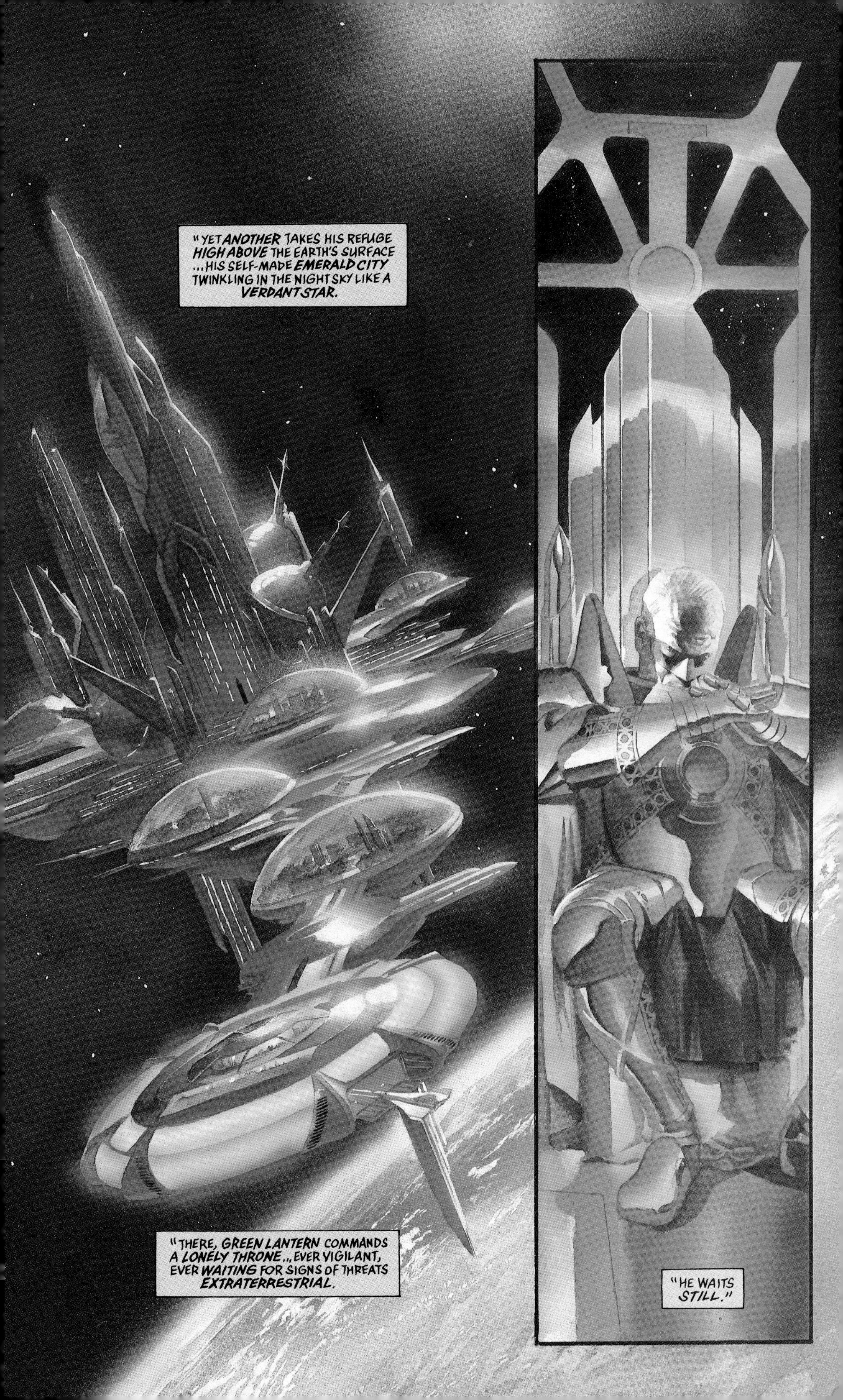
"YET ANOTHER TAKES HIS REFUGE HIGH ABOVE THE EARTH'S SURFACE ...HIS SELF-MADE EMERALD CITY TWINKLING IN THE NIGHT SKY LIKE A VERDANT STAR.
"THERE, GREEN LANTERN COMMANDS A LONELY THRONE... EVER VIGILANT, EVER WAITING FOR SIGNS OF THREATS EXTRATERRESTRIAL.
"HE WAITS STILL."

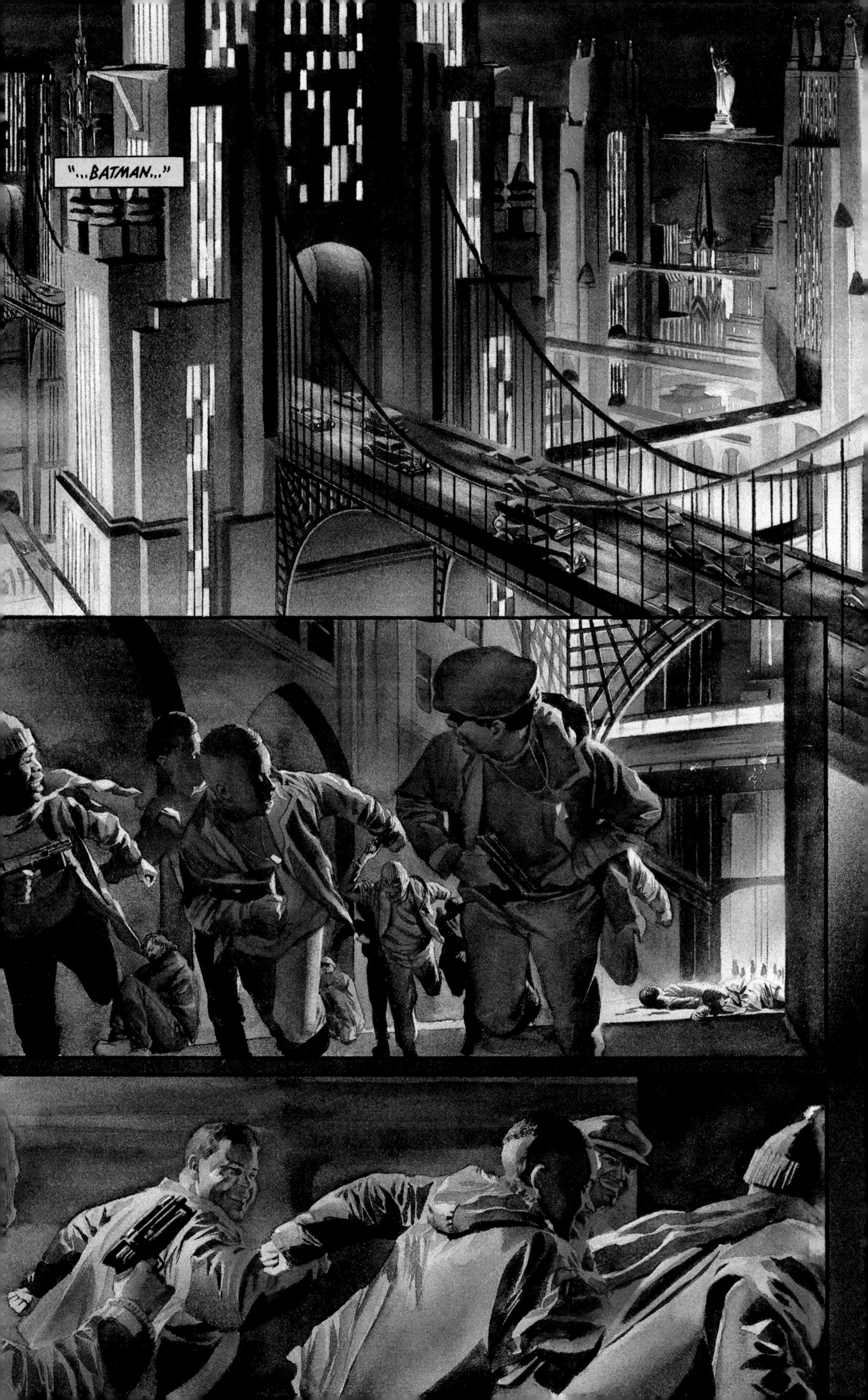
"...BATMAN..."

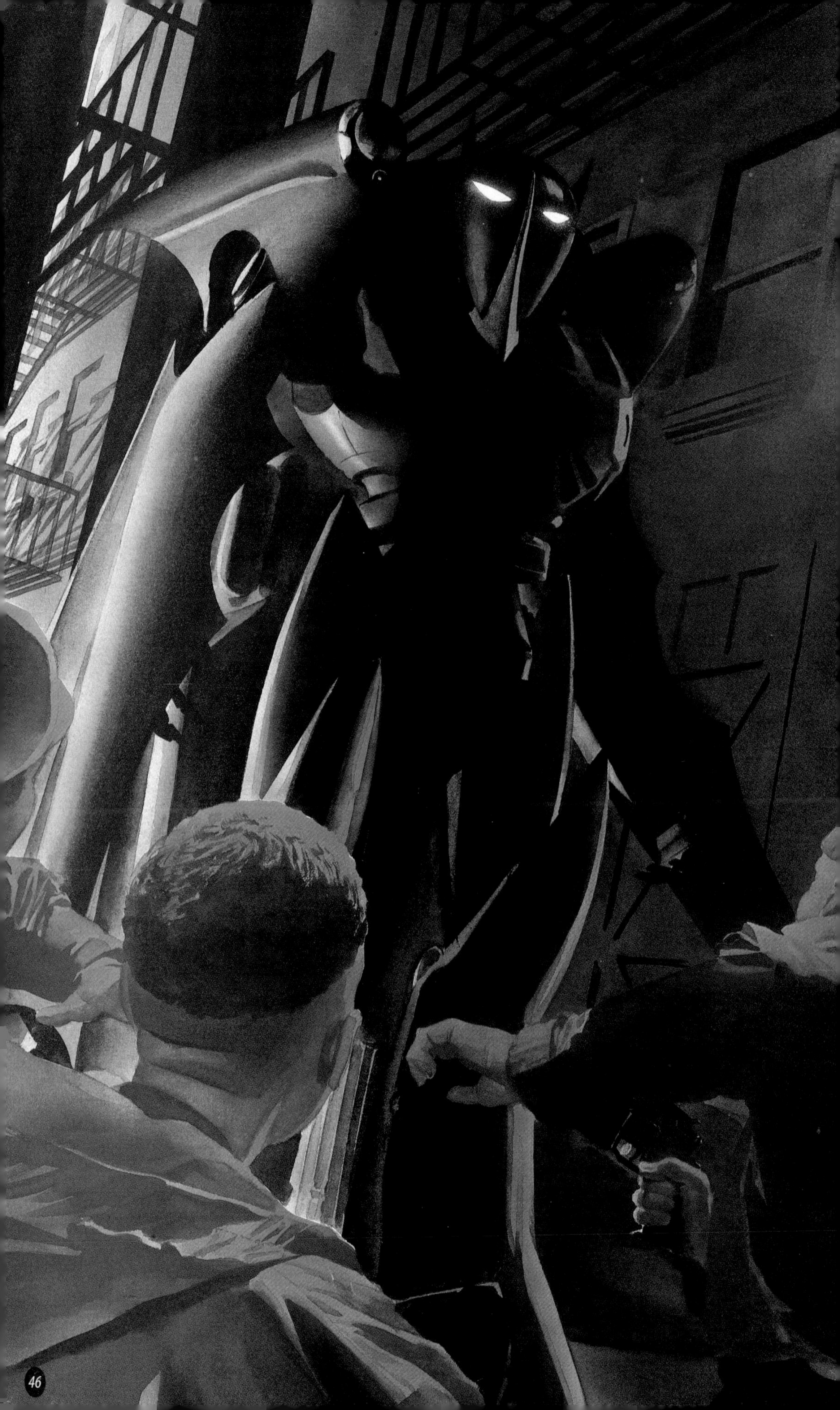

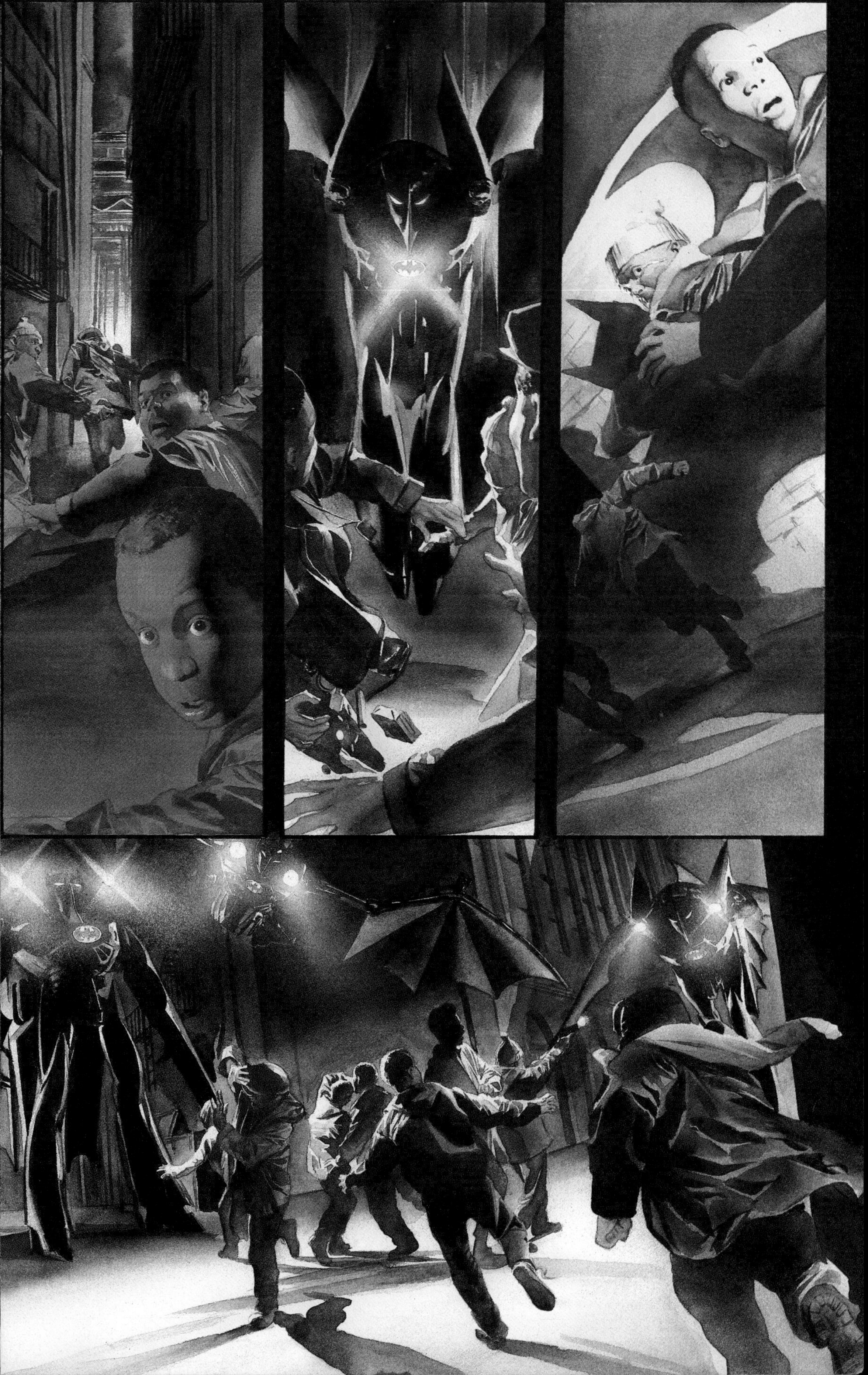

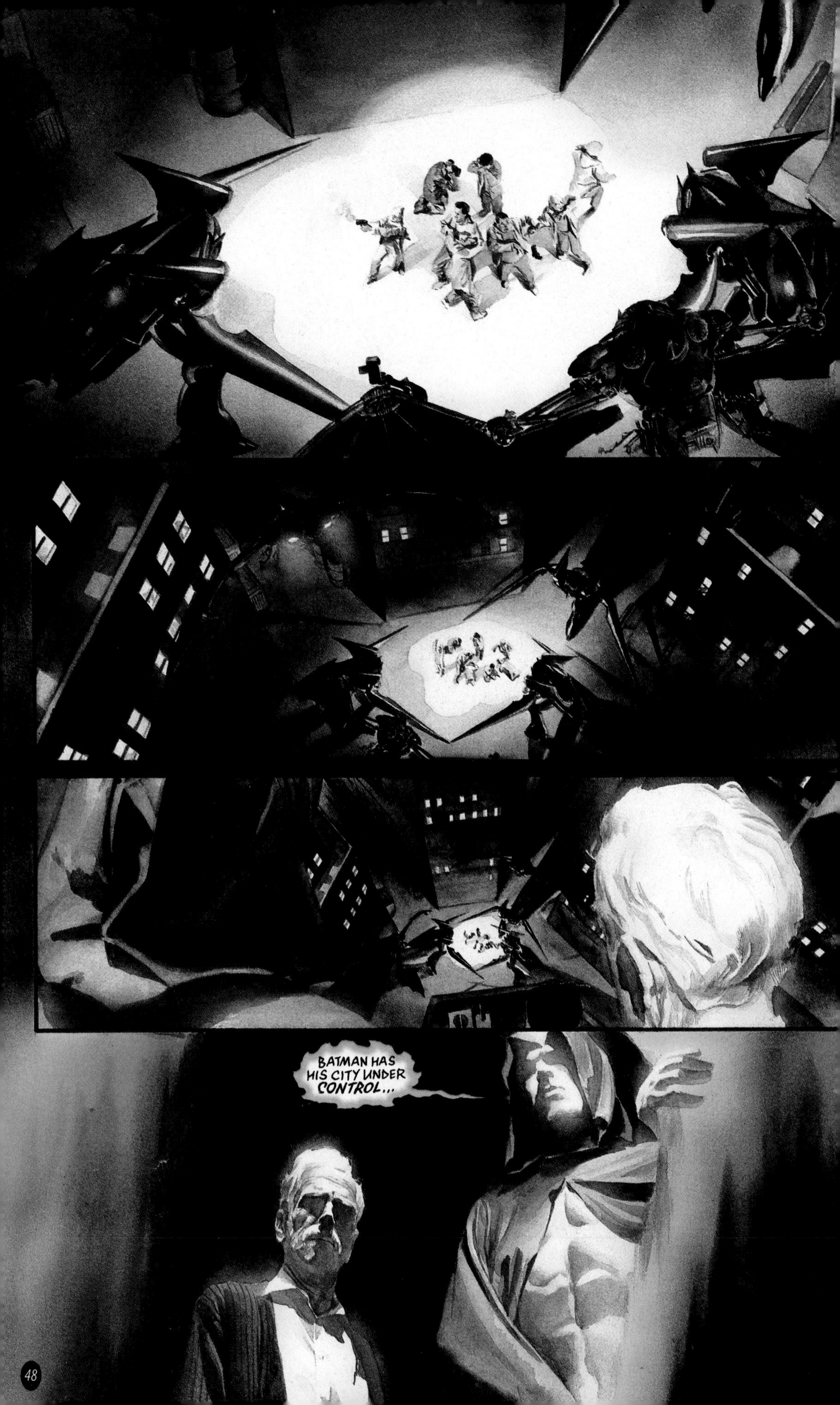
BATMAN HAS
HIS CITY UNDER
CONTROL...

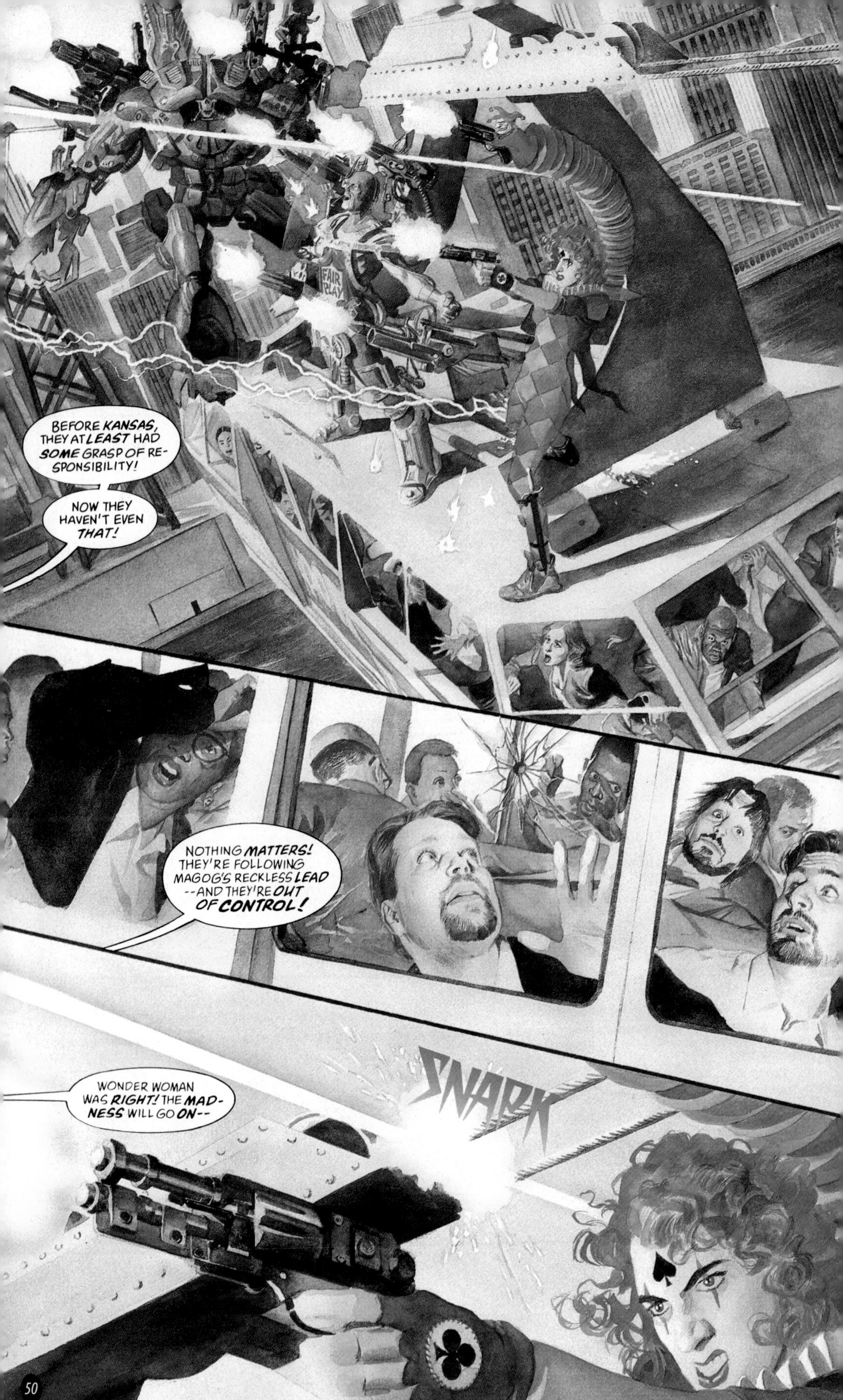
BEFORE KANSAS, THEY AT LEAST HAD SOME GRASP OF RE-SPONSIBILITY!
NOW THEY HAVEN'T EVEN THAT!
FAIR PLAY
NOTHING MATTERS! THEY'RE FOLLOWING MAGOG'S RECKLESS LEAD --AND THEY'RE OUT OF CONTROL!
WONDER WOMAN WAS RIGHT! THE MAD-NESS WILL GO ON--
SNARK

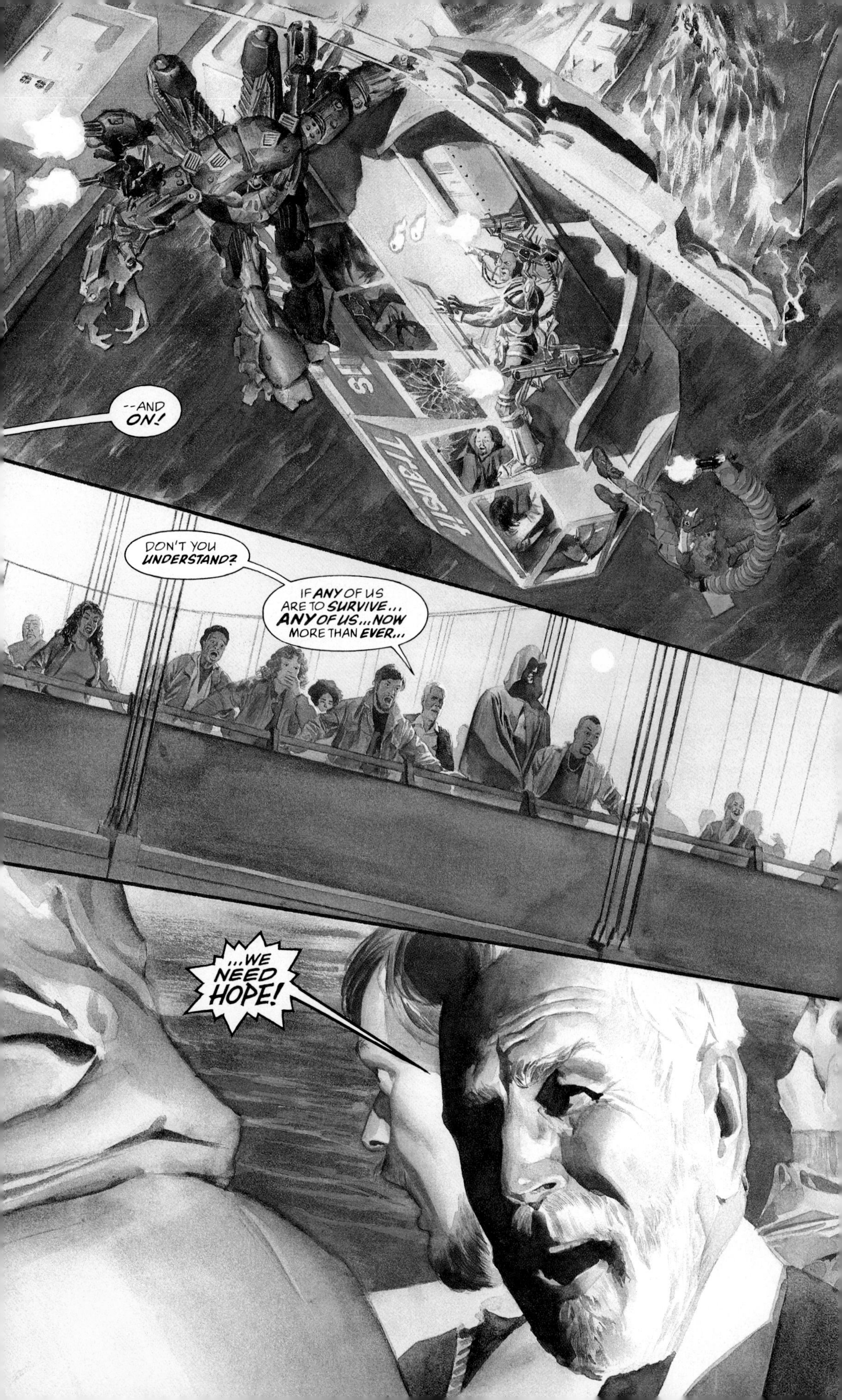
--AND ON!
DON'T YOU UNDERSTAND?
IF ANY OF US ARE TO SURVIVE... ANY OF US...NOW MORE THAN EVER...
...WE NEED HOPE!

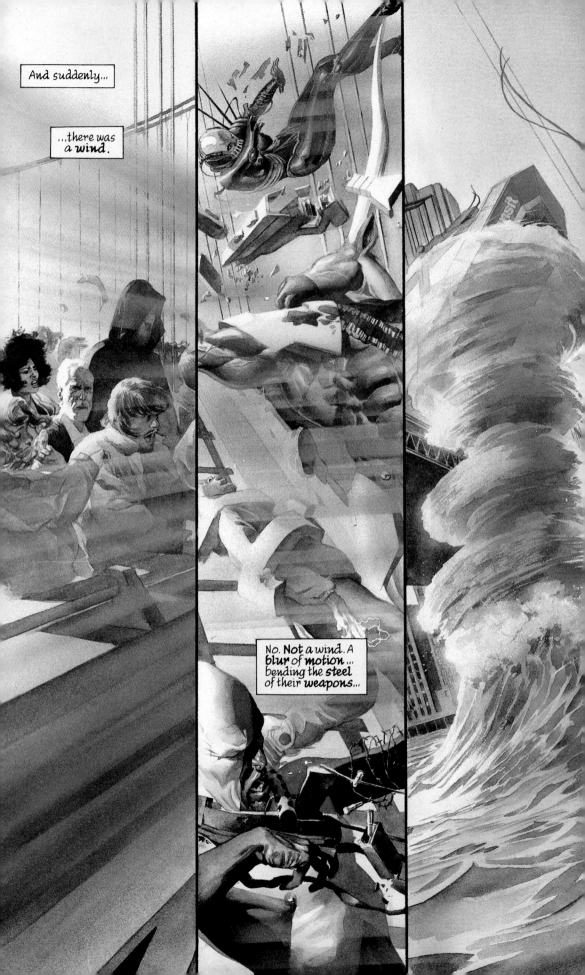

And suddenly...

...there was **a wind**.

No. **Not a wind.** A **blur** of **motion**... bending the **steel** of their **weapons**...

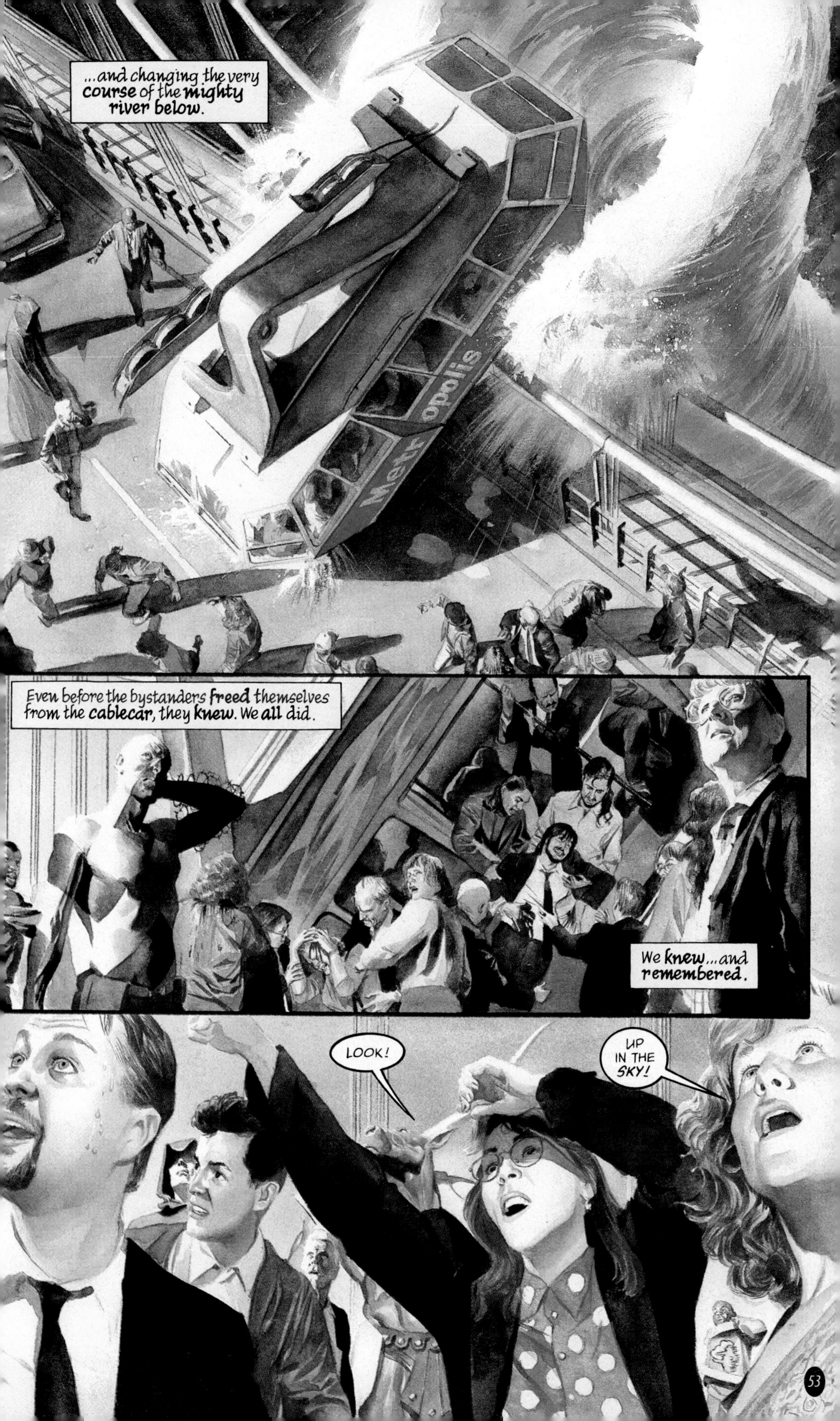
...and changing the very course of the mighty river below.
Metropolis
Even before the bystanders freed themselves from the cablecar, they knew. We all did.
We knew...and remembered.
LOOK!
UP IN THE SKY!

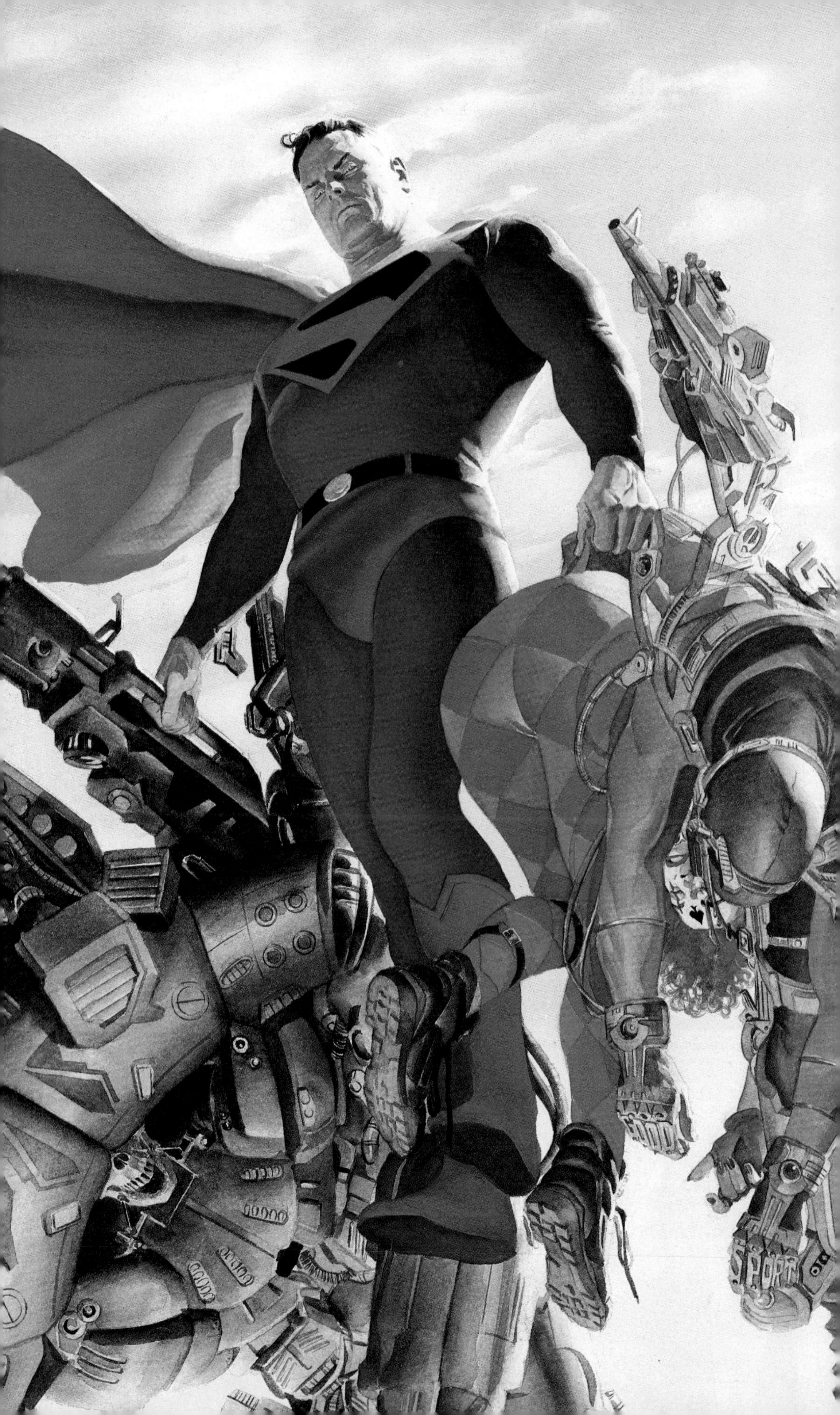

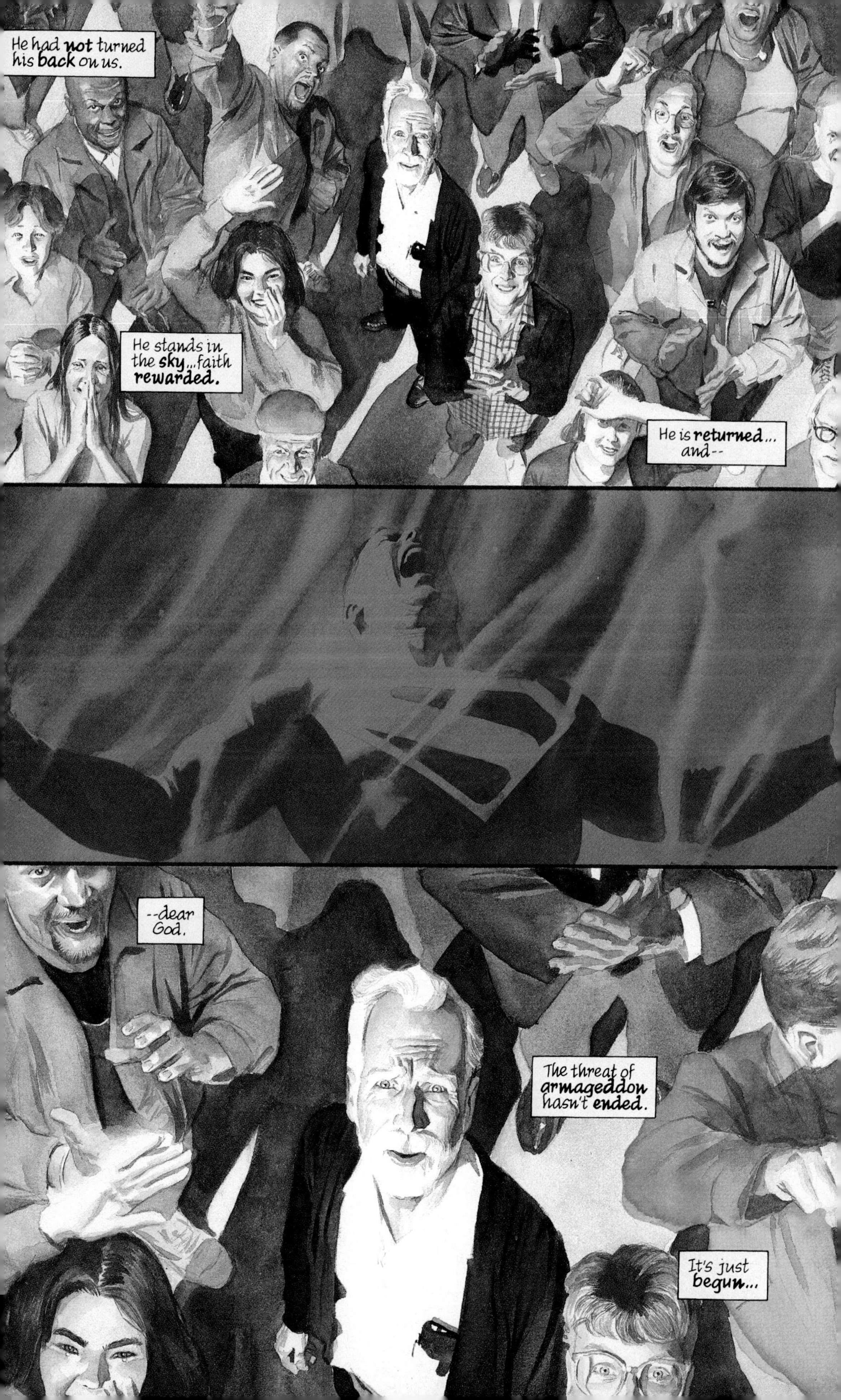
He had not turned his back on us.
He stands in the sky...faith rewarded.
He is returned... and--
--dear God.
The threat of armageddon hasn't ended.
It's just begun...

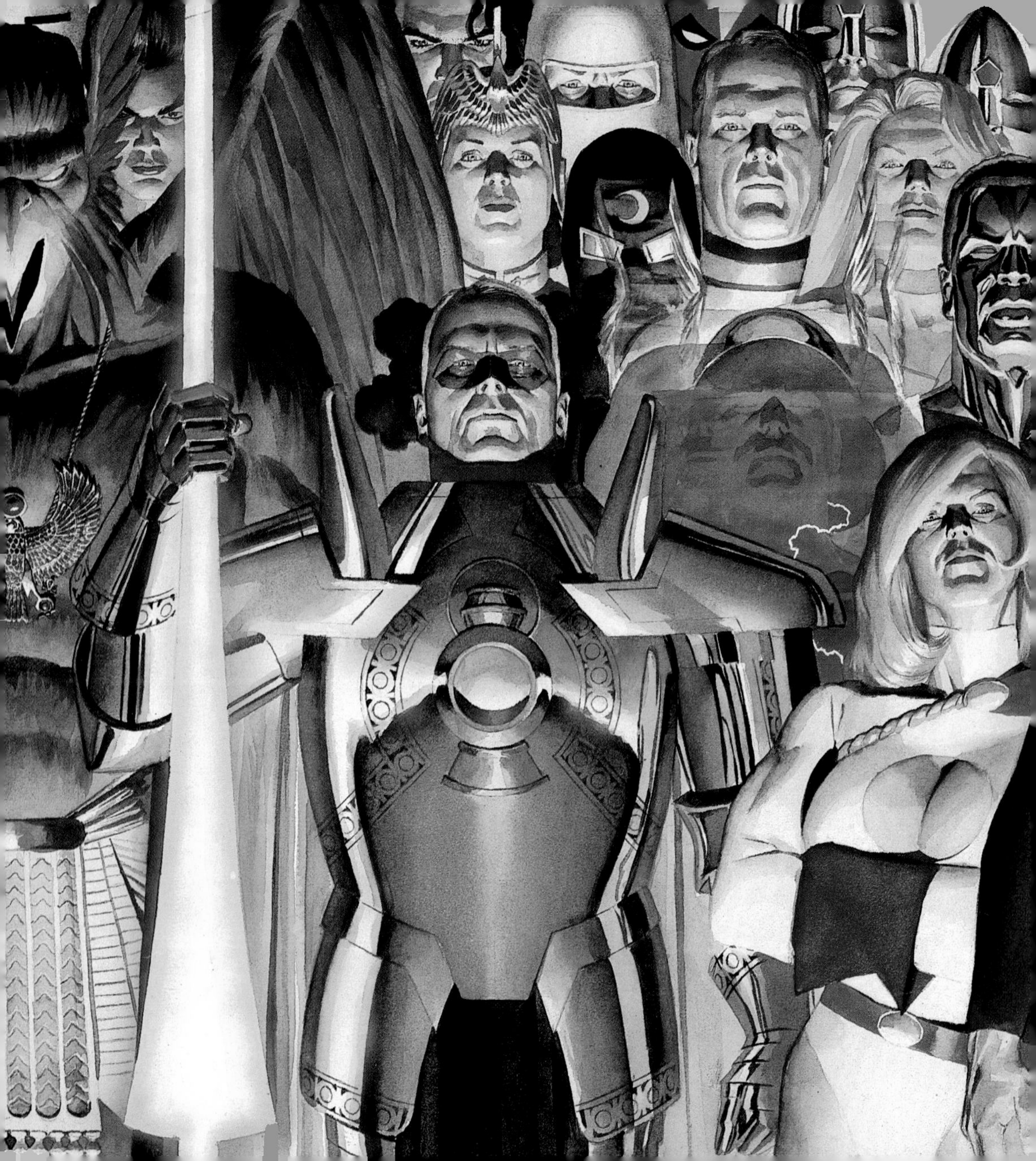

CHAPTER TWO

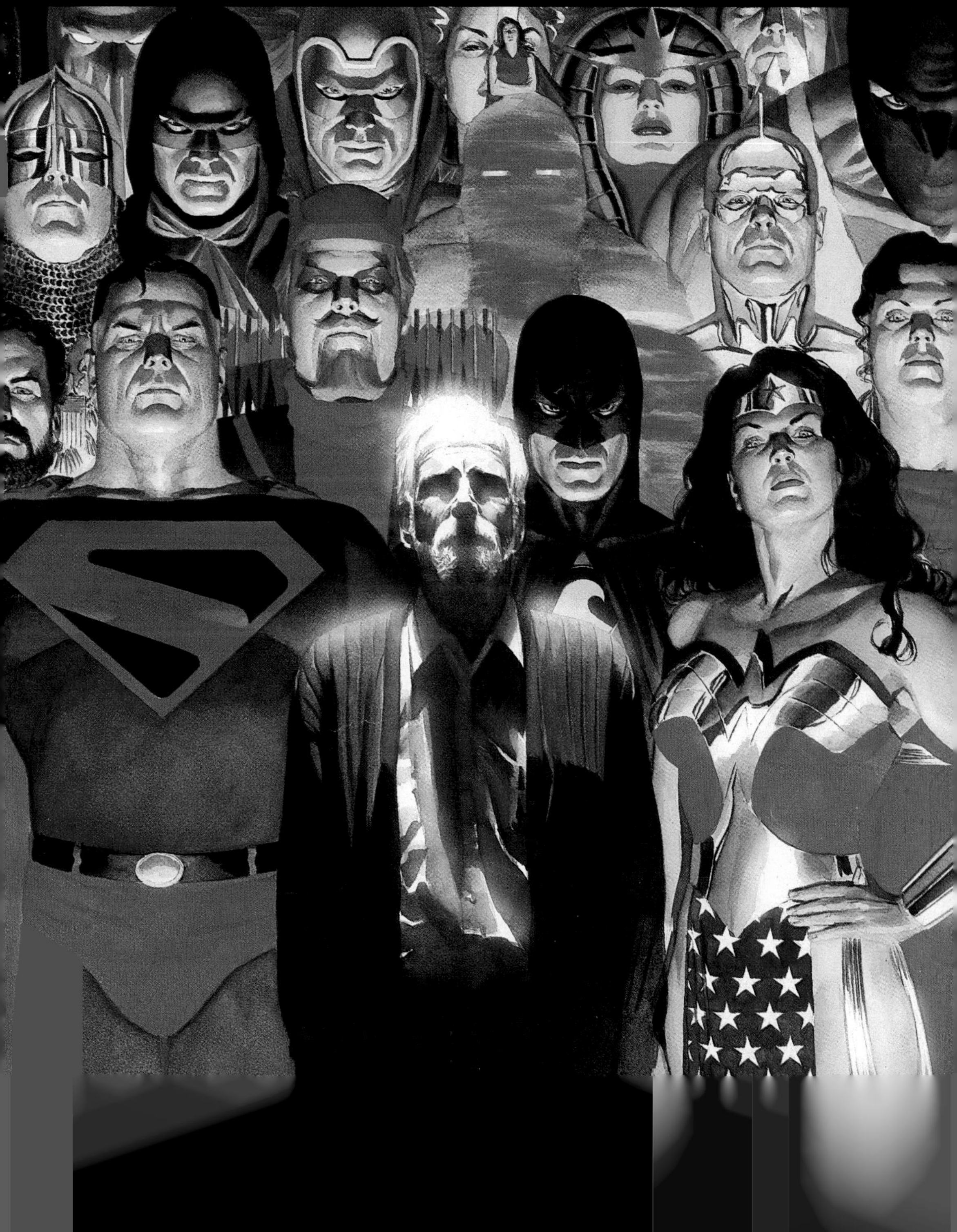

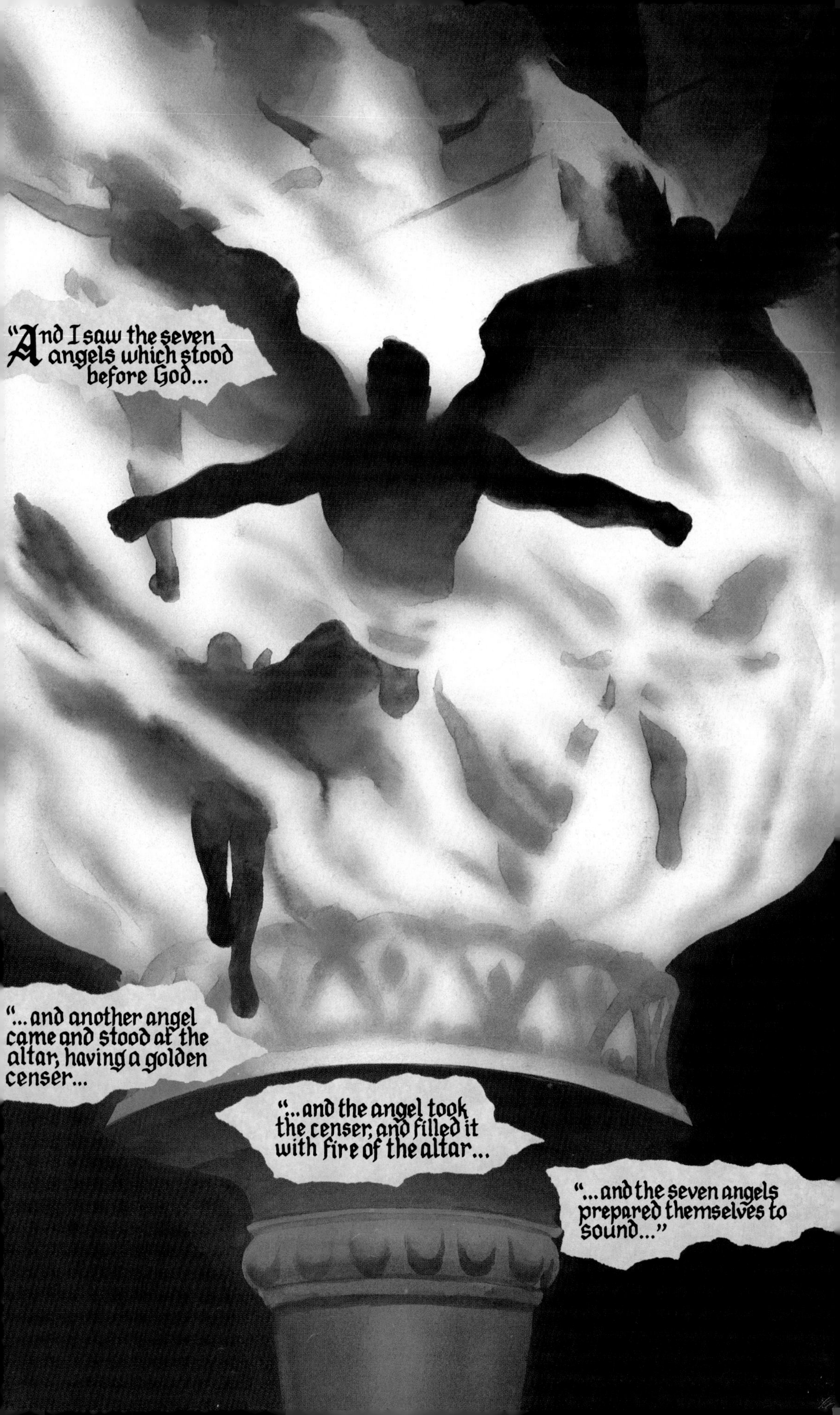
"And I saw the seven angels which stood before God...
"...and another angel came and stood at the altar, having a golden censer...
"...and the angel took the censer, and filled it with fire of the altar...
"...and the seven angels prepared themselves to sound..."

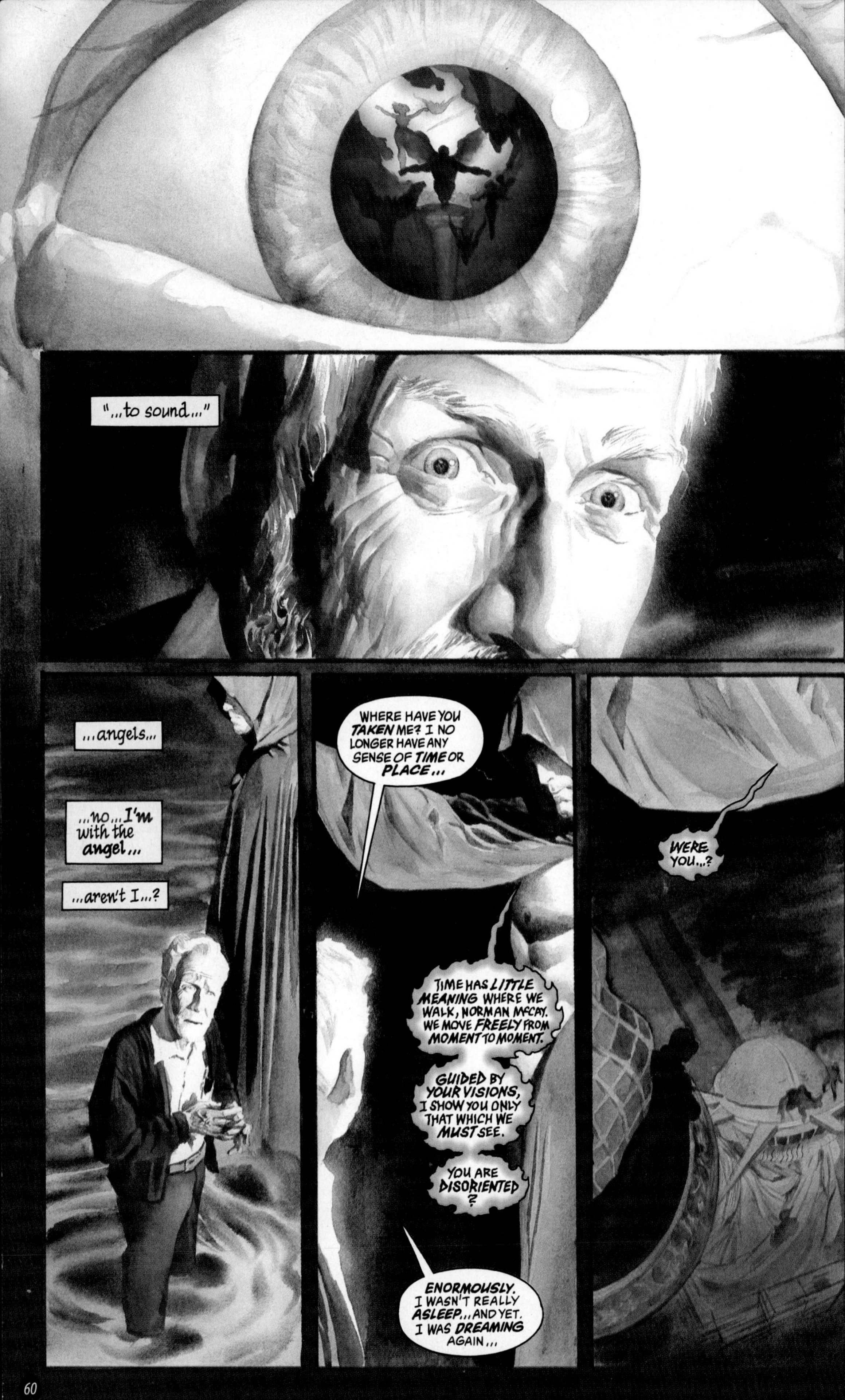
"...to sound..."
...angels...
...no... I'm with the angel...
...aren't I...?
WHERE HAVE YOU TAKEN ME? I NO LONGER HAVE ANY SENSE OF TIME OR PLACE...
WERE YOU...?
TIME HAS LITTLE MEANING WHERE WE WALK, NORMAN McCAY. WE MOVE FREELY FROM MOMENT TO MOMENT.
GUIDED BY YOUR VISIONS, I SHOW YOU ONLY THAT WHICH WE MUST SEE.
YOU ARE DISORIENTED?
ENORMOUSLY. I WASN'T REALLY ASLEEP... AND YET. I WAS DREAMING AGAIN...

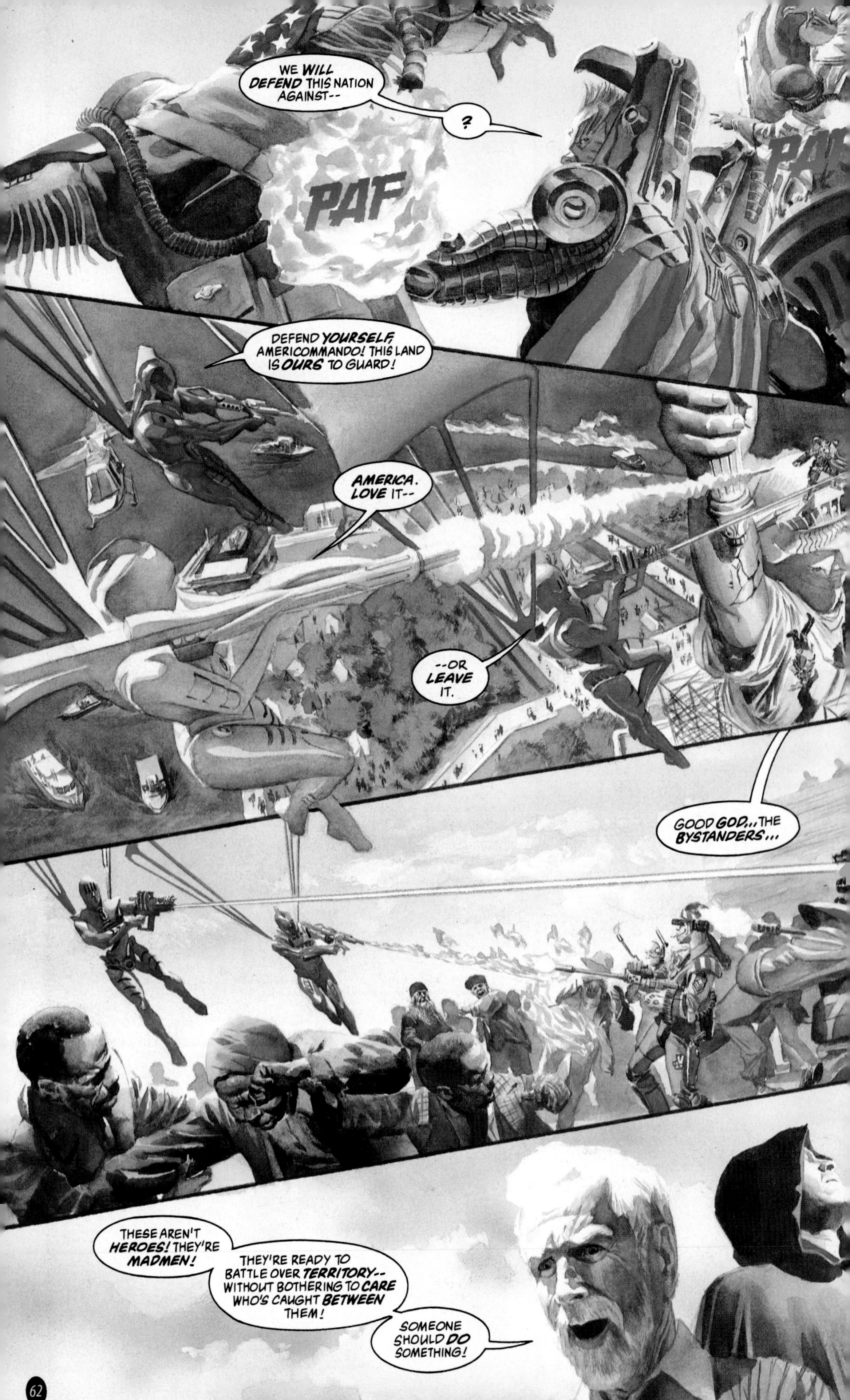

WE WILL DEFEND THIS NATION AGAINST--
?
PAF
PAF
DEFEND YOURSELF, AMERICOMMANDO! THIS LAND IS OURS TO GUARD!
AMERICA. LOVE IT--
--OR LEAVE IT.
GOOD GOD... THE BYSTANDERS...
THESE AREN'T HEROES! THEY'RE MADMEN!
THEY'RE READY TO BATTLE OVER TERRITORY-- WITHOUT BOTHERING TO CARE WHO'S CAUGHT BETWEEN THEM!
SOMEONE SHOULD DO SOMETHING!

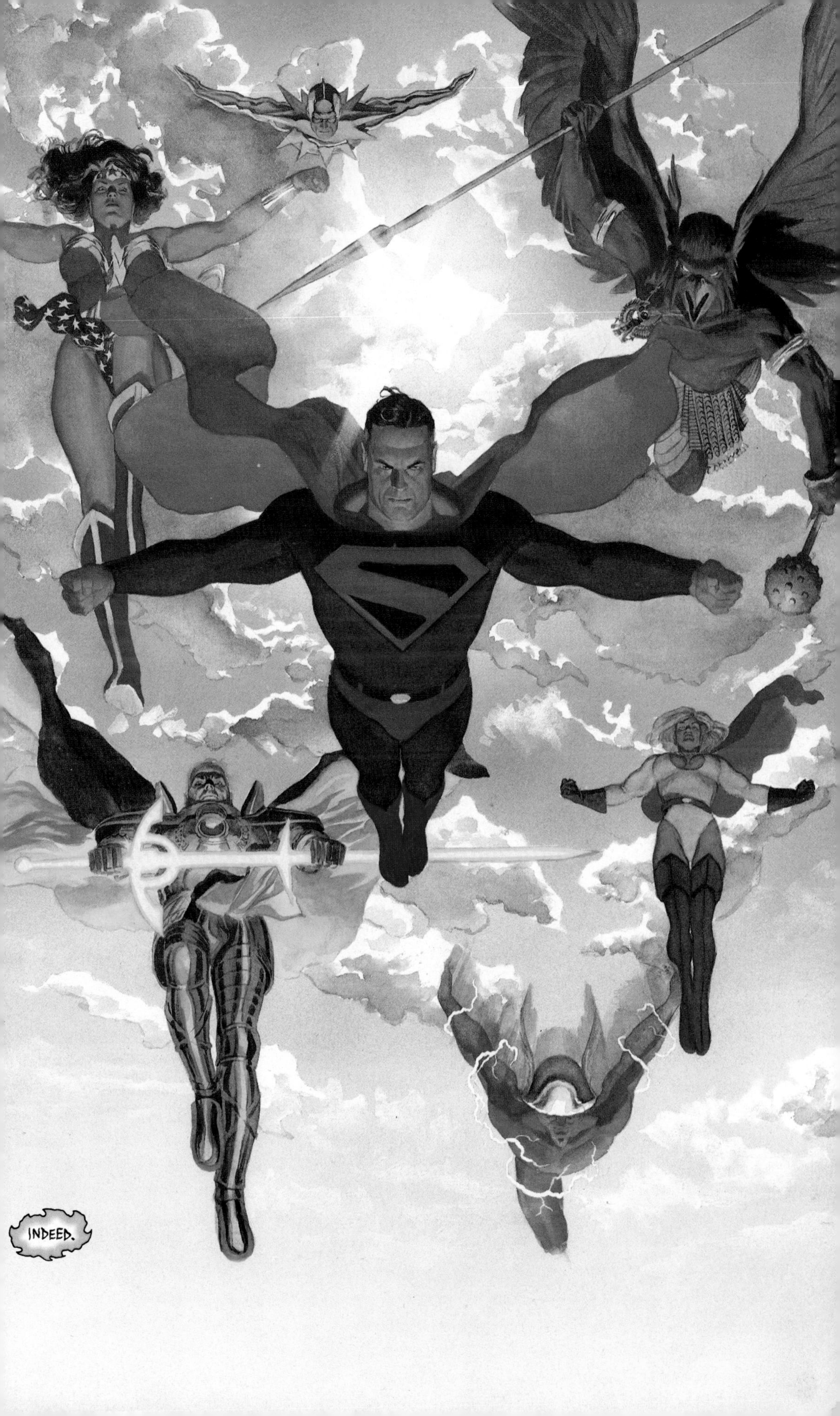
INDEED.

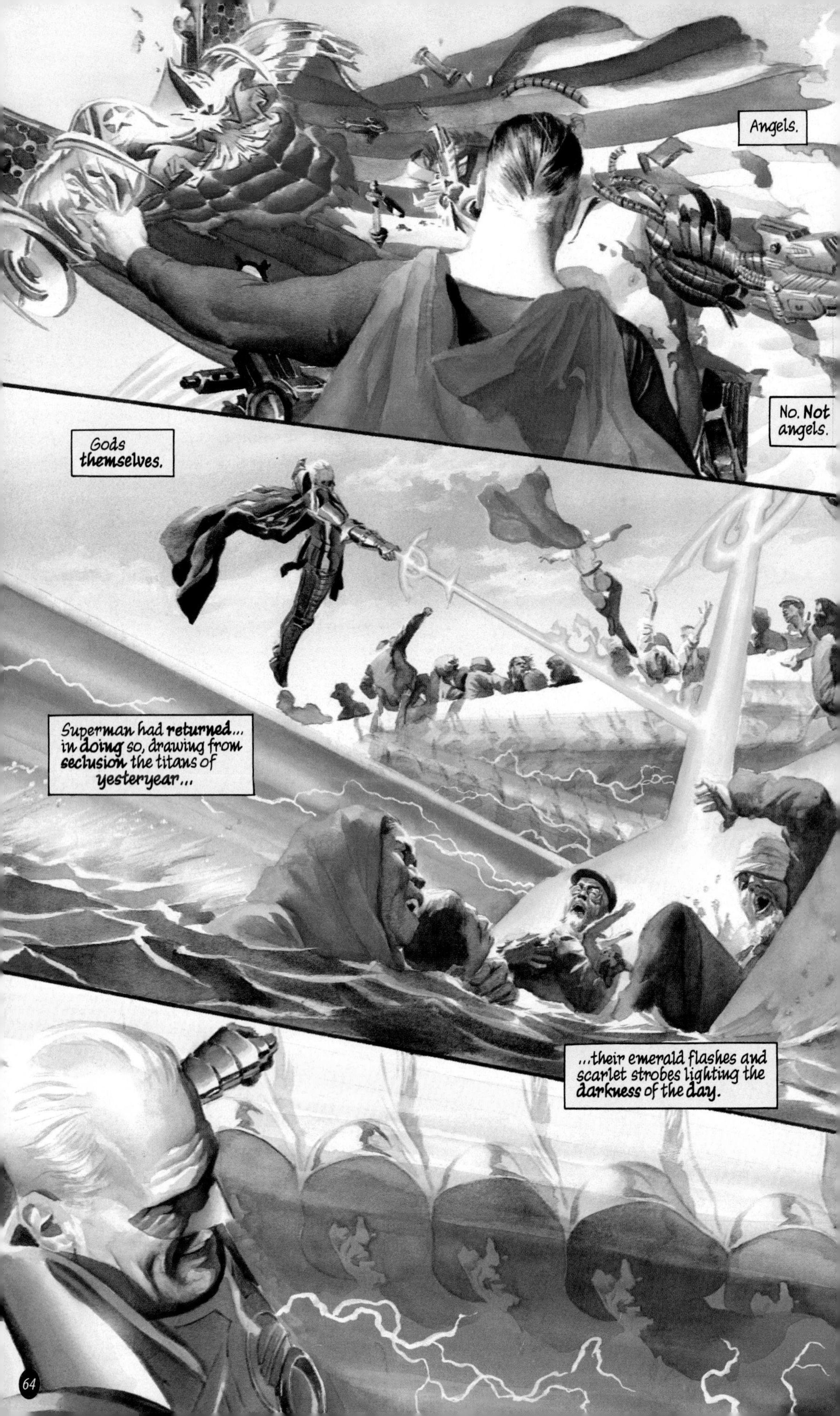

Angels.
No. Not angels.
Gods themselves.
Superman had returned... in doing so, drawing from seclusion the titans of yesteryear...
...their emerald flashes and scarlet strobes lighting the darkness of the day.

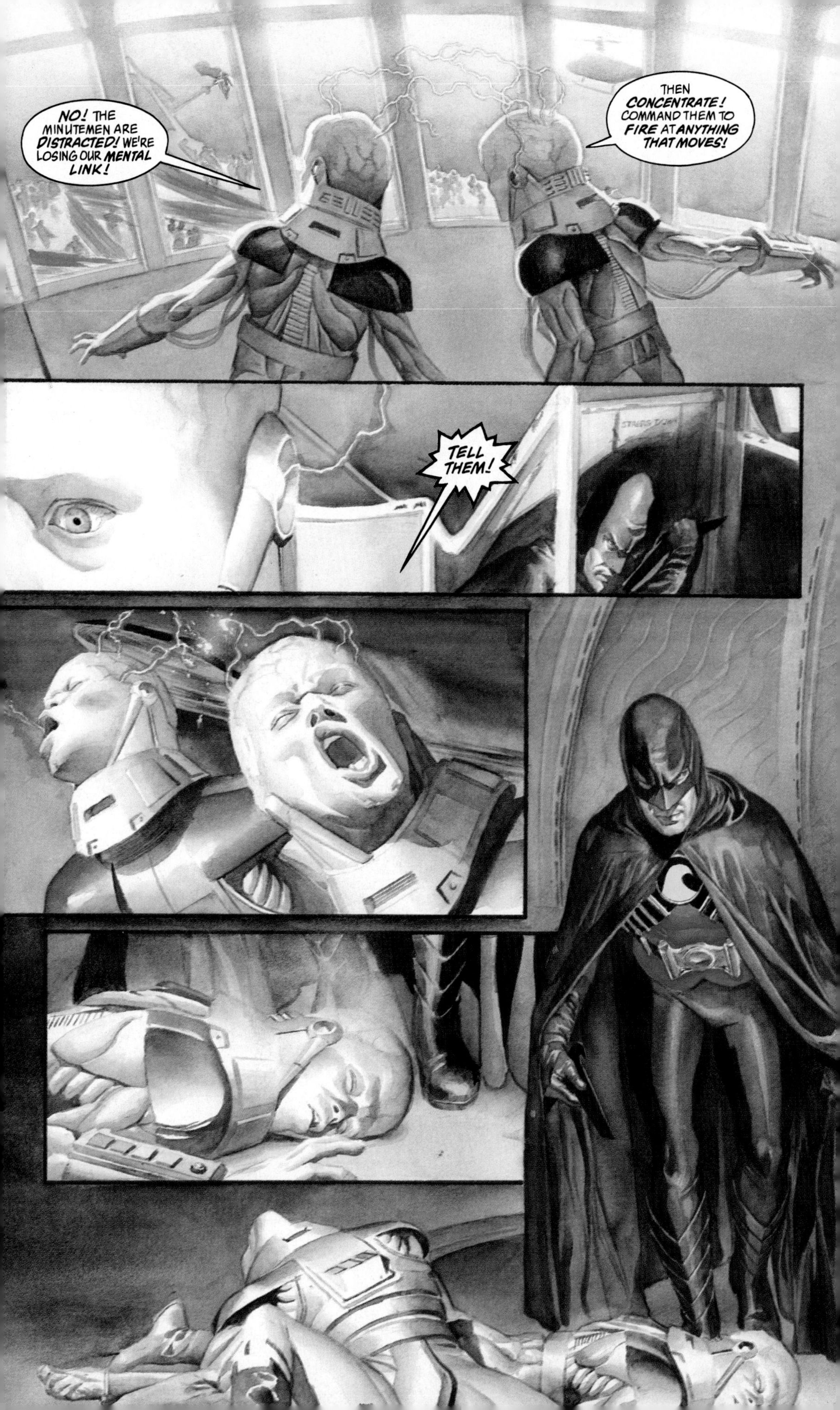
NO! THE MINUTEMEN ARE DISTRACTED! WE'RE LOSING OUR MENTAL LINK!
THEN CONCENTRATE! COMMAND THEM TO FIRE AT ANYTHING THAT MOVES!
TELL THEM!

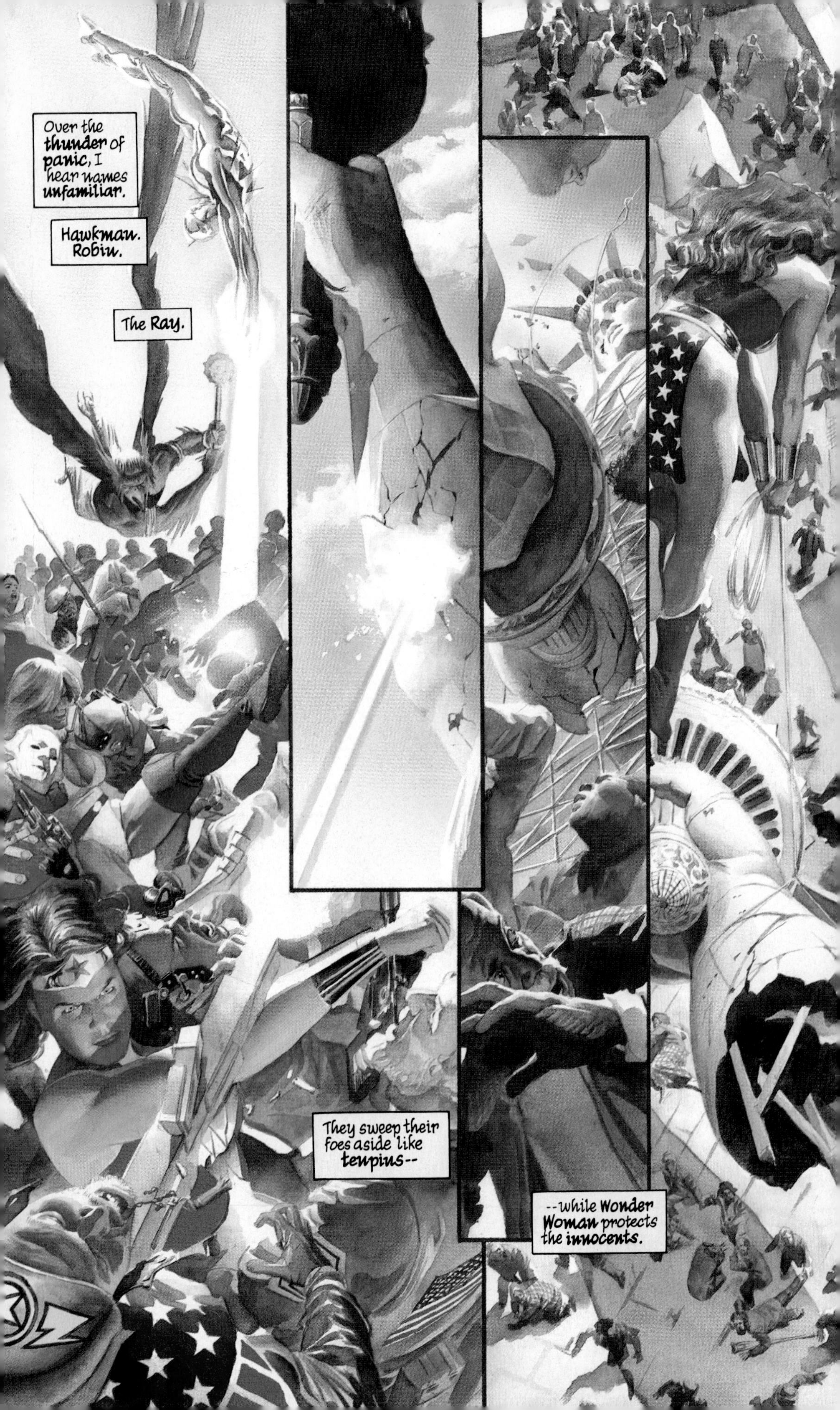

Over the thunder of panic, I hear names unfamiliar.
Hawkman. Robin.
The Ray.
They sweep their foes aside like tenpins--
--while Wonder Woman protects the innocents.

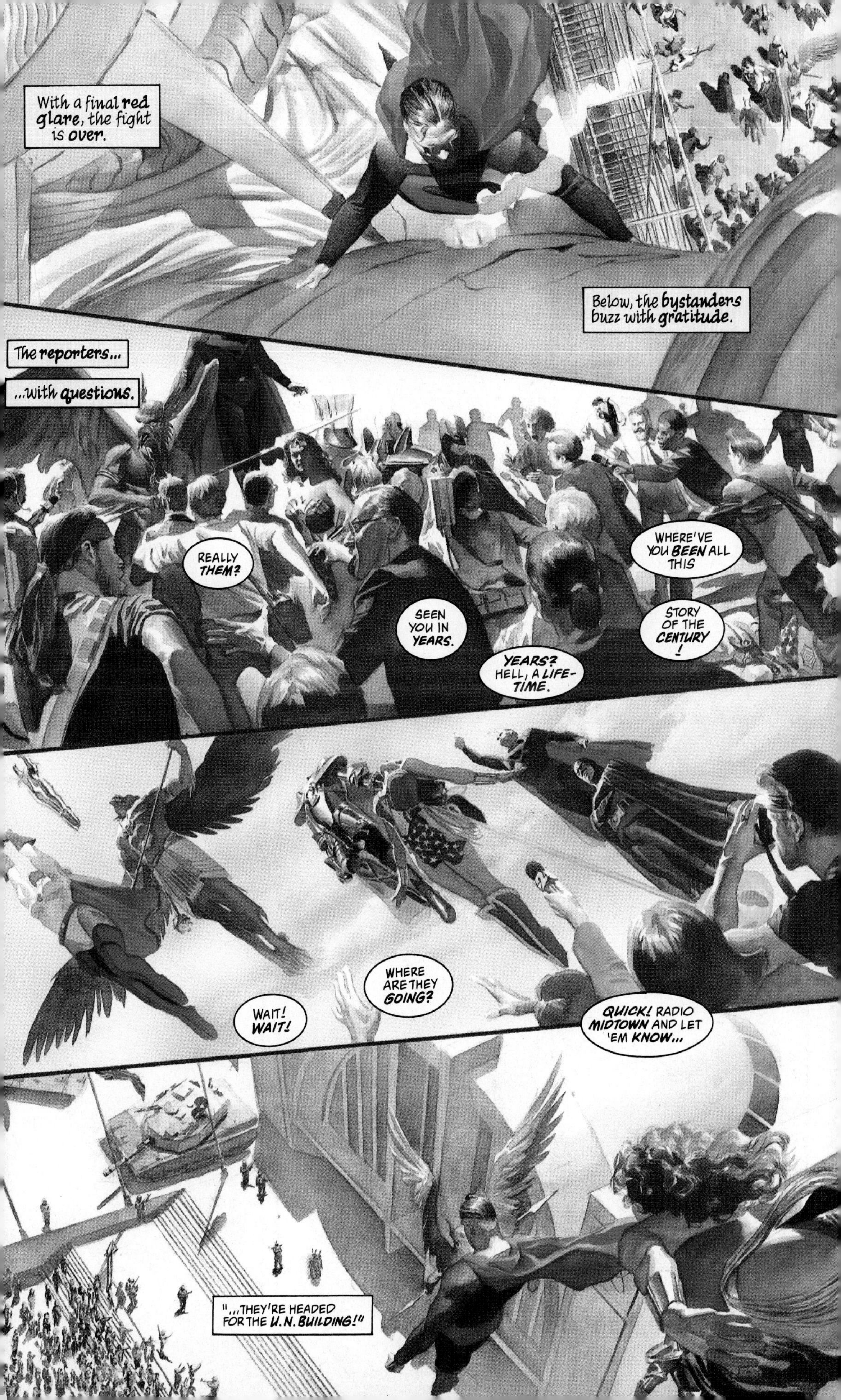
With a final red glare, the fight is over.
Below, the bystanders buzz with gratitude.
The reporters...
...with questions.
REALLY THEM?
SEEN YOU IN YEARS.
YEARS? HELL, A LIFE-TIME.
WHERE'VE YOU BEEN ALL THIS
STORY OF THE CENTURY!
WAIT! WAIT!
WHERE ARE THEY GOING?
QUICK! RADIO MIDTOWN AND LET 'EM KNOW...
"...THEY'RE HEADED FOR THE U.N. BUILDING!"

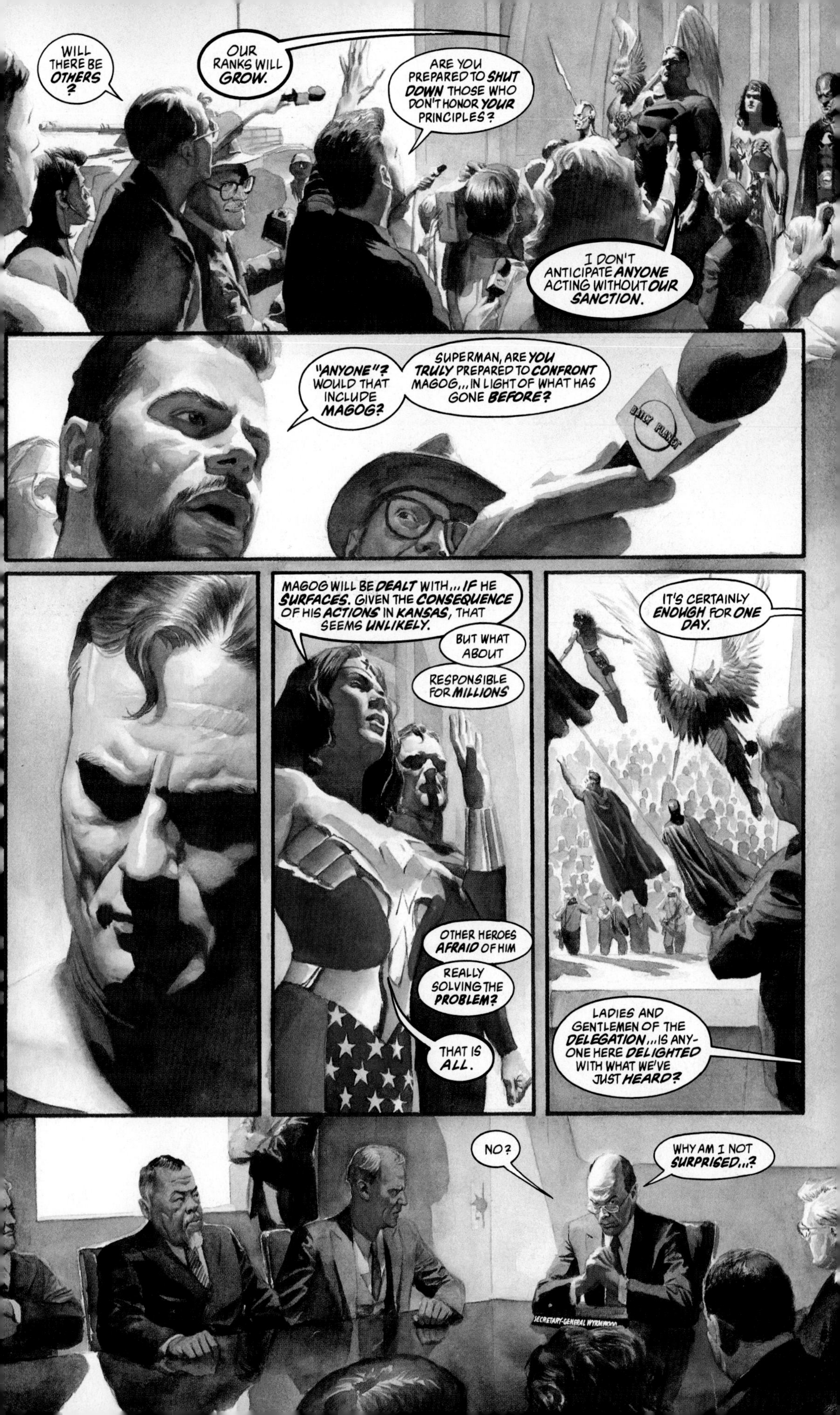

WILL THERE BE OTHERS?
OUR RANKS WILL GROW.
ARE YOU PREPARED TO SHUT DOWN THOSE WHO DON'T HONOR YOUR PRINCIPLES?
I DON'T ANTICIPATE ANYONE ACTING WITHOUT OUR SANCTION.
"ANYONE"? WOULD THAT INCLUDE MAGOG?
SUPERMAN, ARE YOU TRULY PREPARED TO CONFRONT MAGOG... IN LIGHT OF WHAT HAS GONE BEFORE?
DAILY PLANET
MAGOG WILL BE DEALT WITH... IF HE SURFACES. GIVEN THE CONSEQUENCE OF HIS ACTIONS IN KANSAS, THAT SEEMS UNLIKELY.
BUT WHAT ABOUT
RESPONSIBLE FOR MILLIONS
OTHER HEROES AFRAID OF HIM
REALLY SOLVING THE PROBLEM?
THAT IS ALL.
IT'S CERTAINLY ENOUGH FOR ONE DAY.
LADIES AND GENTLEMEN OF THE DELEGATION... IS ANYONE HERE DELIGHTED WITH WHAT WE'VE JUST HEARD?
NO?
WHY AM I NOT SURPRISED...?
SECRETARY-GENERAL WYRMWOOD

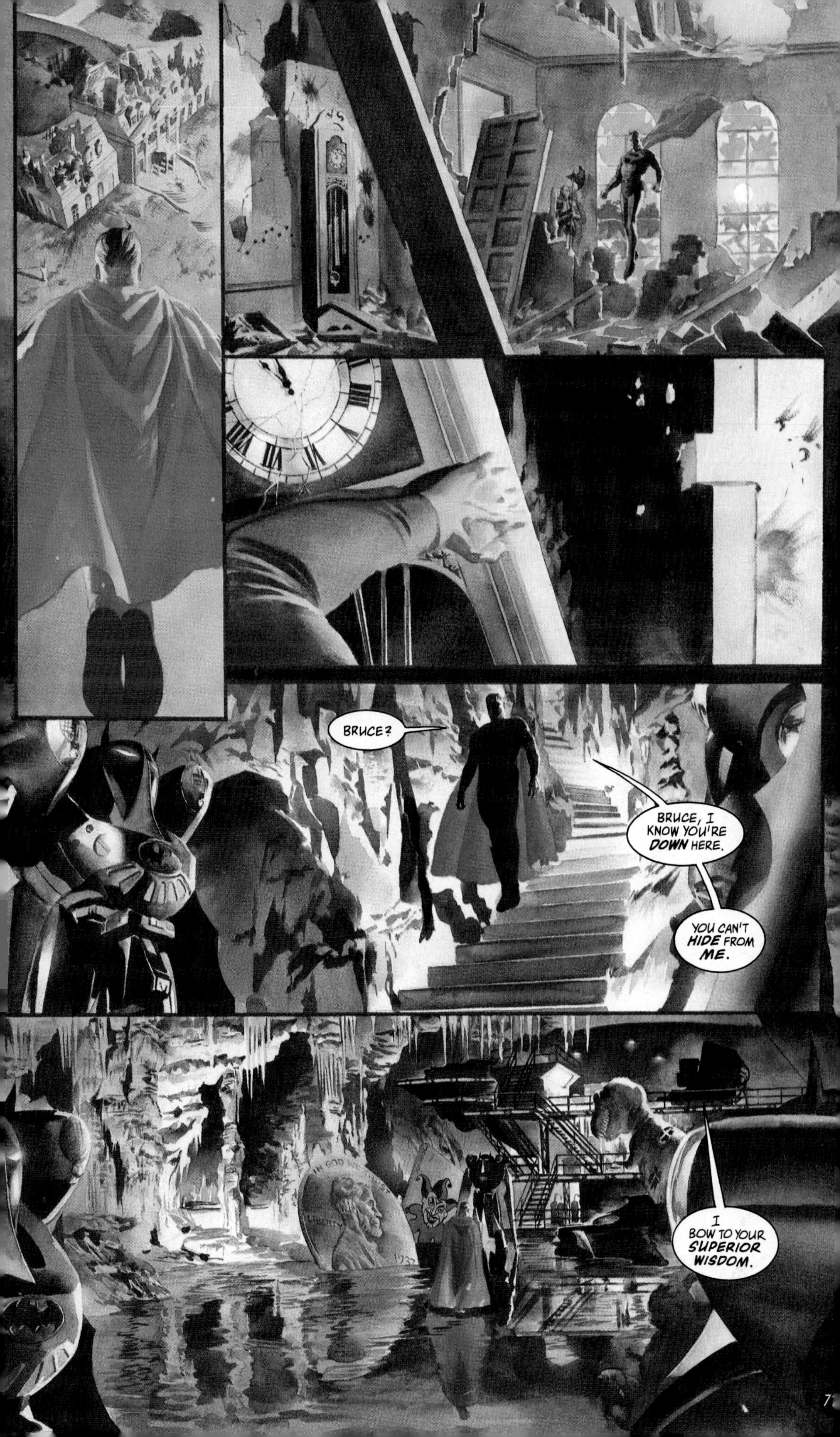
BRUCE?
BRUCE, I KNOW YOU'RE DOWN HERE.
YOU CAN'T HIDE FROM ME.
I BOW TO YOUR SUPERIOR WISDOM.

BRUCE...THE LEAGUE *NEEDS* YOU.

TOO BUSY TO HELP SAVE THE *WORLD*?

THE *CRISIS* AT HAND ISN'T *NEW*, CLARK, WHERE HAVE *YOU* BEEN?

I'M *BUSY.*

OH. I'M SORRY.

TWENTY-FIVE AND THIRTY-TWO... RESUME *PATROL.*

PERHAPS I SHOULD ASK *MAGOG.*

FRICTIONS HAVE BEEN BUILDING TO A HEAD FOR *YEARS*, CLARK.

THE METAHUMAN POPULATION *BOOMED* WHILE YOU WERE GONE... ONCE ORDINARY FOLKS DECIDED YOU AND I WERE TOO *GENTLE* AND *OLD-FASHIONED* TO FACE THE CHALLENGES OF THE 21ST CENTURY.

THEY WANTED THEIR "HEROES" *STRONGER* AND MORE *RUTHLESS.*

BE CAREFUL WHAT YOU *WISH* FOR.

MANEUVER *TWELVE.*

RIGHT *NOW*, THE *METAHUMANS* HAVE THE *KEYS* TO EARTH'S *KINGDOM.* WRESTING *CONTROL* IS A *DELICATE* MATTER.

IT REQUIRES *FINESSE*... AND *METICULOUS*, CAREFUL PLANNING AGAINST THOSE ENEMIES MORE *HIDDEN*... BUT IT *CAN* BE DONE.

WITHOUT, I MIGHT ADD, SUPERMAN AND THE *JUSTICE LEAGUE* BOOMING INTO TOWN-- PUNCHING *NOW*, ASKING QUESTIONS *LATER.*

73

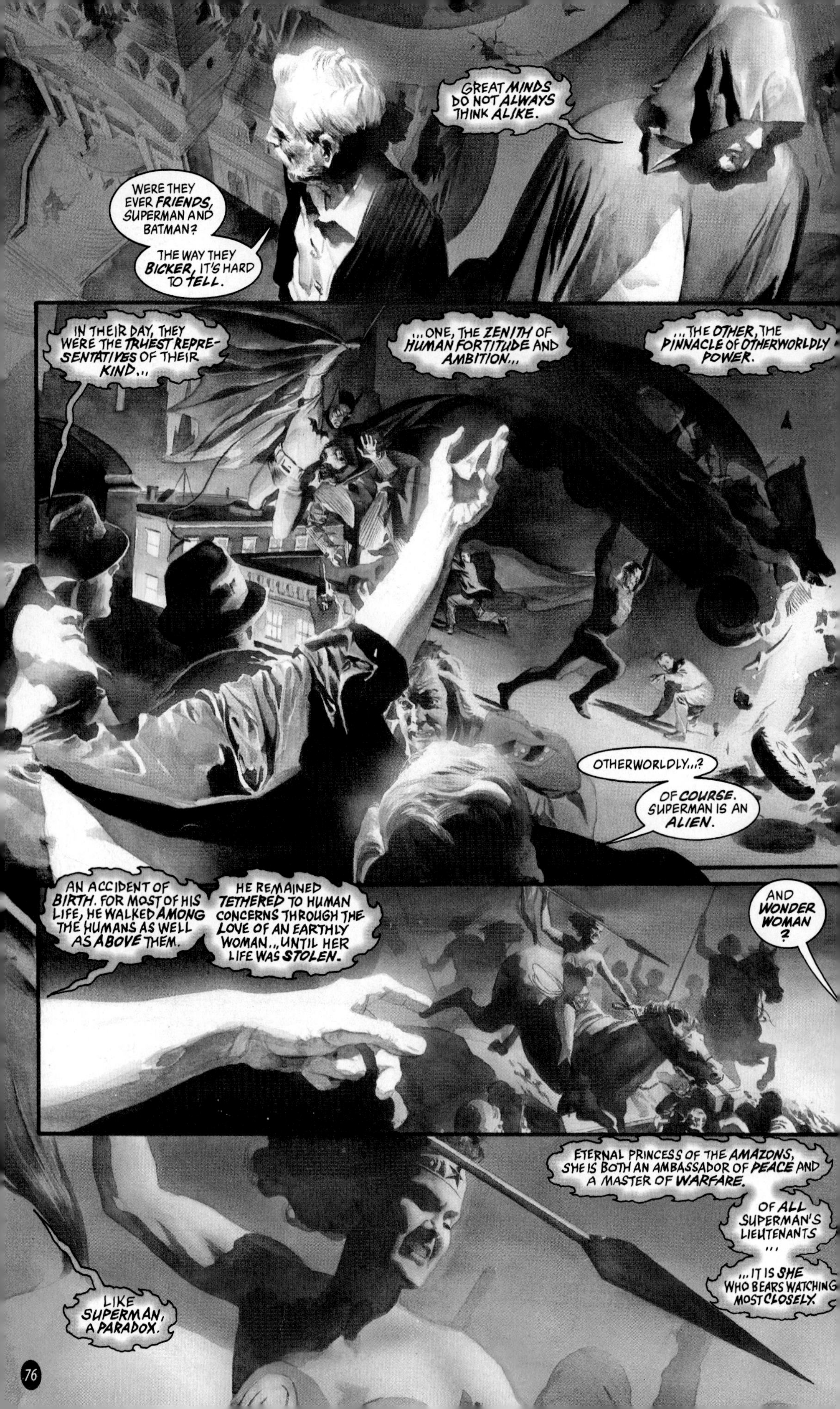
GREAT MINDS DO NOT ALWAYS THINK ALIKE.
WERE THEY EVER FRIENDS, SUPERMAN AND BATMAN?
THE WAY THEY BICKER, IT'S HARD TO TELL.
IN THEIR DAY, THEY WERE THE TRUEST REPRESENTATIVES OF THEIR KIND...
...ONE, THE ZENITH OF HUMAN FORTITUDE AND AMBITION...
...THE OTHER, THE PINNACLE OF OTHERWORLDLY POWER.
OTHERWORLDLY...?
OF COURSE. SUPERMAN IS AN ALIEN.
AN ACCIDENT OF BIRTH. FOR MOST OF HIS LIFE, HE WALKED AMONG THE HUMANS AS WELL AS ABOVE THEM.
HE REMAINED TETHERED TO HUMAN CONCERNS THROUGH THE LOVE OF AN EARTHLY WOMAN... UNTIL HER LIFE WAS STOLEN.
AND WONDER WOMAN?
ETERNAL PRINCESS OF THE AMAZONS, SHE IS BOTH AN AMBASSADOR OF PEACE AND A MASTER OF WARFARE.
LIKE SUPERMAN, A PARADOX.
OF ALL SUPERMAN'S LIEUTENANTS...
...IT IS SHE WHO BEARS WATCHING MOST CLOSELY.

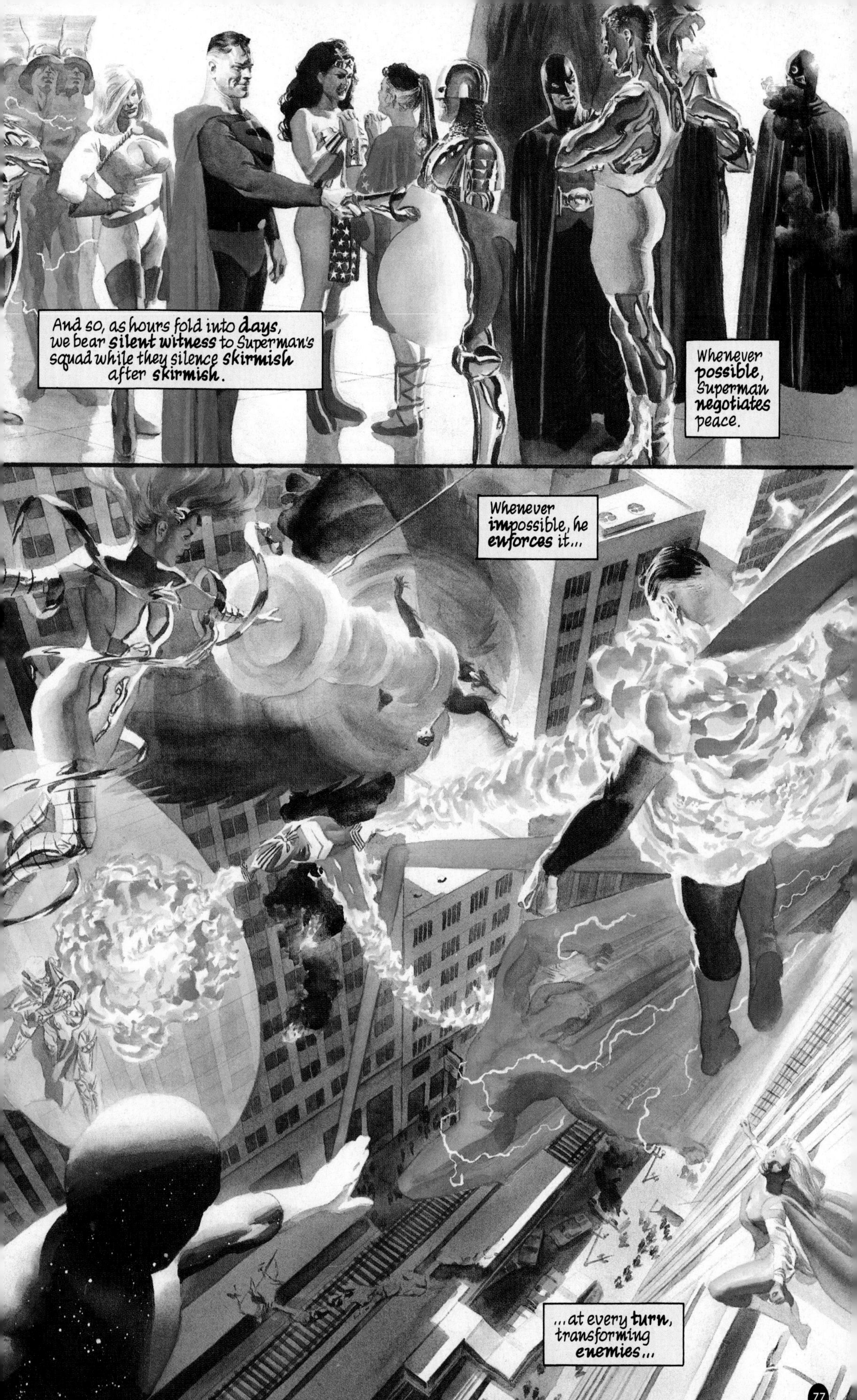

And so, as hours fold into days, we bear silent witness to Superman's squad while they silence skirmish after skirmish.
Whenever possible, Superman negotiates peace.
Whenever impossible, he enforces it...
...at every turn, transforming enemies...

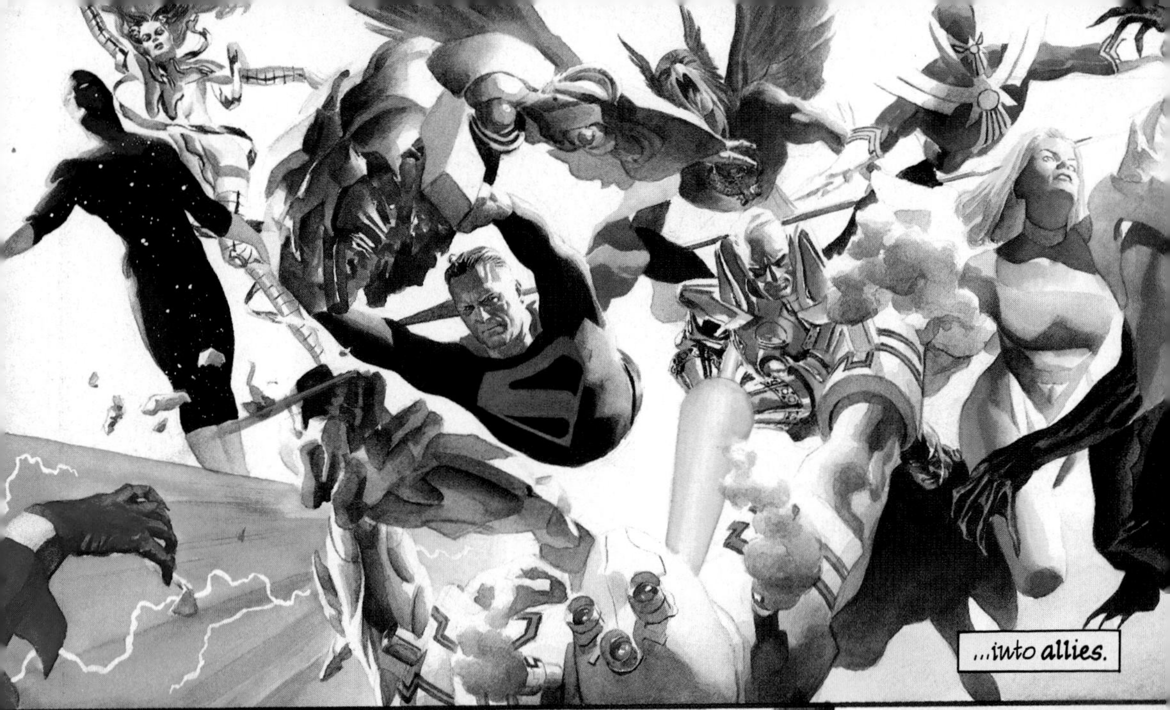
...into allies.

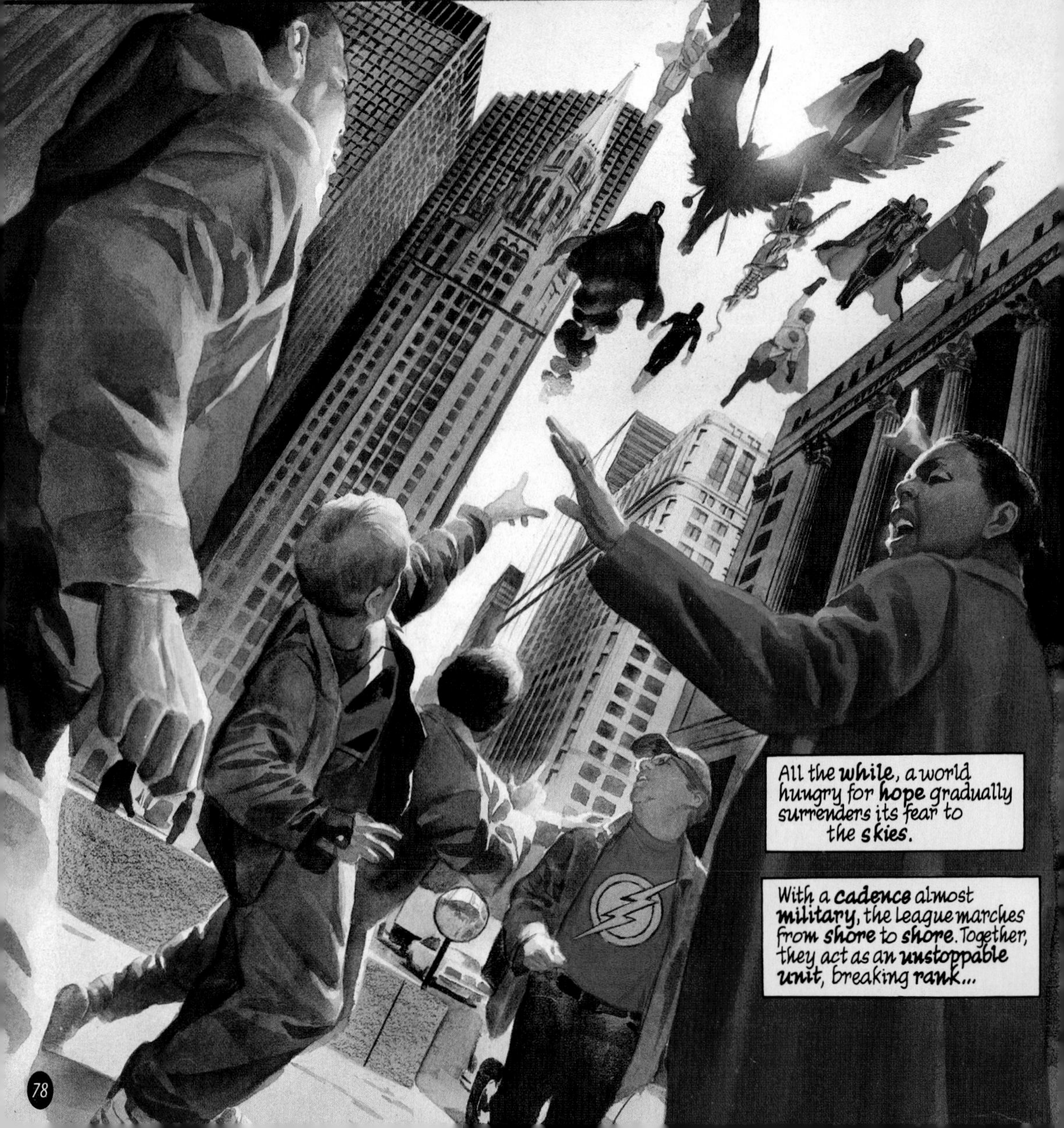
All the while, a world hungry for hope gradually surrenders its fear to the skies.
With a cadence almost military, the League marches from shore to shore. Together, they act as an unstoppable unit, breaking rank...

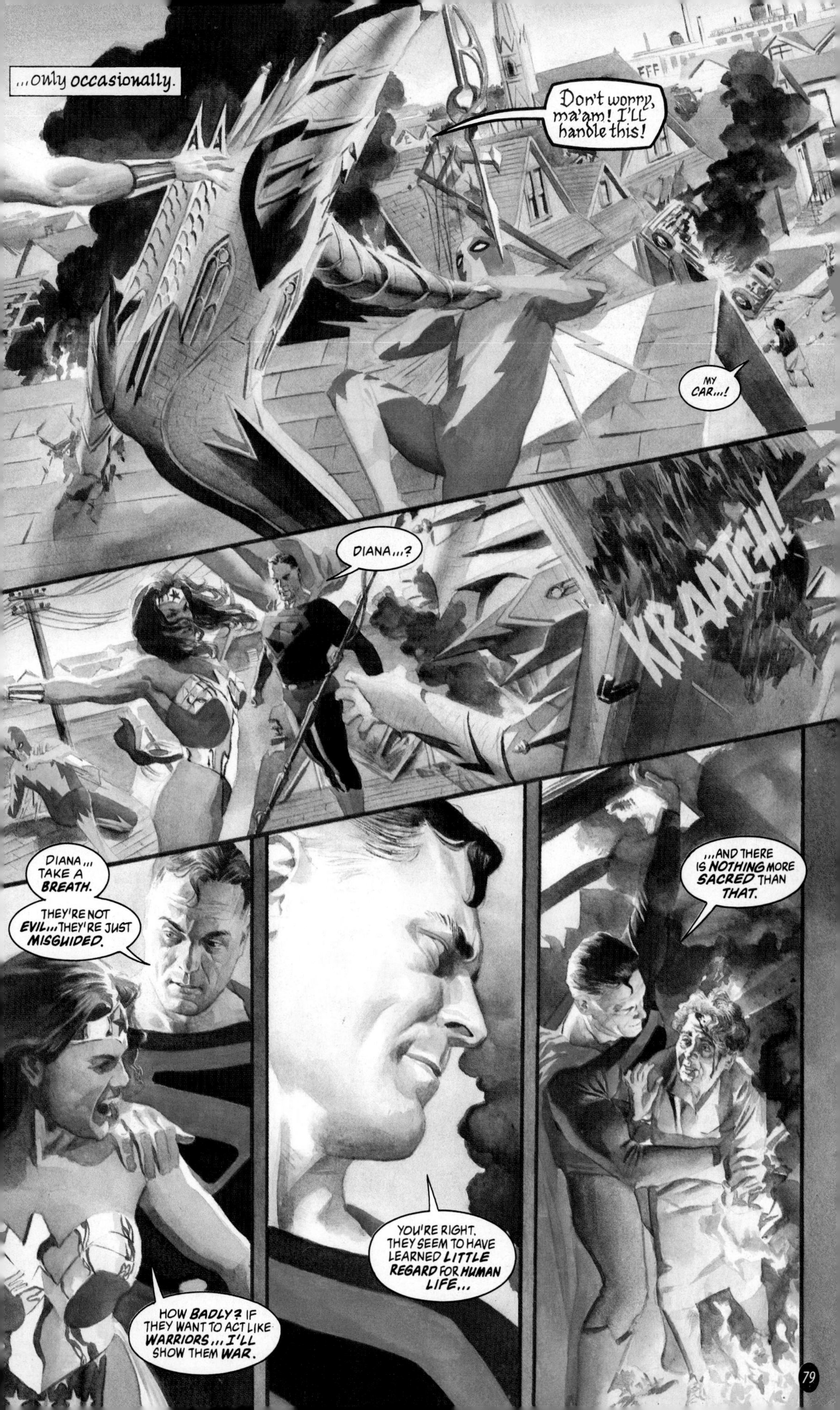
...only occasionally.
Don't worry, ma'am! I'LL handle this!
MY CAR...!
DIANA...?
KRAATCH!
DIANA... TAKE A BREATH.
THEY'RE NOT EVIL... THEY'RE JUST MISGUIDED.
HOW BADLY? IF THEY WANT TO ACT LIKE WARRIORS... I'LL SHOW THEM WAR.
YOU'RE RIGHT. THEY SEEM TO HAVE LEARNED LITTLE REGARD FOR HUMAN LIFE...
...AND THERE IS NOTHING MORE SACRED THAN THAT.

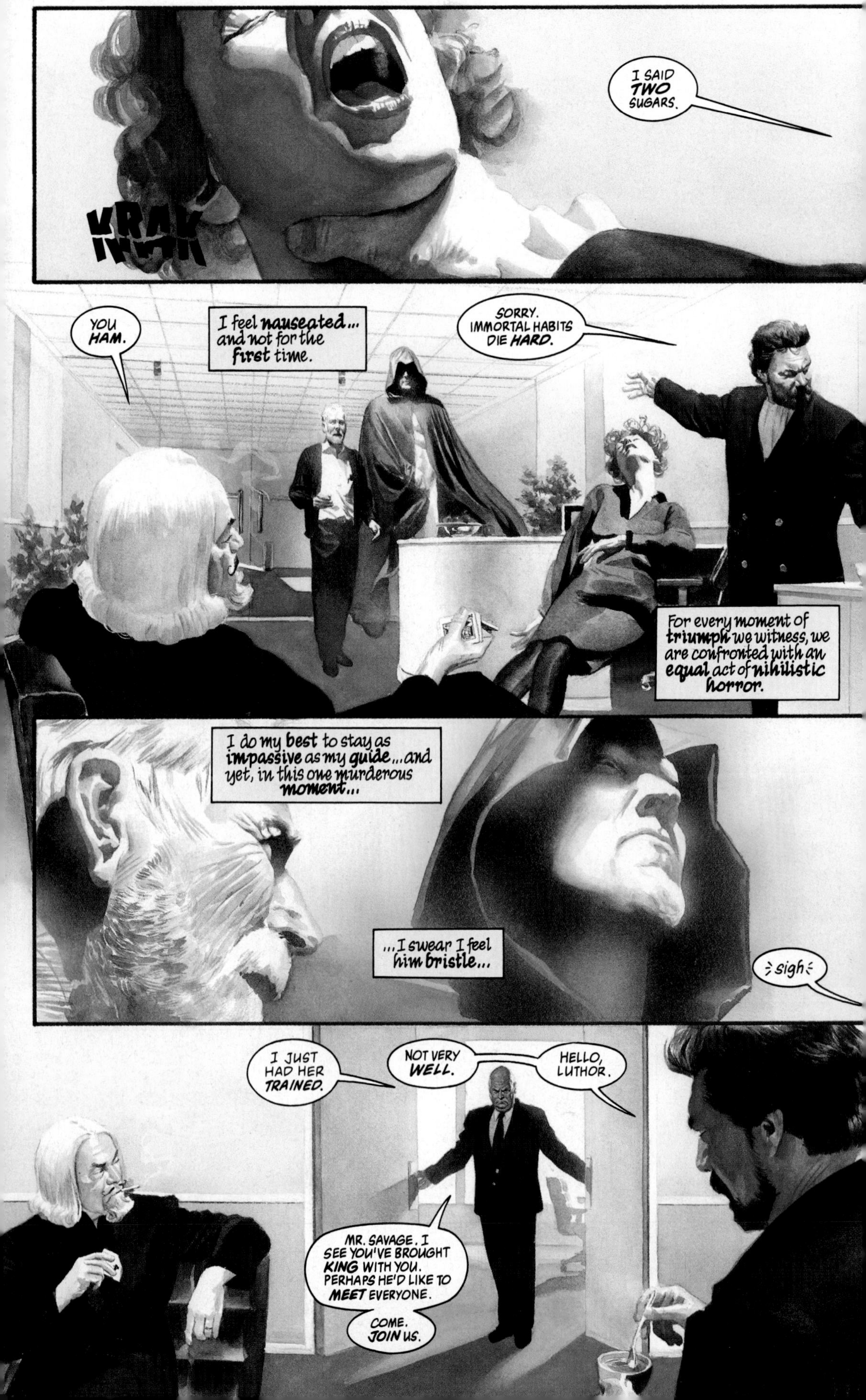
I SAID TWO SUGARS.
KRAK
YOU HAM.
I feel nauseated... and not for the first time.
SORRY. IMMORTAL HABITS DIE HARD.
For every moment of triumph we witness, we are confronted with an equal act of nihilistic horror.
I do my best to stay as impassive as my guide... and yet, in this one murderous moment...
...I swear I feel him bristle...
sigh
I JUST HAD HER TRAINED.
NOT VERY WELL.
HELLO, LUTHOR.
MR. SAVAGE. I SEE YOU'VE BROUGHT KING WITH YOU. PERHAPS HE'D LIKE TO MEET EVERYONE.
COME. JOIN US.

WE CALL OURSELVES THE *MANKIND LIBERATION FRONT.*

YOU *KNOW* IBN AL XU'FFASCH... HEIR TO *RA'S AL GHUL'S* EMPIRE.

THIS IS *LORD NAGA...*

"WHO IS *KOBRA?*"

...*SELINA KYLE...*

"WHO IS *CATWOMAN?*"

...AND HER *COMPANION--EDWARD NIGMA...*

"WHO IS THE *RIDDLER?*"

...WHO SHOULD BE *REMINDED* THAT HE IS HERE *SOLELY* AS A *GRACE* TO MS. KYLE.

SIMMER DOWN, EDDIE...

GENTLEMEN... I NEED A *STATUS REPORT.*

XU'FFASCH, WHERE DO WE STAND WITH *MEDICAL AT-TENTION* AND *DISASTER RELIEF* FOR THE *KANSAS* VICTIMS?

DELAYED... PERHAPS FOR *WEEKS.*

SPLENDID.

TECH DISPERSAL THIS QUARTER, NAGA?

WE HAVE INTEGRATED ANOTHER *SIX SCORE* VIGILANTES.

GIVEN THE *ARKHAM* AND *BELLE REVE* SURVIVORS WE RE-OUTFITTED AND RENAMED, WE ARE NOW RESPONSIBLE FOR *EIGHT PERCENT* OF THE "SUPER-HERO" POPULATION.

EXCELLENT.

81

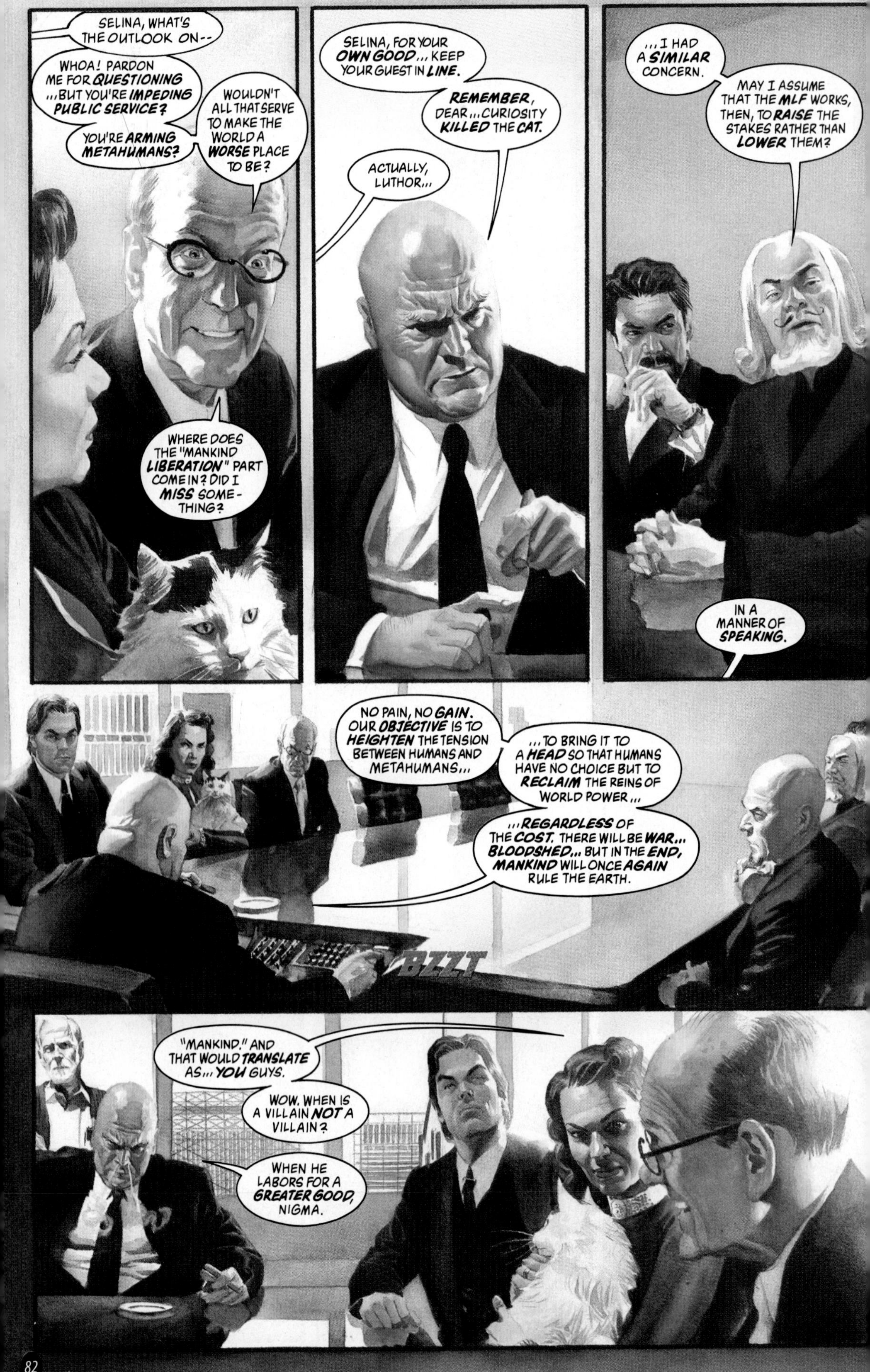

SELINA, WHAT'S THE OUTLOOK ON--
WHOA! PARDON ME FOR QUESTIONING ...BUT YOU'RE IMPEDING PUBLIC SERVICE?
YOU'RE ARMING METAHUMANS?
WOULDN'T ALL THAT SERVE TO MAKE THE WORLD A WORSE PLACE TO BE?
WHERE DOES THE "MANKIND LIBERATION" PART COME IN? DID I MISS SOME-THING?
SELINA, FOR YOUR OWN GOOD... KEEP YOUR GUEST IN LINE.
REMEMBER, DEAR... CURIOSITY KILLED THE CAT.
ACTUALLY, LUTHOR...
...I HAD A SIMILAR CONCERN.
MAY I ASSUME THAT THE MLF WORKS, THEN, TO RAISE THE STAKES RATHER THAN LOWER THEM?
IN A MANNER OF SPEAKING.
NO PAIN, NO GAIN. OUR OBJECTIVE IS TO HEIGHTEN THE TENSION BETWEEN HUMANS AND METAHUMANS...
...TO BRING IT TO A HEAD SO THAT HUMANS HAVE NO CHOICE BUT TO RECLAIM THE REINS OF WORLD POWER...
...REGARDLESS OF THE COST. THERE WILL BE WAR... BLOODSHED... BUT IN THE END, MANKIND WILL ONCE AGAIN RULE THE EARTH.
BZZT
"MANKIND." AND THAT WOULD TRANSLATE AS... YOU GUYS.
WOW. WHEN IS A VILLAIN NOT A VILLAIN?
WHEN HE LABORS FOR A GREATER GOOD, NIGMA.

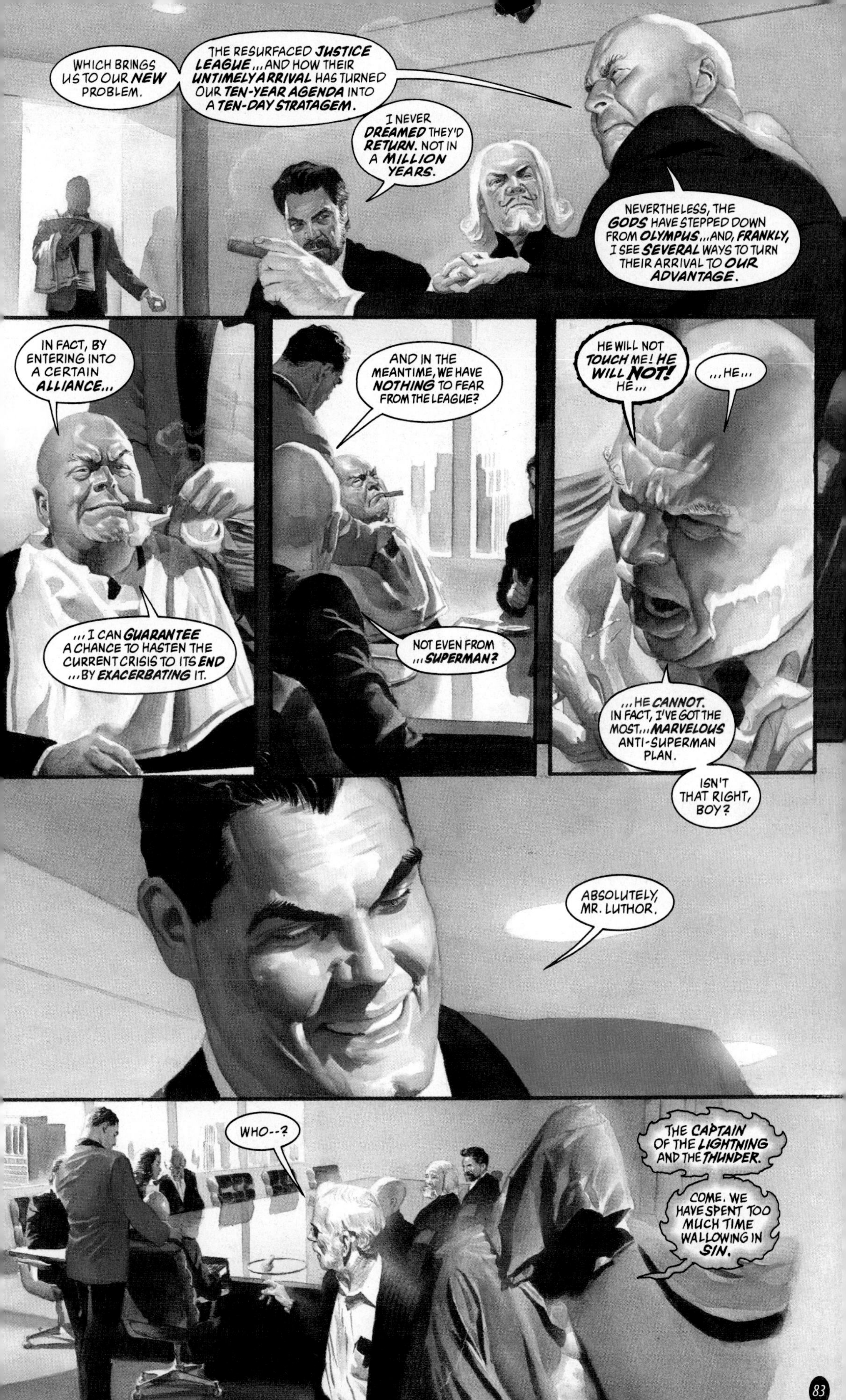
WHICH BRINGS US TO OUR NEW PROBLEM.
THE RESURFACED JUSTICE LEAGUE,,, AND HOW THEIR UNTIMELY ARRIVAL HAS TURNED OUR TEN-YEAR AGENDA INTO A TEN-DAY STRATAGEM.
I NEVER DREAMED THEY'D RETURN. NOT IN A MILLION YEARS.
NEVERTHELESS, THE GODS HAVE STEPPED DOWN FROM OLYMPUS,,, AND, FRANKLY, I SEE SEVERAL WAYS TO TURN THEIR ARRIVAL TO OUR ADVANTAGE.
IN FACT, BY ENTERING INTO A CERTAIN ALLIANCE,,,
,,, I CAN GUARANTEE A CHANCE TO HASTEN THE CURRENT CRISIS TO ITS END ,,, BY EXACERBATING IT.
AND IN THE MEANTIME, WE HAVE NOTHING TO FEAR FROM THE LEAGUE?
NOT EVEN FROM ,,, SUPERMAN?
HE WILL NOT TOUCH ME! HE WILL NOT! HE,,,
,,, HE,,,
,,, HE CANNOT. IN FACT, I'VE GOT THE MOST,,, MARVELOUS ANTI-SUPERMAN PLAN.
ISN'T THAT RIGHT, BOY?
ABSOLUTELY, MR. LUTHOR.
WHO--?
THE CAPTAIN OF THE LIGHTNING AND THE THUNDER.
COME. WE HAVE SPENT TOO MUCH TIME WALLOWING IN SIN.

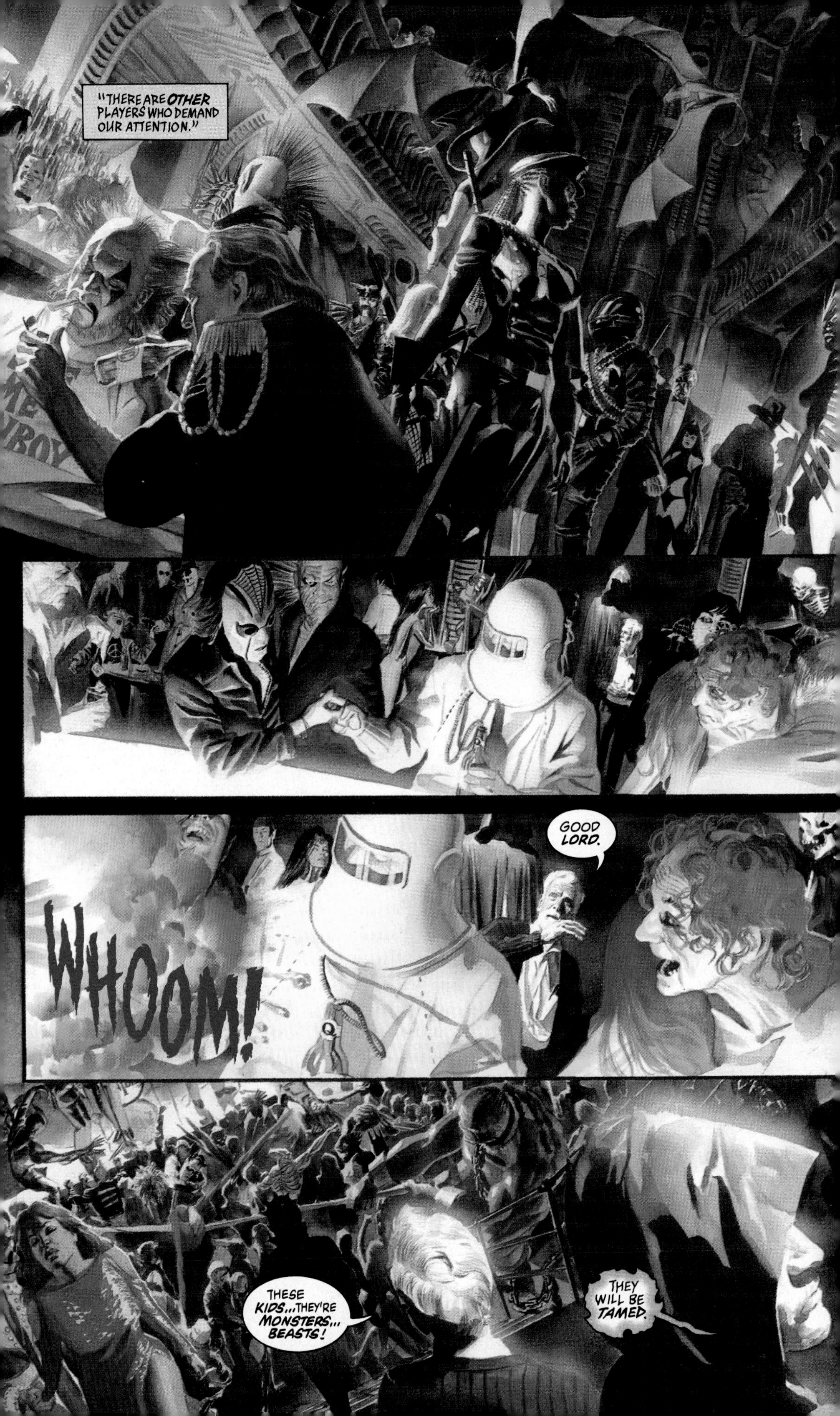
"THERE ARE OTHER PLAYERS WHO DEMAND OUR ATTENTION."
WHOOM!
GOOD LORD.
THESE KIDS... THEY'RE MONSTERS... BEASTS!
THEY WILL BE TAMED.

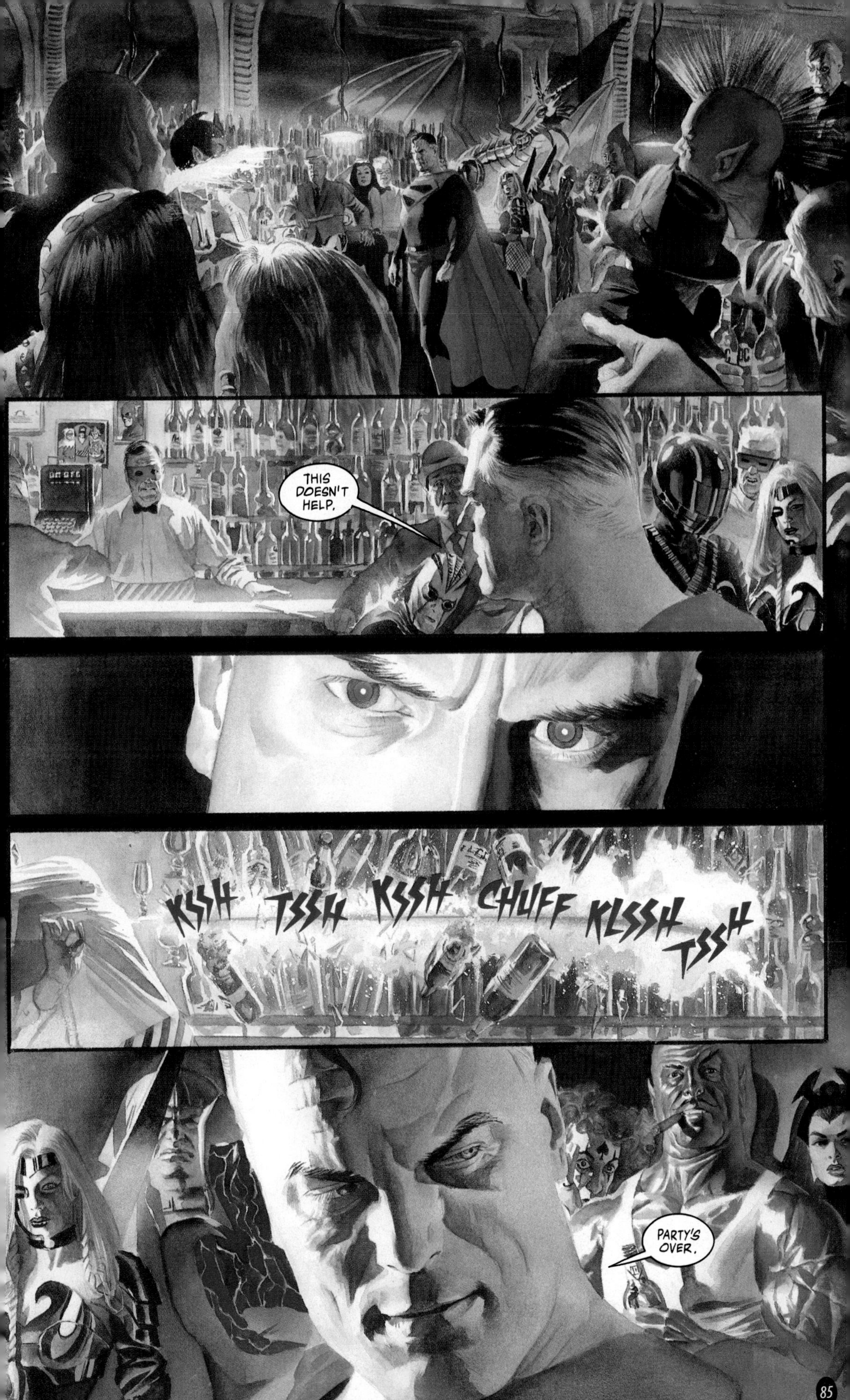
THIS DOESN'T HELP.
KSSH TSSH KSSH CHUFF KLSSH TSSH
PARTY'S OVER.

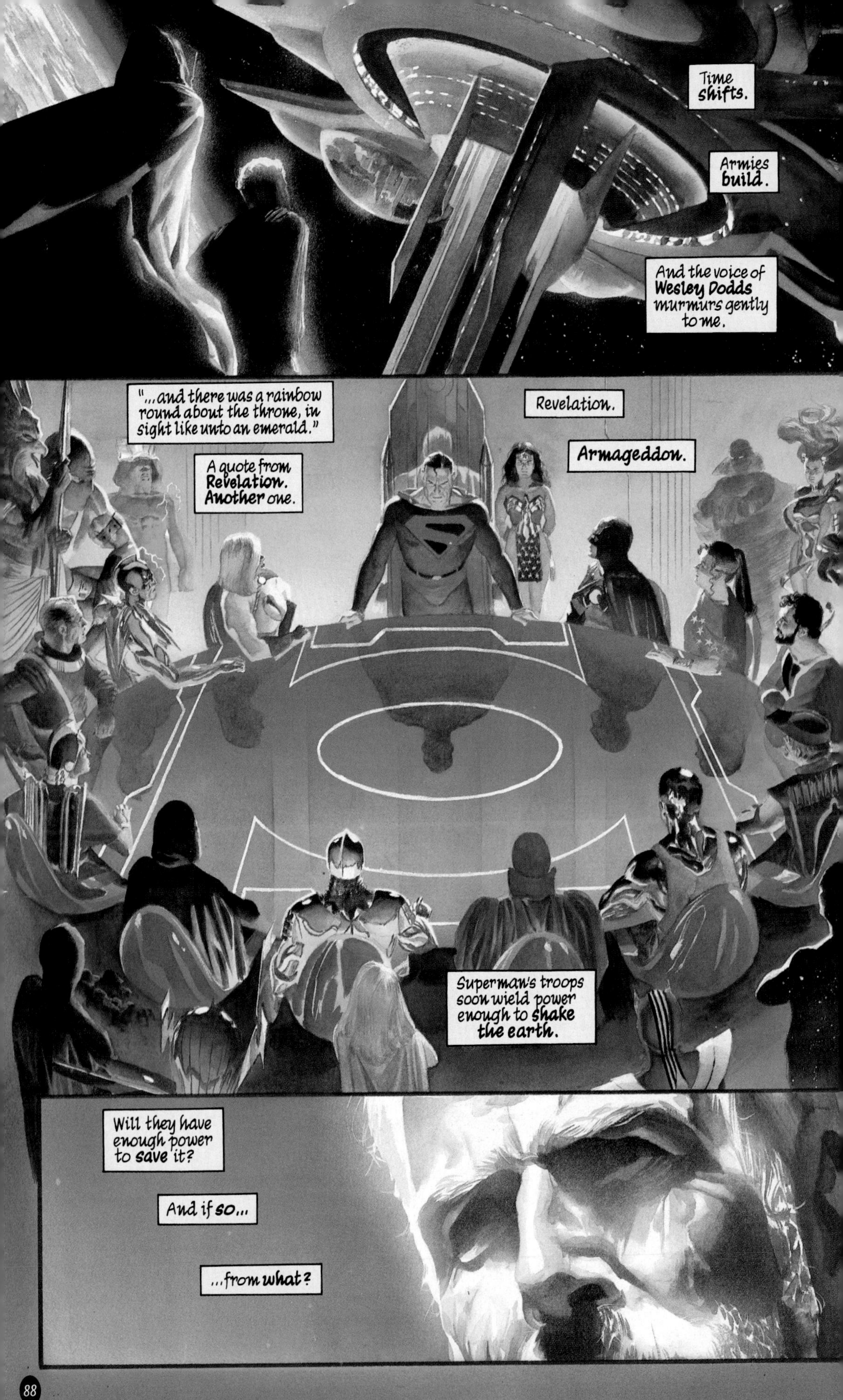
Time shifts.
Armies build.
And the voice of Wesley Dodds murmurs gently to me.
"...and there was a rainbow round about the throne, in sight like unto an emerald."
A quote from Revelation. Another one.
Revelation.
Armageddon.
Superman's troops soon wield power enough to shake the earth.
Will they have enough power to save it?
And if so...
...from what?

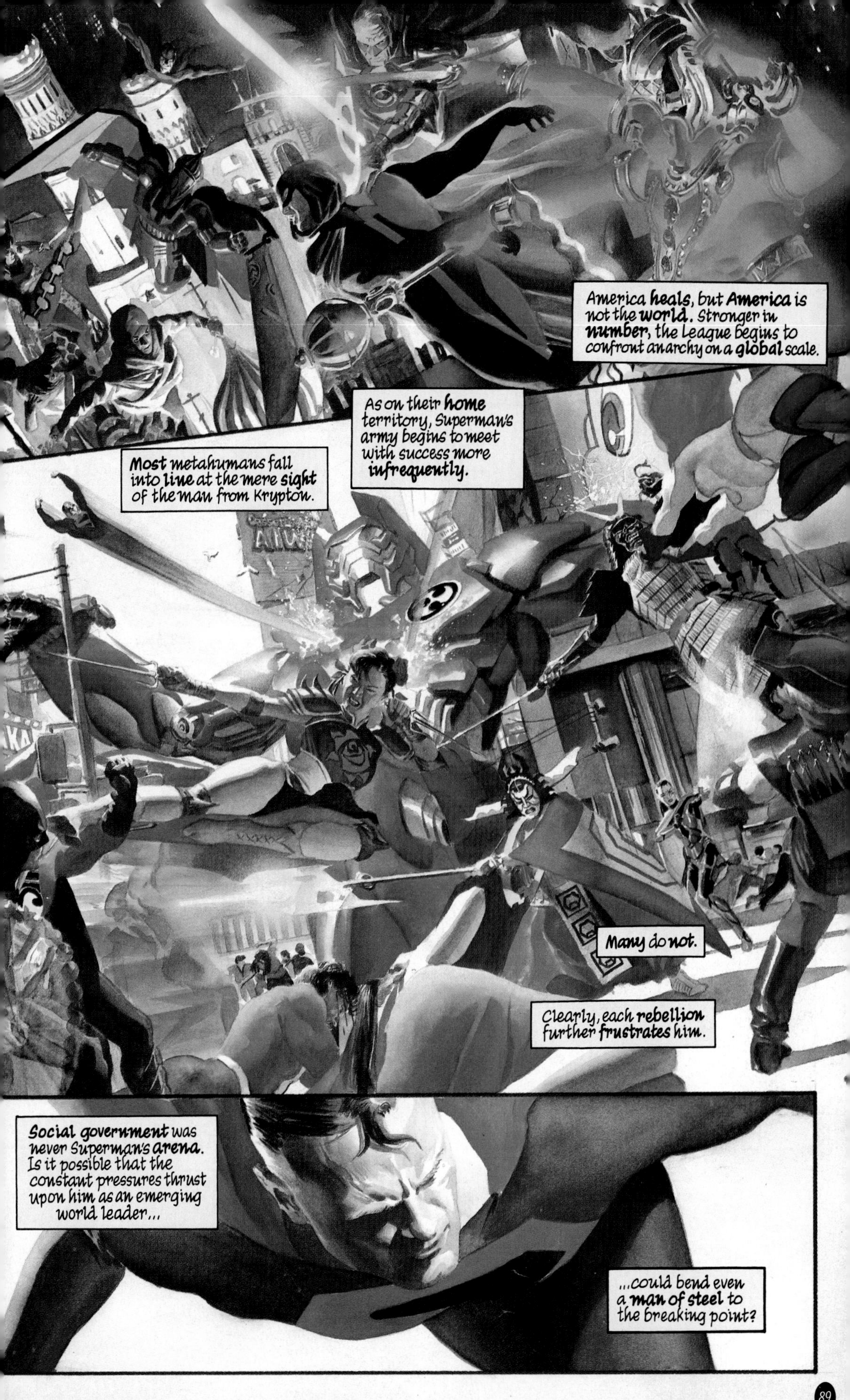
America heals, but America is not the world. Stronger in number, the League begins to confront anarchy on a global scale.
Most metahumans fall into line at the mere sight of the man from Krypton.
As on their home territory, Superman's army begins to meet with success more infrequently.
Many do not.
Clearly, each rebellion further frustrates him.
Social government was never Superman's arena. Is it possible that the constant pressures thrust upon him as an emerging world leader...
...could bend even a man of steel to the breaking point?

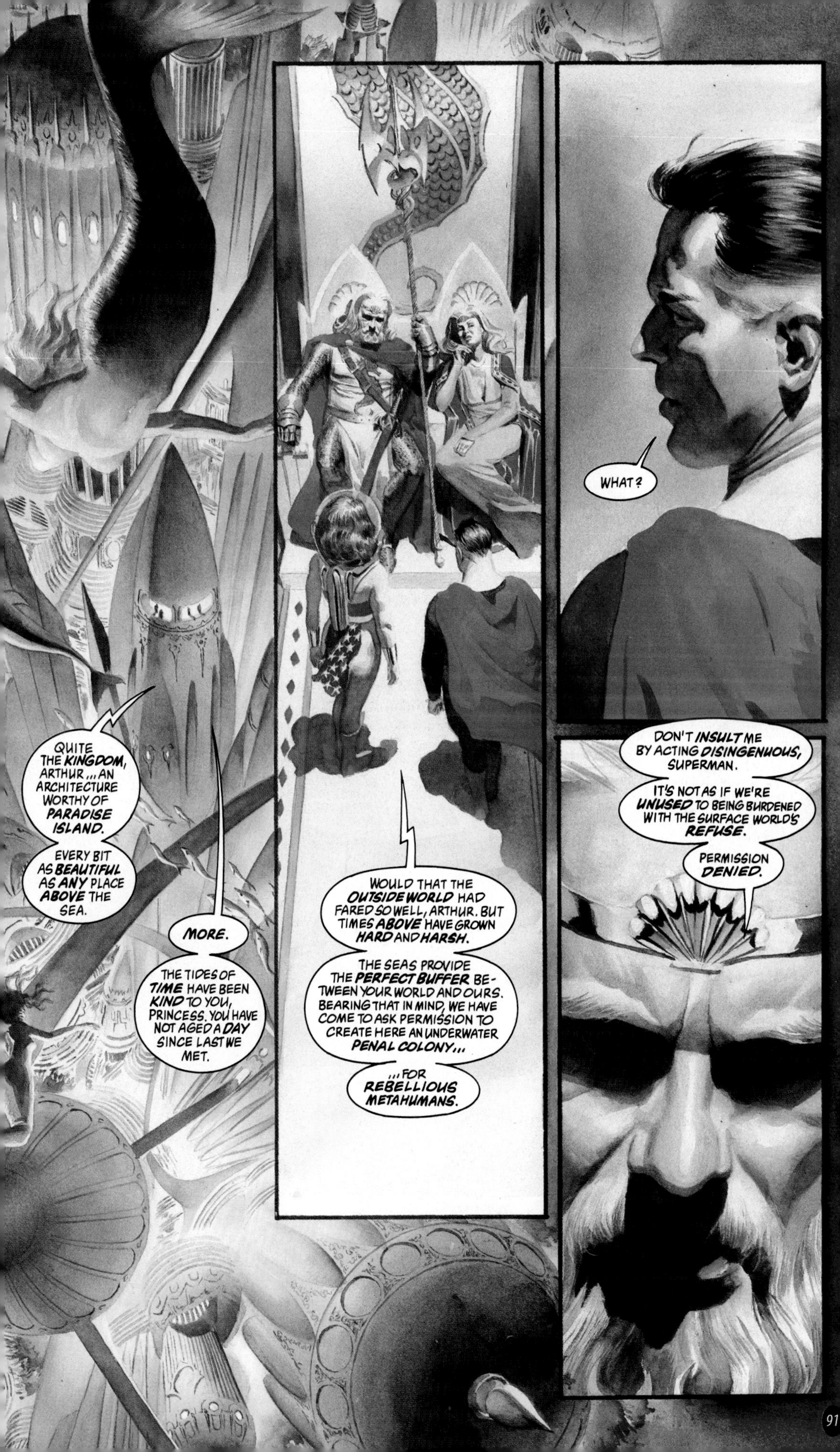
QUITE THE KINGDOM, ARTHUR ... AN ARCHITECTURE WORTHY OF PARADISE ISLAND.
EVERY BIT AS BEAUTIFUL AS ANY PLACE ABOVE THE SEA.
MORE.
THE TIDES OF TIME HAVE BEEN KIND TO YOU, PRINCESS. YOU HAVE NOT AGED A DAY SINCE LAST WE MET.
WOULD THAT THE OUTSIDE WORLD HAD FARED SO WELL, ARTHUR. BUT TIMES ABOVE HAVE GROWN HARD AND HARSH.
THE SEAS PROVIDE THE PERFECT BUFFER BETWEEN YOUR WORLD AND OURS. BEARING THAT IN MIND, WE HAVE COME TO ASK PERMISSION TO CREATE HERE AN UNDERWATER PENAL COLONY...
...FOR REBELLIOUS METAHUMANS.
WHAT?
DON'T INSULT ME BY ACTING DISINGENUOUS, SUPERMAN.
IT'S NOT AS IF WE'RE UNUSED TO BEING BURDENED WITH THE SURFACE WORLD'S REFUSE.
PERMISSION DENIED.

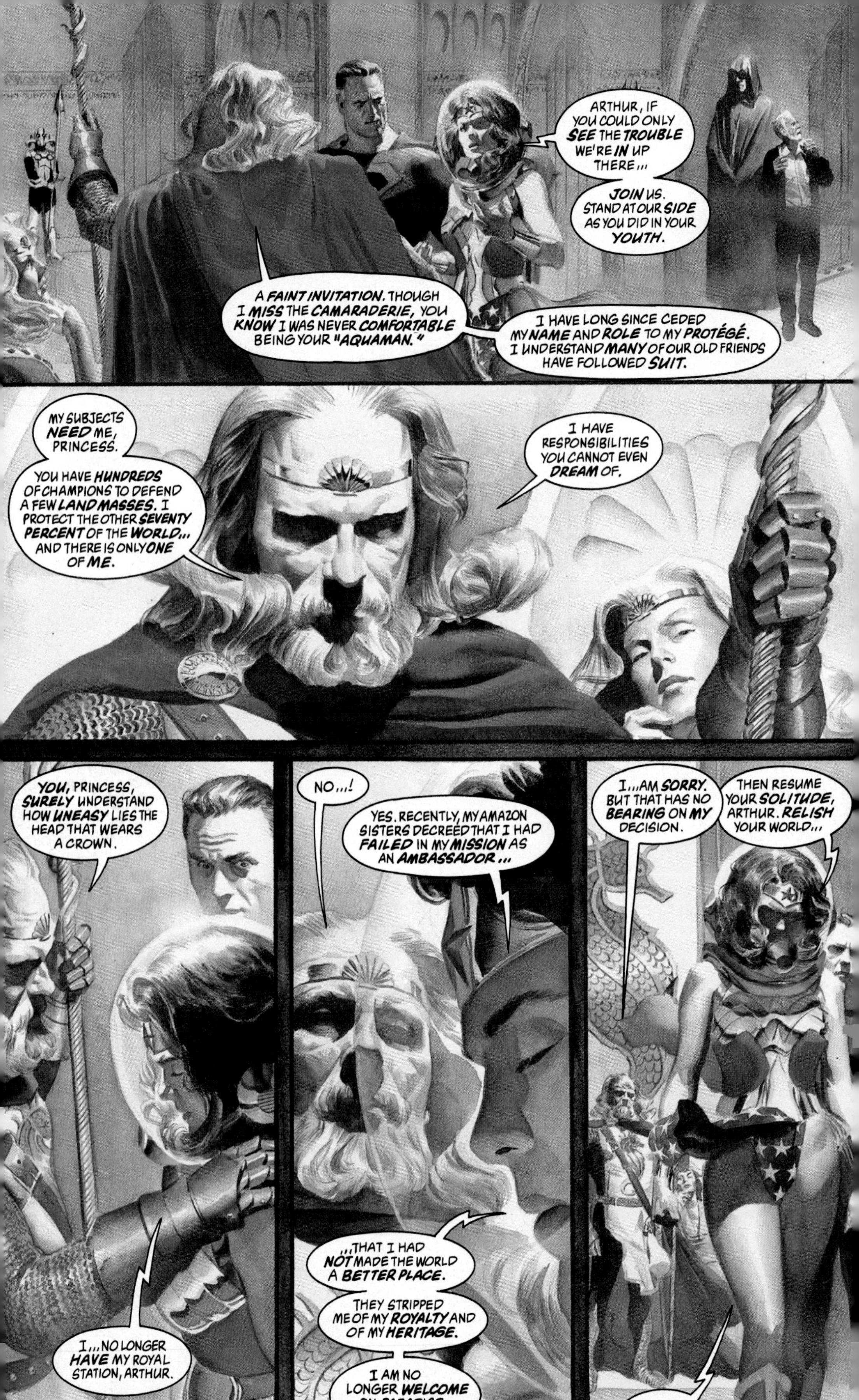

ARTHUR, IF YOU COULD ONLY SEE THE TROUBLE WE'RE IN UP THERE...
JOIN US. STAND AT OUR SIDE AS YOU DID IN YOUR YOUTH.
A FAINT INVITATION. THOUGH I MISS THE CAMARADERIE, YOU KNOW I WAS NEVER COMFORTABLE BEING YOUR "AQUAMAN."
I HAVE LONG SINCE CEDED MY NAME AND ROLE TO MY PROTÉGÉ. I UNDERSTAND MANY OF OUR OLD FRIENDS HAVE FOLLOWED SUIT.
MY SUBJECTS NEED ME, PRINCESS.
YOU HAVE HUNDREDS OF CHAMPIONS TO DEFEND A FEW LAND MASSES. I PROTECT THE OTHER SEVENTY PERCENT OF THE WORLD... AND THERE IS ONLY ONE OF ME.
I HAVE RESPONSIBILITIES YOU CANNOT EVEN DREAM OF.
YOU, PRINCESS, SURELY UNDERSTAND HOW UNEASY LIES THE HEAD THAT WEARS A CROWN.
I... NO LONGER HAVE MY ROYAL STATION, ARTHUR.
NO...!
YES. RECENTLY, MY AMAZON SISTERS DECREED THAT I HAD FAILED IN MY MISSION AS AN AMBASSADOR...
...THAT I HAD NOT MADE THE WORLD A BETTER PLACE.
THEY STRIPPED ME OF MY ROYALTY AND OF MY HERITAGE.
I AM NO LONGER WELCOME ON PARADISE ISLAND.
I... AM SORRY. BUT THAT HAS NO BEARING ON MY DECISION.
THEN RESUME YOUR SOLITUDE, ARTHUR. RELISH YOUR WORLD...
...FOR SO LONG AS IT LASTS.

93

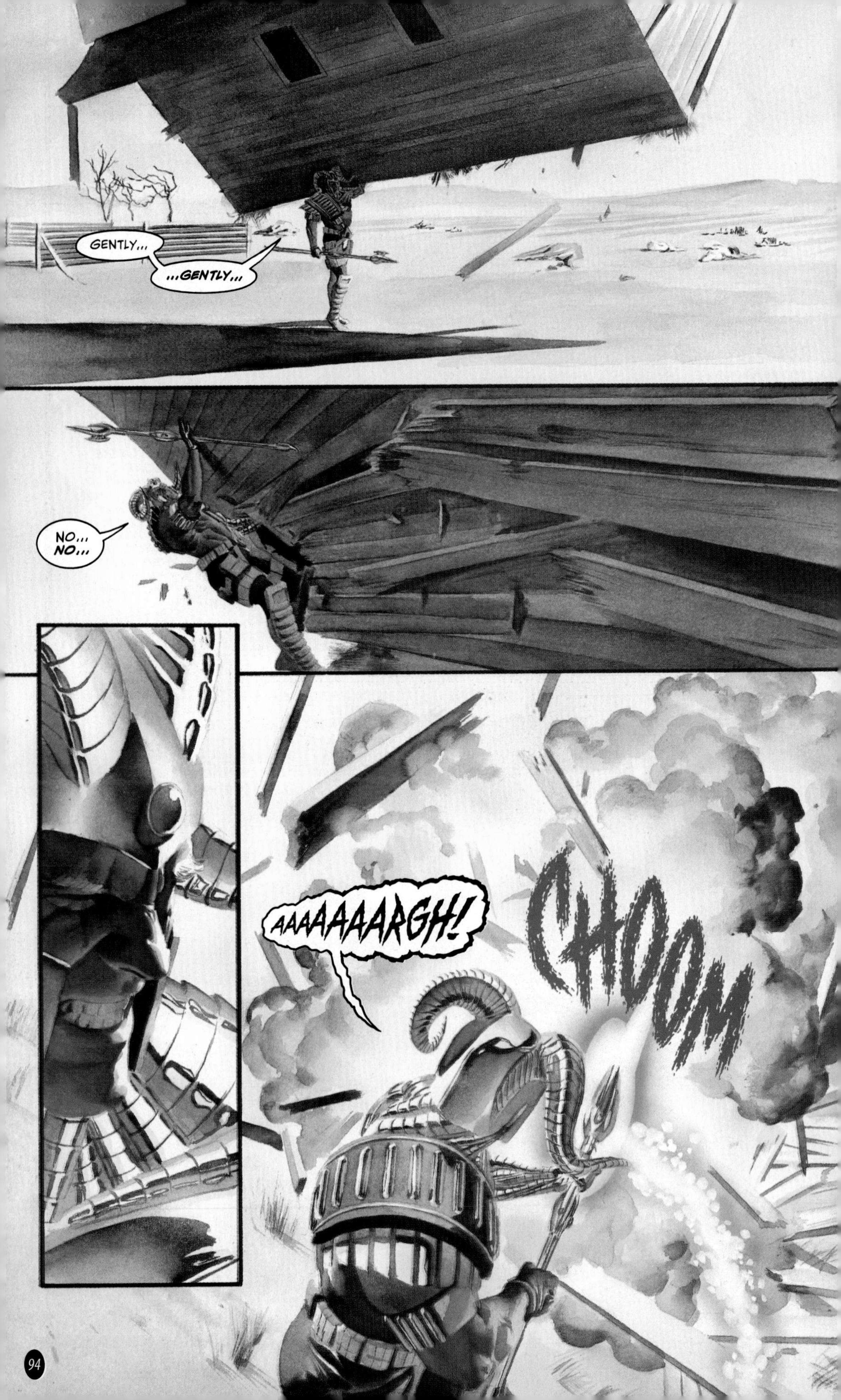

GENTLY...
...GENTLY...
NO... NO...
AAAAAAARGH!
CHOOM

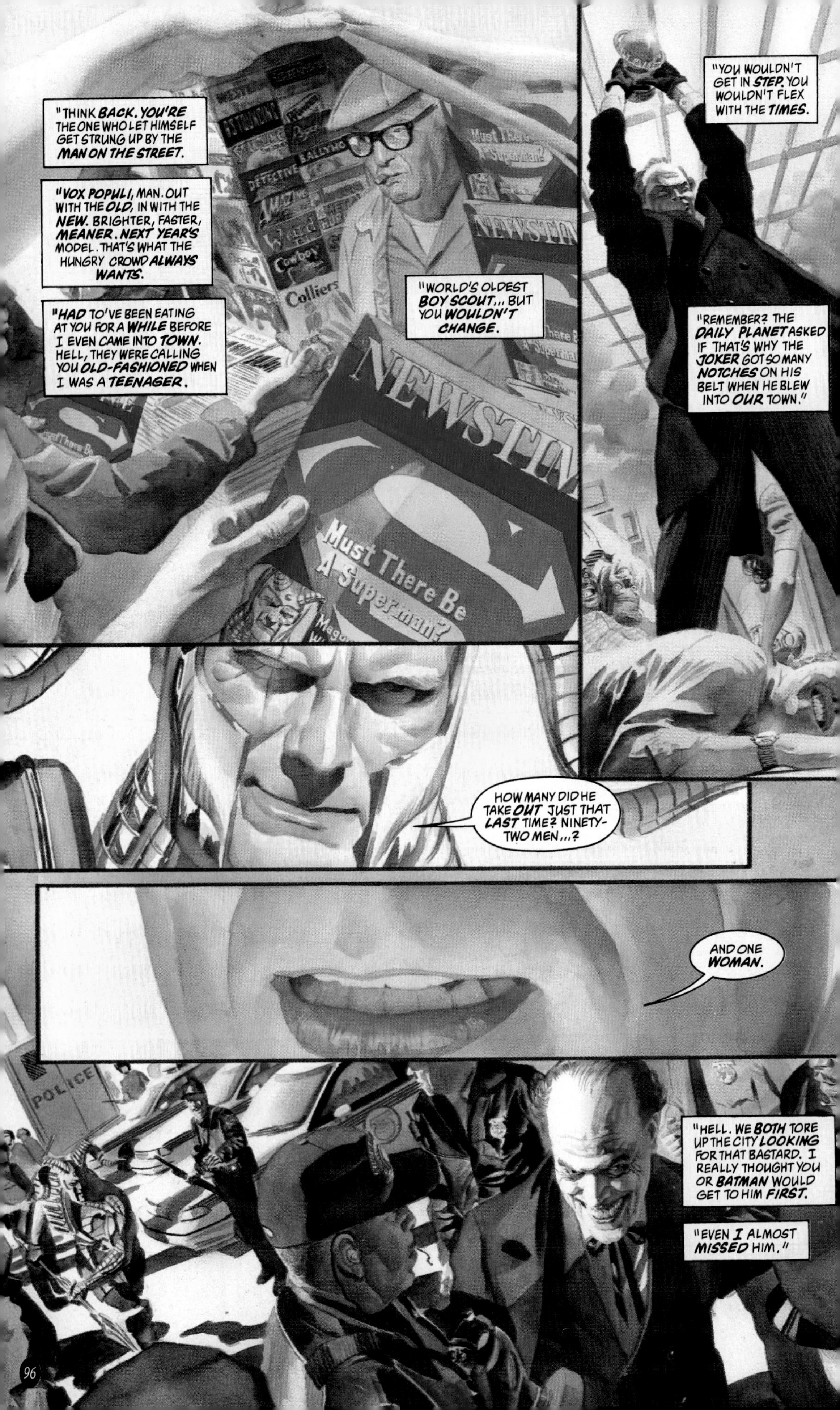
"THINK BACK. YOU'RE THE ONE WHO LET HIMSELF GET STRUNG UP BY THE MAN ON THE STREET.
"VOX POPULI, MAN. OUT WITH THE OLD, IN WITH THE NEW. BRIGHTER, FASTER, MEANER. NEXT YEAR'S MODEL. THAT'S WHAT THE HUNGRY CROWD ALWAYS WANTS.
"HAD TO'VE BEEN EATING AT YOU FOR A WHILE BEFORE I EVEN CAME INTO TOWN. HELL, THEY WERE CALLING YOU OLD-FASHIONED WHEN I WAS A TEENAGER.
"WORLD'S OLDEST BOY SCOUT... BUT YOU WOULDN'T CHANGE.
Must There Be A Superman?
"YOU WOULDN'T GET IN STEP. YOU WOULDN'T FLEX WITH THE TIMES.
"REMEMBER? THE DAILY PLANET ASKED IF THAT'S WHY THE JOKER GOT SO MANY NOTCHES ON HIS BELT WHEN HE BLEW INTO OUR TOWN."
HOW MANY DID HE TAKE OUT JUST THAT LAST TIME? NINETY-TWO MEN...?
AND ONE WOMAN.
"HELL. WE BOTH TORE UP THE CITY LOOKING FOR THAT BASTARD. I REALLY THOUGHT YOU OR BATMAN WOULD GET TO HIM FIRST.
"EVEN I ALMOST MISSED HIM."
POLICE

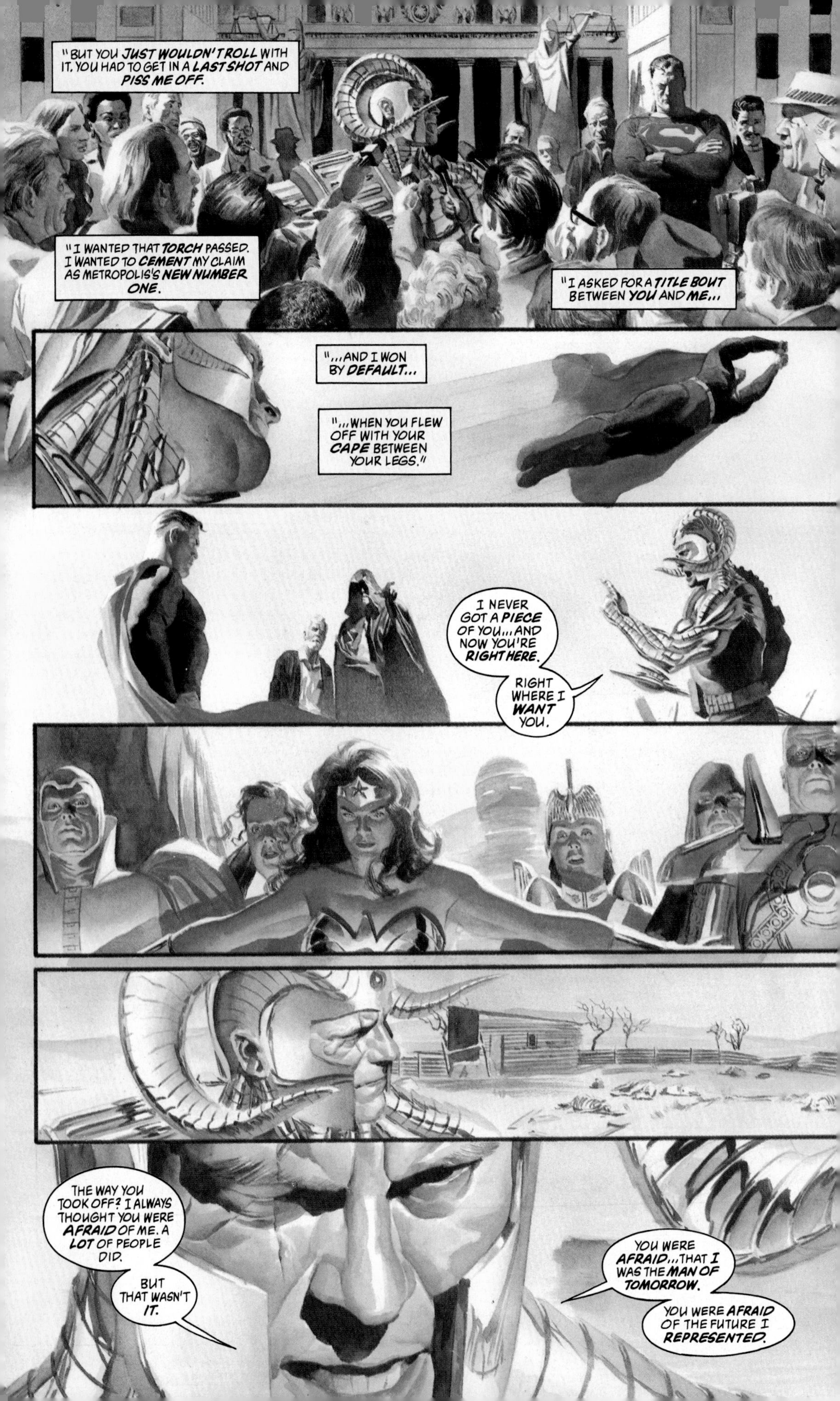
"BUT YOU JUST WOULDN'T ROLL WITH IT. YOU HAD TO GET IN A LAST SHOT AND PISS ME OFF.
"I WANTED THAT TORCH PASSED. I WANTED TO CEMENT MY CLAIM AS METROPOLIS'S NEW NUMBER ONE.
"I ASKED FOR A TITLE BOUT BETWEEN YOU AND ME...
"...AND I WON BY DEFAULT...
"...WHEN YOU FLEW OFF WITH YOUR CAPE BETWEEN YOUR LEGS."
I NEVER GOT A PIECE OF YOU... AND NOW YOU'RE RIGHT HERE.
RIGHT WHERE I WANT YOU.
THE WAY YOU TOOK OFF? I ALWAYS THOUGHT YOU WERE AFRAID OF ME. A LOT OF PEOPLE DID.
BUT THAT WASN'T IT.
YOU WERE AFRAID... THAT I WAS THE MAN OF TOMORROW.
YOU WERE AFRAID OF THE FUTURE I REPRESENTED.

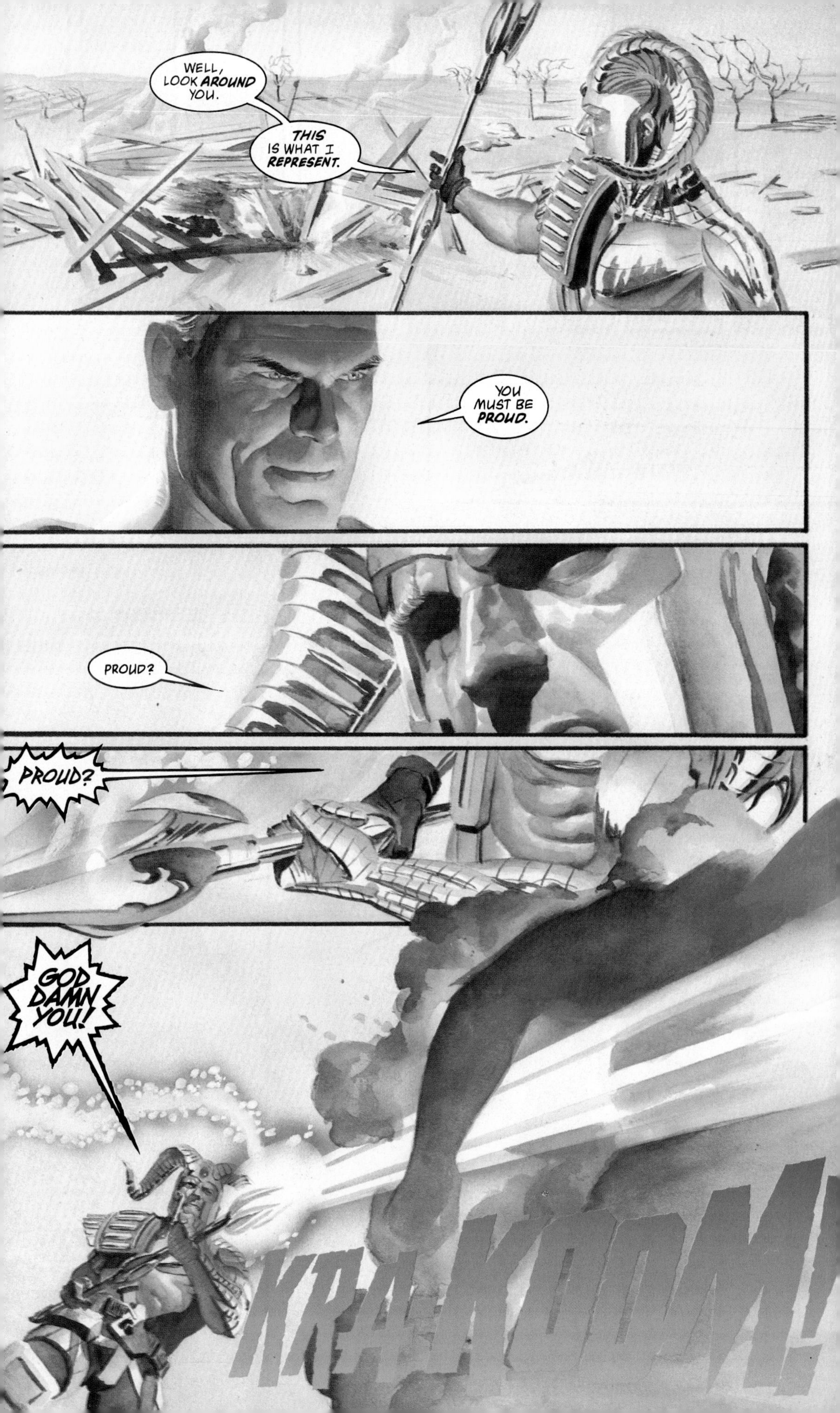
WELL, LOOK AROUND YOU.
THIS IS WHAT I REPRESENT.
YOU MUST BE PROUD.
PROUD?
PROUD?
GOD DAMN YOU!
KRA-KOOM!

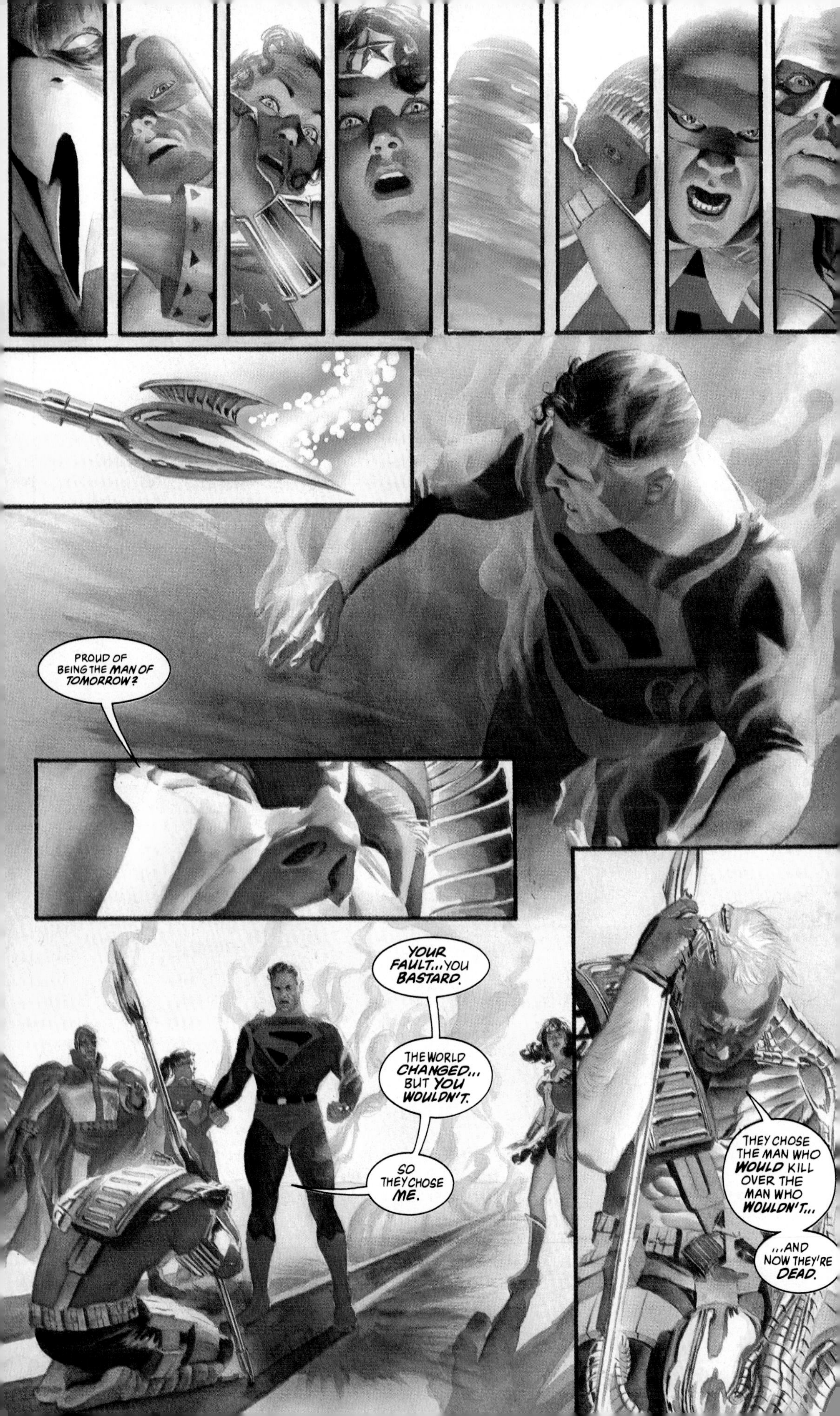
PROUD OF BEING THE MAN OF TOMORROW?
YOUR FAULT... YOU BASTARD.
THE WORLD CHANGED... BUT YOU WOULDN'T.
SO THEY CHOSE ME.
THEY CHOSE THE MAN WHO WOULD KILL OVER THE MAN WHO WOULDN'T...
...AND NOW THEY'RE DEAD.

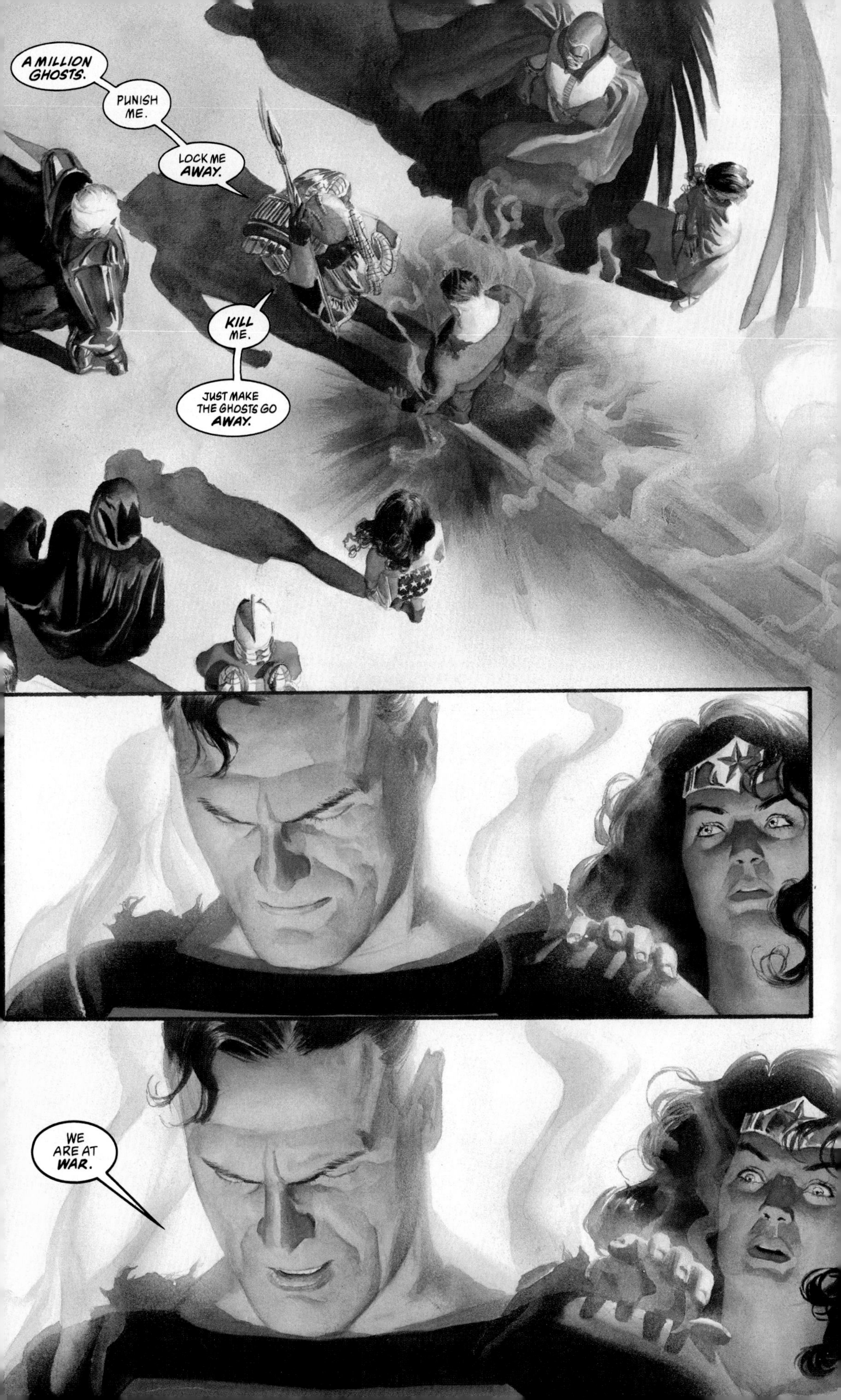
A MILLION GHOSTS.
PUNISH ME.
LOCK ME AWAY.
KILL ME.
JUST MAKE THE GHOSTS GO AWAY.
WE ARE AT WAR.

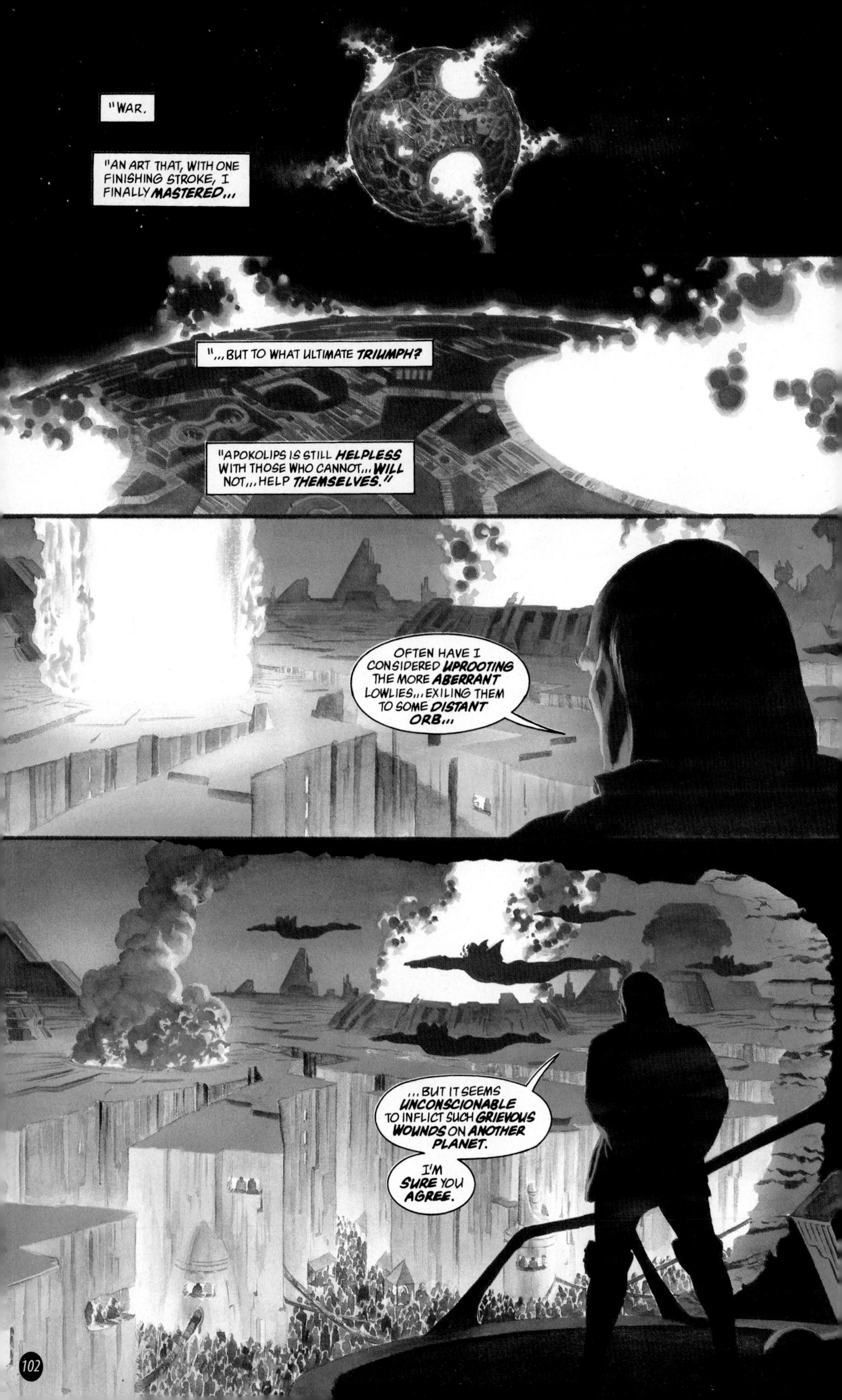
"WAR.
"AN ART THAT, WITH ONE FINISHING STROKE, I FINALLY MASTERED...
"...BUT TO WHAT ULTIMATE TRIUMPH?
"APOKOLIPS IS STILL HELPLESS WITH THOSE WHO CANNOT... WILL NOT... HELP THEMSELVES."
OFTEN HAVE I CONSIDERED UPROOTING THE MORE ABERRANT LOWLIES... EXILING THEM TO SOME DISTANT ORB...
...BUT IT SEEMS UNCONSCIONABLE TO INFLICT SUCH GRIEVOUS WOUNDS ON ANOTHER PLANET.
I'M SURE YOU AGREE.

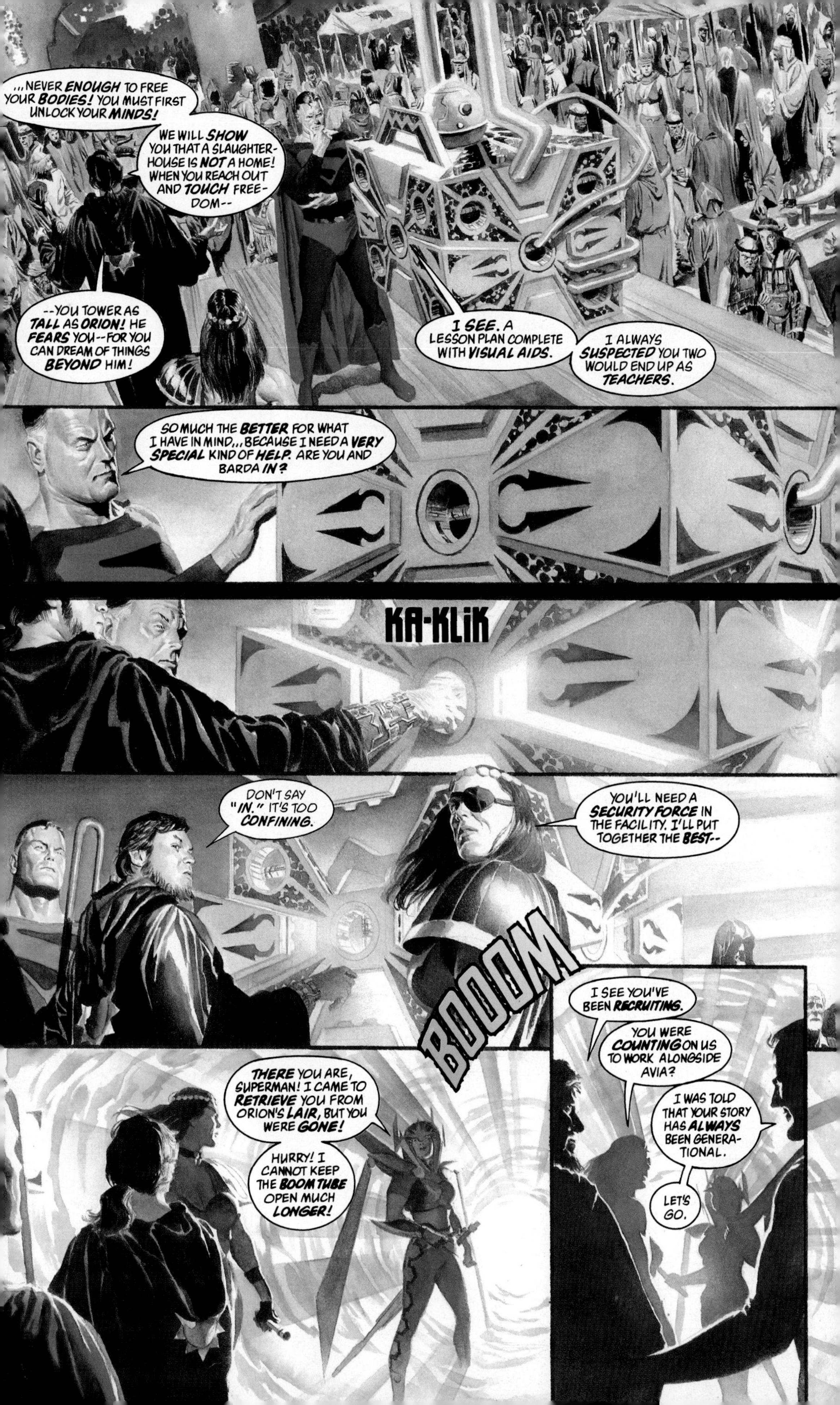
...NEVER ENOUGH TO FREE YOUR BODIES! YOU MUST FIRST UNLOCK YOUR MINDS!
WE WILL SHOW YOU THAT A SLAUGHTER-HOUSE IS NOT A HOME! WHEN YOU REACH OUT AND TOUCH FREE-DOM--
--YOU TOWER AS TALL AS ORION! HE FEARS YOU--FOR YOU CAN DREAM OF THINGS BEYOND HIM!
I SEE. A LESSON PLAN COMPLETE WITH VISUAL AIDS.
I ALWAYS SUSPECTED YOU TWO WOULD END UP AS TEACHERS.
SO MUCH THE BETTER FOR WHAT I HAVE IN MIND,,, BECAUSE I NEED A VERY SPECIAL KIND OF HELP. ARE YOU AND BARDA IN?
KA-KLIK
DON'T SAY "IN." IT'S TOO CONFINING.
YOU'LL NEED A SECURITY FORCE IN THE FACILITY. I'LL PUT TOGETHER THE BEST--
BOOOM
THERE YOU ARE, SUPERMAN! I CAME TO RETRIEVE YOU FROM ORION'S LAIR, BUT YOU WERE GONE!
HURRY! I CANNOT KEEP THE BOOM TUBE OPEN MUCH LONGER!
I SEE YOU'VE BEEN RECRUITING.
YOU WERE COUNTING ON US TO WORK ALONGSIDE AVIA?
I WAS TOLD THAT YOUR STORY HAS ALWAYS BEEN GENERA-TIONAL.
LET'S GO.

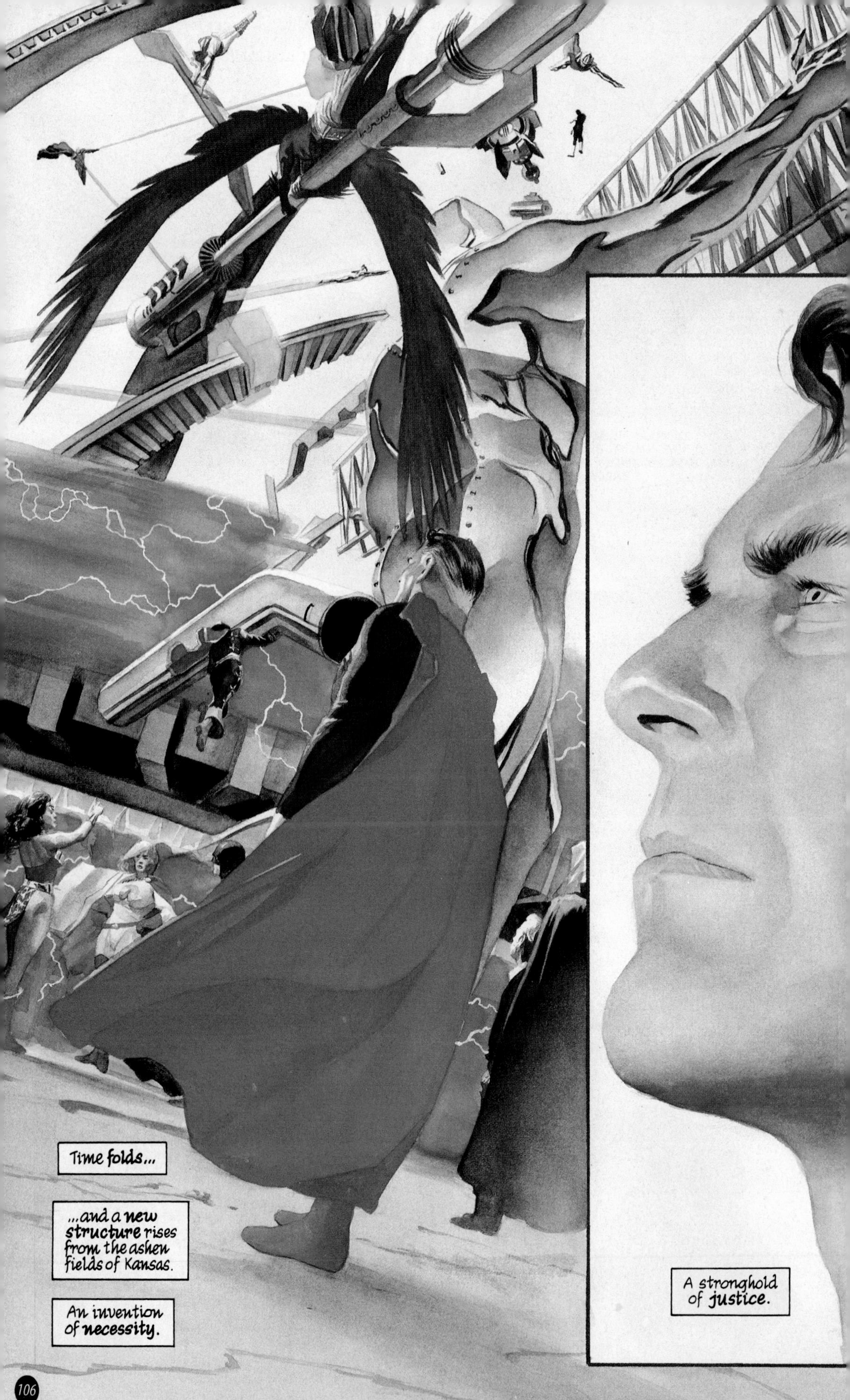
Time folds...
...and a new structure rises from the ashen fields of Kansas.
An invention of necessity.
A stronghold of justice.

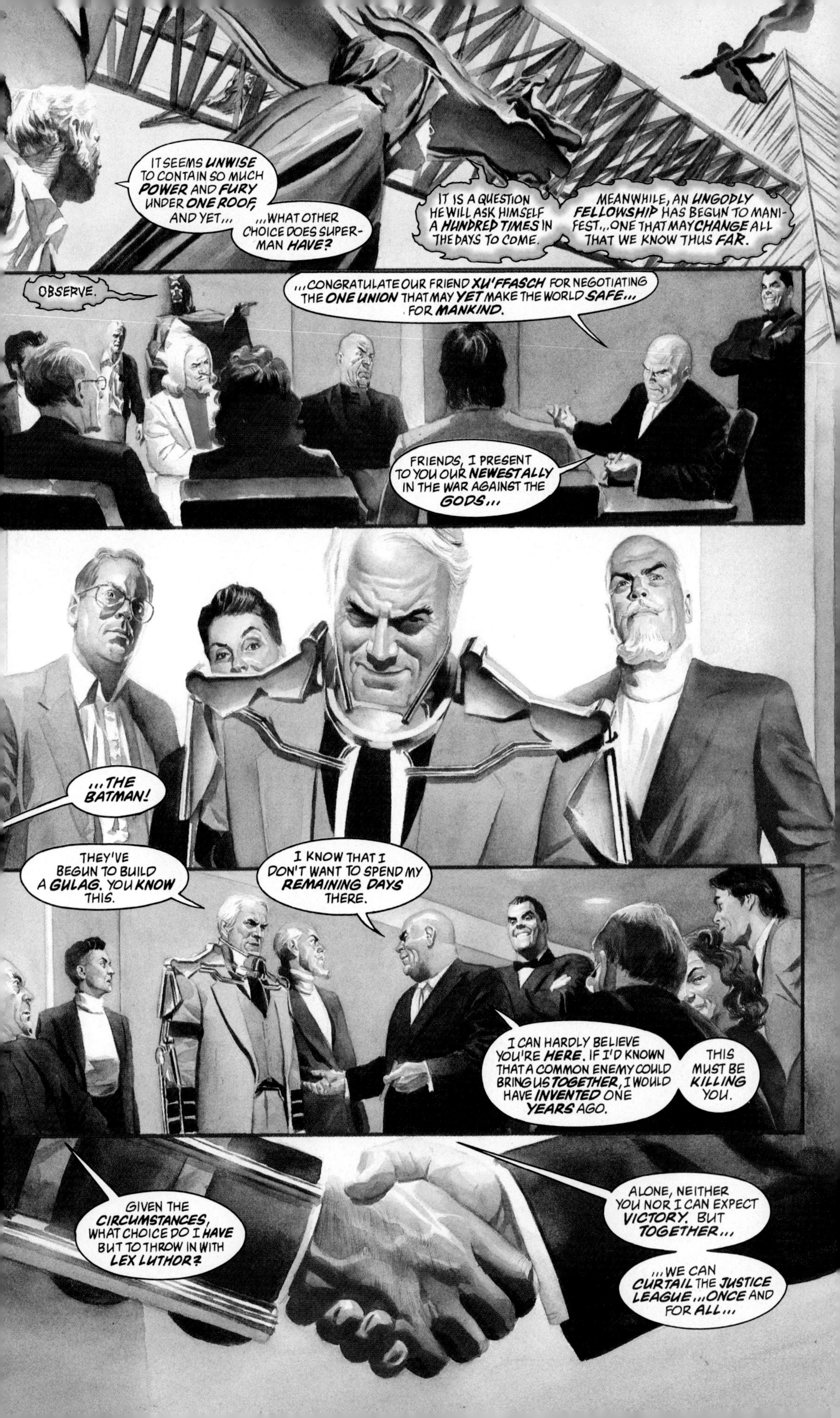

IT SEEMS UNWISE TO CONTAIN SO MUCH POWER AND FURY UNDER ONE ROOF, AND YET...
...WHAT OTHER CHOICE DOES SUPER-MAN HAVE?
IT IS A QUESTION HE WILL ASK HIMSELF A HUNDRED TIMES IN THE DAYS TO COME.
MEANWHILE, AN UNGODLY FELLOWSHIP HAS BEGUN TO MANI-FEST...ONE THAT MAY CHANGE ALL THAT WE KNOW THUS FAR.
OBSERVE.
...CONGRATULATE OUR FRIEND XU'FFASCH FOR NEGOTIATING THE ONE UNION THAT MAY YET MAKE THE WORLD SAFE... FOR MANKIND.
FRIENDS, I PRESENT TO YOU OUR NEWEST ALLY IN THE WAR AGAINST THE GODS...
...THE BATMAN!
THEY'VE BEGUN TO BUILD A GULAG. YOU KNOW THIS.
I KNOW THAT I DON'T WANT TO SPEND MY REMAINING DAYS THERE.
I CAN HARDLY BELIEVE YOU'RE HERE. IF I'D KNOWN THAT A COMMON ENEMY COULD BRING US TOGETHER, I WOULD HAVE INVENTED ONE YEARS AGO.
THIS MUST BE KILLING YOU.
GIVEN THE CIRCUMSTANCES, WHAT CHOICE DO I HAVE BUT TO THROW IN WITH LEX LUTHOR?
ALONE, NEITHER YOU NOR I CAN EXPECT VICTORY. BUT TOGETHER...
...WE CAN CURTAIL THE JUSTICE LEAGUE...ONCE AND FOR ALL...

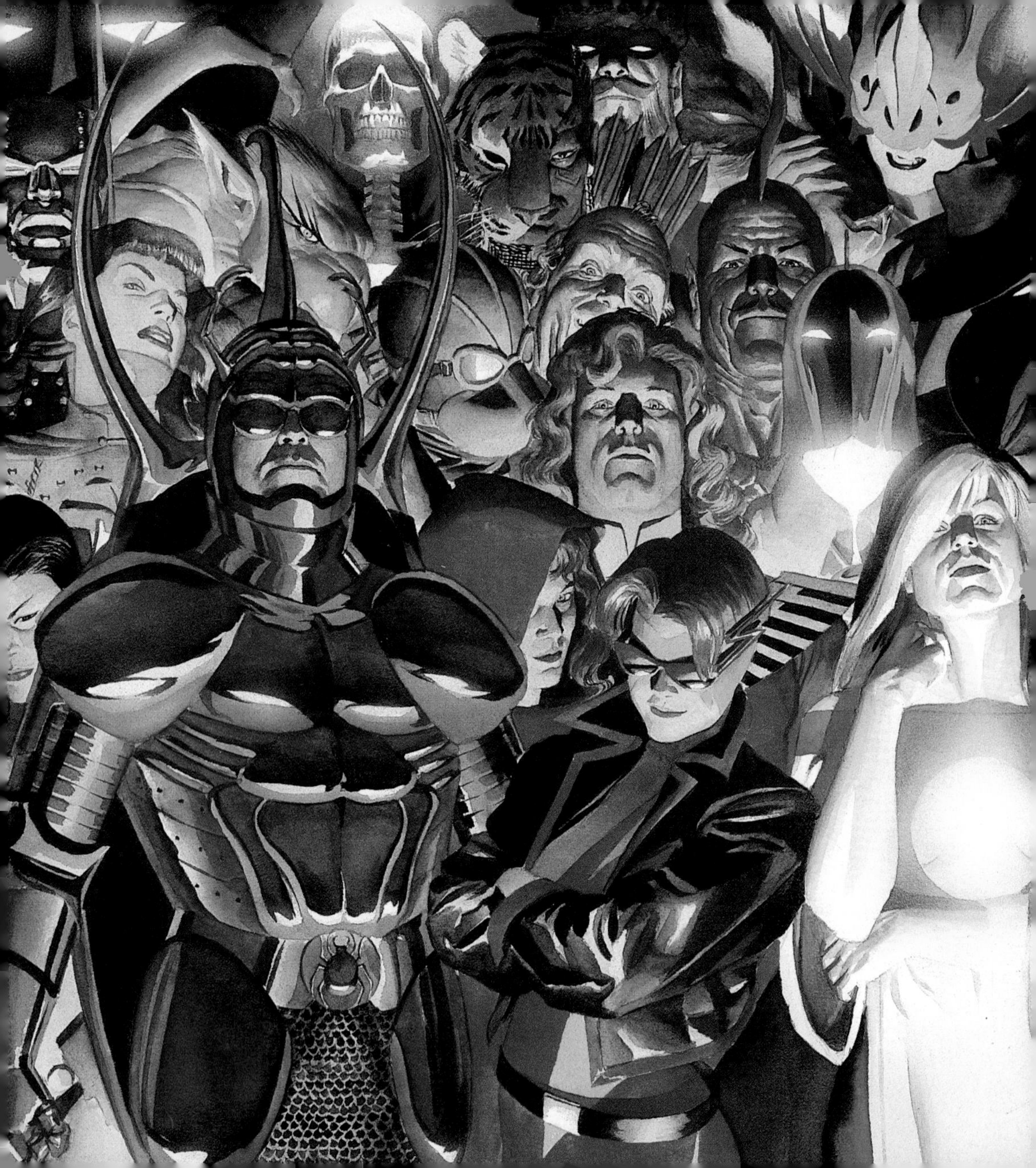

CHAPTER THREE

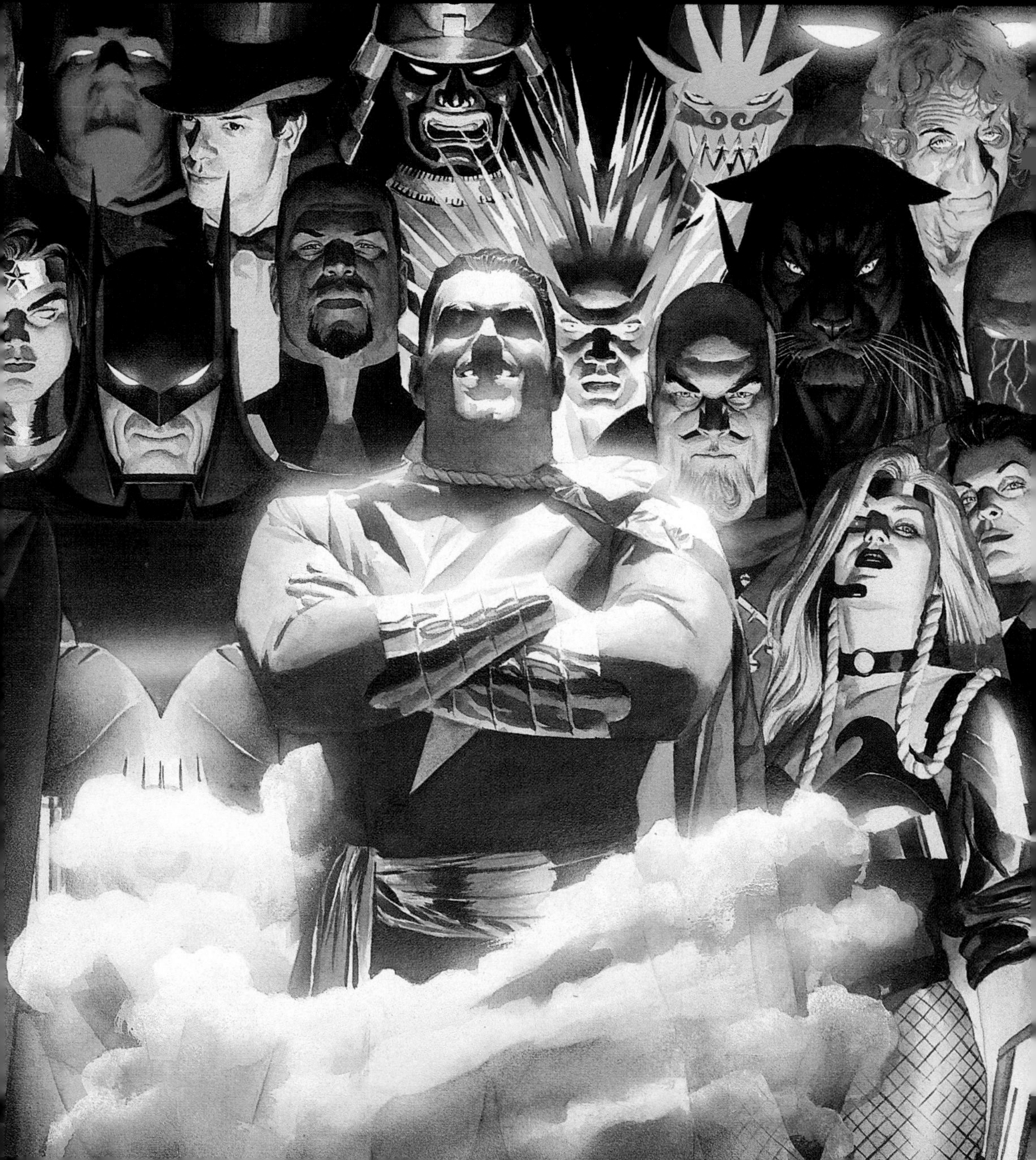

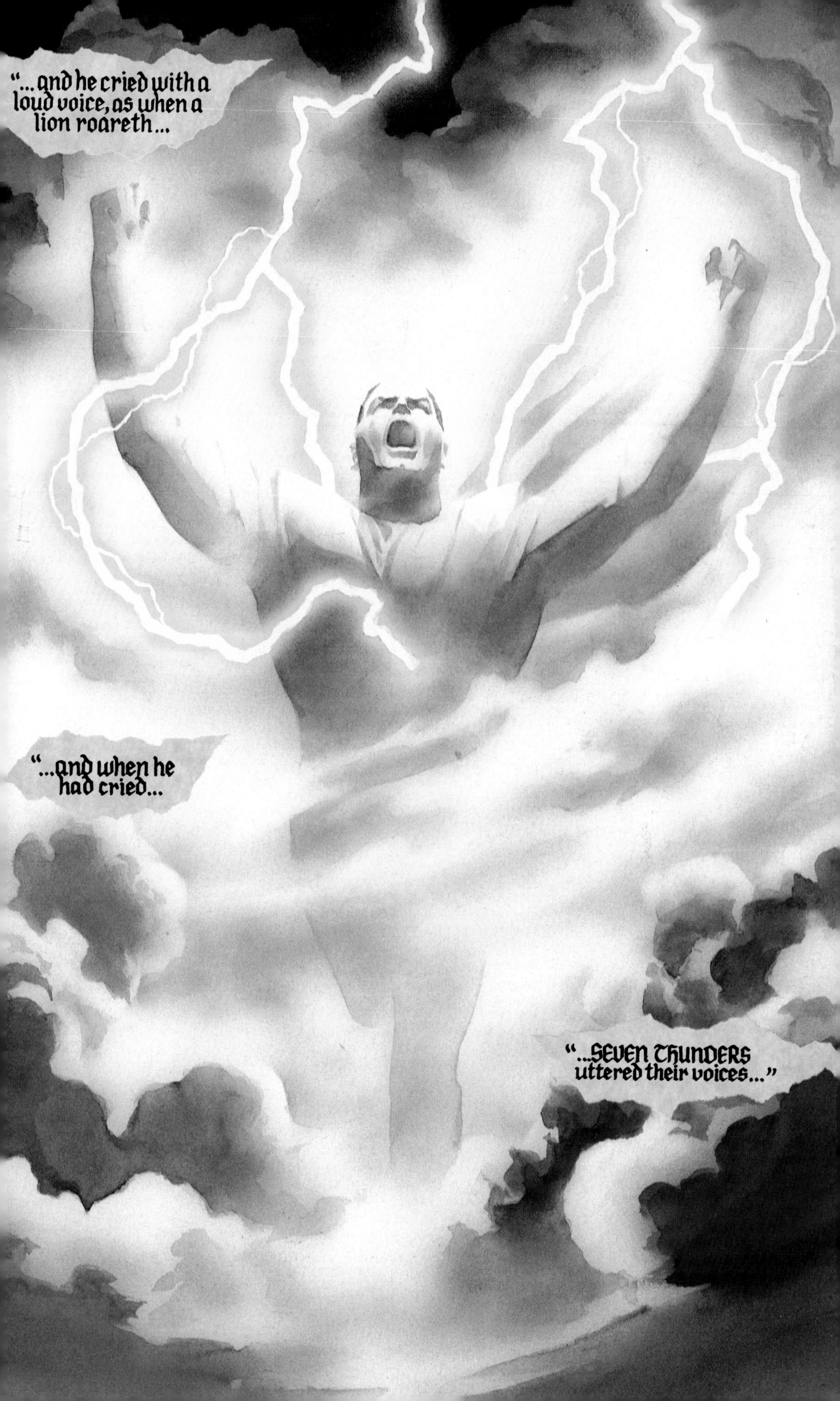
"...and he cried with a loud voice, as when a lion roareth...
"...and when he had cried...
"...SEVEN THUNDERS uttered their voices..."

ANOTHER *VISION?*

THEY'RE COMING MORE AND MORE *QUICKLY.*

DREAMS OF *ARMAGEDDON.*

CERTAINLY, YOU MUST *SHARE* THEM. HOW *ELSE* DO YOU EXPLAIN THE ROAD WE *WALK?*

HOW ELSE DO YOU *UNERRINGLY* LEAD US TO THE TABLEAUS AND REALITIES *BEHIND* MY DREAMS?

I SEE MANY THINGS, NORMAN McCAY... BUT THE *FUTURE* IS NOT ONE OF THEM.

I DO NOT LEAD *YOU. YOU* LEAD *ME...*

ONLY *YOU* FORESEE THE ROAD TO *RAGNAROK.*

And with *that* pronouncement, we begin *once more* to wander the Earth like spirits. Time *ebbs* and *flows* around us.

...INEXORABLY...

...TO AN IMMINENT HOUR WHEN JUDGMENT MUST BE *PASSED...* AND JUSTICE *SERVED.*

Many of the places I see are *new* and strange.

Others...

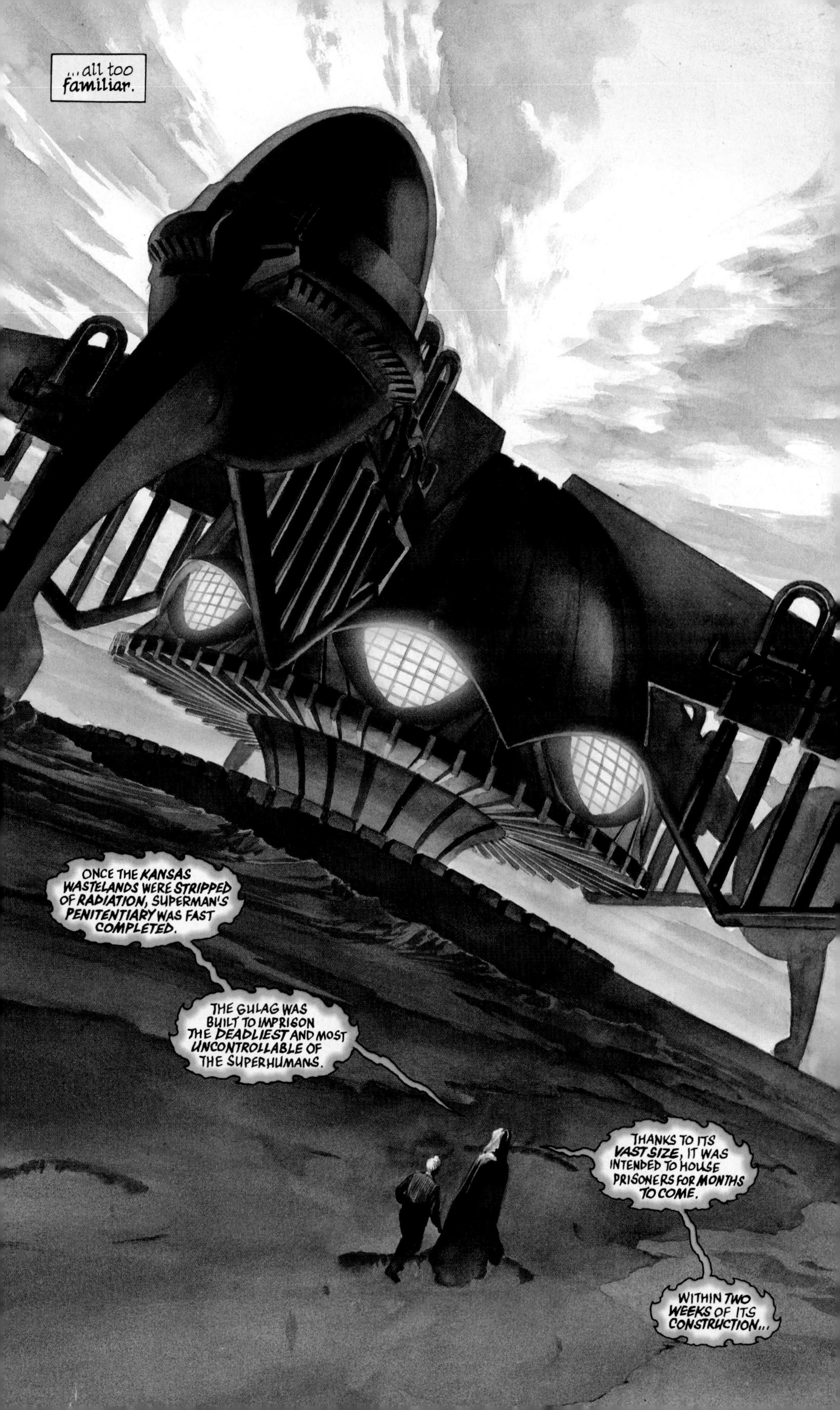
...all too familiar.
ONCE THE KANSAS WASTELANDS WERE STRIPPED OF RADIATION, SUPERMAN'S PENITENTIARY WAS FAST COMPLETED.
THE GULAG WAS BUILT TO IMPRISON THE DEADLIEST AND MOST UNCONTROLLABLE OF THE SUPERHUMANS.
THANKS TO ITS VAST SIZE, IT WAS INTENDED TO HOUSE PRISONERS FOR MONTHS TO COME.
WITHIN TWO WEEKS OF ITS CONSTRUCTION...

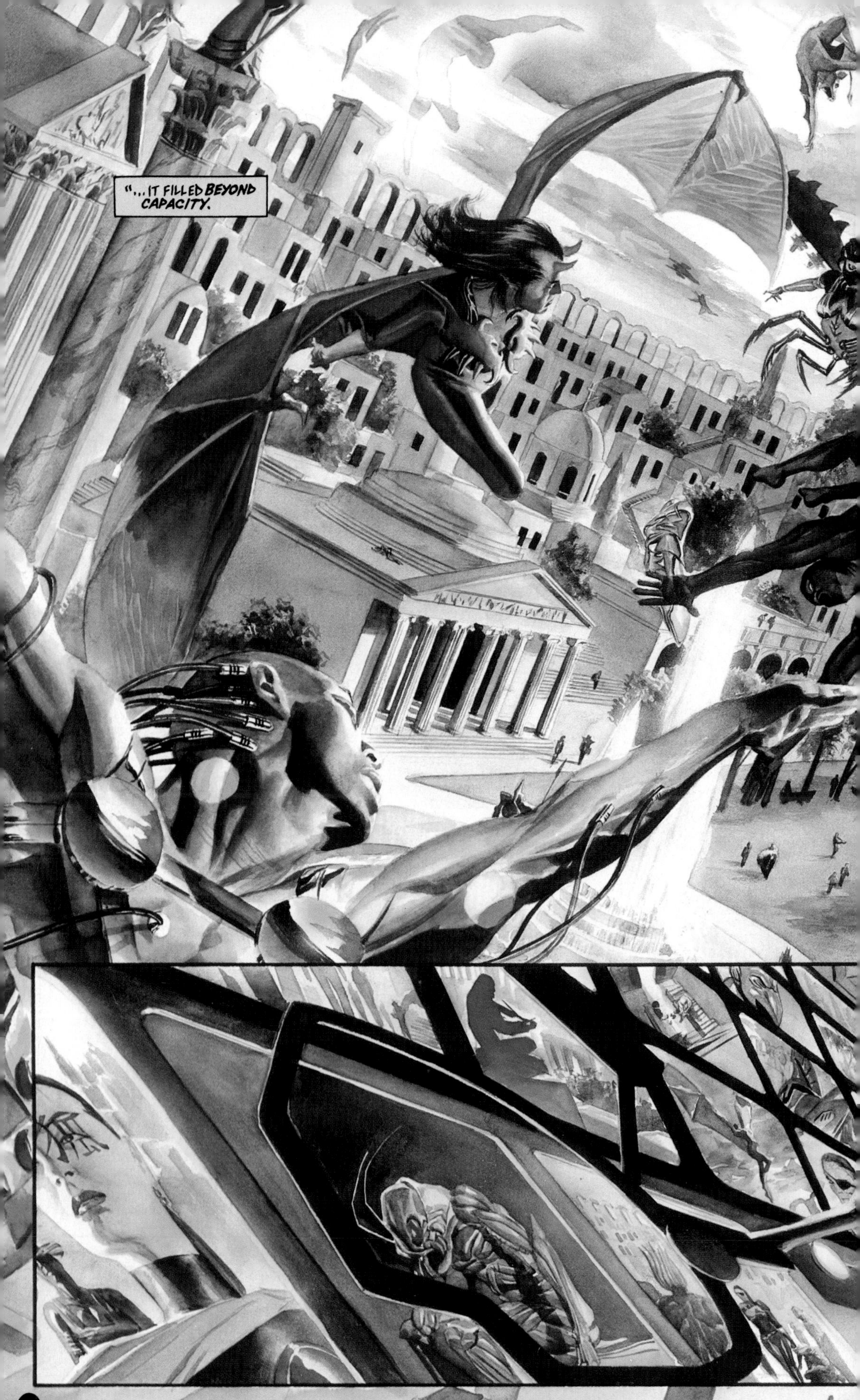
"...IT FILLED BEYOND CAPACITY.

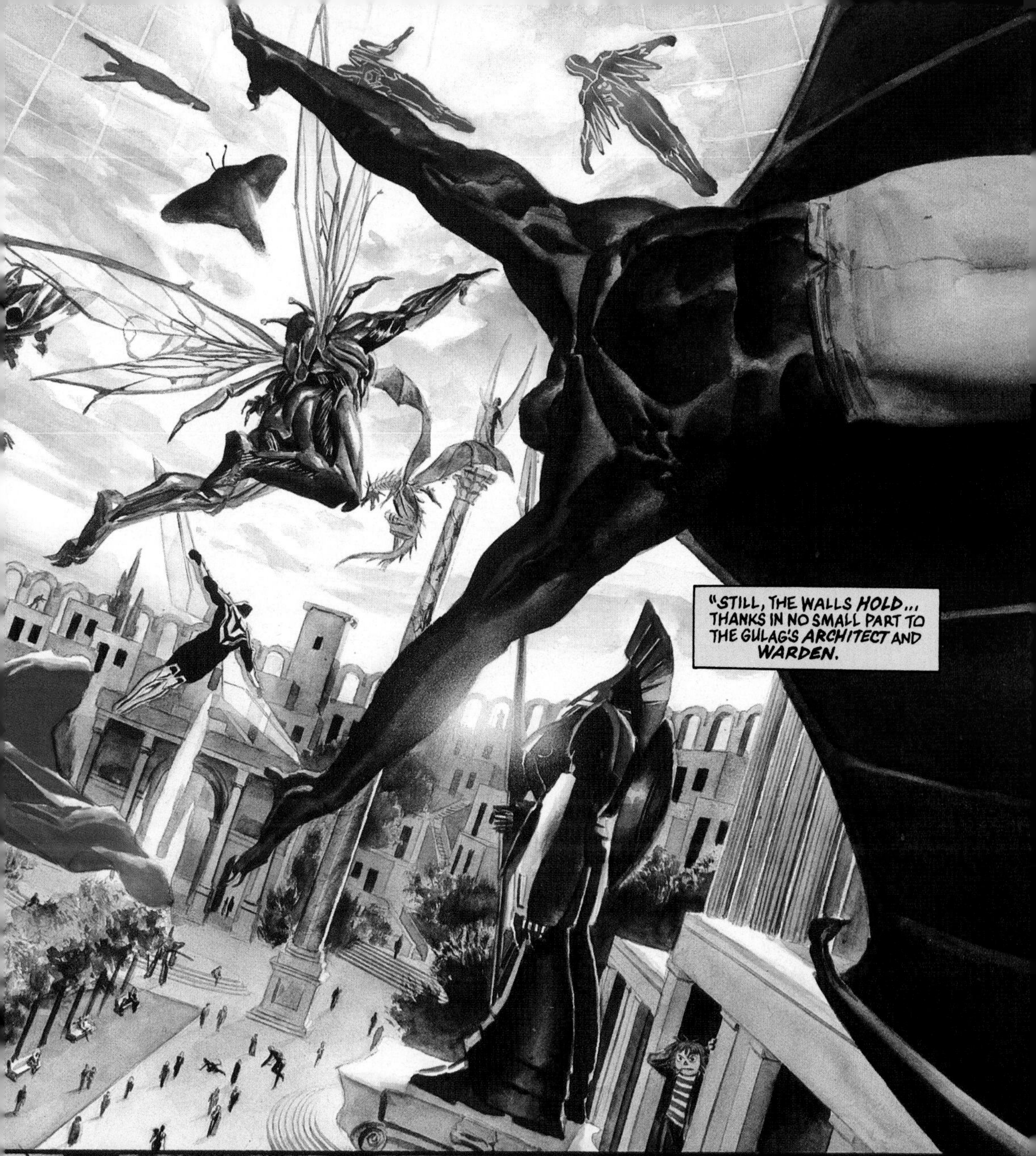
"STILL, THE WALLS HOLD... THANKS IN NO SMALL PART TO THE GULAG'S ARCHITECT AND WARDEN.

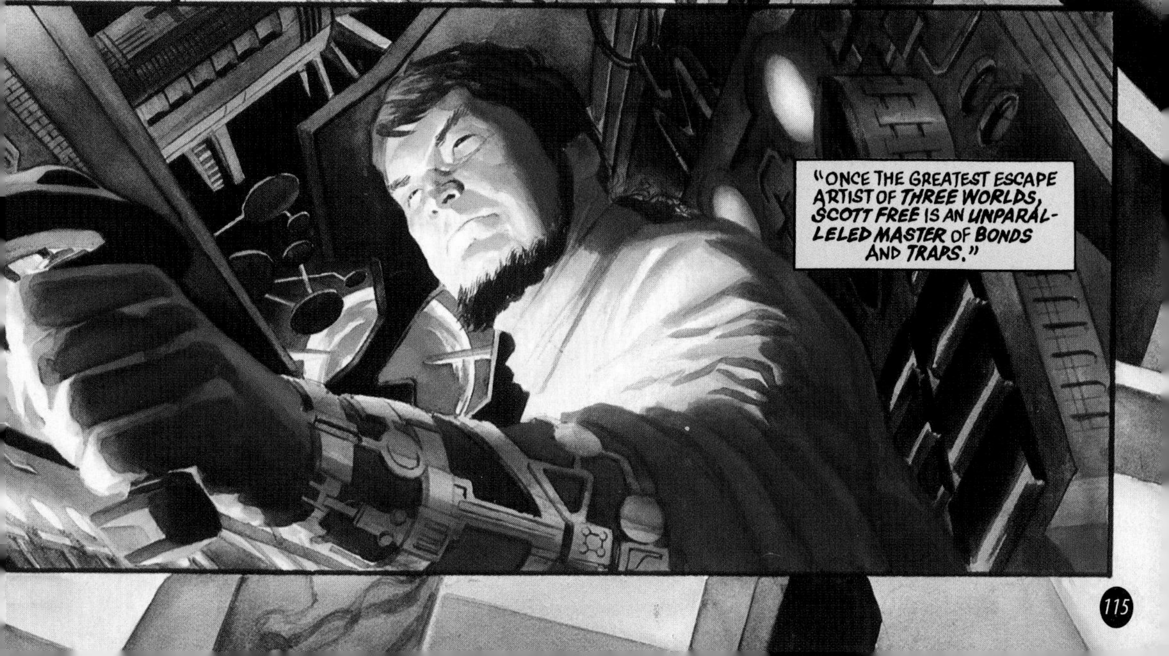
"ONCE THE GREATEST ESCAPE ARTIST OF THREE WORLDS, SCOTT FREE IS AN UNPARAL-LELED MASTER OF BONDS AND TRAPS."

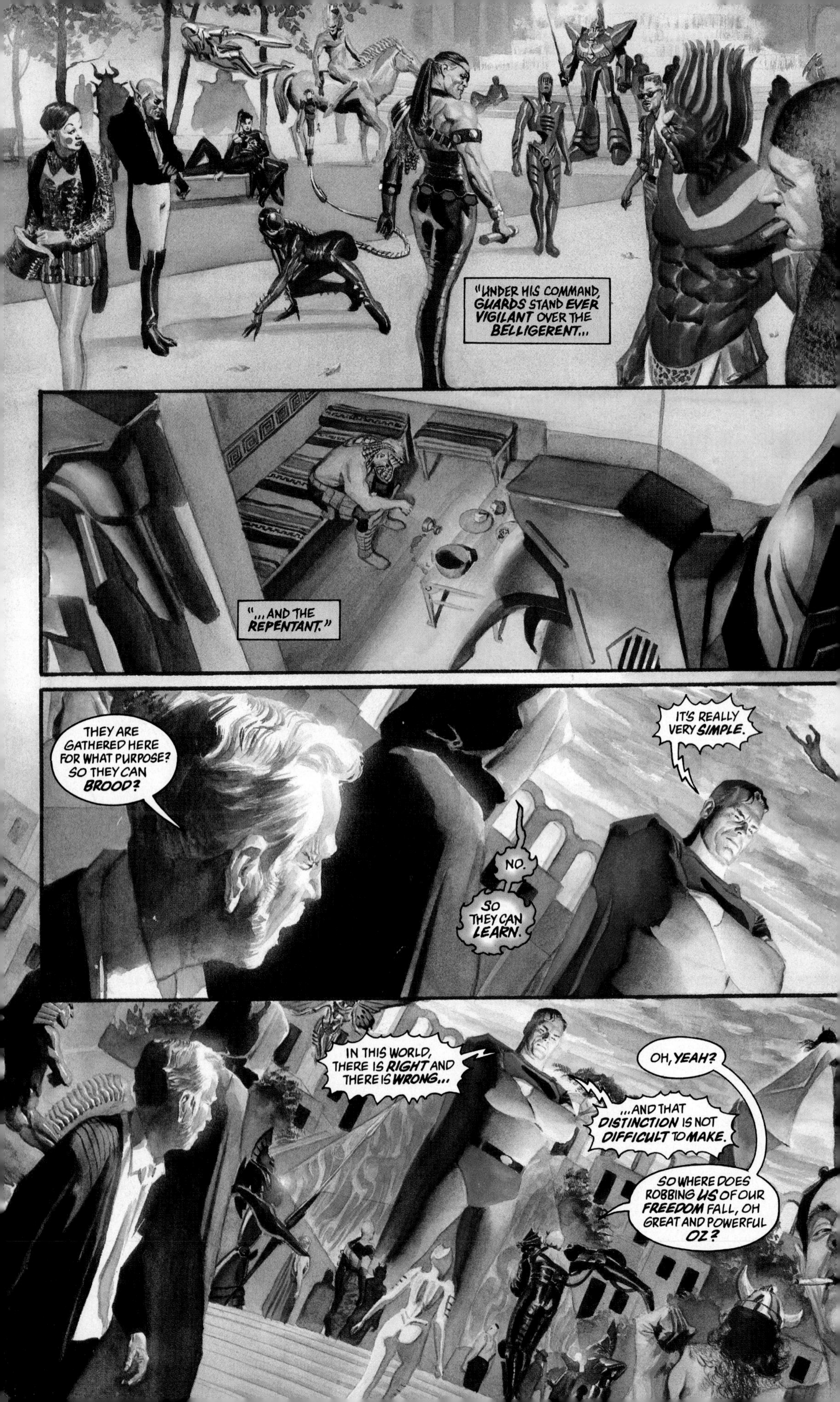
"UNDER HIS COMMAND, GUARDS STAND EVER VIGILANT OVER THE BELLIGERENT...
"...AND THE REPENTANT."
THEY ARE GATHERED HERE FOR WHAT PURPOSE? SO THEY CAN BROOD?
IT'S REALLY VERY SIMPLE.
NO.
SO THEY CAN LEARN.
IN THIS WORLD, THERE IS RIGHT AND THERE IS WRONG...
...AND THAT DISTINCTION IS NOT DIFFICULT TO MAKE.
OH, YEAH?
SO WHERE DOES ROBBING US OF OUR FREEDOM FALL, OH GREAT AND POWERFUL OZ?

PLEASE UNDERSTAND OUR *INTENT. NONE* OF YOU ARE HERE FOR *PUNISHMENT.* YOU'RE HERE FOR *EDUCATION.*

WE'RE HERE BECAUSE OF *FORCED BUSSING,* YOU STUPID *RECORDING!*

HOW MANY DIFFERENT WAYS CAN YOU *SPEW* THAT POLLYANNA *CRAP?*

THE *POWERS* WE HAVE... THE THINGS WE *DO...* THEY'RE MEANT TO *INSPIRE* ORDINARY CITIZENS...NOT *INTIMIDATE* THEM. NOT *TERRIFY* THEM.

DAY AFTER *DAY,* HE TALKS TO US LIKE *WE'RE* THE *BAD GUYS!*

WE *CANNOT* ACT AS *JUDGE* AND JURY. WE ADHERE TO A *MORAL CODE* BASED ON THE *PRESERVATION* OF *LIFE...*

EASY FOR *HIM* TO SAY. DID *HE* EVER HAVE TO FIGHT THE *SLAUGHTER BRIGADE* ?

HE STICKS US IN *HERE* JUST BECAUSE WE DON'T KISS *BABIES* AND SALUTE THE FRIG-GIN' *FLAG!*

I'M *SICK* OF THIS *MEDIEVAL THINKING!* HIS *CODE'S* JUST AS *EMPTY--*

WHO BAGGED *ECLIPSO,* HUH? WHO TOASTED *RA'S AL GHUL?* GUYS LIKE *US,* THAT'S WHO! WE SAVED LIVES, MAN!

"MAN OF TOMORROW," MY *ASS.* TRY "MAN OF THE *NINETEEN-FIFTIES!"* TIMES *CHANGE...* BUT HE *STILL* EXPECTS *EVERYONE* TO LIVE UP TO SOME *COBWEBBED CODE!*

--AS THIS *STUPID HOLOGRAM!*

KRSZZAK

SORRY YOU *FEEL* THAT WAY.

UH-OH...

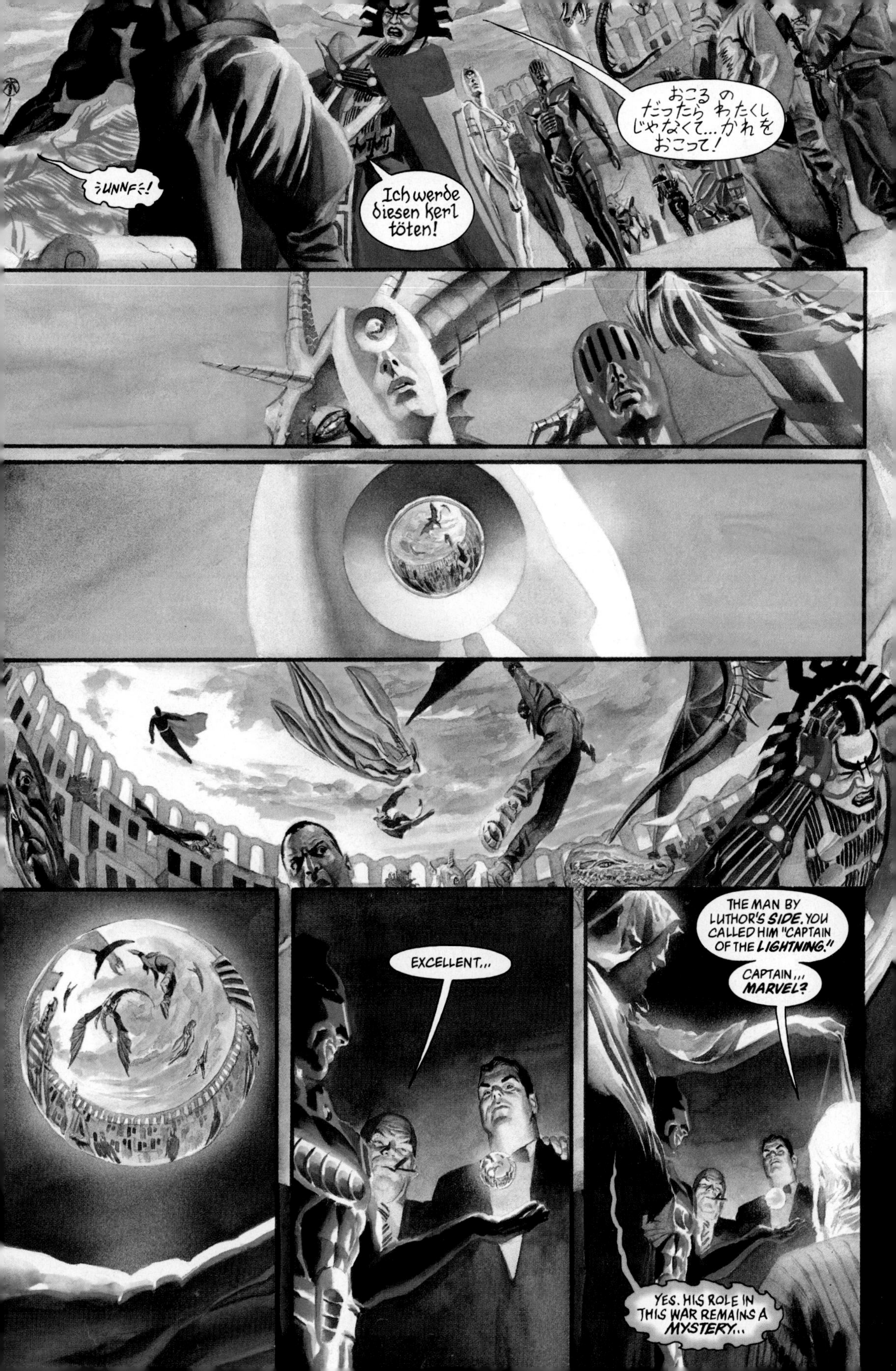

おこるの だったら わたくし じゃなくて…かれを おこって!
UNNF!
Ich werde diesen kerl töten!
EXCELLENT...
THE MAN BY LUTHOR'S SIDE. YOU CALLED HIM "CAPTAIN OF THE LIGHTNING."
CAPTAIN... MARVEL?
YES. HIS ROLE IN THIS WAR REMAINS A MYSTERY...

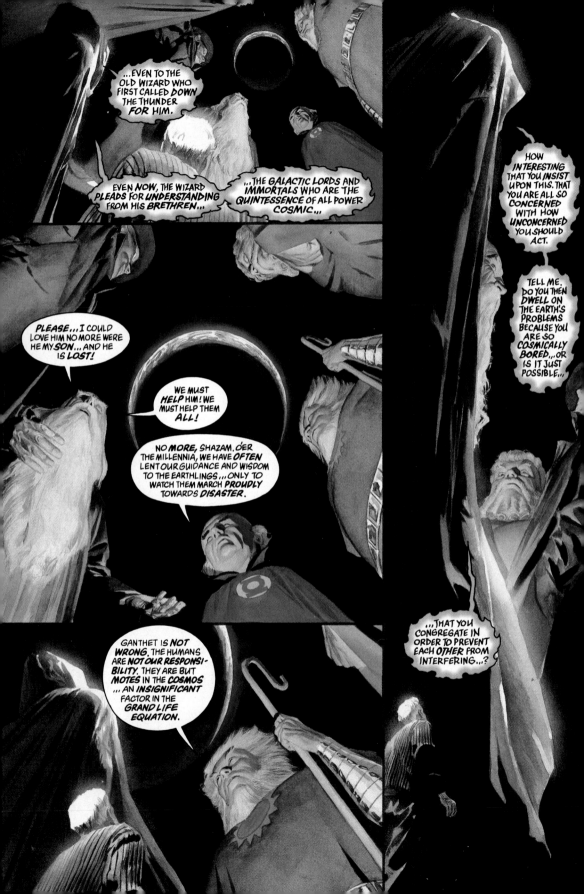

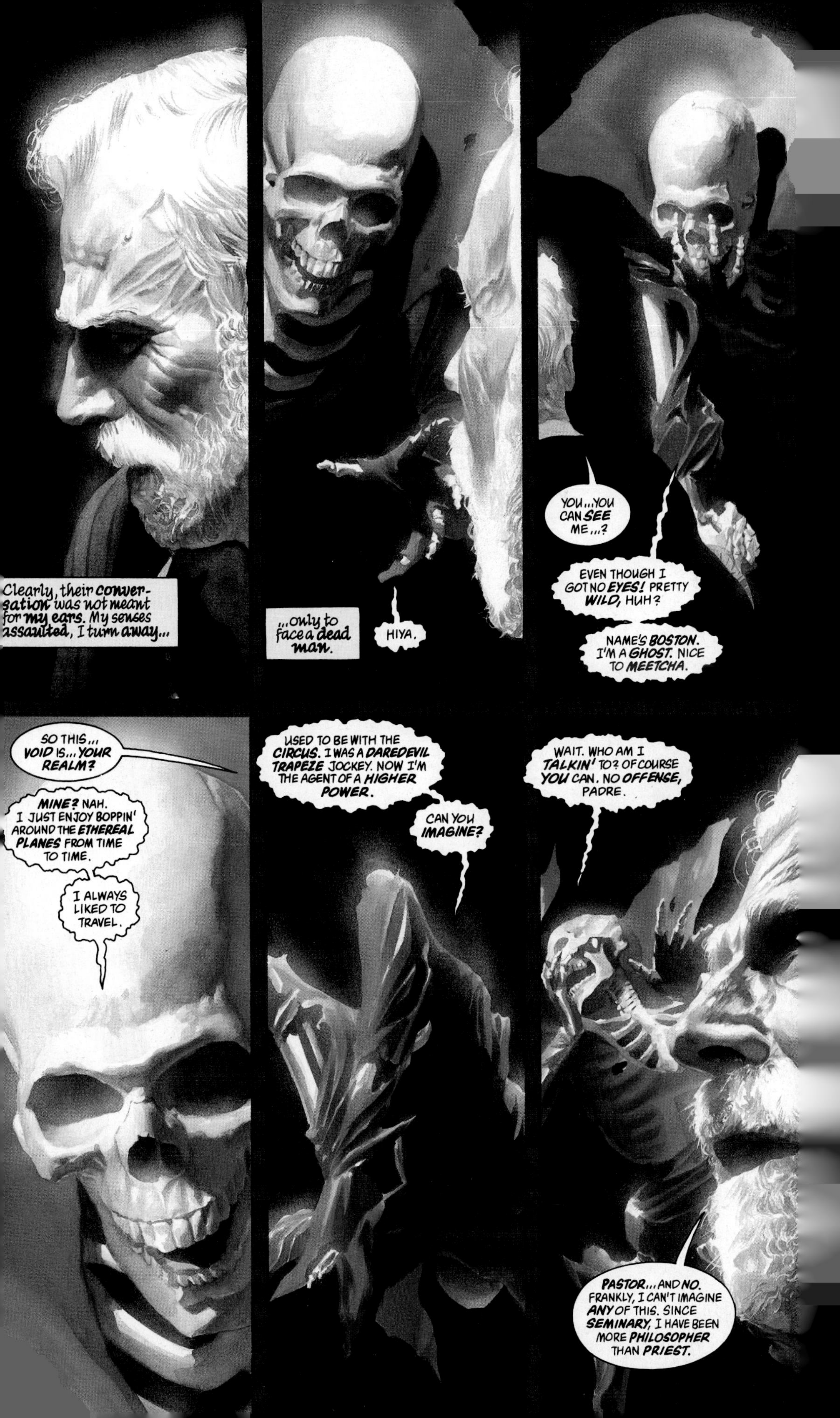
Clearly, their conversation was not meant for my ears. My senses assaulted, I turn away...
...only to face a dead man.
HIYA.
YOU...YOU CAN SEE ME...?
EVEN THOUGH I GOT NO EYES! PRETTY WILD, HUH?
NAME'S BOSTON. I'M A GHOST. NICE TO MEETCHA.
SO THIS... VOID IS... YOUR REALM?
MINE? NAH. I JUST ENJOY BOPPIN' AROUND THE ETHEREAL PLANES FROM TIME TO TIME.
I ALWAYS LIKED TO TRAVEL.
USED TO BE WITH THE CIRCUS. I WAS A DAREDEVIL TRAPEZE JOCKEY. NOW I'M THE AGENT OF A HIGHER POWER.
CAN YOU IMAGINE?
WAIT. WHO AM I TALKIN' TO? OF COURSE YOU CAN. NO OFFENSE, PADRE.
PASTOR... AND NO. FRANKLY, I CAN'T IMAGINE ANY OF THIS. SINCE SEMINARY, I HAVE BEEN MORE PHILOSOPHER THAN PRIEST.

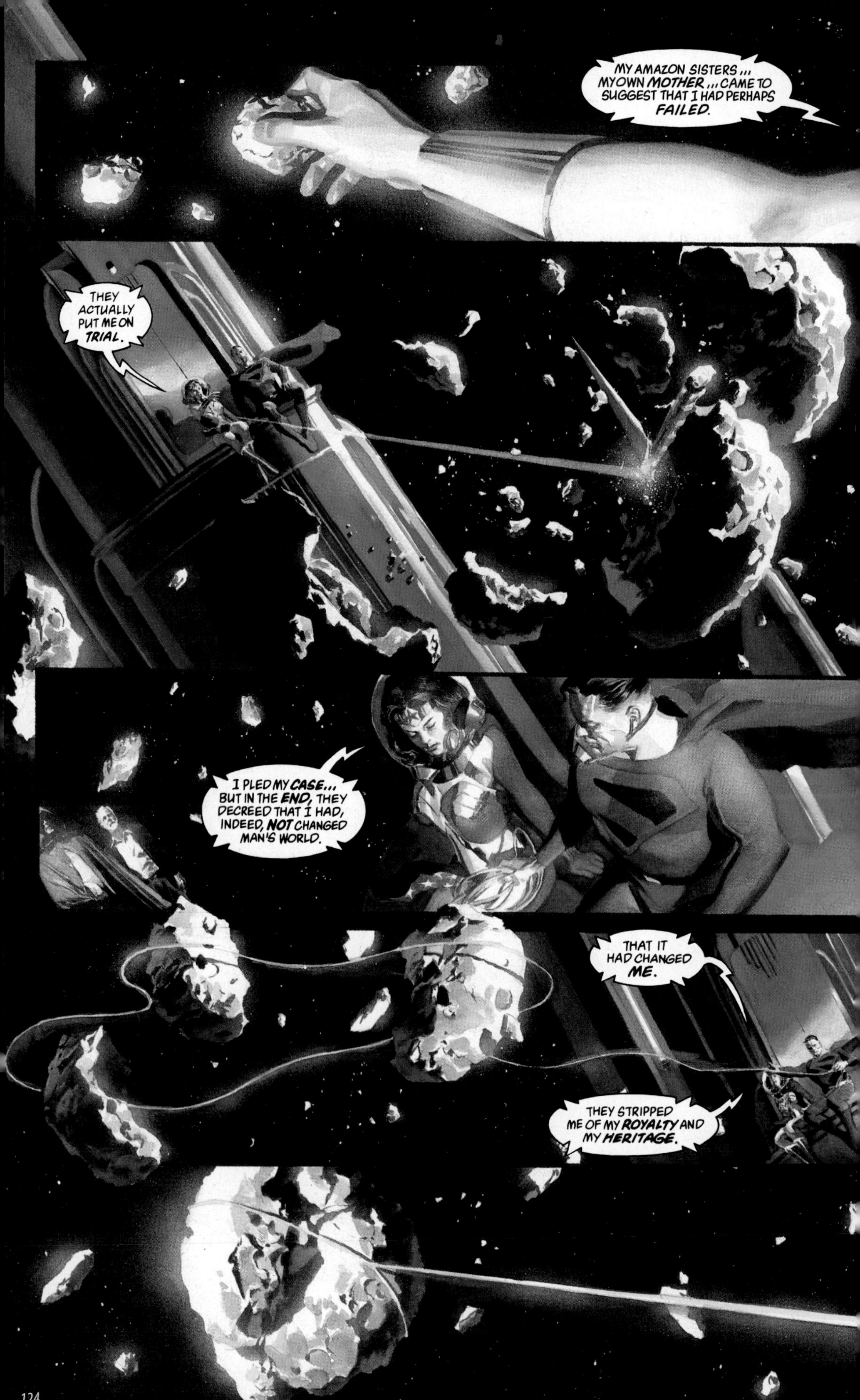
MY AMAZON SISTERS ... MY OWN MOTHER ... CAME TO SUGGEST THAT I HAD PERHAPS FAILED.
THEY ACTUALLY PUT ME ON TRIAL.
I PLED MY CASE... BUT IN THE END, THEY DECREED THAT I HAD, INDEED, NOT CHANGED MAN'S WORLD.
THAT IT HAD CHANGED ME.
THEY STRIPPED ME OF MY ROYALTY AND MY HERITAGE.

OUR OLD FRIEND SIVANA SAW TO THAT, DIDN'T HE?
HERE. LET ME GET THAT.
INGENIOUS LITTLE BUGGER, SIVANA WAS. DO YOU SUPPOSE THAT WHEN THEY COINED THE TERM "MAD SCIENTIST," THEY WERE THINKING OF HIM?
I'LL BET THEY WERE.
WELL, REST IN PEACE, SIVANA. SCIENCE...
...MARCHES ON.
♫ THE WORMS CRAWL IN... THE WORMS CRAWL OUT... ♪
SHU...SHA... SHAZ...
OH, NO, NO. THERE'LL BE NO RETREAT.
NOT YET.
I STILL HAVE A VERY SPECIAL JOB FOR YOU...

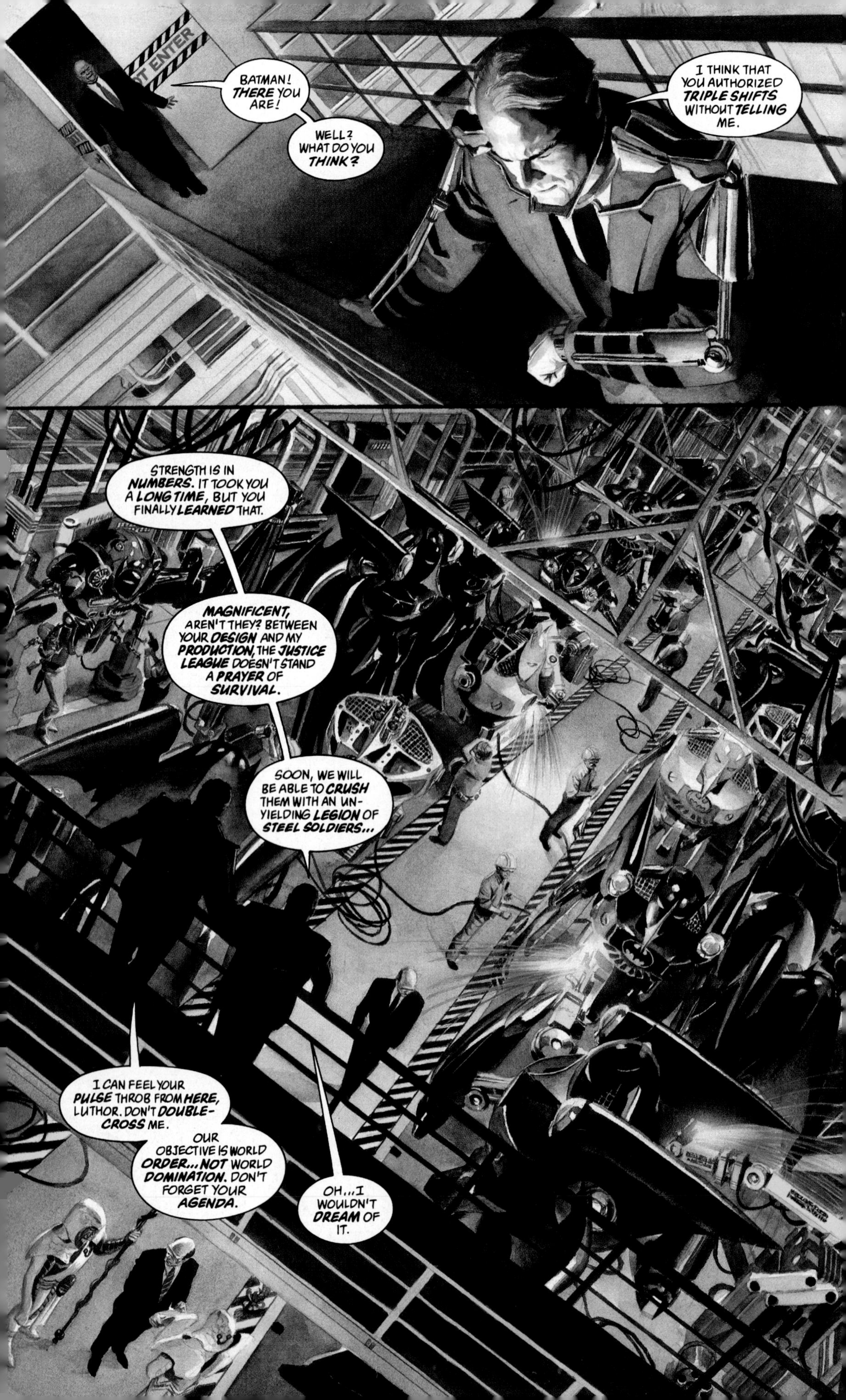
BATMAN! THERE YOU ARE!
WELL? WHAT DO YOU THINK?
I THINK THAT YOU AUTHORIZED TRIPLE SHIFTS WITHOUT TELLING ME.
STRENGTH IS IN NUMBERS. IT TOOK YOU A LONG TIME, BUT YOU FINALLY LEARNED THAT.
MAGNIFICENT, AREN'T THEY? BETWEEN YOUR DESIGN AND MY PRODUCTION, THE JUSTICE LEAGUE DOESN'T STAND A PRAYER OF SURVIVAL.
SOON, WE WILL BE ABLE TO CRUSH THEM WITH AN UN-YIELDING LEGION OF STEEL SOLDIERS...
I CAN FEEL YOUR PULSE THROB FROM HERE, LUTHOR. DON'T DOUBLE-CROSS ME.
OUR OBJECTIVE IS WORLD ORDER... NOT WORLD DOMINATION. DON'T FORGET YOUR AGENDA.
OH...I WOULDN'T DREAM OF IT.

I *KNOW* WHAT YOU'RE *THINKING*. I DO!

I'M *AWARE* OF THAT, OLD FRIEND.

BUT LET'S NOT DO THIS *TELEPATH-ICALLY*. YOU WON'T STAY *FOCUSED*.

TALK TO ME.

JUST *RELAX*...AND *TALK*.

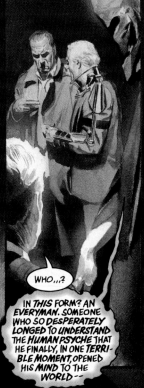

WHO...?

IN *THIS* FORM? AN *EVERYMAN*. SOMEONE WHO SO DESPERATELY *LONGED* TO UNDERSTAND THE *HUMAN PSYCHE* THAT HE FINALLY, IN ONE *TERRIBLE* MOMENT, OPENED HIS *MIND* TO THE *WORLD*--

--AND WAS FOREVER *SHATTERED* BY ITS *THOUGHTS*.

HE WAS ONCE A *MARTIAN CHAMPION*.

NOW HE IS NOT MUCH OF *ANYTHING*.

J'ONN... CAN YOU *VERIFY*?

I WUH-WILL *ATTEMPT*...

TOO MUCH NOISE! *TOO MUCH*--

SHH. SHH. IT'S *OKAY*.

WHAT *N-NOW*? I WANT TO *STAY*, I WANT TO...MUH-*MATTER*, I...

OH. YOU...YOU DON'T THINK I'LL *H-HELP*...

J'ONN, YOU FOUGHT THE GOOD FIGHT LONGER THAN *ANY* OF US.

YOU'VE DONE *ALL* THAT'S EVER BEEN *ASKED* OF YOU...

...AND TODAY WAS *NO EXCEPTION*.

YOU'VE PAID YOUR *DUES*, OLD FRIEND. GO HOME AND *REST*.

DREAM OF *RED SANDS* AND *SILENT STARS*.

131

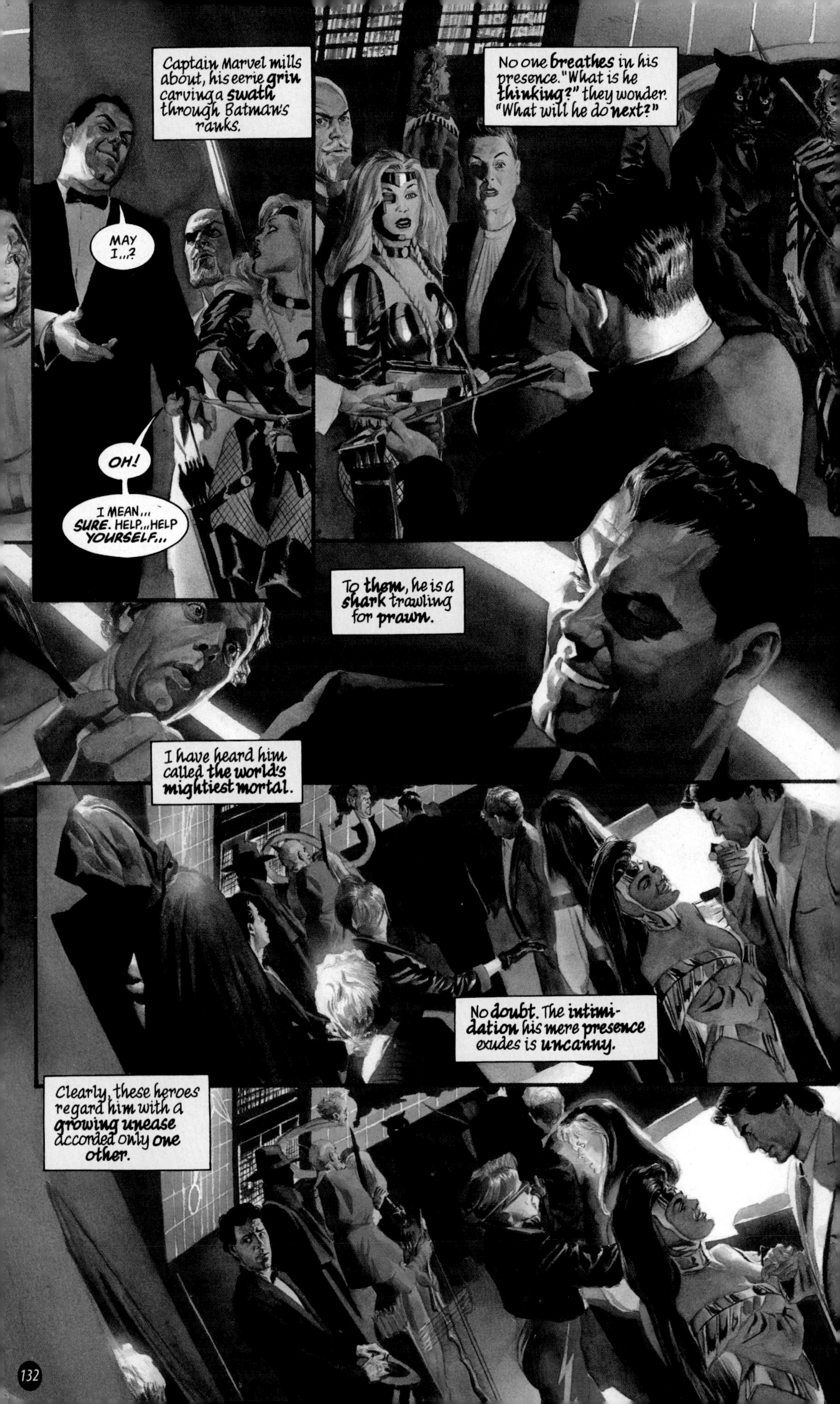

Captain Marvel mills about, his eerie grin carving a swath through Batman's ranks.
MAY I...?
OH!
I MEAN... SURE. HELP... HELP YOURSELF...
No one breathes in his presence. "What is he thinking?" they wonder. "What will he do next?"
To them, he is a shark trawling for prawn.
I have heard him called the world's mightiest mortal.
No doubt. The intimidation his mere presence exudes is uncanny.
Clearly, these heroes regard him with a growing unease accorded only one other.

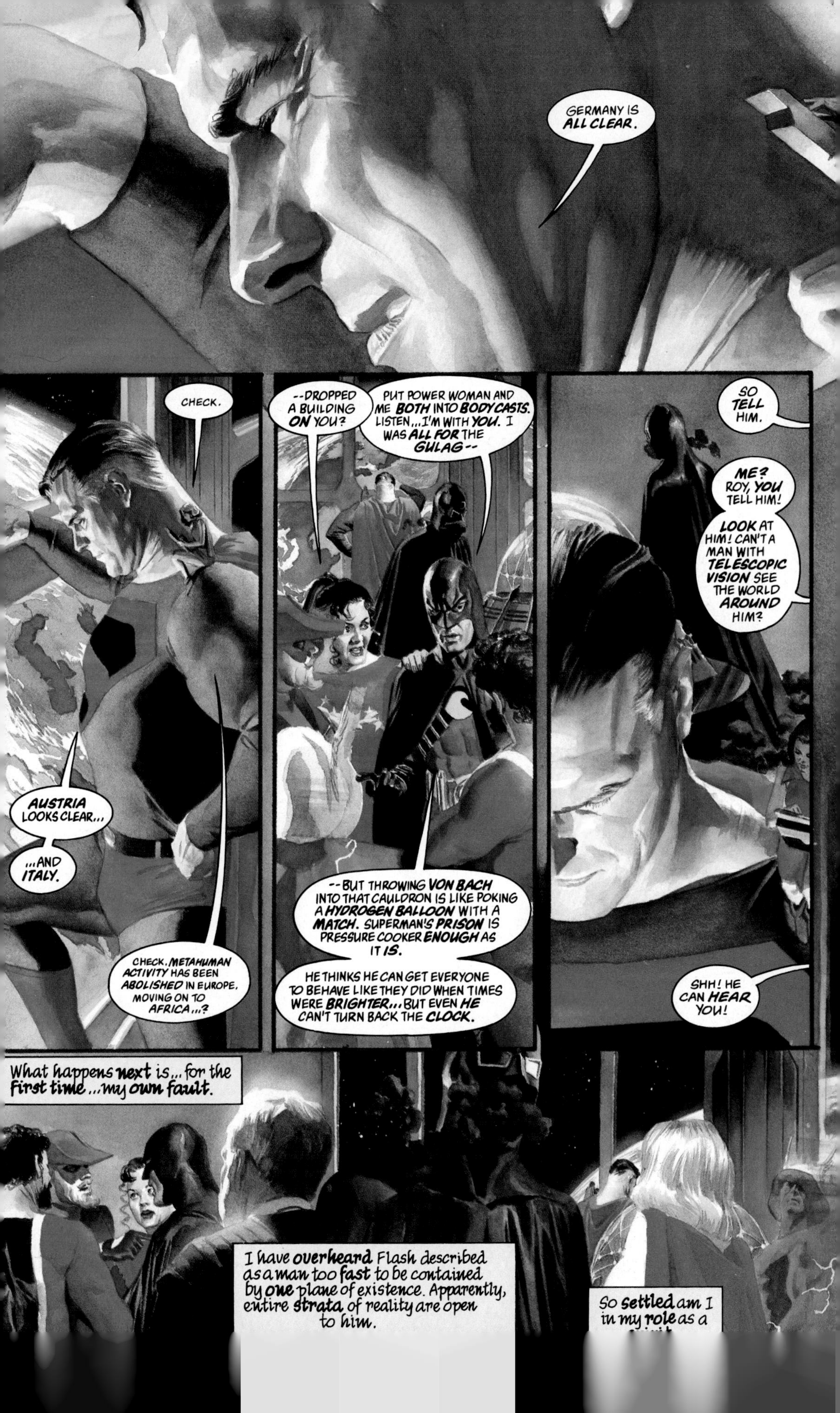
GERMANY IS ALL CLEAR.
CHECK.
AUSTRIA LOOKS CLEAR...
...AND ITALY.
CHECK. METAHUMAN ACTIVITY HAS BEEN ABOLISHED IN EUROPE. MOVING ON TO AFRICA...?
--DROPPED A BUILDING ON YOU?
PUT POWER WOMAN AND ME BOTH INTO BODY CASTS. LISTEN... I'M WITH YOU. I WAS ALL FOR THE GULAG--
--BUT THROWING VON BACH INTO THAT CAULDRON IS LIKE POKING A HYDROGEN BALLOON WITH A MATCH. SUPERMAN'S PRISON IS PRESSURE COOKER ENOUGH AS IT IS.
HE THINKS HE CAN GET EVERYONE TO BEHAVE LIKE THEY DID WHEN TIMES WERE BRIGHTER... BUT EVEN HE CAN'T TURN BACK THE CLOCK.
SO TELL HIM.
ME? ROY, YOU TELL HIM!
LOOK AT HIM! CAN'T A MAN WITH TELESCOPIC VISION SEE THE WORLD AROUND HIM?
SHH! HE CAN HEAR YOU!
What happens next is... for the first time... my own fault.
I have overheard Flash described as a man too fast to be contained by one plane of existence. Apparently, entire strata of reality are open to him.
So settled am I in my role as a

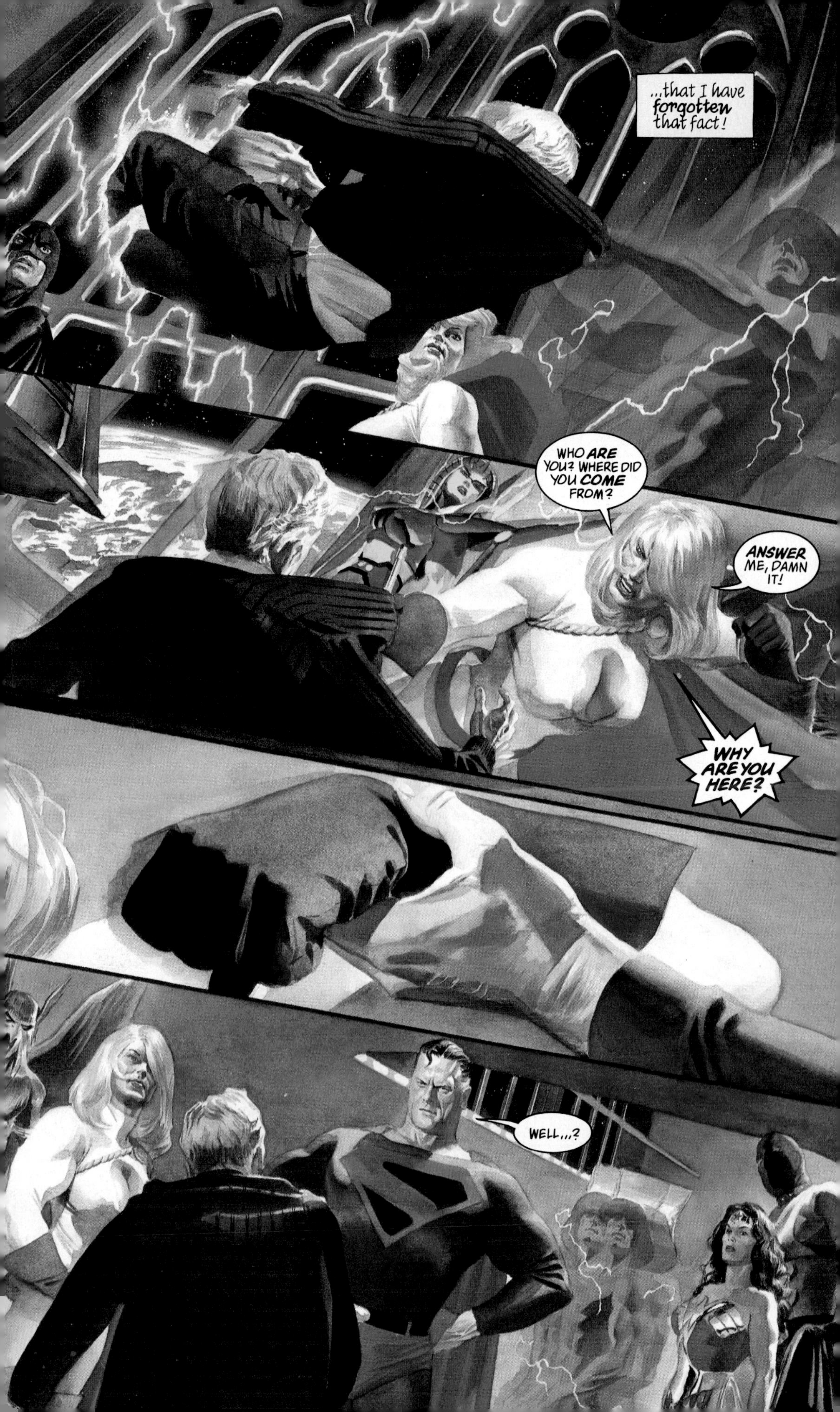
...that I have forgotten that fact!
WHO ARE YOU? WHERE DID YOU COME FROM?
ANSWER ME, DAMN IT!
WHY ARE YOU HERE?
WELL...?

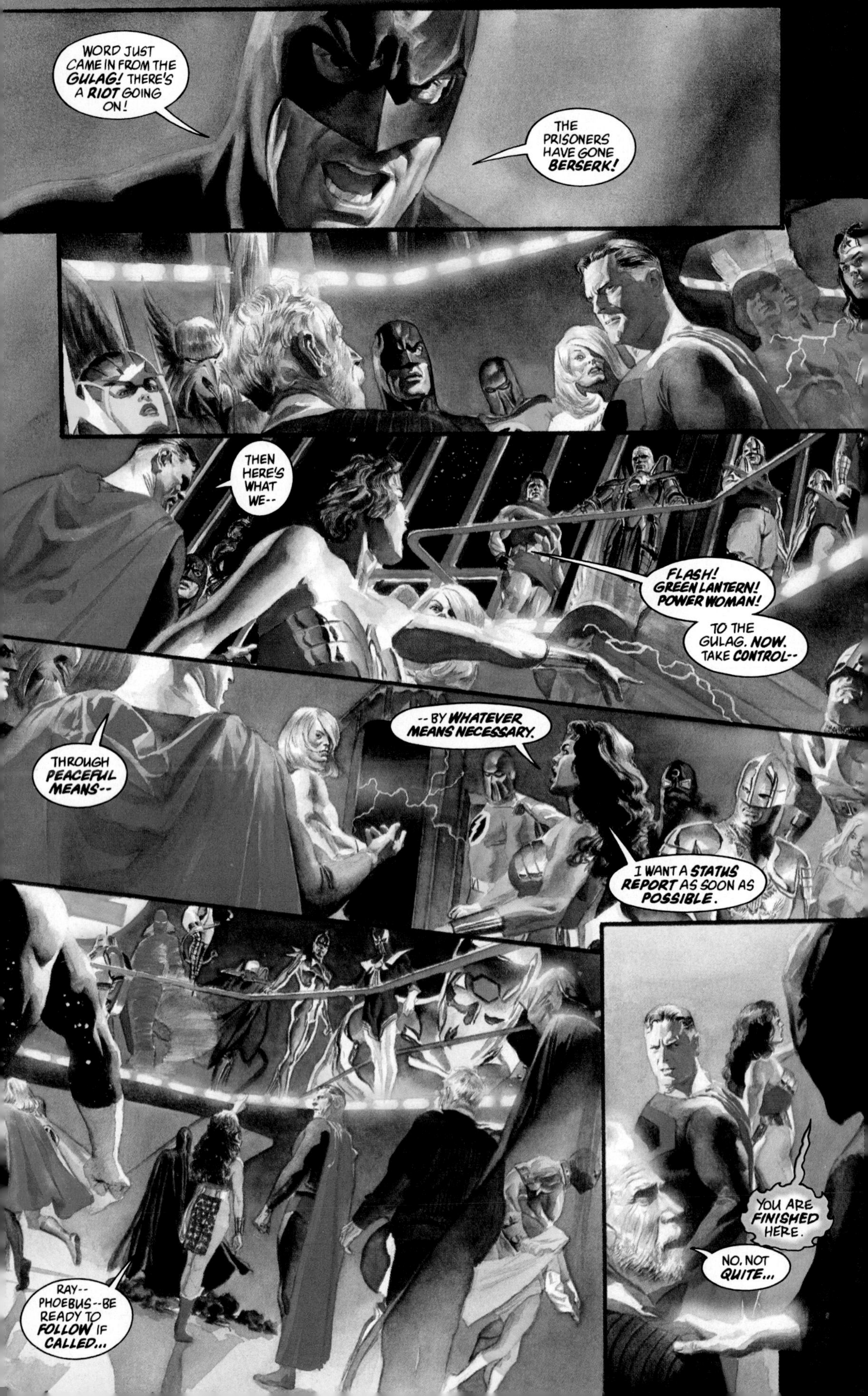

WORD JUST CAME IN FROM THE GULAG! THERE'S A RIOT GOING ON!
THE PRISONERS HAVE GONE BERSERK!
THEN HERE'S WHAT WE--
FLASH! GREEN LANTERN! POWER WOMAN!
TO THE GULAG. NOW. TAKE CONTROL--
THROUGH PEACEFUL MEANS--
--BY WHATEVER MEANS NECESSARY.
I WANT A STATUS REPORT AS SOON AS POSSIBLE.
RAY--PHOEBUS--BE READY TO FOLLOW IF CALLED...
YOU ARE FINISHED HERE.
NO, NOT QUITE...

WHY DID I...?

--FROM SOMEONE.

WHERE DID THE OLD MAN GO? WHO *WAS* HE?

THEY CAN'T *HELP* BUT KNOW ABOUT THE *GULAG* BY NOW.

I DON'T *KNOW*.

WHY DID YOU UNDERMINE MY *AUTHORITY*?

I SAW A *CRISIS*. I *REACTED* IN A *CONFIDENT* AND *UNQUALIFIED MANNER*. THE OTHERS *NEED* TO SEE THAT SORT OF AUTHORITY--

PULL YOURSELF *TOGETHER*. WE'RE *OVERDUE* FOR A MEETING WITH THE *U.N.*

THEN I *GUARANTEE* THEY'RE WONDERING WHEN WE STARTED MAKING UP OUR *OWN LAWS*. LET'S *GO*.

WE HAVE TO *CONVINCE* THEM THAT WE'RE THE *GOOD GUYS*."

...*FLATTERED* THAT THE MIGHTY *JUSTICE LEAGUE* HAS FINALLY DEEMED THE *HUMAN* RACE WORTHY OF *CONVERSATION*.

THERE'S NO NEED FOR *SARCASM*, SECRETARY-GENERAL.

FORGIVE ME.

WE'RE SIMPLY NO LONGER *ACCUSTOMED* TO BEING *ADVISED* OR *CONSULTED*. IMAGINE OUR *SURPRISE*, FOR INSTANCE, TO LEARN THAT THE *CENTER* OF THE U.S. NOW HARBORS A *META-HUMAN PRISON*.

YOU *INSIST* THAT-- HARD AS THIS IS TO *BELIEVE* -- IT POSES *NO PREVAILING DANGER*.

SECRETARY GENERAL WYRMWOOD

THAT THOSE *INCARCERATED* ARE *FULLY DOCILE* AND EAGER TO *ACCLIMATE*.

IS THAT *TRUE*, SUPERMAN?

NOT ENTIRELY.

THE *GULAG* IS A *WORK IN PROGRESS*. THE LEAGUE *MUST* FIND A WAY TO *GUIDE* THOSE WHO *INSIST* UPON WORKING *AGAINST* THE *COMMON GOOD.*

I *ADMIT* TO SOME *DANGER*,... BUT I CHOSE TO PUT THE RENEGADES *TOGETHER* WHERE WE CAN *MONITOR* THEM AND *TEACH* THEM.

INSIDE A GIANT *POWDER KEG.* SUPERMAN, THE *CONFIDENCE* AND *HOPE* YOUR REEMERGENCE ENGENDERED IS *FAST ERODING.*

GLOBAL ECONOMY IS STILL *CATASTROPHIC*...WORLD TRAUMA, *STAGGERING.* WE *WILL NOT RISK* ANOTHER *KANSAS.* I CAN *PROMISE* YOU THAT.

MEANING...?

MEANING THAT WE MUST *BEGIN* TO DECIDE *SOME* THINGS FOR *OURSELVES.* GOOD DAY.

STOP LOOKING SO *STUNNED.* DO YOU *HONESTLY BELIEVE* THEY'LL *SIT BACK* AND LET *US* SOLVE THE PROBLEM AT *OUR* LEISURE?

THEY'RE *SCARED*... AND THEIR *FEARS* MAY SOON TRUMP *OUR* SOLUTIONS. WE HAVE TO *ACT.*

...THE LEAGUE WILL BE *FORCED* TO TAKE A *FINAL, DECISIVE ACTION*...

KAL, WHETHER YOU LIKE IT OR *NOT,* YOU'RE A *WORLD LEADER*...AND THE LEAGUE IS GETTING *TIRED* OF WAITING FOR YOU TO *ADJUST* TO THAT ROLE.

AS FAR AS *I'M* CONCERNED, IF THE SITUATION WITH THE *GULAG* PRISONERS GETS *ONE MICRON WORSE*...

138

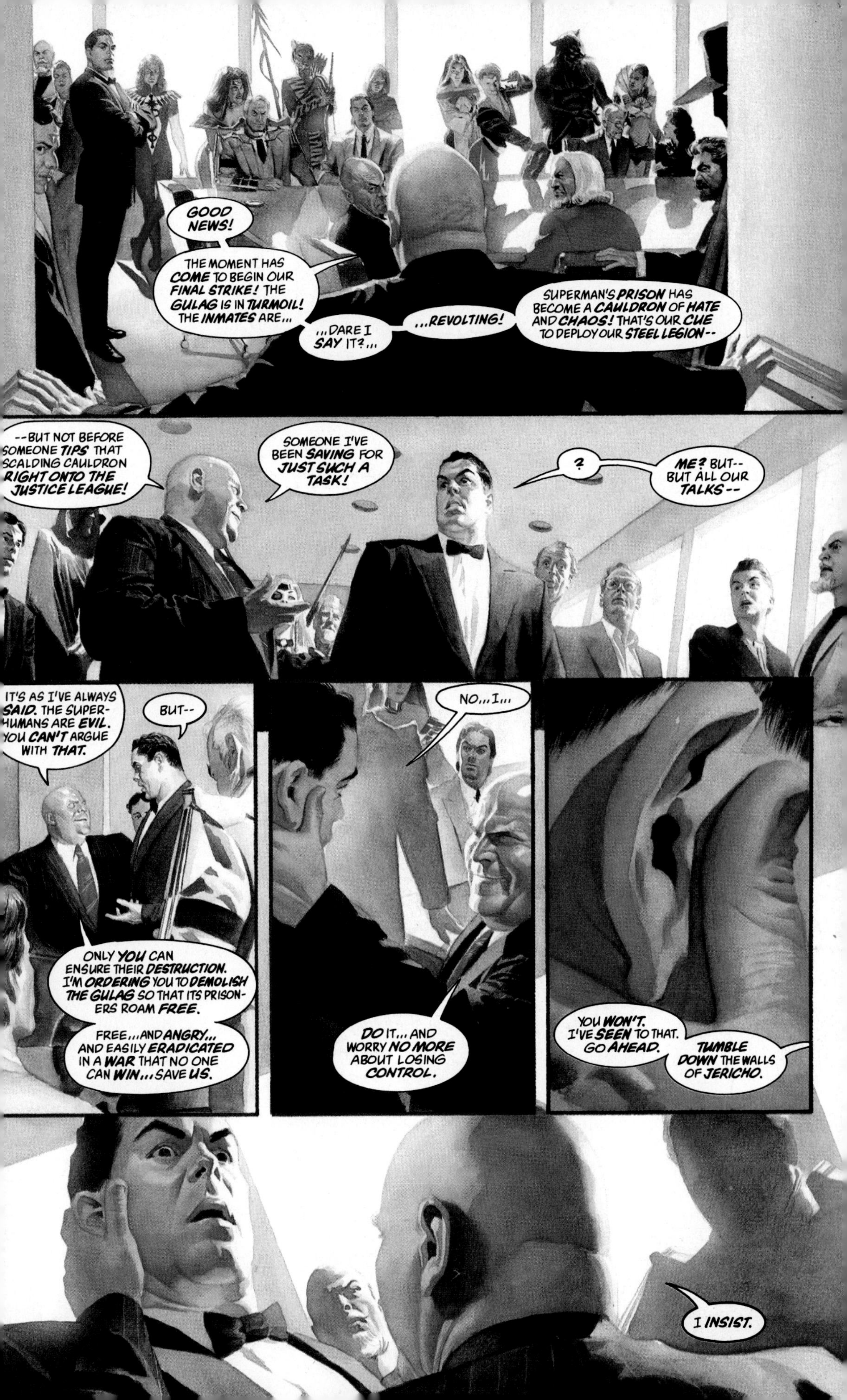
GOOD NEWS!
THE MOMENT HAS COME TO BEGIN OUR FINAL STRIKE! THE GULAG IS IN TURMOIL! THE INMATES ARE...
...DARE I SAY IT?...
...REVOLTING!
SUPERMAN'S PRISON HAS BECOME A CAULDRON OF HATE AND CHAOS! THAT'S OUR CUE TO DEPLOY OUR STEEL LEGION--
--BUT NOT BEFORE SOMEONE TIPS THAT SCALDING CAULDRON RIGHT ONTO THE JUSTICE LEAGUE!
SOMEONE I'VE BEEN SAVING FOR JUST SUCH A TASK!
?
ME? BUT-- BUT ALL OUR TALKS--
IT'S AS I'VE ALWAYS SAID. THE SUPER-HUMANS ARE EVIL. YOU CAN'T ARGUE WITH THAT.
BUT--
ONLY YOU CAN ENSURE THEIR DESTRUCTION. I'M ORDERING YOU TO DEMOLISH THE GULAG SO THAT ITS PRISON-ERS ROAM FREE.
FREE...AND ANGRY... AND EASILY ERADICATED IN A WAR THAT NO ONE CAN WIN...SAVE US.
NO...I...
DO IT...AND WORRY NO MORE ABOUT LOSING CONTROL.
YOU WON'T. I'VE SEEN TO THAT. GO AHEAD.
TUMBLE DOWN THE WALLS OF JERICHO.
I INSIST.

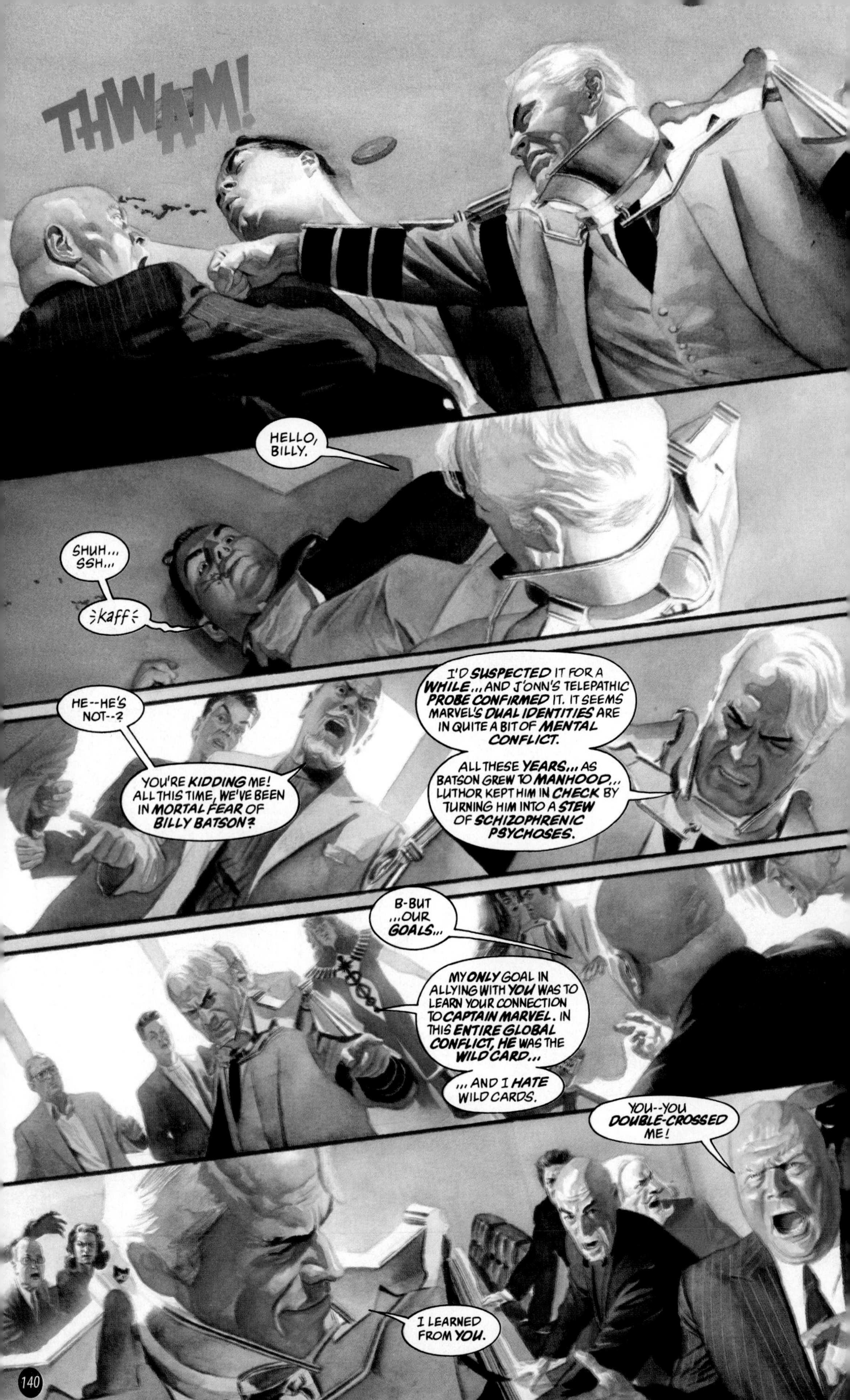
THWAM!
HELLO, BILLY.
SHUH... SSH...
kaff
HE--HE'S NOT--?
YOU'RE KIDDING ME! ALL THIS TIME, WE'VE BEEN IN MORTAL FEAR OF BILLY BATSON?
I'D SUSPECTED IT FOR A WHILE... AND J'ONN'S TELEPATHIC PROBE CONFIRMED IT. IT SEEMS MARVEL'S DUAL IDENTITIES ARE IN QUITE A BIT OF MENTAL CONFLICT.
ALL THESE YEARS... AS BATSON GREW TO MANHOOD... LUTHOR KEPT HIM IN CHECK BY TURNING HIM INTO A STEW OF SCHIZOPHRENIC PSYCHOSES.
B-BUT ...OUR GOALS...
MY ONLY GOAL IN ALLYING WITH YOU WAS TO LEARN YOUR CONNECTION TO CAPTAIN MARVEL. IN THIS ENTIRE GLOBAL CONFLICT, HE WAS THE WILD CARD...
...AND I HATE WILD CARDS.
YOU--YOU DOUBLE-CROSSED ME!
I LEARNED FROM YOU.

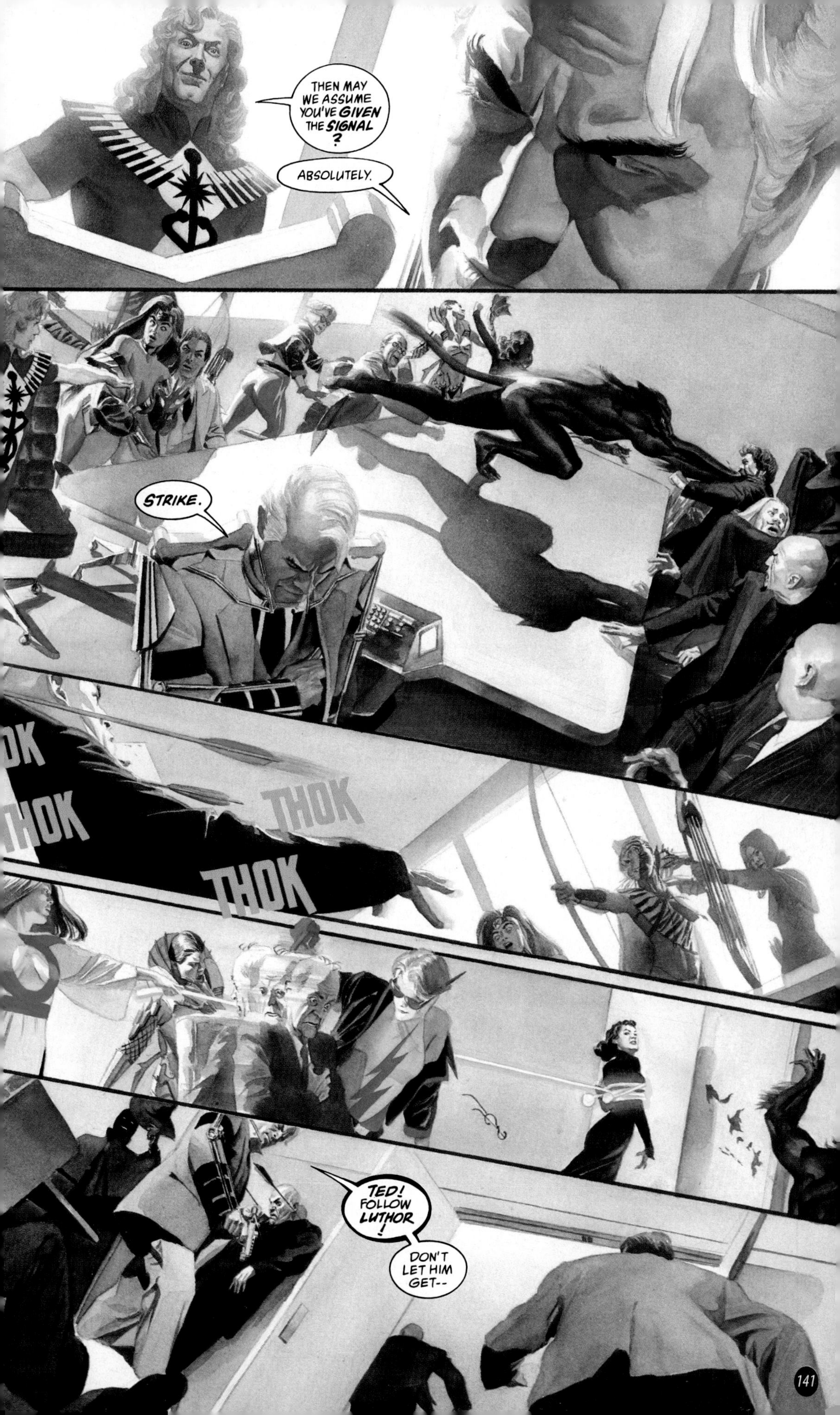
THEN MAY WE ASSUME YOU'VE GIVEN THE SIGNAL?
ABSOLUTELY.
STRIKE.
THOK
THOK
THOK
THOK
TED! FOLLOW LUTHOR!
DON'T LET HIM GET--

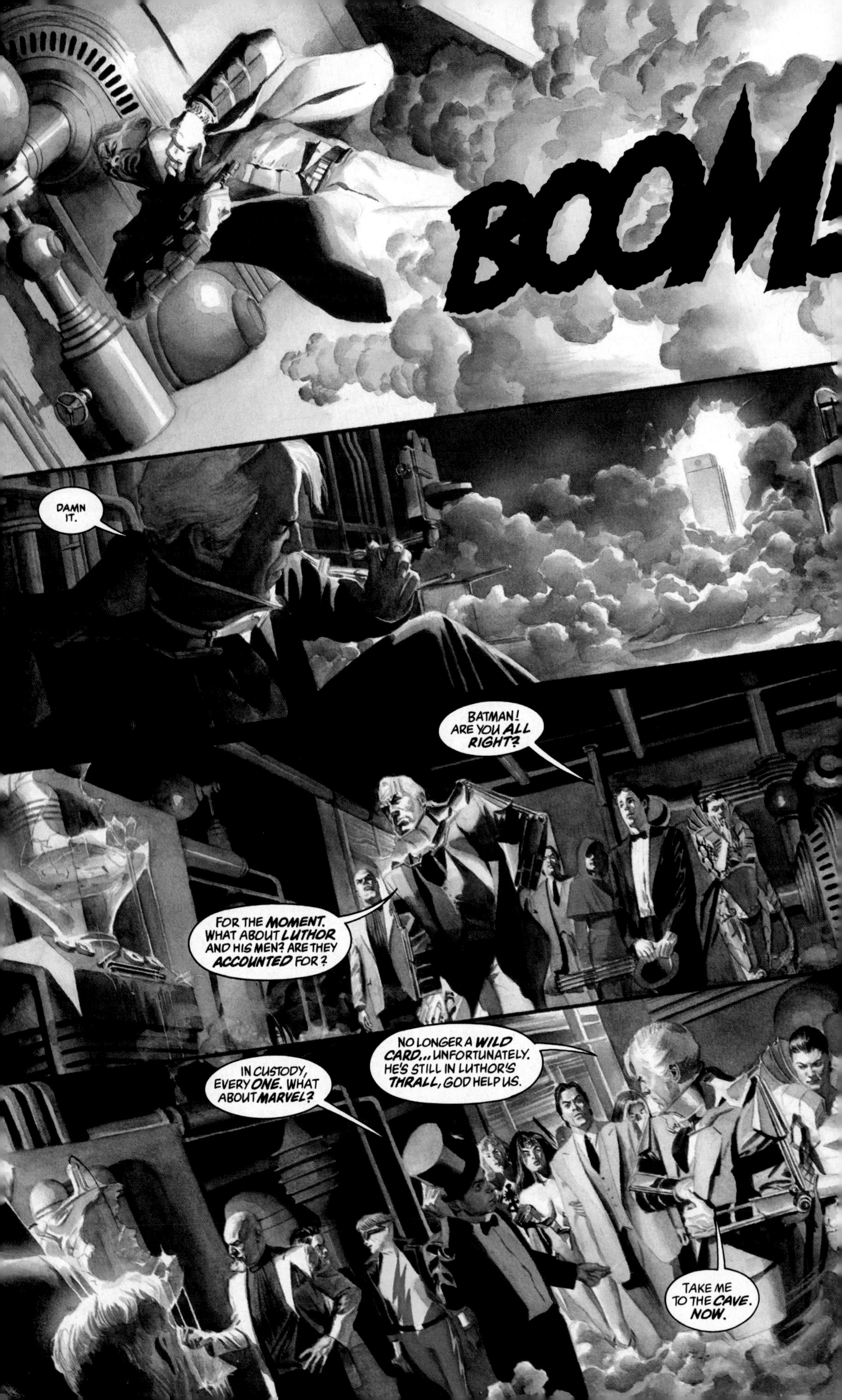
BOOM!
DAMN IT.
BATMAN! ARE YOU ALL RIGHT?
FOR THE MOMENT. WHAT ABOUT LUTHOR AND HIS MEN? ARE THEY ACCOUNTED FOR?
IN CUSTODY, EVERY ONE. WHAT ABOUT MARVEL?
NO LONGER A WILD CARD... UNFORTUNATELY. HE'S STILL IN LUTHOR'S THRALL, GOD HELP US.
TAKE ME TO THE CAVE. NOW.

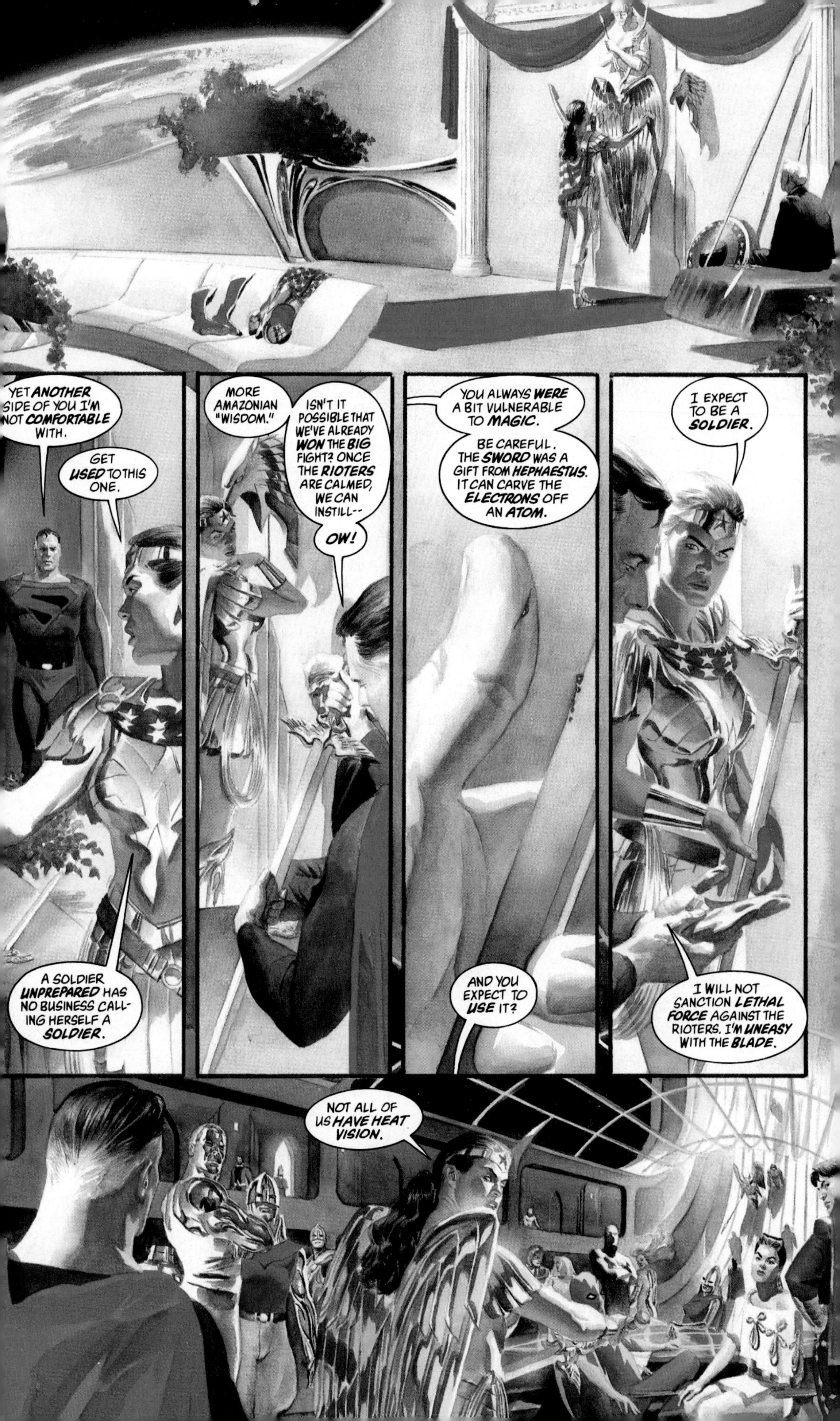
YET ANOTHER SIDE OF YOU I'M NOT COMFORTABLE WITH.
GET USED TO THIS ONE.
A SOLDIER UNPREPARED HAS NO BUSINESS CALLING HERSELF A SOLDIER.
MORE AMAZONIAN "WISDOM."
ISN'T IT POSSIBLE THAT WE'VE ALREADY WON THE BIG FIGHT? ONCE THE RIOTERS ARE CALMED, WE CAN INSTILL--
OW!
YOU ALWAYS WERE A BIT VULNERABLE TO MAGIC.
BE CAREFUL. THE SWORD WAS A GIFT FROM HEPHAESTUS. IT CAN CARVE THE ELECTRONS OFF AN ATOM.
AND YOU EXPECT TO USE IT?
I EXPECT TO BE A SOLDIER.
I WILL NOT SANCTION LETHAL FORCE AGAINST THE RIOTERS. I'M UNEASY WITH THE BLADE.
NOT ALL OF US HAVE HEAT VISION.

THERE ARE LINES WE **DO NOT CROSS!** WE HAVE **RULES!**

AND THE **PRISONERS DON'T!** THAT'S **WHY** THEY'RE **PRISONERS!** AND IF THEY DON'T **REMAIN** PRISONERS, YOUR **BIG, BLUE MARBLE** TEETERS ON THE **BRINK!**

YOU MADE THE DECISION TO INCARCER-ATE THEM FOR THE **GOOD OF MANKIND,** RE-MEMBER?

AND MAYBE THAT WAS MY **MISTAKE.** MAYBE I **SHOULD** HAVE LET THE HUMANS DECIDE HOW TO--

--HEAR ME? SEND HELP!

≳KOFF≲

FOR **GOD'S SAKE,** CAN YOU **HEAR** ME?

GL?

WE'RE... WE'RE IN **TROUBLE!** THE FIGHT AT THE **GULAG** GOES WORSE THAN WE EX-PECTED!

THE PRISONERS HAVE ALREADY BEGUN TO **BREACH THE WALLS!** THEY CAN'T **HOLD** MUCH LONGER--NOR CAN **WE!**

THEY'VE ALREADY...

...THEY'VE **KILLED** CAPTAIN COMET...

NO!

THWAM!

146

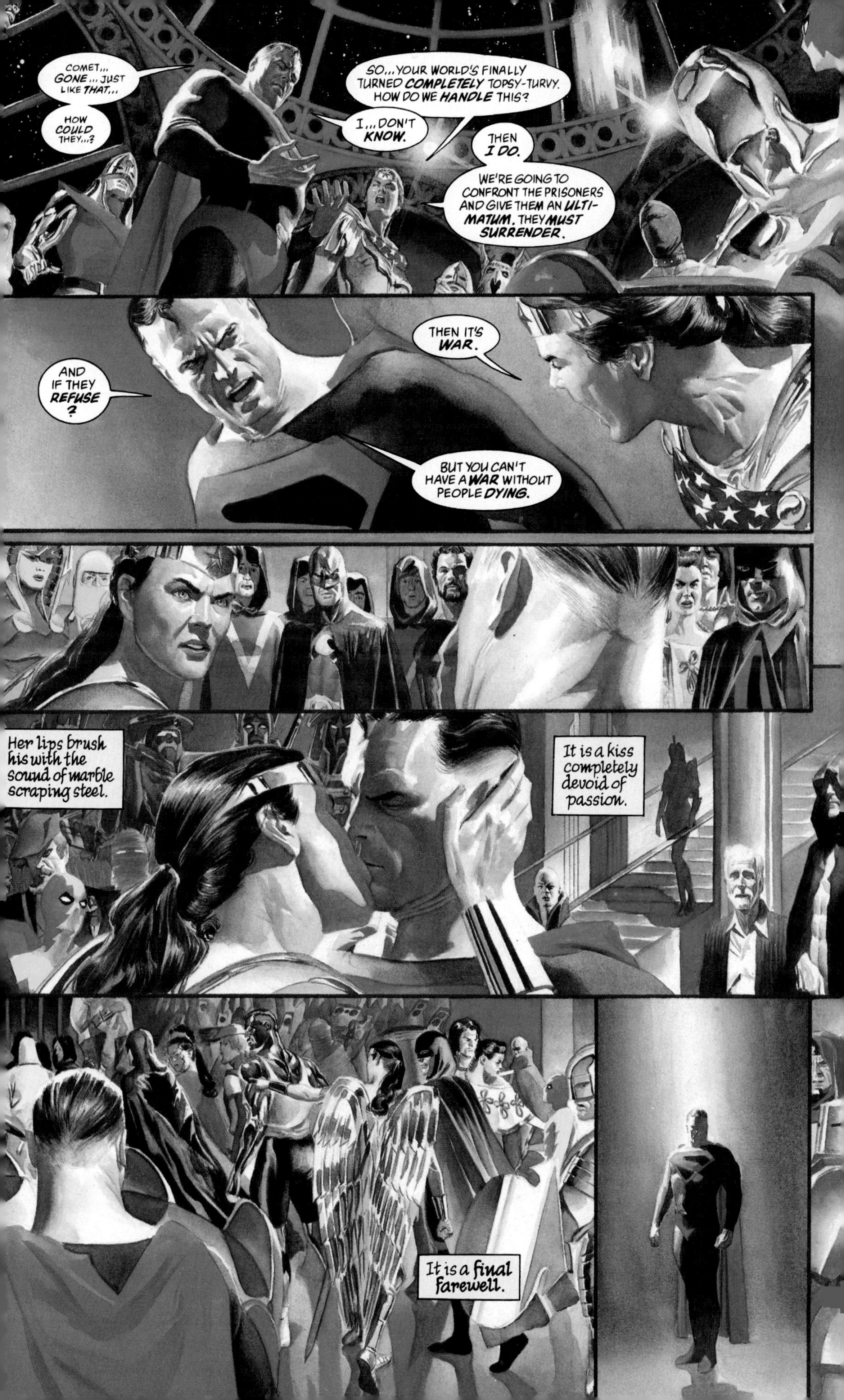
COMET... GONE... JUST LIKE THAT...
HOW COULD THEY...?
SO... YOUR WORLD'S FINALLY TURNED COMPLETELY TOPSY-TURVY. HOW DO WE HANDLE THIS?
I... DON'T KNOW.
THEN I DO.
WE'RE GOING TO CONFRONT THE PRISONERS AND GIVE THEM AN ULTI-MATUM. THEY MUST SURRENDER.
AND IF THEY REFUSE?
THEN IT'S WAR.
BUT YOU CAN'T HAVE A WAR WITHOUT PEOPLE DYING.
Her lips brush his with the sound of marble scraping steel.
It is a kiss completely devoid of passion.
It is a final farewell.

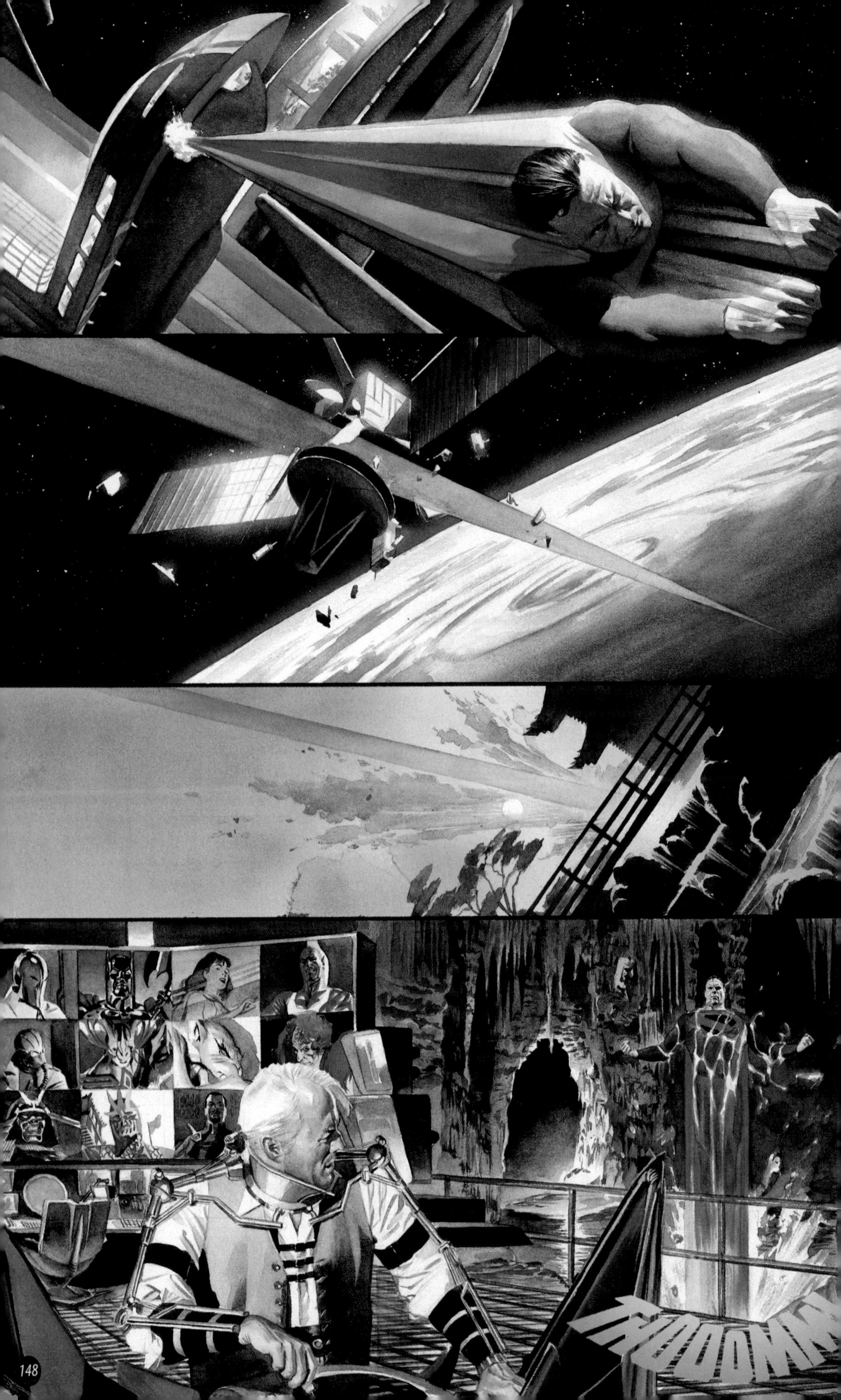
THOOOMM

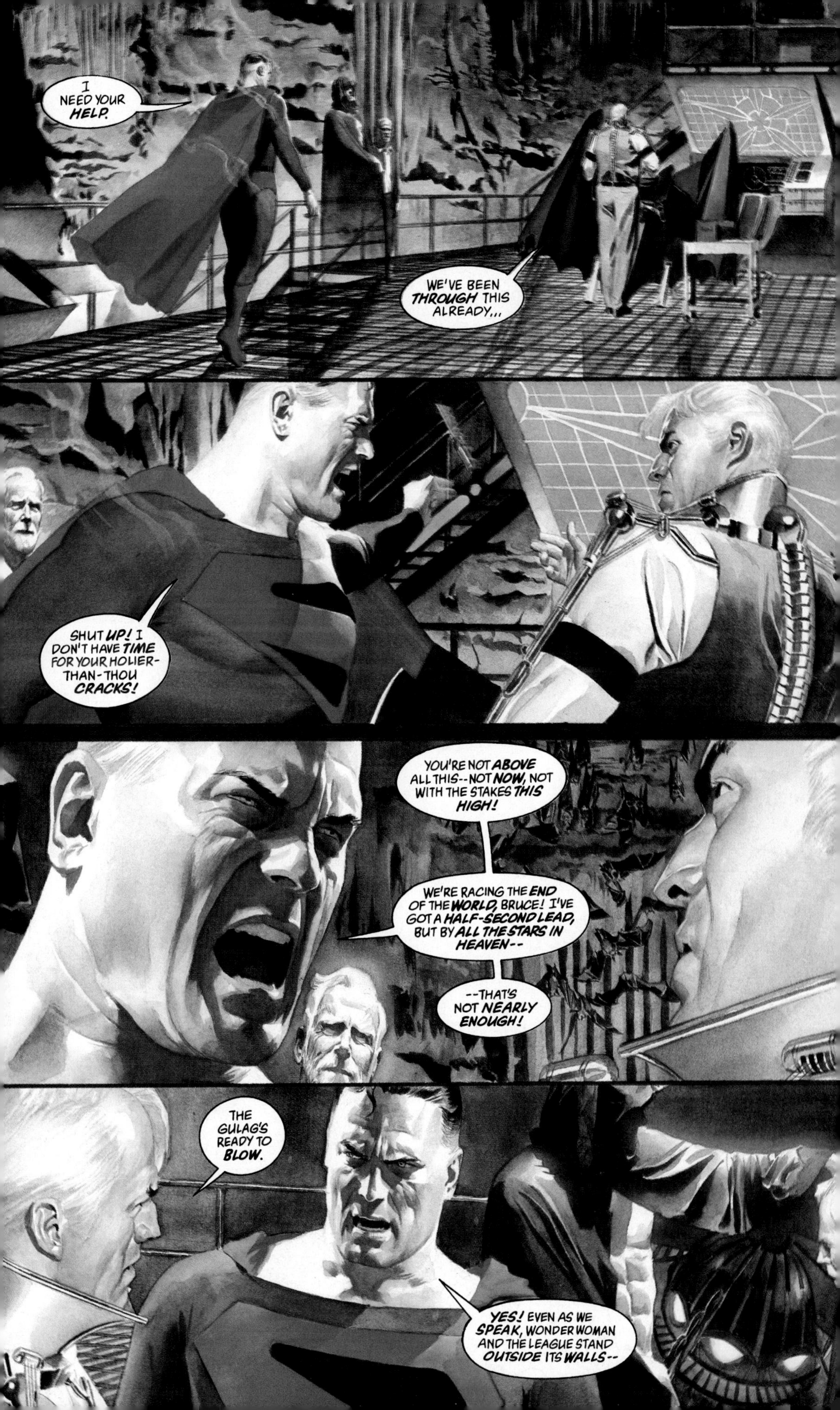
I NEED YOUR HELP.
WE'VE BEEN THROUGH THIS ALREADY...
SHUT UP! I DON'T HAVE TIME FOR YOUR HOLIER-THAN-THOU CRACKS!
YOU'RE NOT ABOVE ALL THIS--NOT NOW, NOT WITH THE STAKES THIS HIGH!
WE'RE RACING THE END OF THE WORLD, BRUCE! I'VE GOT A HALF-SECOND LEAD, BUT BY ALL THE STARS IN HEAVEN--
--THAT'S NOT NEARLY ENOUGH!
THE GULAG'S READY TO BLOW.
YES! EVEN AS WE SPEAK, WONDER WOMAN AND THE LEAGUE STAND OUTSIDE ITS WALLS--

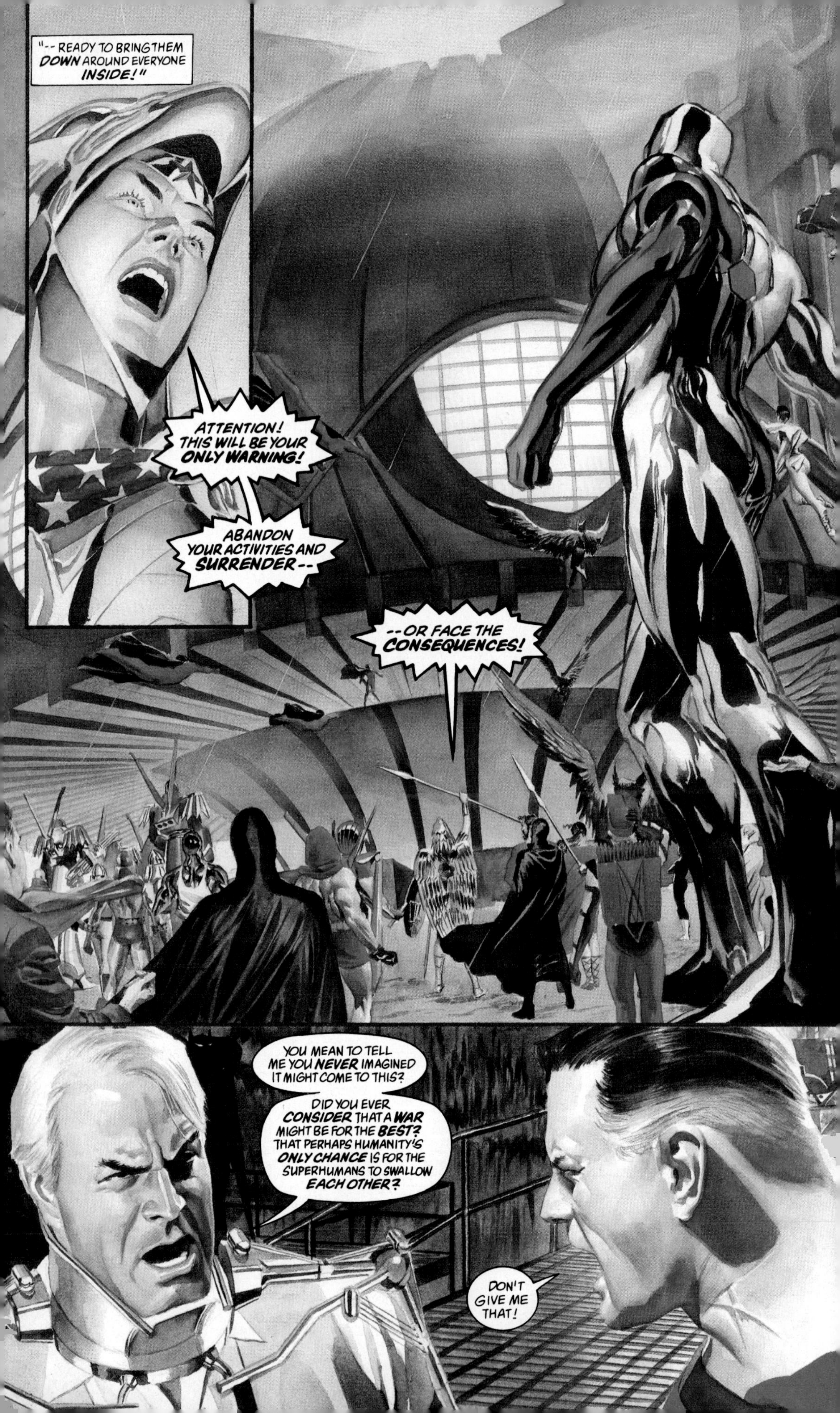
"-- READY TO BRING THEM DOWN AROUND EVERYONE INSIDE!"
ATTENTION! THIS WILL BE YOUR ONLY WARNING!
ABANDON YOUR ACTIVITIES AND SURRENDER --
-- OR FACE THE CONSEQUENCES!
YOU MEAN TO TELL ME YOU NEVER IMAGINED IT MIGHT COME TO THIS?
DID YOU EVER CONSIDER THAT A WAR MIGHT BE FOR THE BEST? THAT PERHAPS HUMANITY'S ONLY CHANCE IS FOR THE SUPERHUMANS TO SWALLOW EACH OTHER?
DON'T GIVE ME THAT!

THE DELIBERATE TAKING OF HUMAN--EVEN *SUPER-HUMAN*--LIFE GOES AGAINST EVERY BELIEF I *HAVE*--AND THAT *YOU* HAVE.

THAT'S THE *ONE THING* WE'VE *ALWAYS* HAD IN *COMMON.* IT'S WHAT *MADE* US WHAT WE *ARE.*

WE CAN *STILL INTERCEDE.* GATHER YOUR FORCES. TOGETHER, WE CAN BE THE *WORLD'S FINEST TEAM.*

I WILL TELL YOU THIS *ONE THING.* THERE'S A PLAYER YOU HAVEN'T *COUNTED* ON.

CAPTAIN MARVEL.

MARVEL...?

HE'S BEEN *BRAINWASHED...SEVERELY.* ONCE, THERE WAS A GOOD KID INSIDE HIM, BUT HE'S BEEN DRIVEN *OUT*--

--AND I DON'T KNOW HOW YOU'D EVER *FIND* HIM AGAIN.

MORE THAN ANYONE IN THE WORLD, WHEN YOU SCRATCH EVERYTHING ELSE AWAY FROM *BATMAN,* YOU'RE LEFT WITH SOMEONE WHO *DOESN'T WANT TO SEE* ANYBODY DIE.

TELL ME YOU'LL *HELP* ME.

MARVEL'S HEADED FOR THE *GULAG,* CLARK.

HE'S GOING TO BREAK IT *WIDE OPEN* ONTO THE *JUSTICE LEAGUE.*

SO *THAT'S* WHAT THAT FEELS LIKE...

WHAT DO YOU EXPECT *ME* TO DO AGAINST...

151

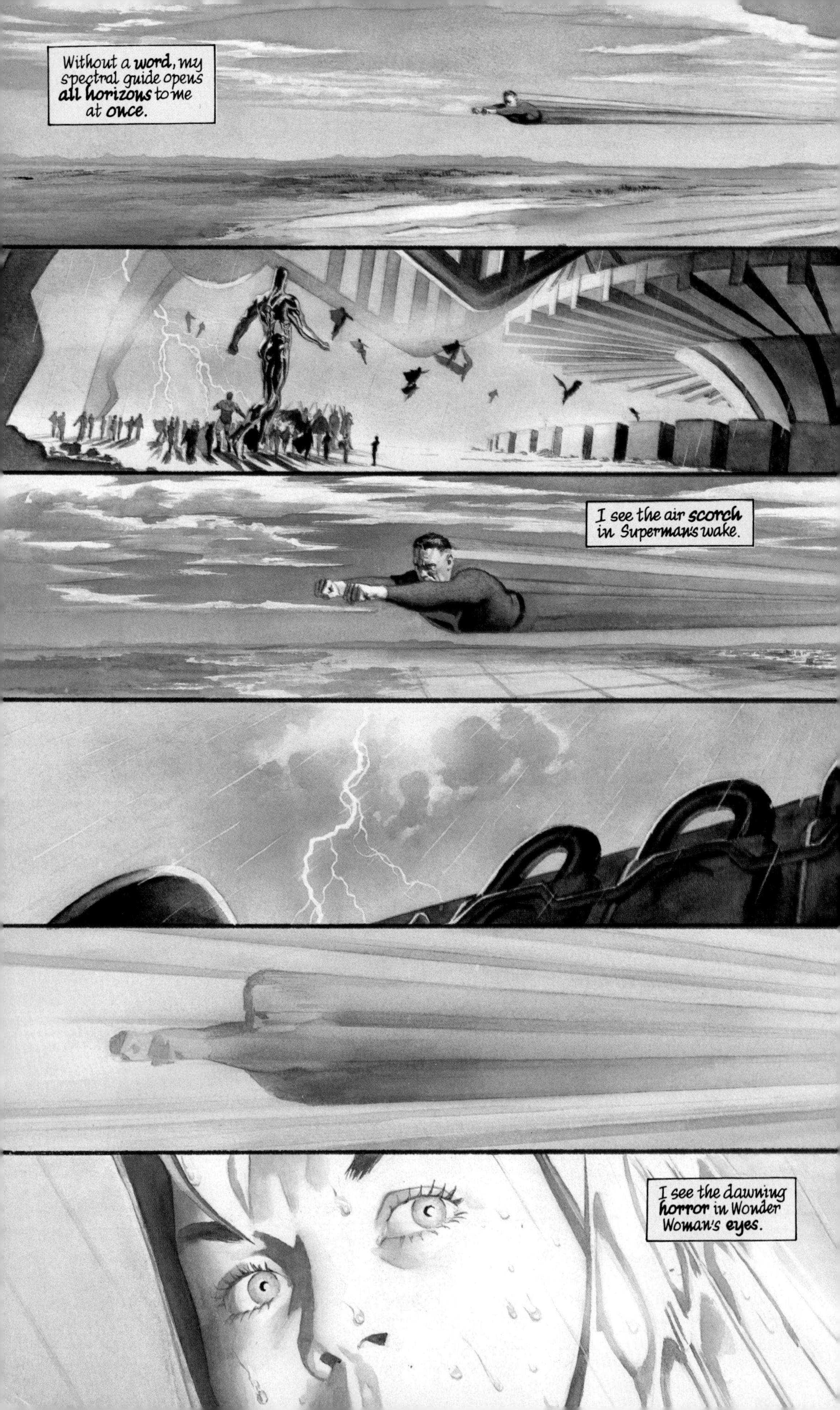

Without a **word**, my spectral guide opens **all horizons** to me at **once**.
I see the air **scorch** in Superman's wake.
I see the dawning **horror** in Wonder Woman's **eyes**.

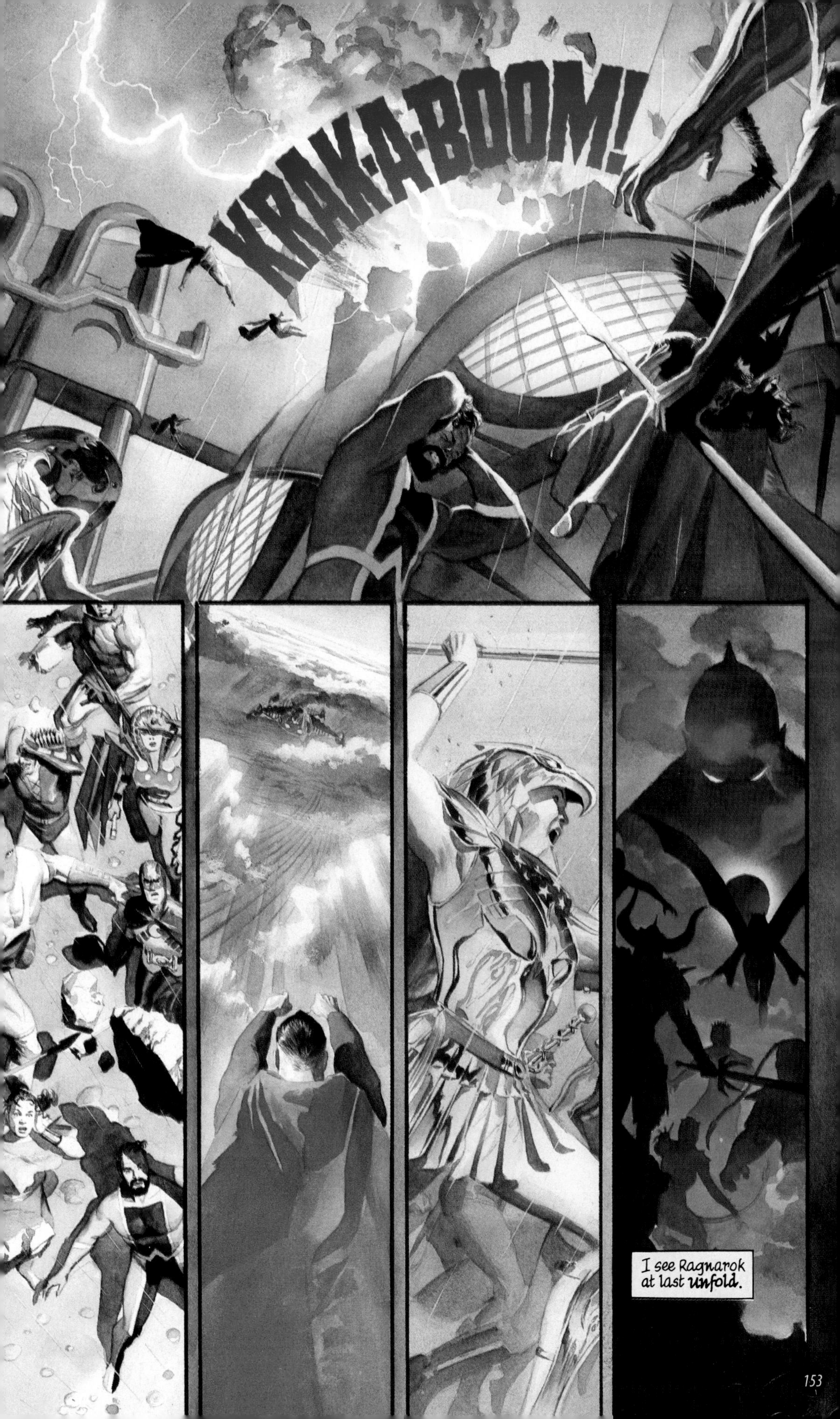

KRAK-A-BOOM!
I see Ragnarok at last unfold.

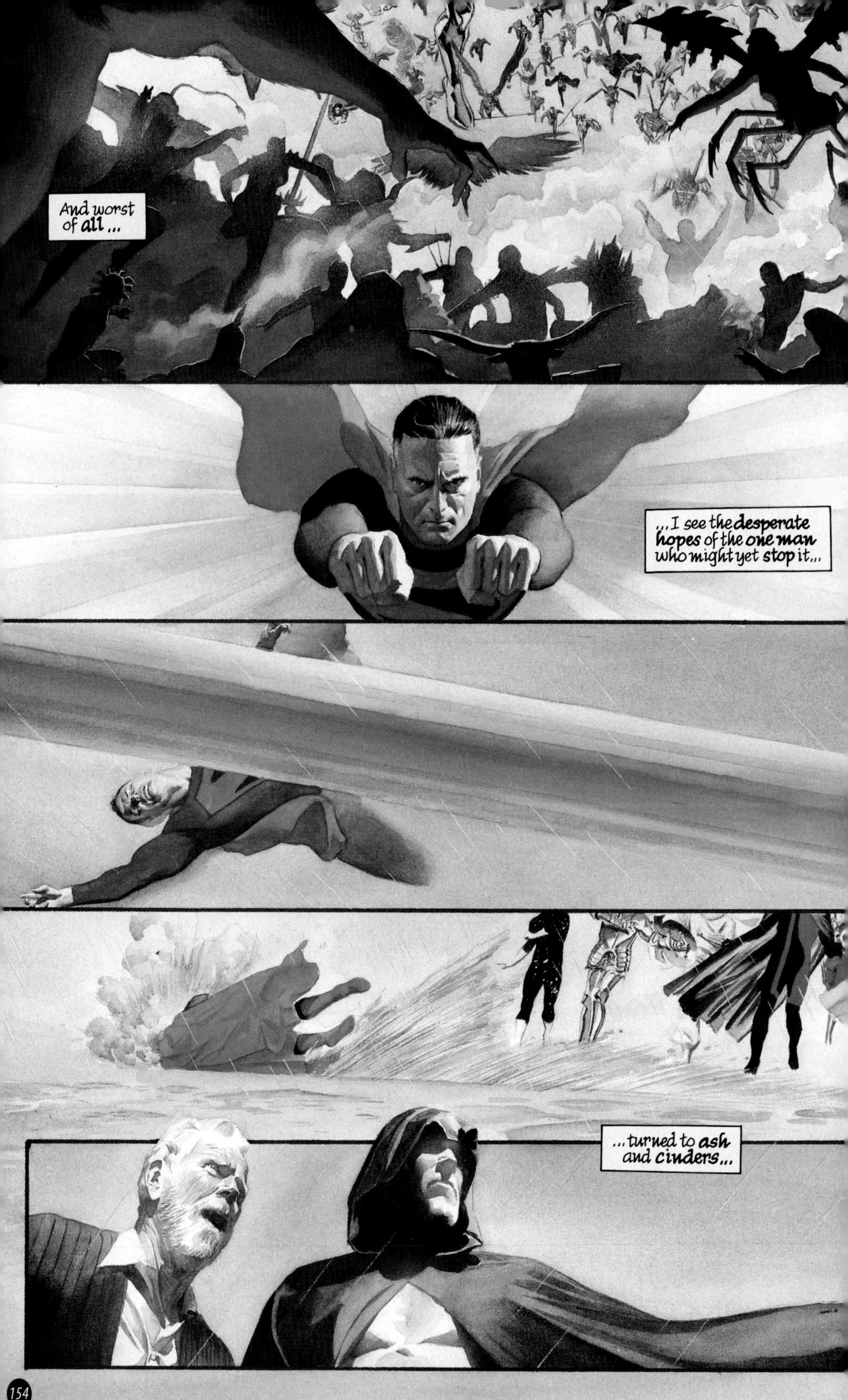
And worst of all...
...I see the desperate hopes of the one man who might yet stop it...
...turned to ash and cinders...

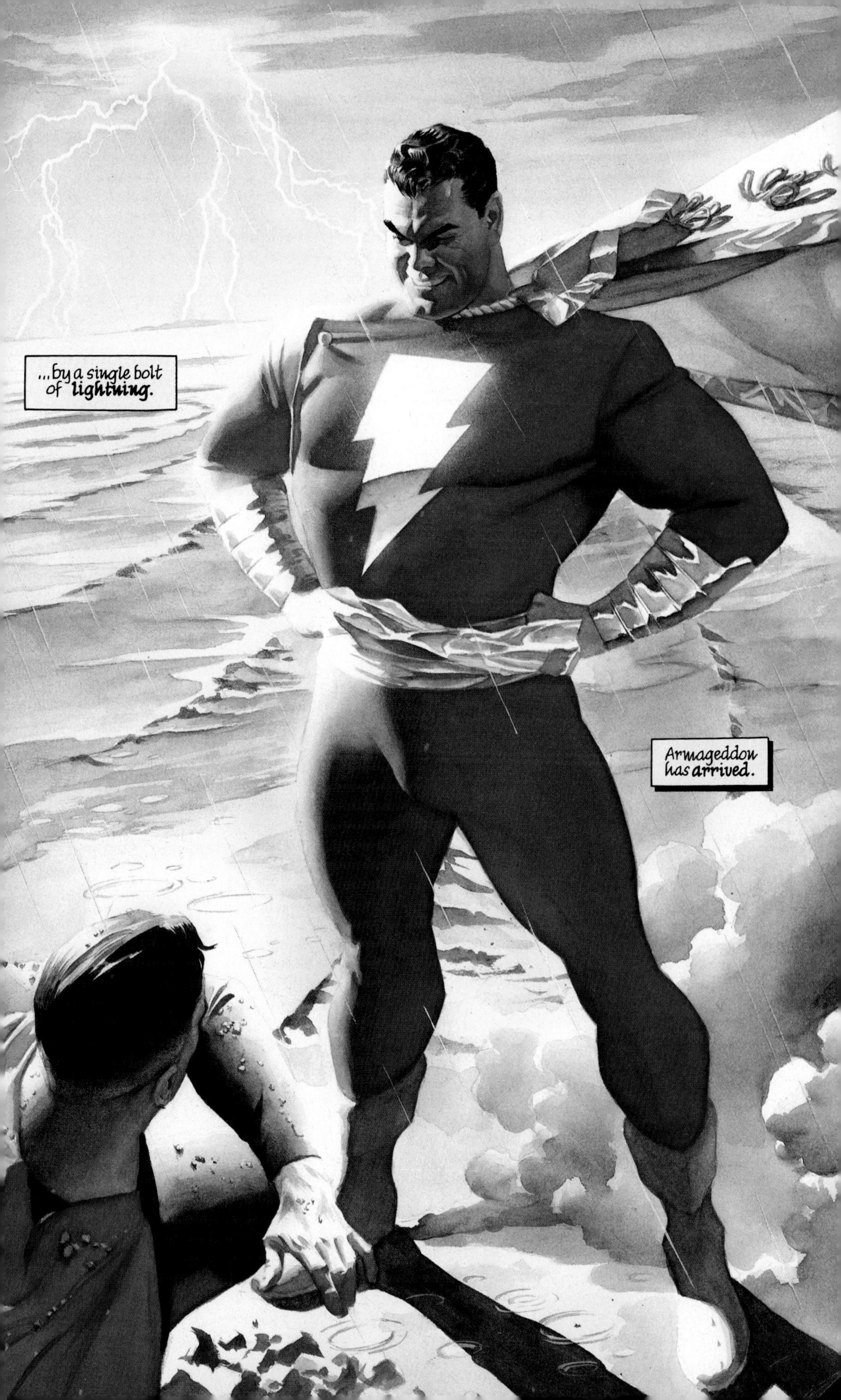
...by a single bolt of **lightning**.
Armageddon has **arrived**.

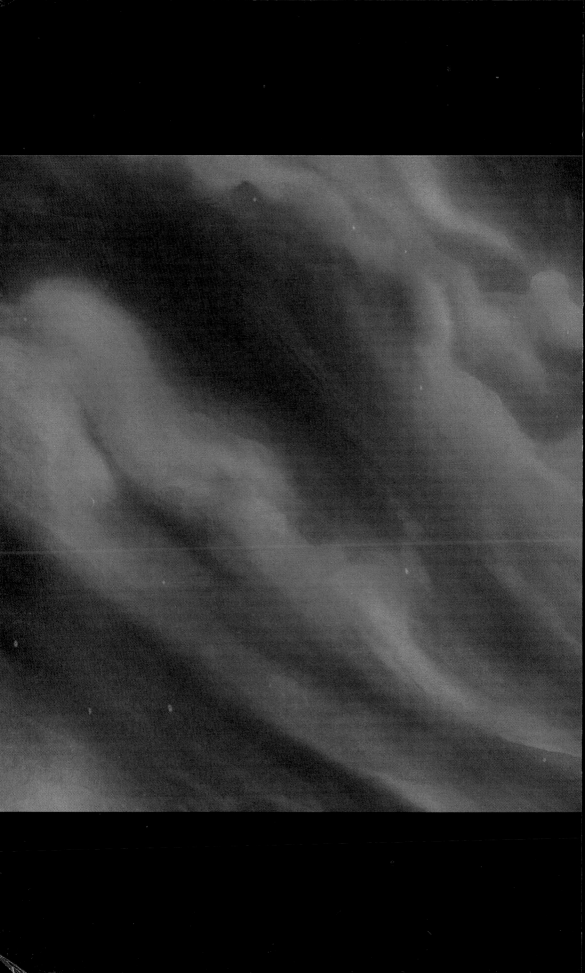

CHAPTER FOUR

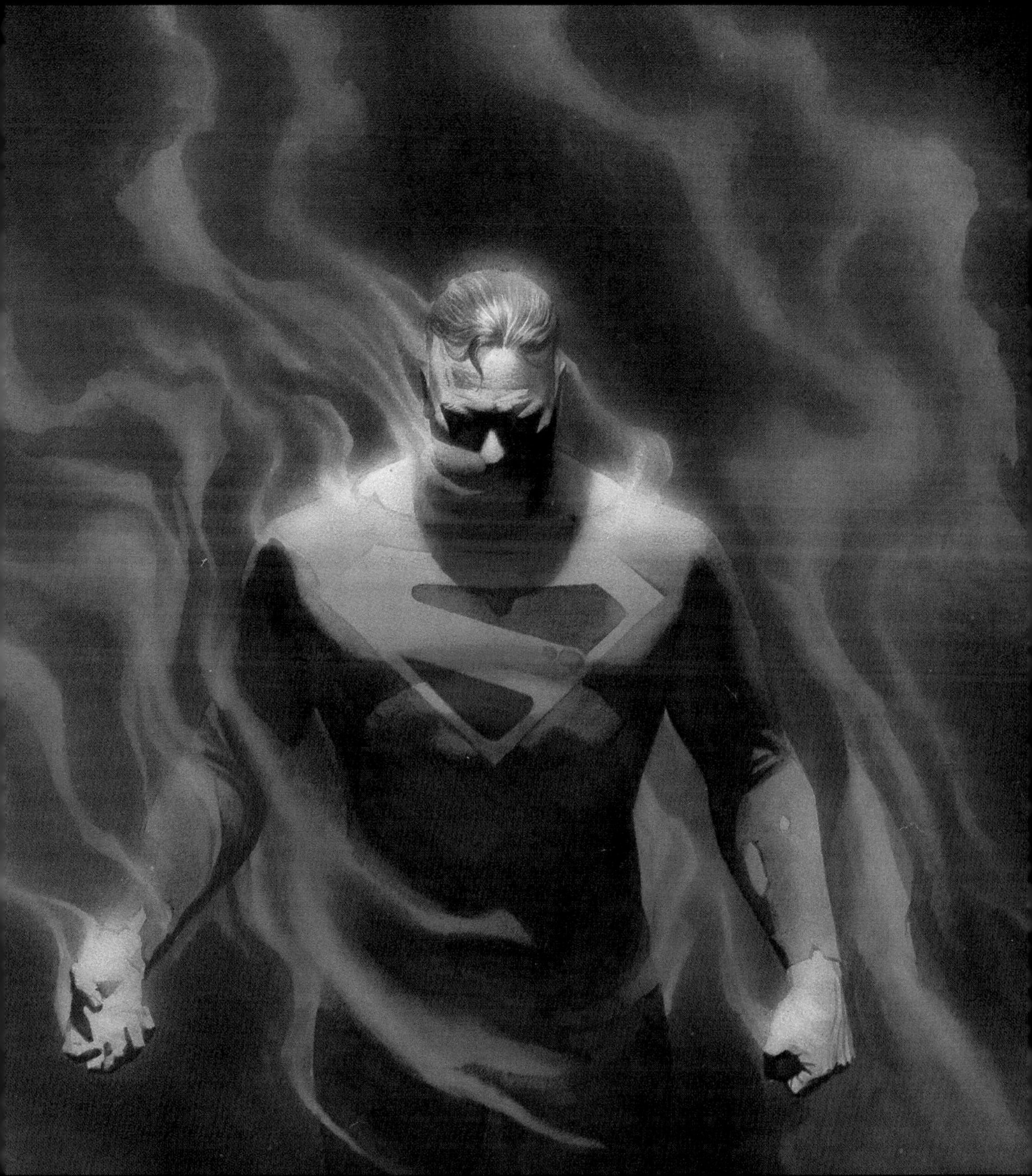

Never-Ending Battle

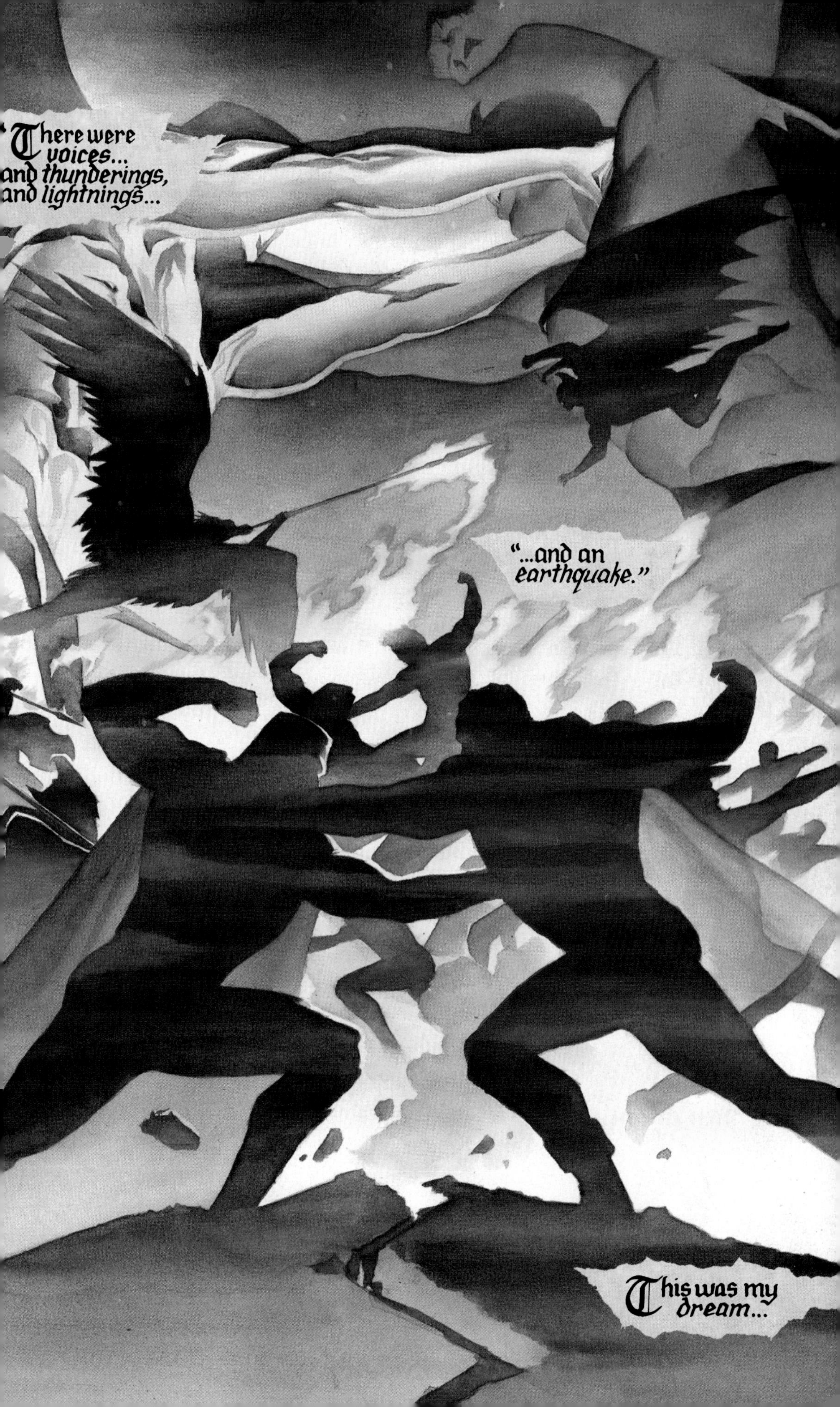
There were voices... and thunderings, and lightnings...
"...and an earthquake."
This was my dream...

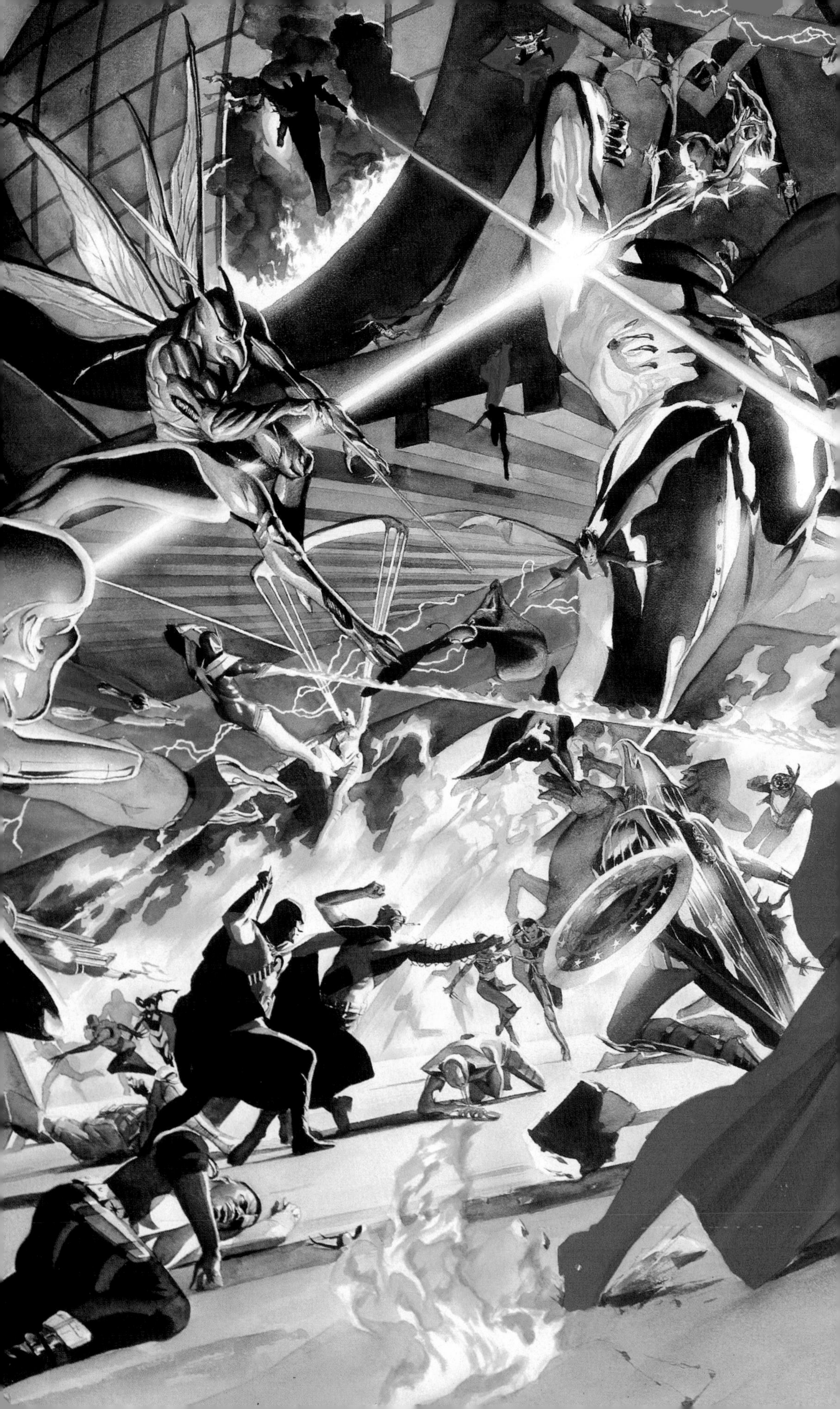

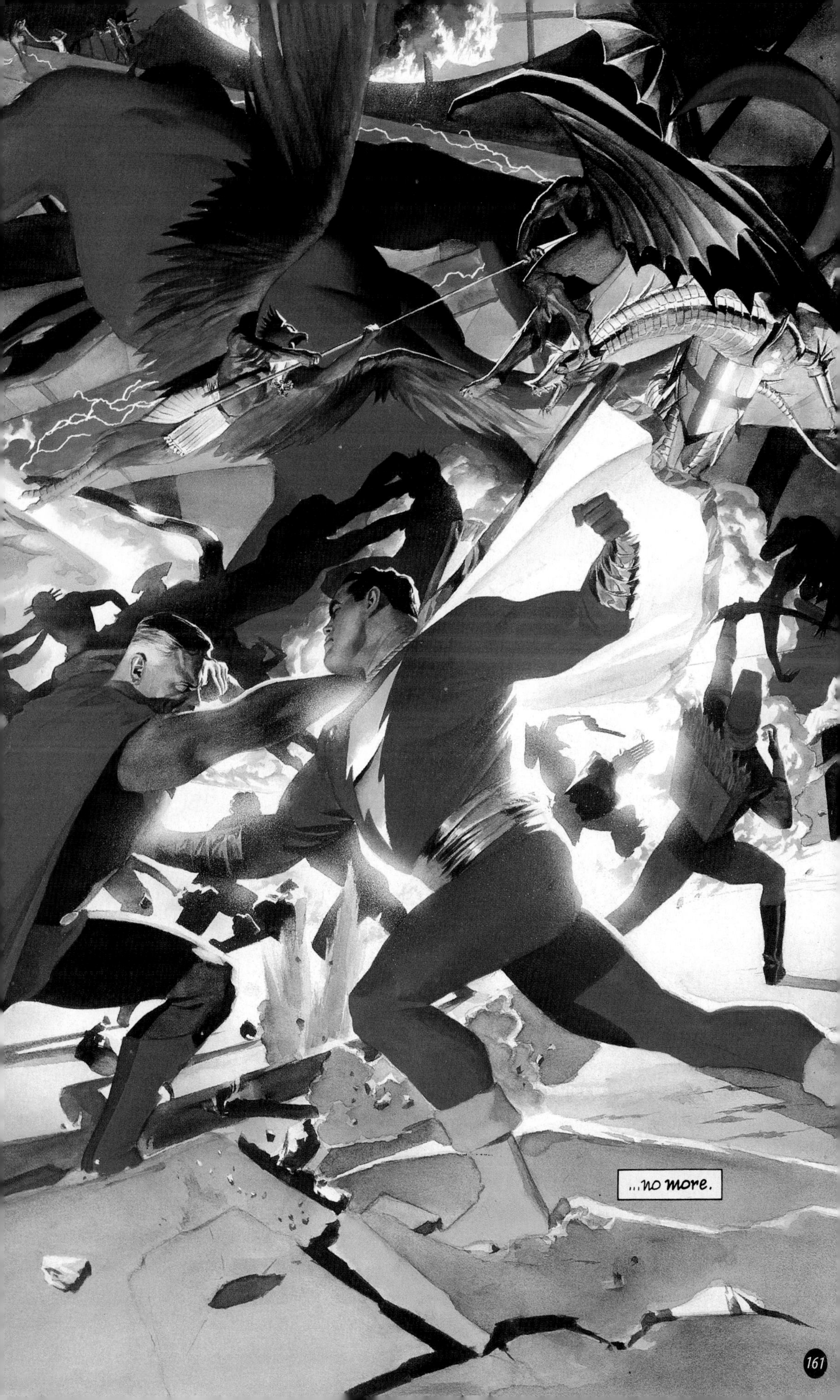
...no more.

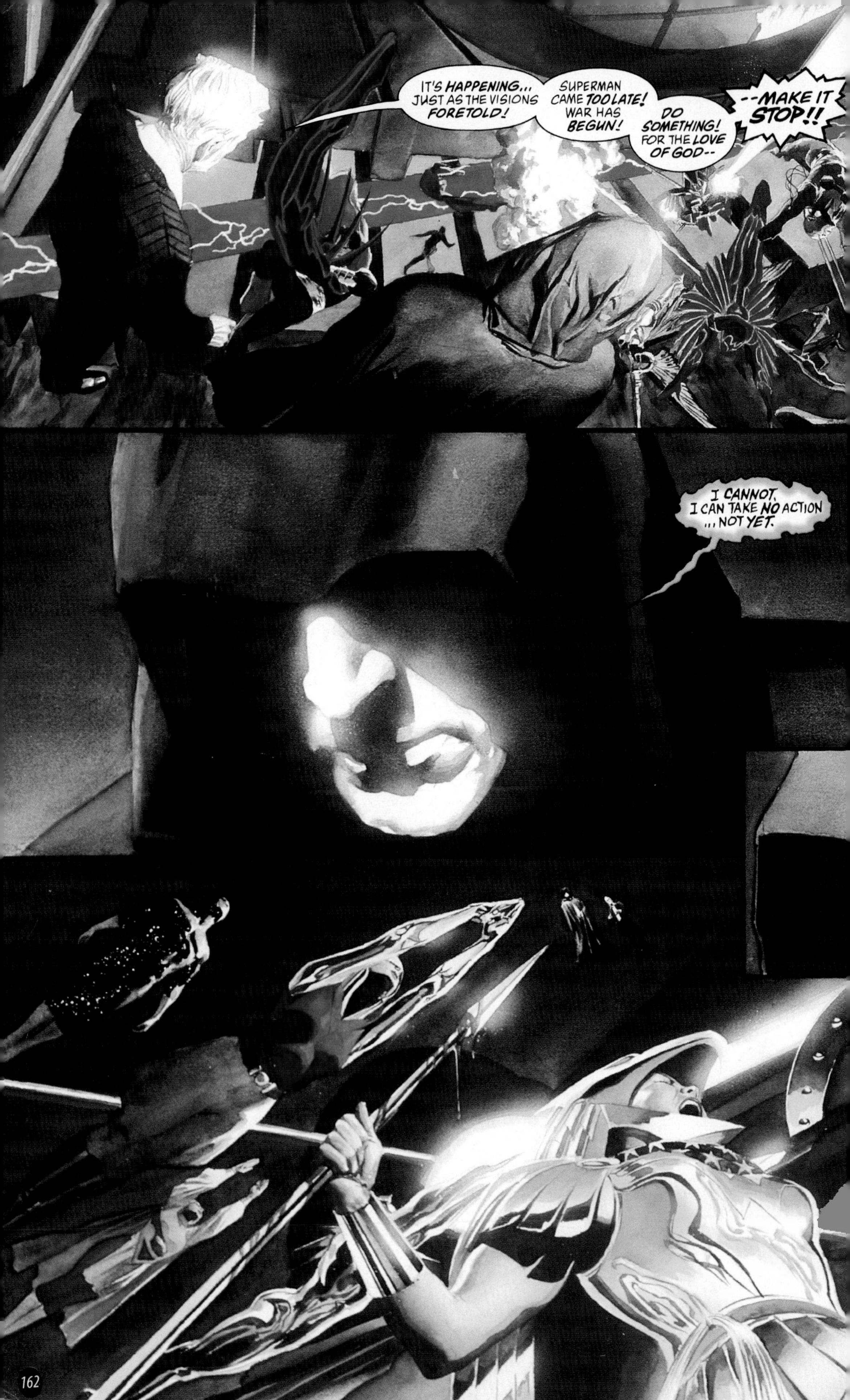

IT'S HAPPENING... JUST AS THE VISIONS FORETOLD!
SUPERMAN CAME TOO LATE! WAR HAS BEGUN!
DO SOMETHING! FOR THE LOVE OF GOD--
--MAKE IT STOP!!
I CANNOT. I CAN TAKE NO ACTION ...NOT YET.

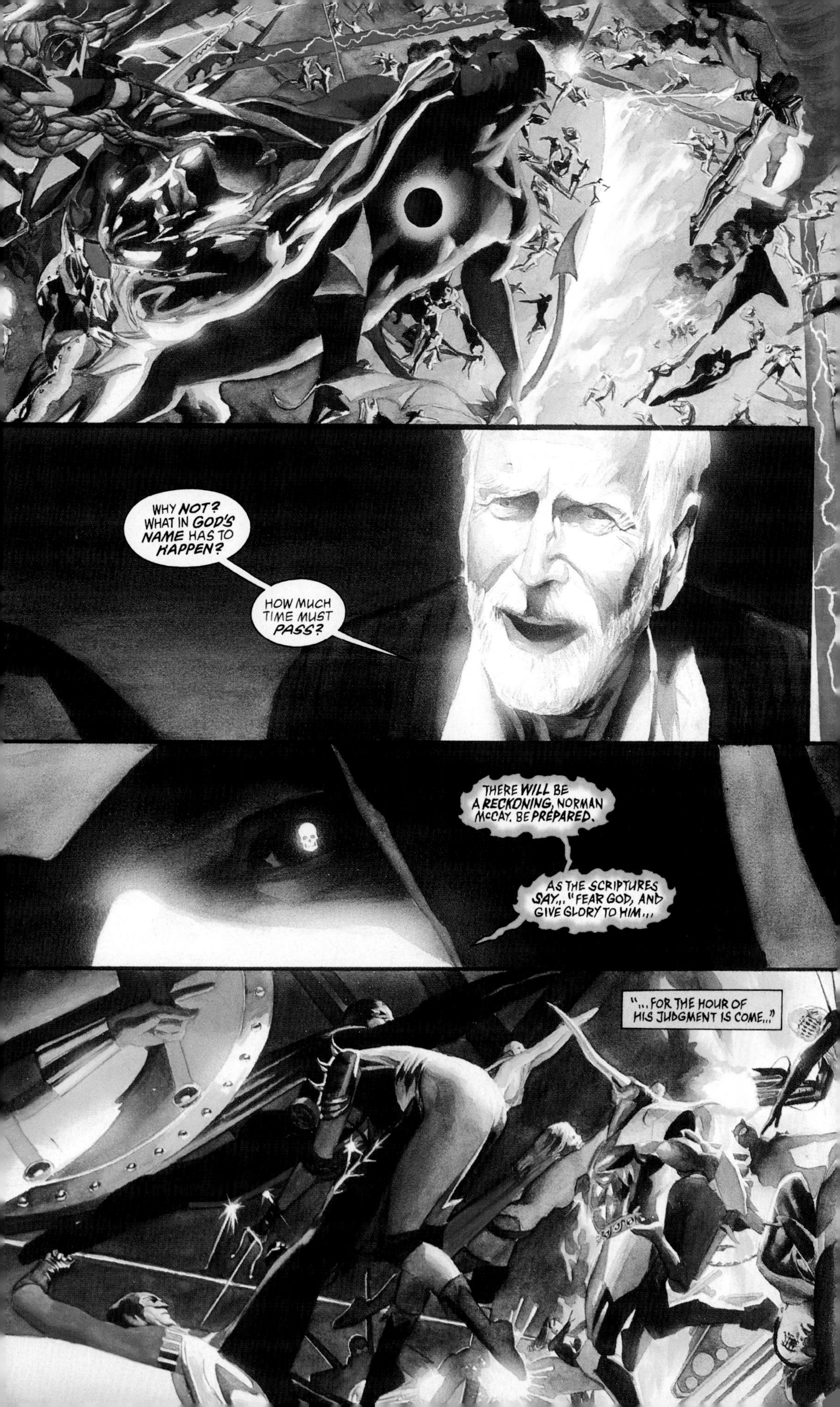
WHY NOT? WHAT IN GOD'S NAME HAS TO HAPPEN?
HOW MUCH TIME MUST PASS?
THERE WILL BE A RECKONING, NORMAN McCAY. BE PREPARED.
AS THE SCRIPTURES SAY... "FEAR GOD, AND GIVE GLORY TO HIM...
"...FOR THE HOUR OF HIS JUDGMENT IS COME..."

--MULTI-MEGATON NUCLEAR EXPLOSIVES HELD IN RESERVE FOR *JUST THIS MOMENT.*

TAKE A *GOOD LOOK* AT MANKIND'S *LAST HOPE.*

CAPABLE OF VAPORIZING A *COUNTY.* SHEATHED IN A FORCE-FIELD *UNBREACHABLE* BY ALL CATALOGUED METAHUMAN POWERS. DEPLOYMENT SYSTEM...

...VIRTUALLY *UNDETECTABLE.*

ALL OUR PROJECTIONS ESTIMATE THAT *ONE* WILL DO THE *JOB.*

AS *SECRETARY-GENERAL* OF THIS *NEW UNITED NATIONS...* I AM EMPOWERED TO SANCTION THE USE OF *THREE.*

THREE? UNACCEPT-ABLE!

SURELY *KILL* CIVILIANS, *TOO*

RISK OF *INFLAMING*

INSIST ON *SOME OTHER WAY* OF

LISTEN TO ME AND *UNDERSTAND!* THERE IS *NOTHING RATIONAL* ABOUT DISPATCHING *TACTICAL NUKES* INTO THE *HEART* OF MY *OWN COUNTRY*--

--BUT THESE ARE *NOT RATIONAL TIMES!* WE ARE AT THE *FLASHPOINT* OF *HUMAN EXISTENCE!*

WHAT THEN?

MY *GOD*...YOU CAN *HEAR* THE *BATTLE* EVEN *HERE!* AT *ANY MOMENT,* IT THREATENS TO *SPREAD FORTH* AND ENGULF THE *WORLD!* WHAT *THEN?*

165

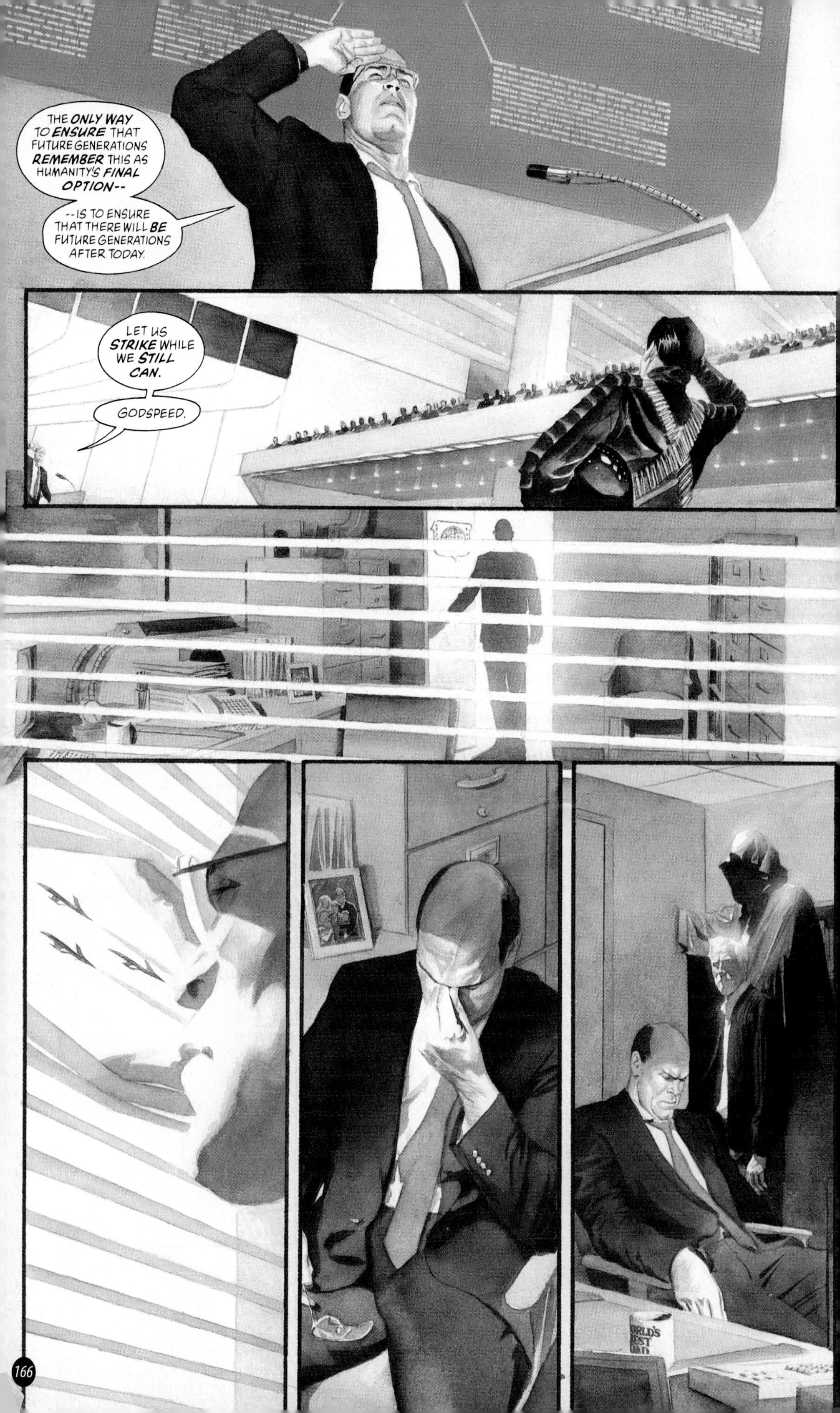
THE ONLY WAY TO ENSURE THAT FUTURE GENERATIONS REMEMBER THIS AS HUMANITY'S FINAL OPTION--
--IS TO ENSURE THAT THERE WILL BE FUTURE GENERATIONS AFTER TODAY.
LET US STRIKE WHILE WE STILL CAN.
GODSPEED.

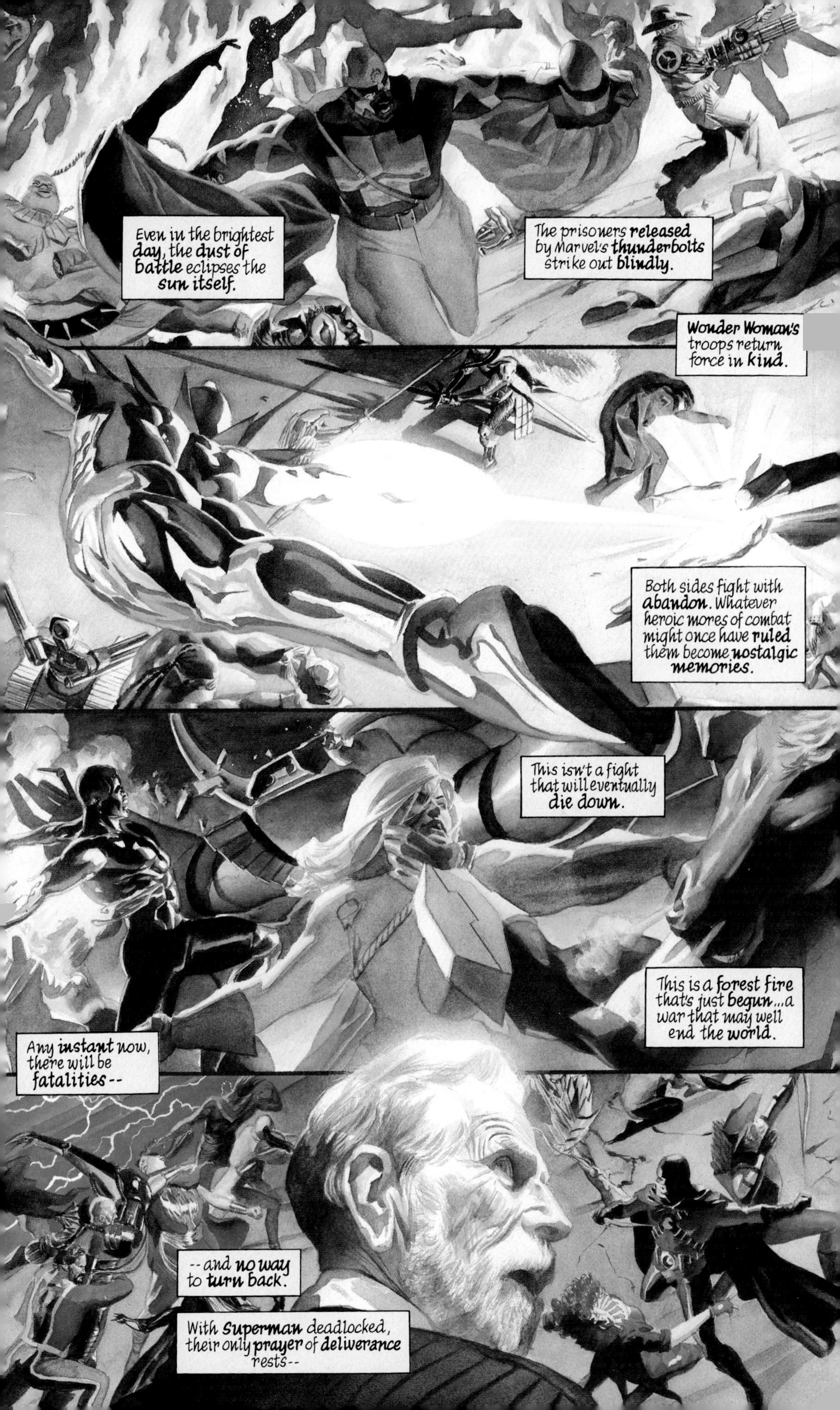

Even in the brightest day, the dust of battle eclipses the sun itself.
The prisoners released by Marvel's thunderbolts strike out blindly.
Wonder Woman's troops return force in kind.
Both sides fight with abandon. Whatever heroic mores of combat might once have ruled them become nostalgic memories.
This isn't a fight that will eventually die down.
This is a forest fire that's just begun...a war that may well end the world.
Any instant now, there will be fatalities--
--and no way to turn back.
With Superman deadlocked, their only prayer of deliverance rests--

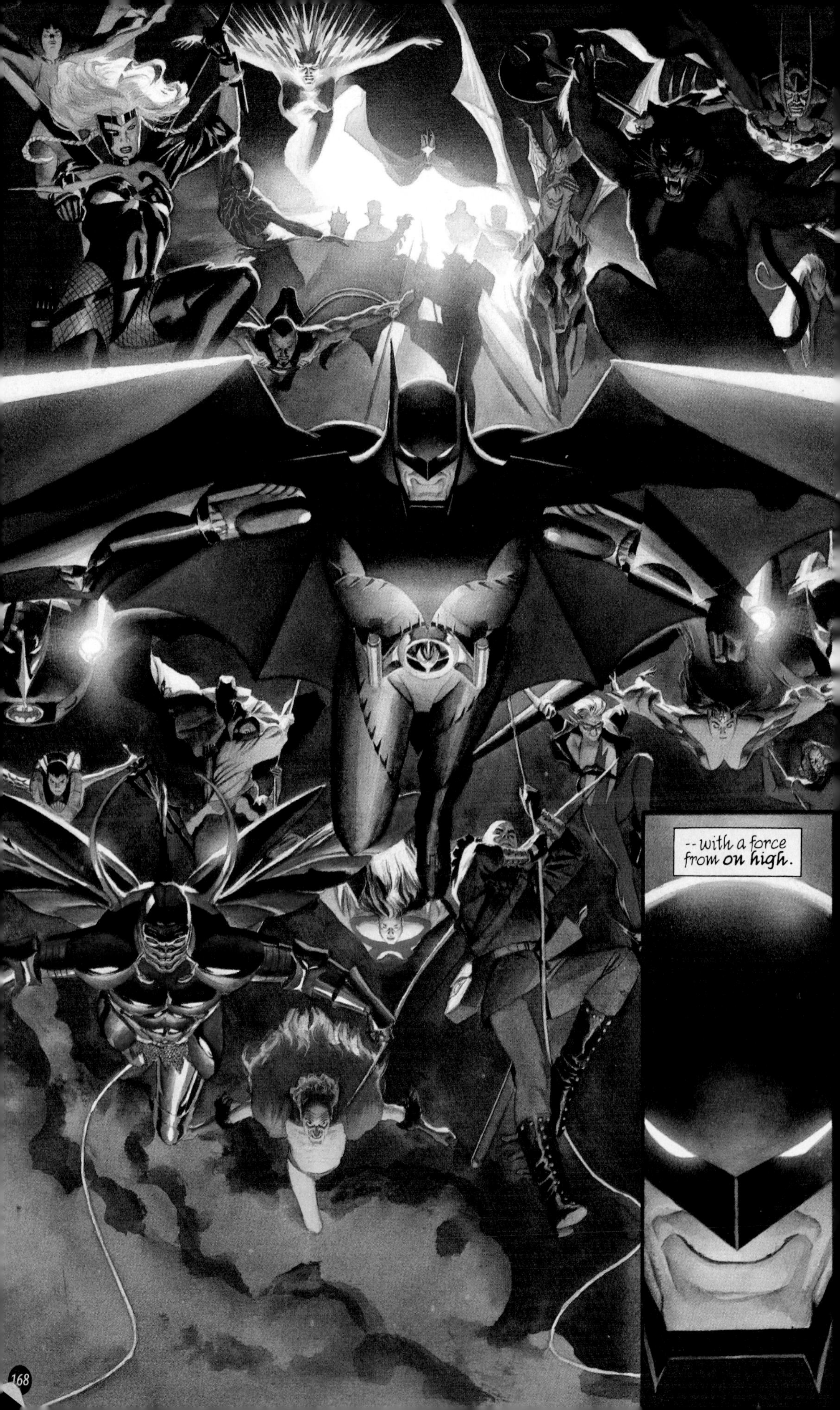
--with a force
from on high.

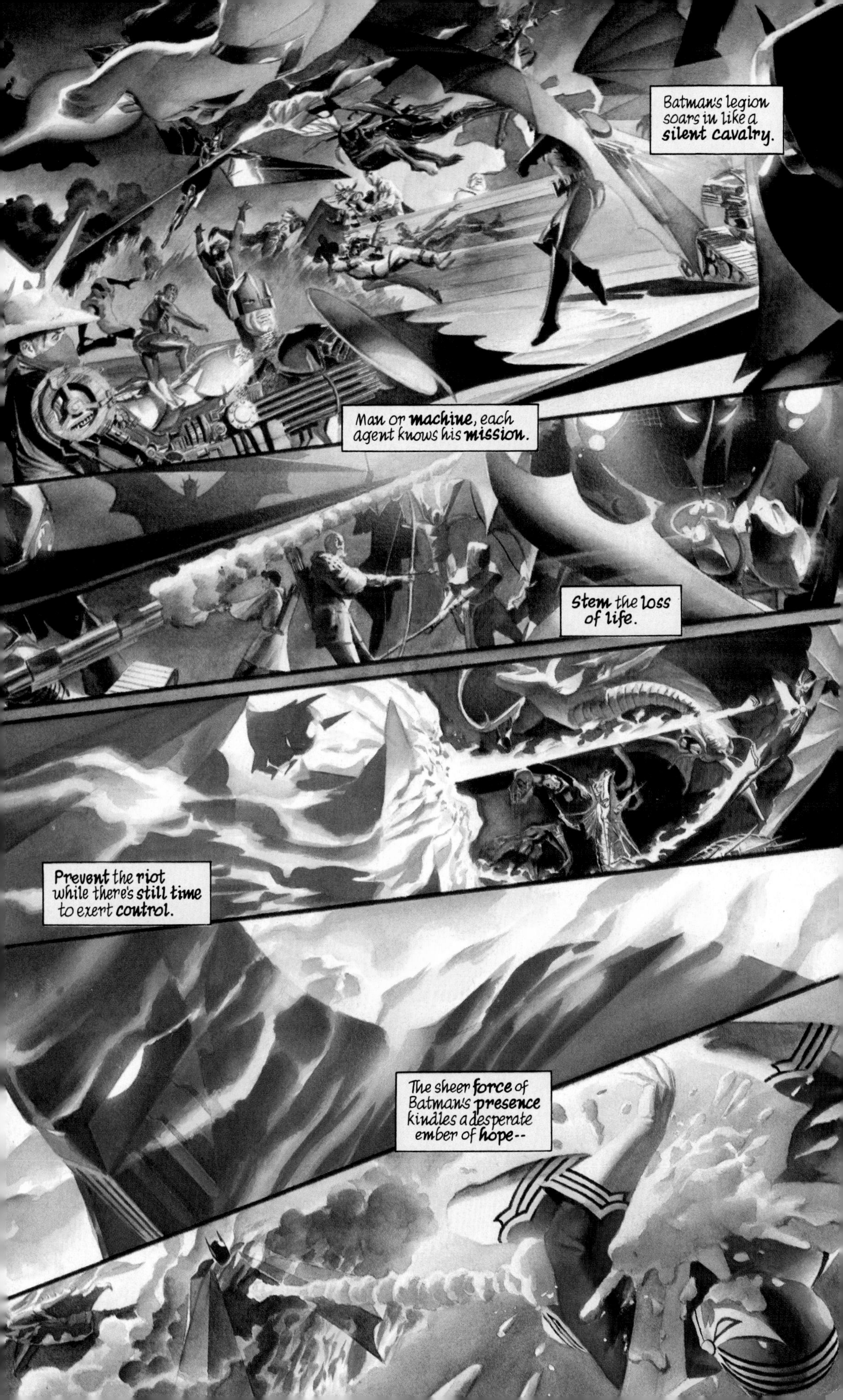
Batman's legion soars in like a **silent cavalry**.
Man or **machine**, each agent knows his **mission**.
Stem the loss of **life**.
Prevent the **riot** while there's **still time** to exert **control**.
The sheer **force** of Batman's **presence** kindles a desperate ember of **hope**--

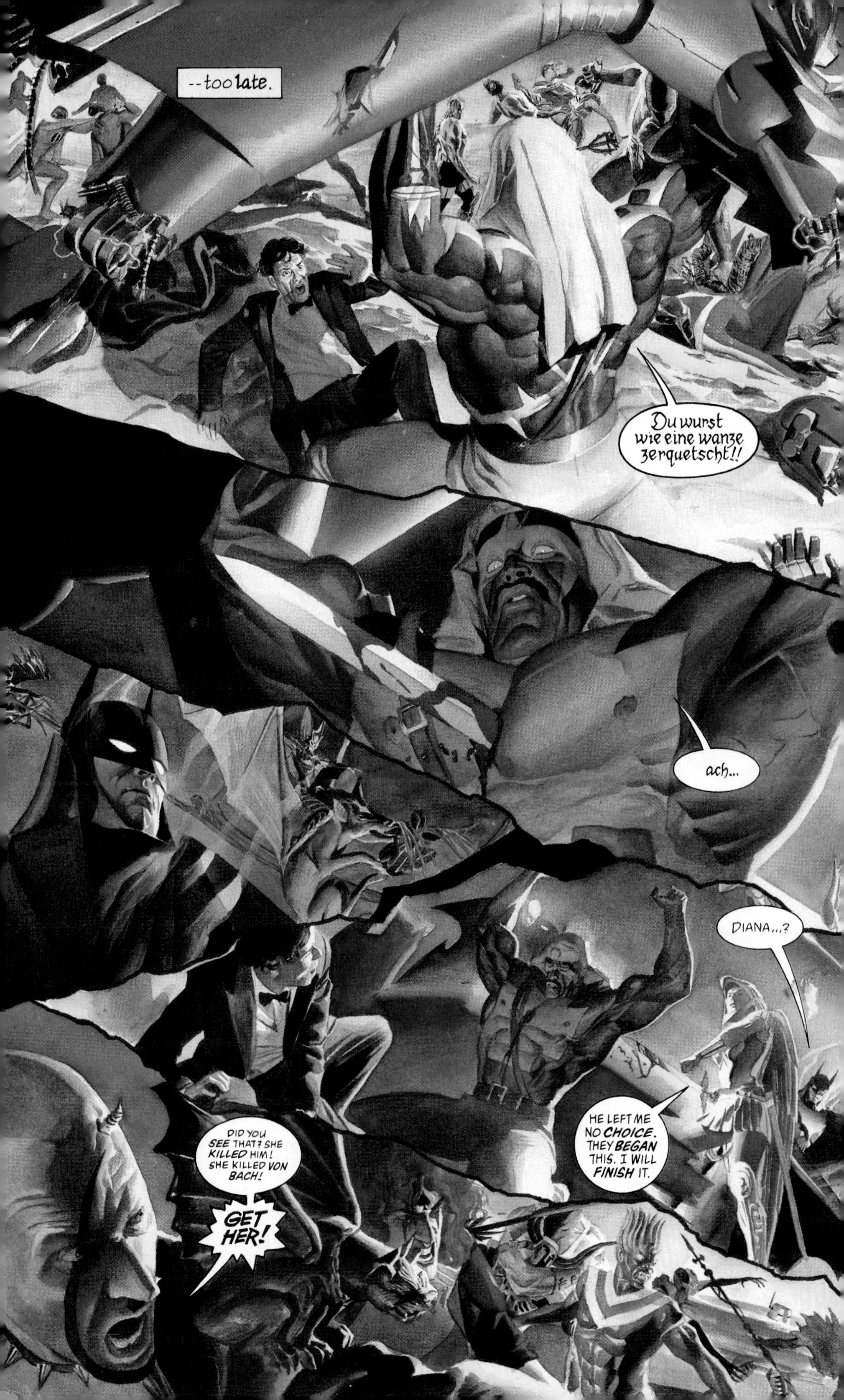
--too late.
Du wurst wie eine wanze zerquetscht!!
ach...
DIANA...?
HE LEFT ME NO CHOICE. THEY BEGAN THIS. I WILL FINISH IT.
DID YOU SEE THAT? SHE KILLED HIM! SHE KILLED VON BACH!
GET HER!

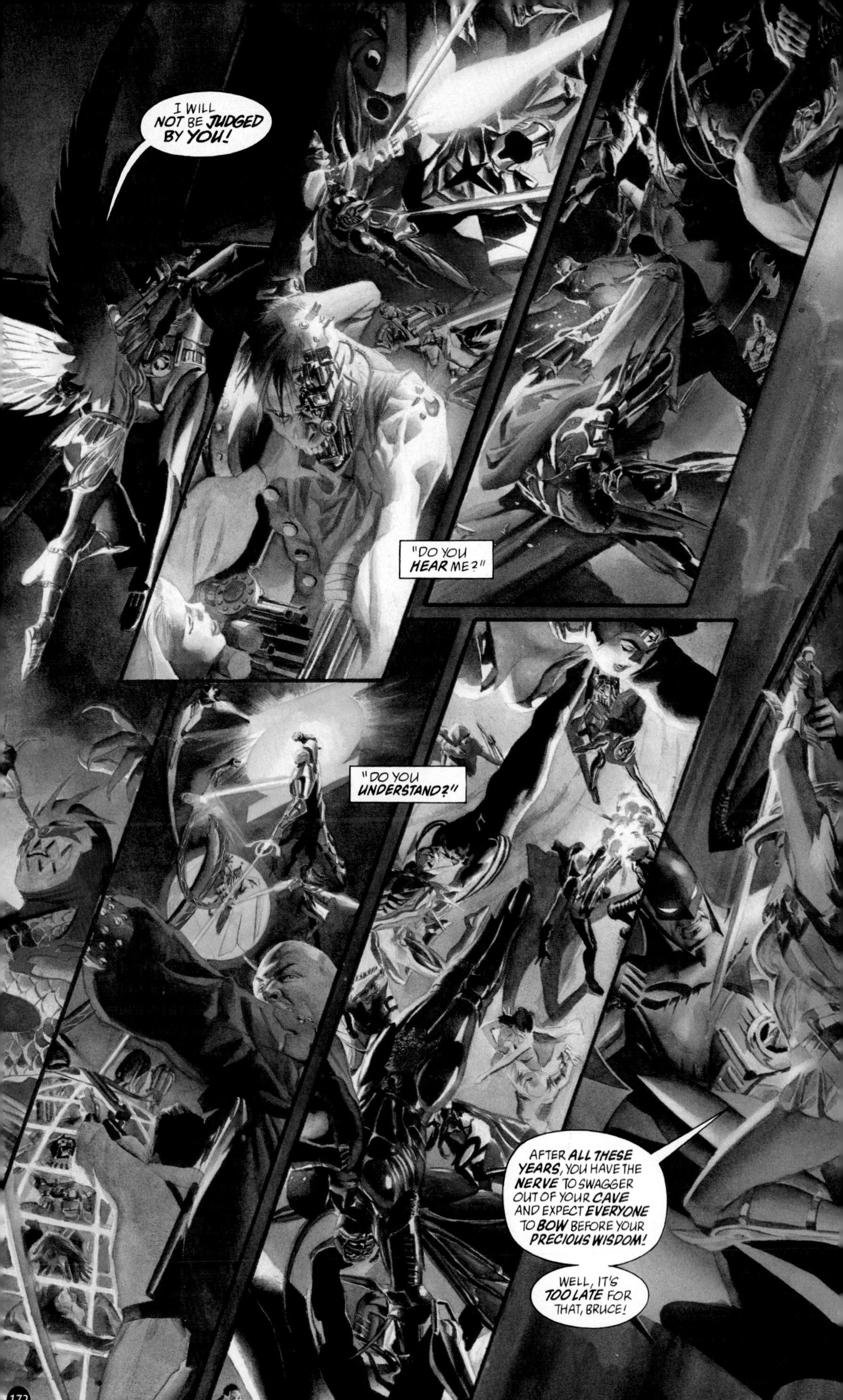
I WILL NOT BE JUDGED BY YOU!
"DO YOU HEAR ME?"
"DO YOU UNDERSTAND?"
AFTER ALL THESE YEARS, YOU HAVE THE NERVE TO SWAGGER OUT OF YOUR CAVE AND EXPECT EVERYONE TO BOW BEFORE YOUR PRECIOUS WISDOM!
WELL, IT'S TOO LATE FOR THAT, BRUCE!

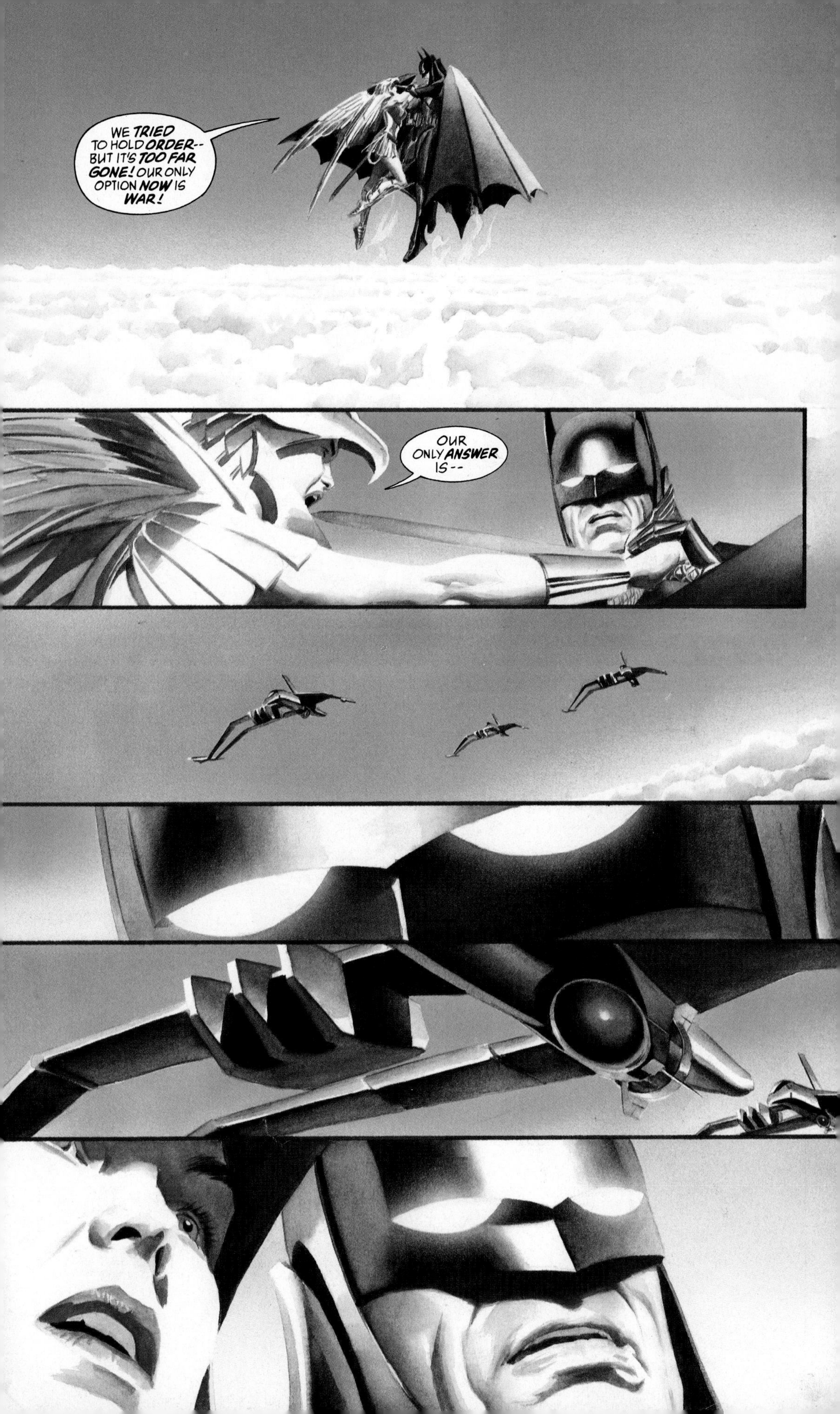

WE TRIED TO HOLD ORDER-- BUT IT'S TOO FAR GONE! OUR ONLY OPTION NOW IS WAR!
OUR ONLY ANSWER IS--

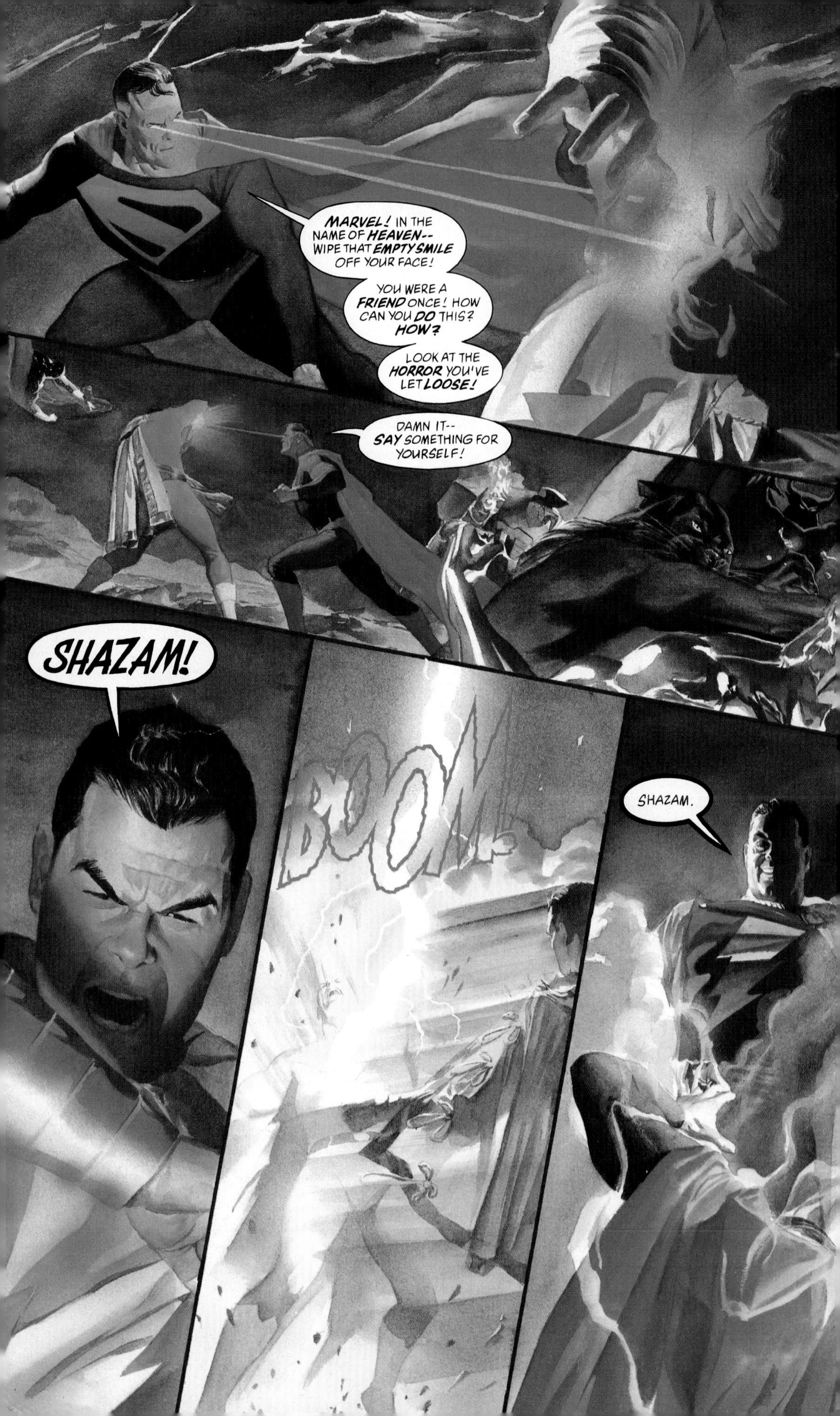

MARVEL! IN THE NAME OF HEAVEN-- WIPE THAT EMPTY SMILE OFF YOUR FACE!
YOU WERE A FRIEND ONCE! HOW CAN YOU DO THIS? HOW?
LOOK AT THE HORROR YOU'VE LET LOOSE!
DAMN IT-- SAY SOMETHING FOR YOURSELF!
SHAZAM!
BOOM!
SHAZAM.

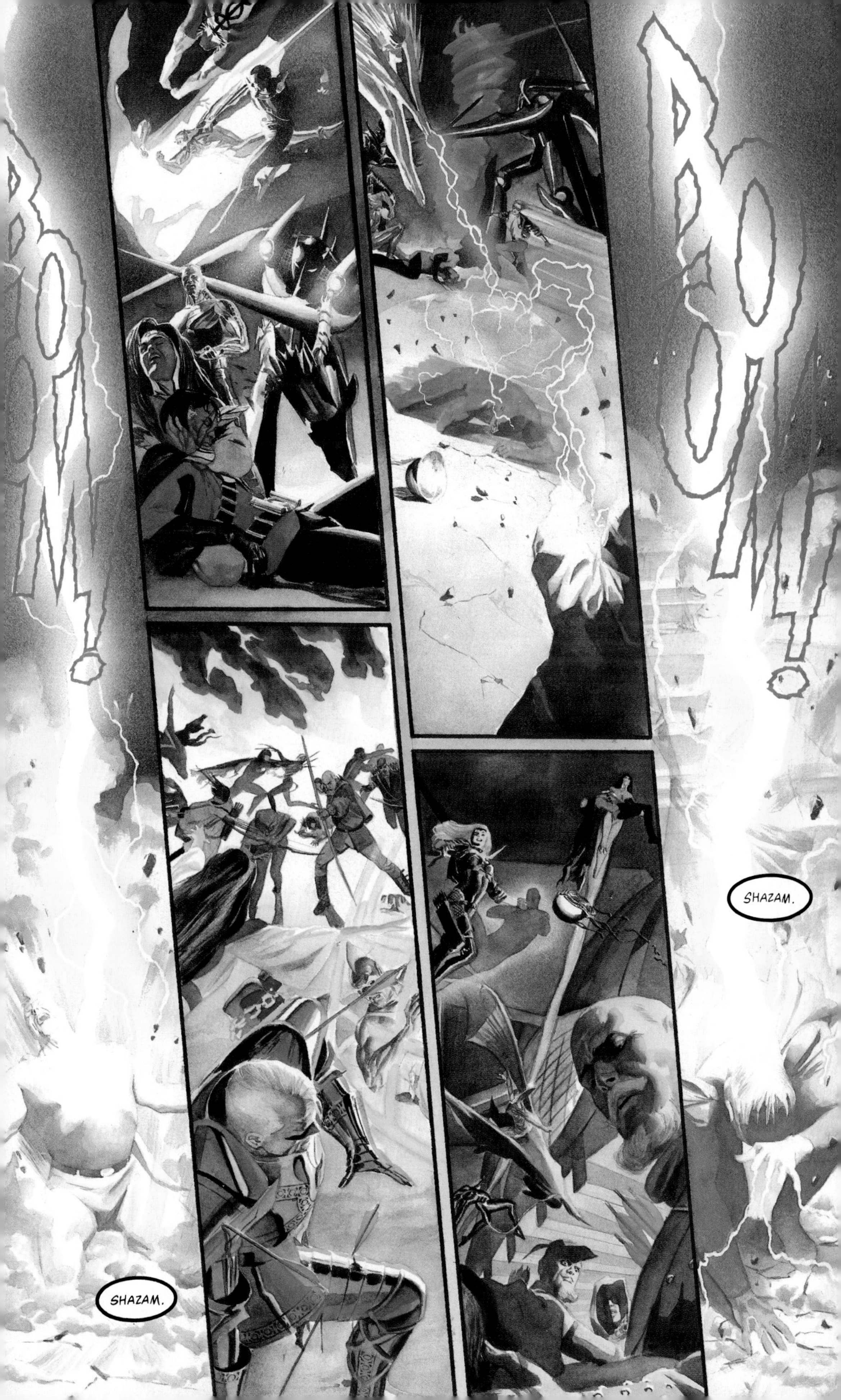
BOOM!
BOOM!
SHAZAM.
SHAZAM.

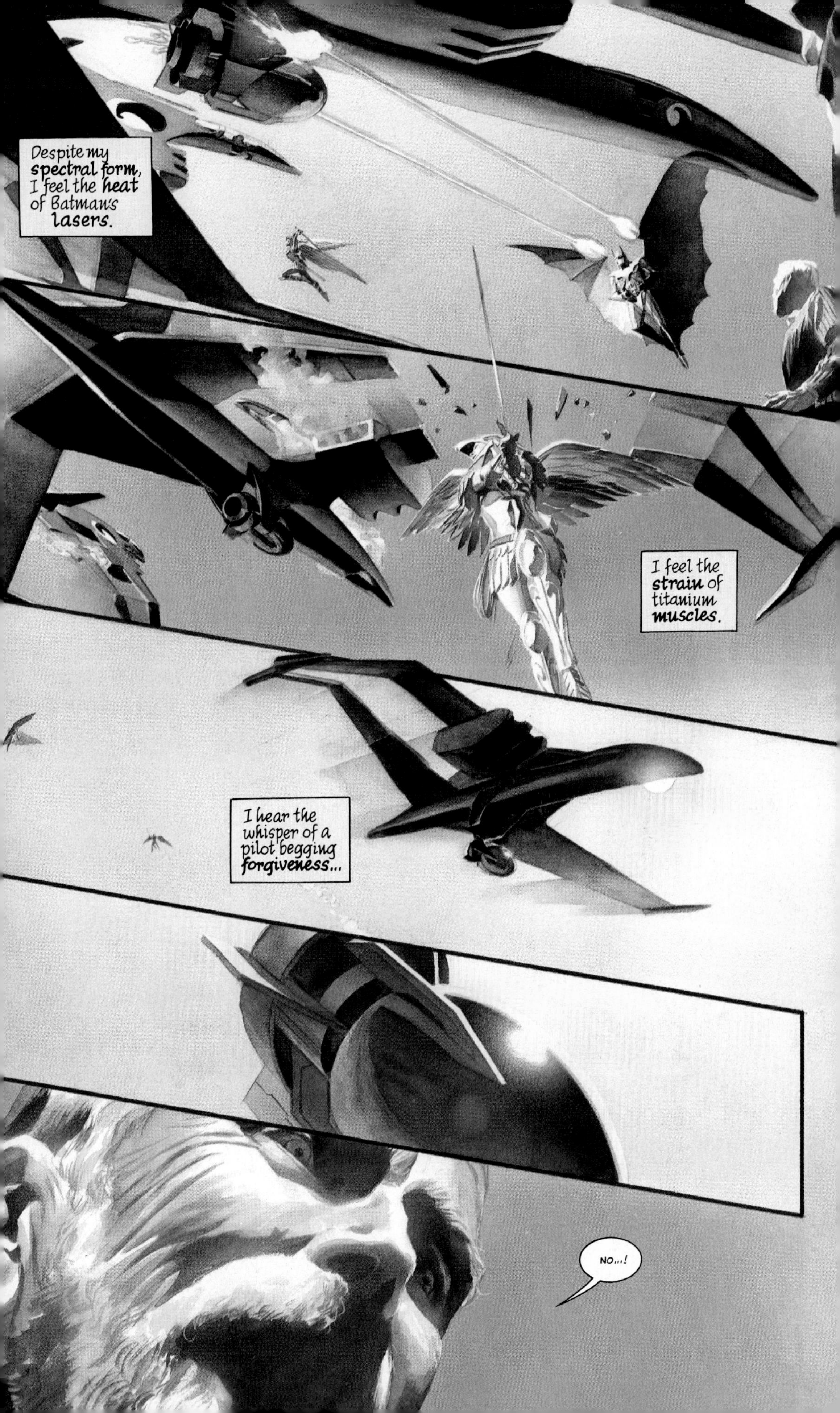

Despite my spectral form, I feel the heat of Batman's lasers.
I feel the strain of titanium muscles.
I hear the whisper of a pilot begging forgiveness...
NO...!

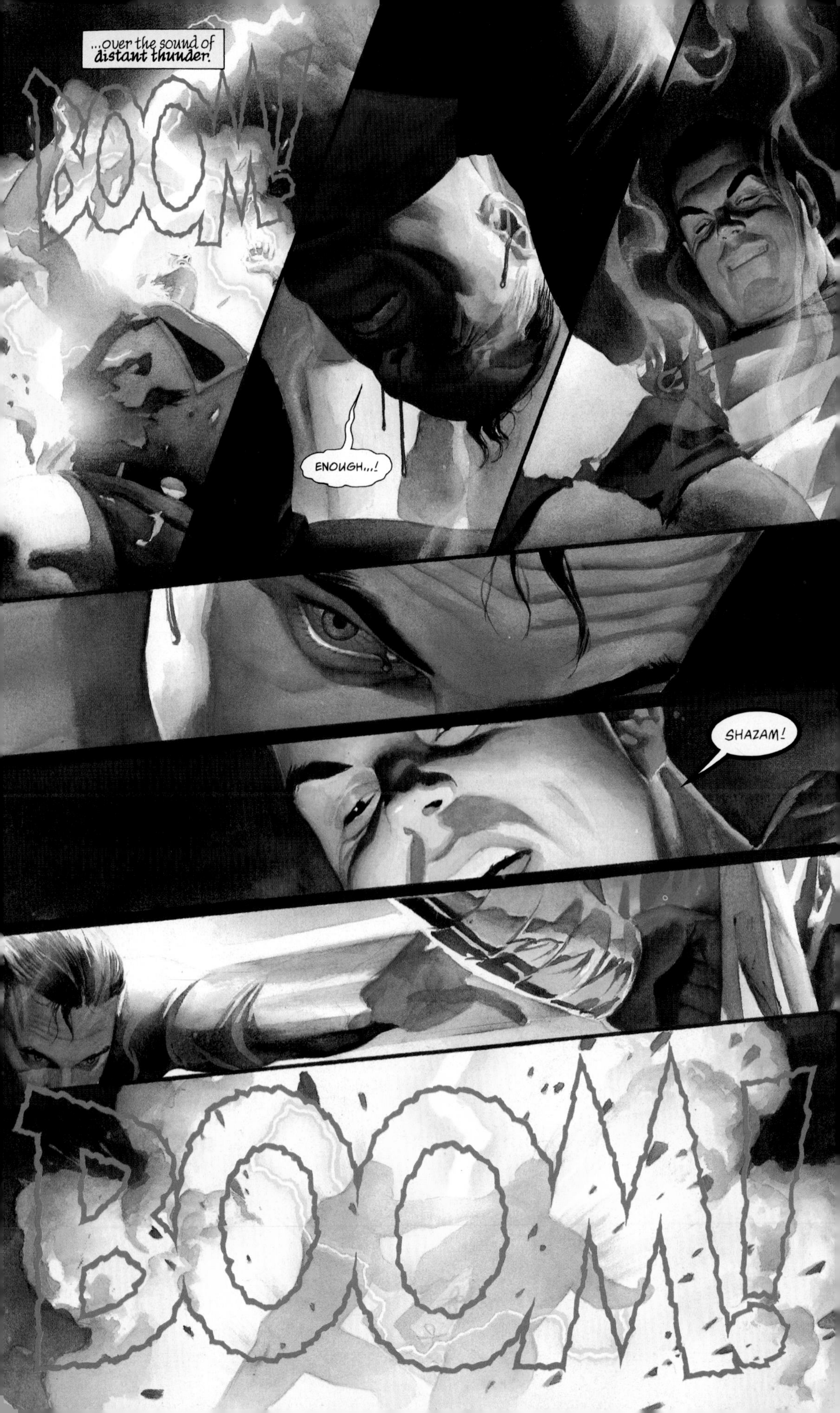
...over the sound of distant thunder.
BOOM!
ENOUGH...!
SHAZAM!
BOOM!

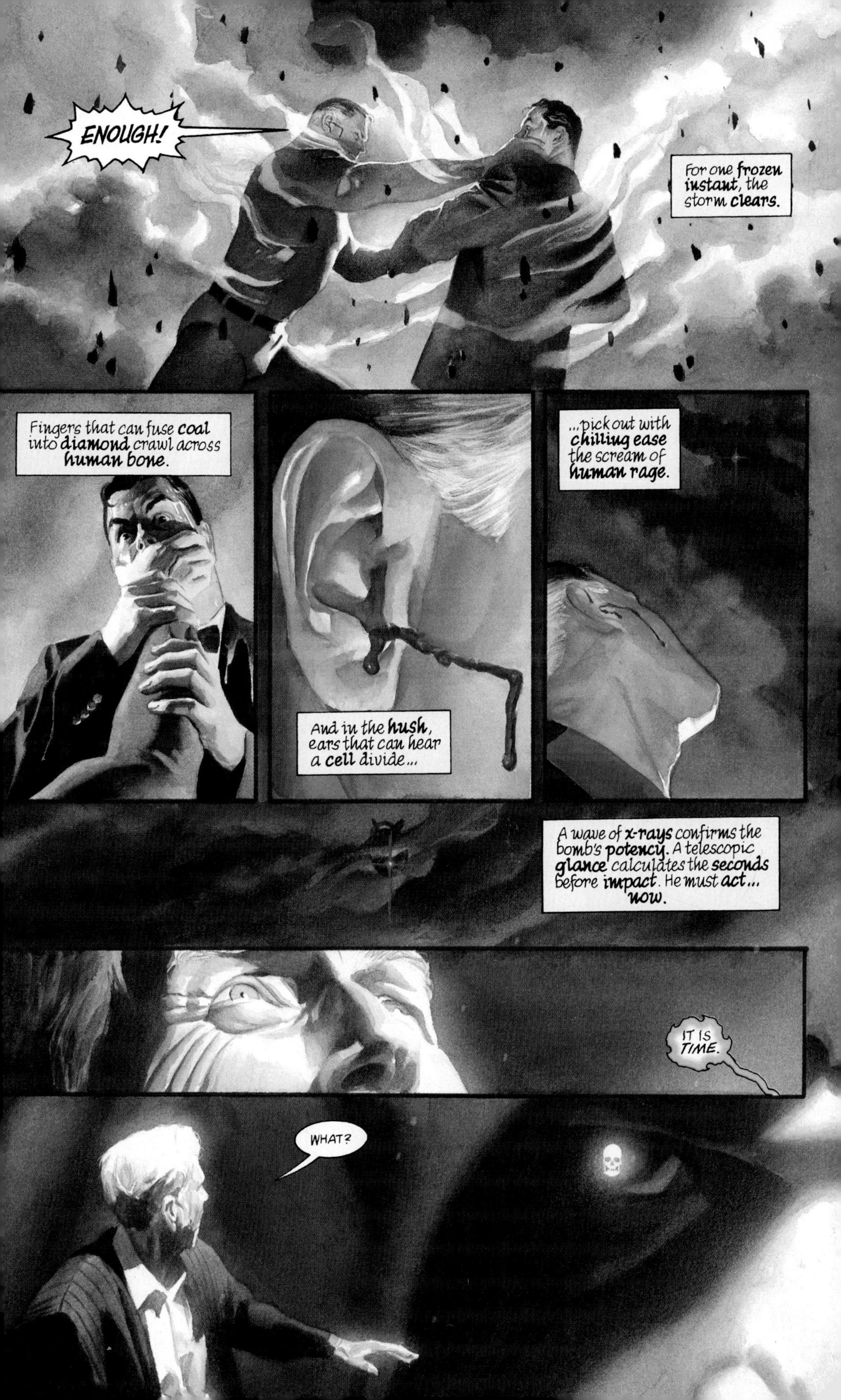
ENOUGH!
For one frozen instant, the storm clears.
Fingers that can fuse coal into diamond crawl across human bone.
And in the hush, ears that can hear a cell divide...
...pick out with chilling ease the scream of human rage.
A wave of x-rays confirms the bomb's potency. A telescopic glance calculates the seconds before impact. He must act... now.
IT IS TIME.
WHAT?

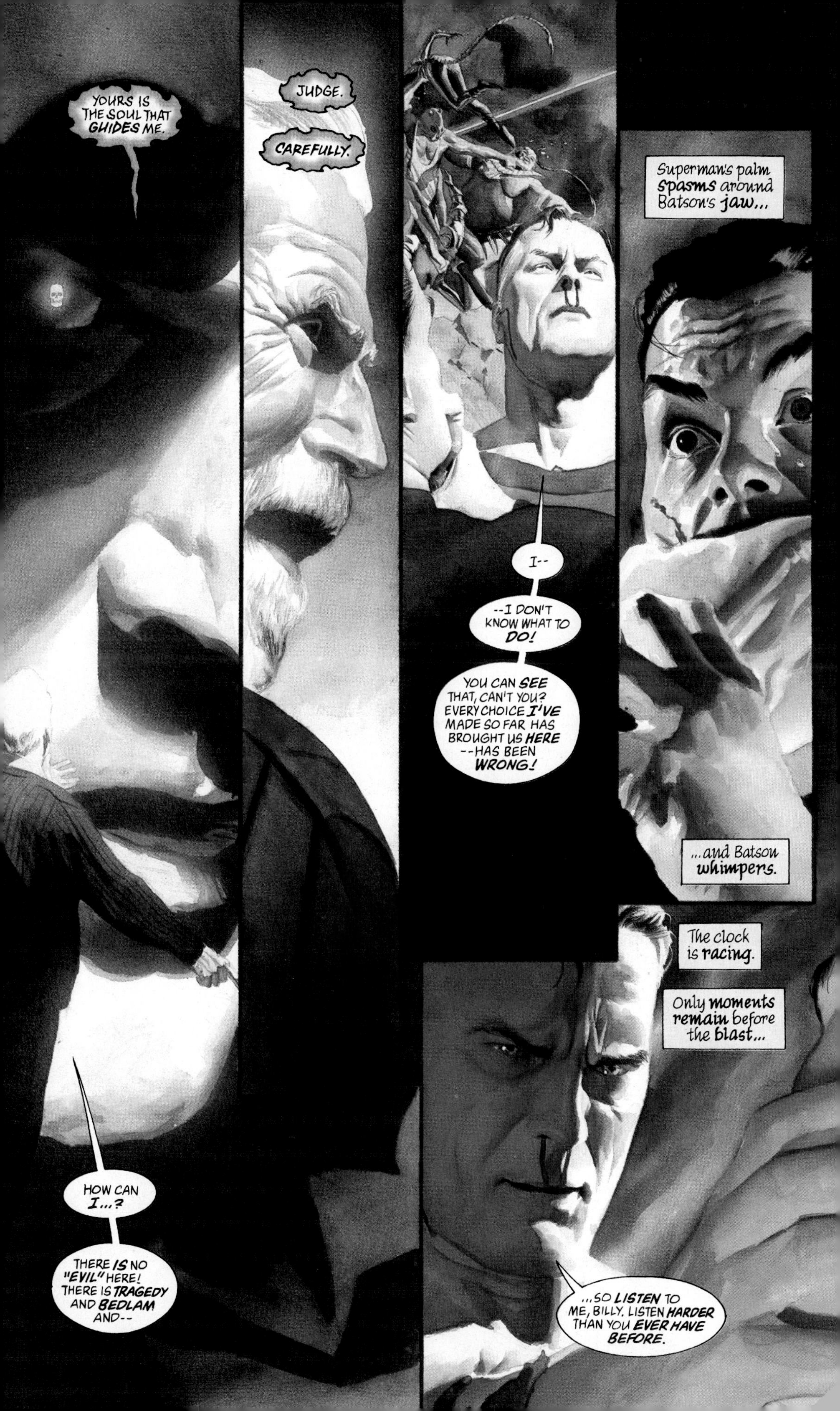
YOURS IS THE SOUL THAT GUIDES ME.
JUDGE.
CAREFULLY.
I--
--I DON'T KNOW WHAT TO DO!
YOU CAN SEE THAT, CAN'T YOU? EVERY CHOICE I'VE MADE SO FAR HAS BROUGHT US HERE --HAS BEEN WRONG!
Superman's palm spasms around Batson's jaw...
...and Batson whimpers.
HOW CAN I...?
THERE IS NO "EVIL" HERE! THERE IS TRAGEDY AND BEDLAM AND--
The clock is racing.
Only moments remain before the blast...
...SO LISTEN TO ME, BILLY. LISTEN HARDER THAN YOU EVER HAVE BEFORE.

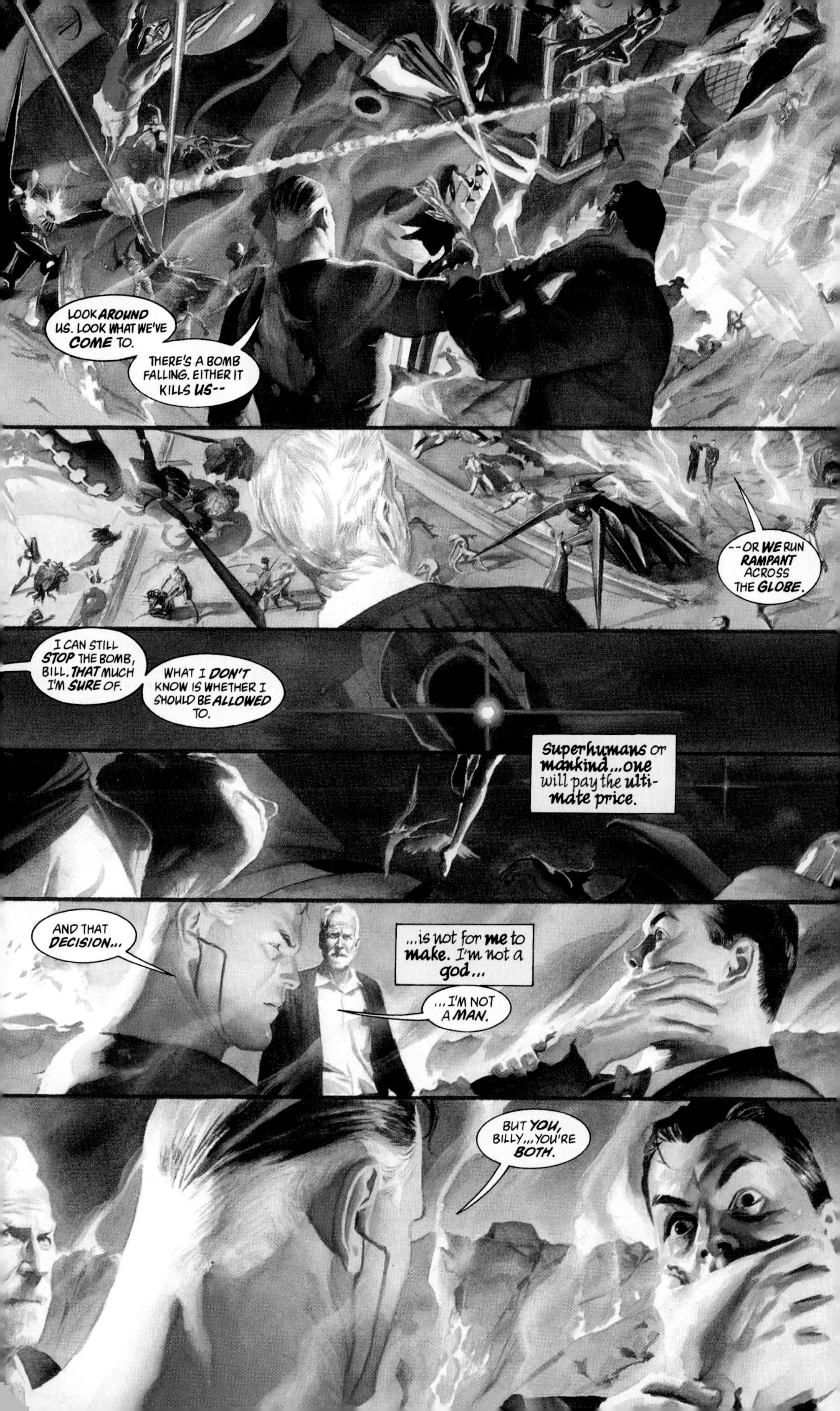
LOOK AROUND US. LOOK WHAT WE'VE COME TO.
THERE'S A BOMB FALLING. EITHER IT KILLS US--
--OR WE RUN RAMPANT ACROSS THE GLOBE.
I CAN STILL STOP THE BOMB, BILL. THAT MUCH I'M SURE OF.
WHAT I DON'T KNOW IS WHETHER I SHOULD BE ALLOWED TO.
Superhumans or mankind...one will pay the ultimate price.
AND THAT DECISION...
...is not for me to make. I'm not a god...
...I'M NOT A MAN.
BUT YOU, BILLY... YOU'RE BOTH.

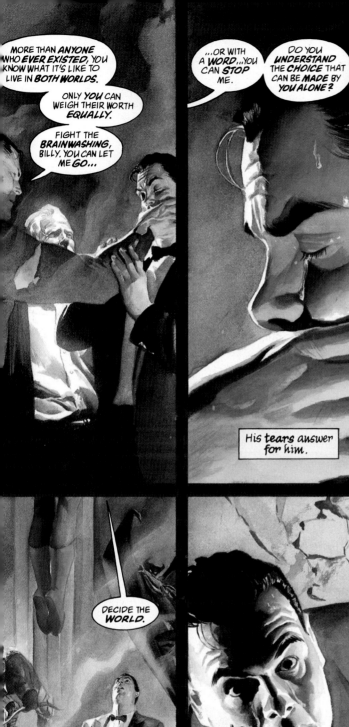

MORE THAN *ANYONE* WHO *EVER EXISTED*, YOU KNOW WHAT IT'S LIKE TO LIVE IN *BOTH WORLDS*.

ONLY *YOU* CAN WEIGH THEIR WORTH *EQUALLY*.

FIGHT THE *BRAINWASHING*, BILLY. YOU CAN LET ME *GO*...

...OR WITH A *WORD*,...YOU CAN *STOP* ME.

DO YOU *UNDERSTAND* THE *CHOICE* THAT CAN BE *MADE* BY *YOU ALONE*?

His *tears* answer for him.

THEN *DECIDE*.

DECIDE THE *WORLD*.

And *when* he cries...

SHAZAM.

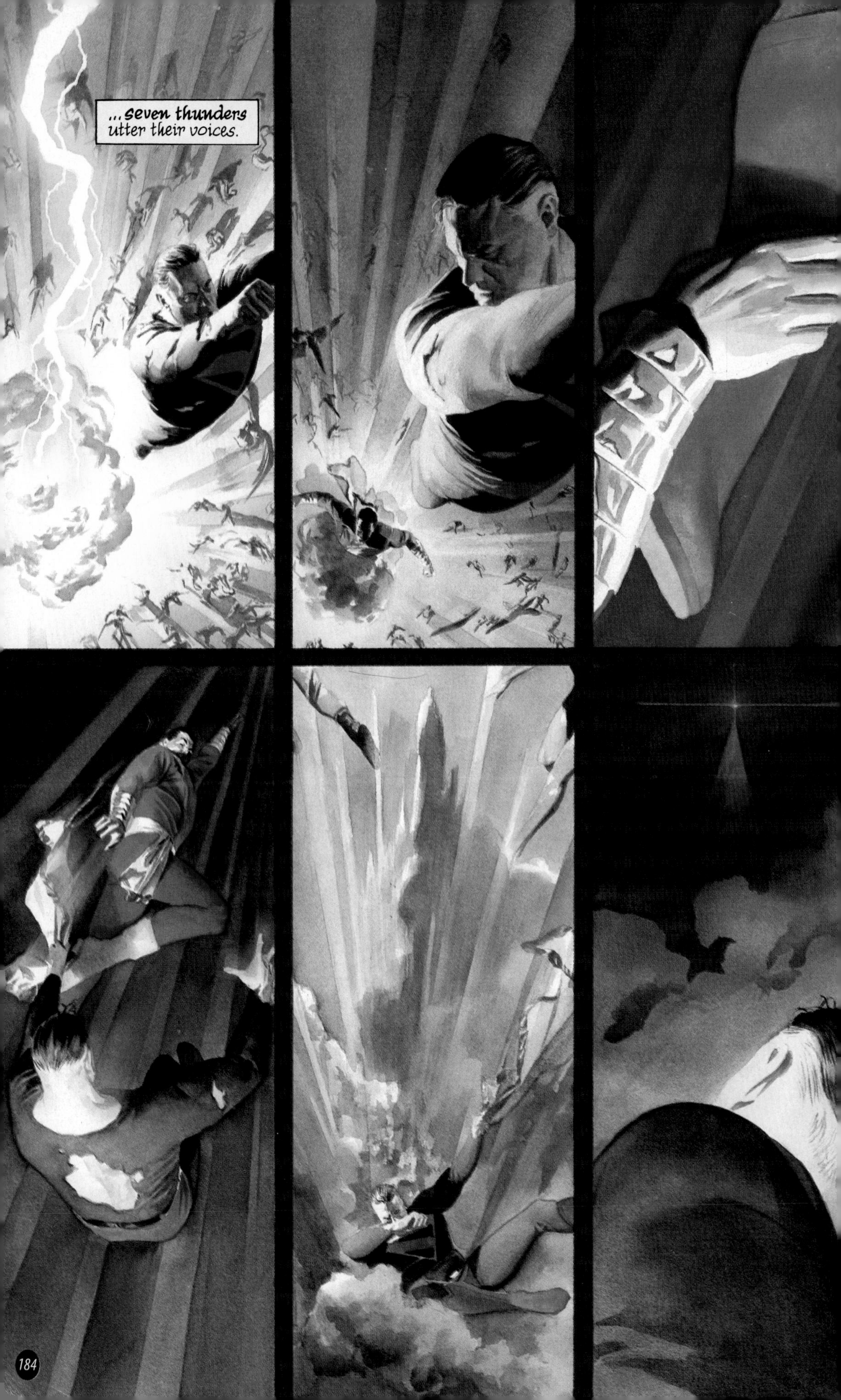
...seven thunders utter their voices.

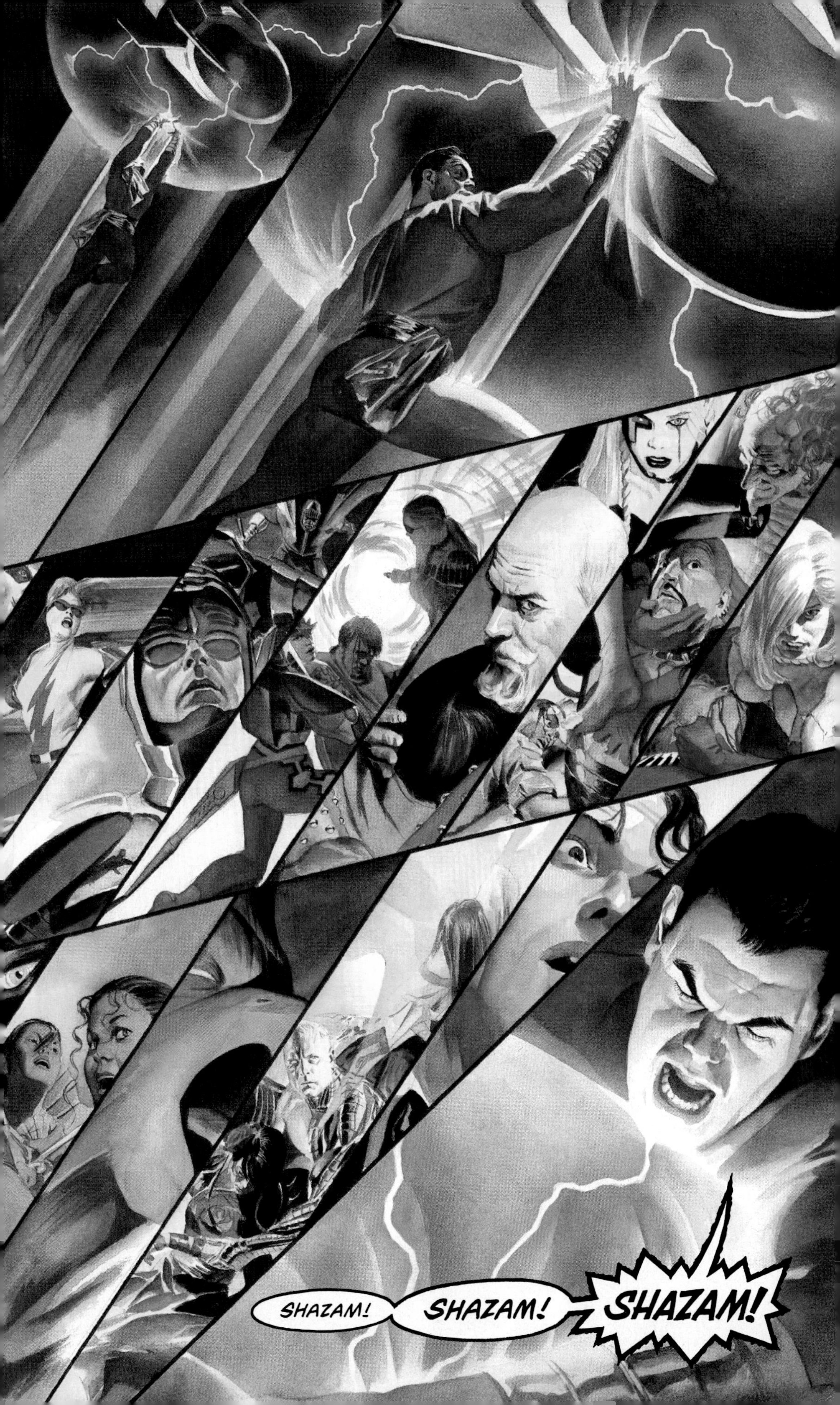
SHAZAM!
SHAZAM!
SHAZAM!

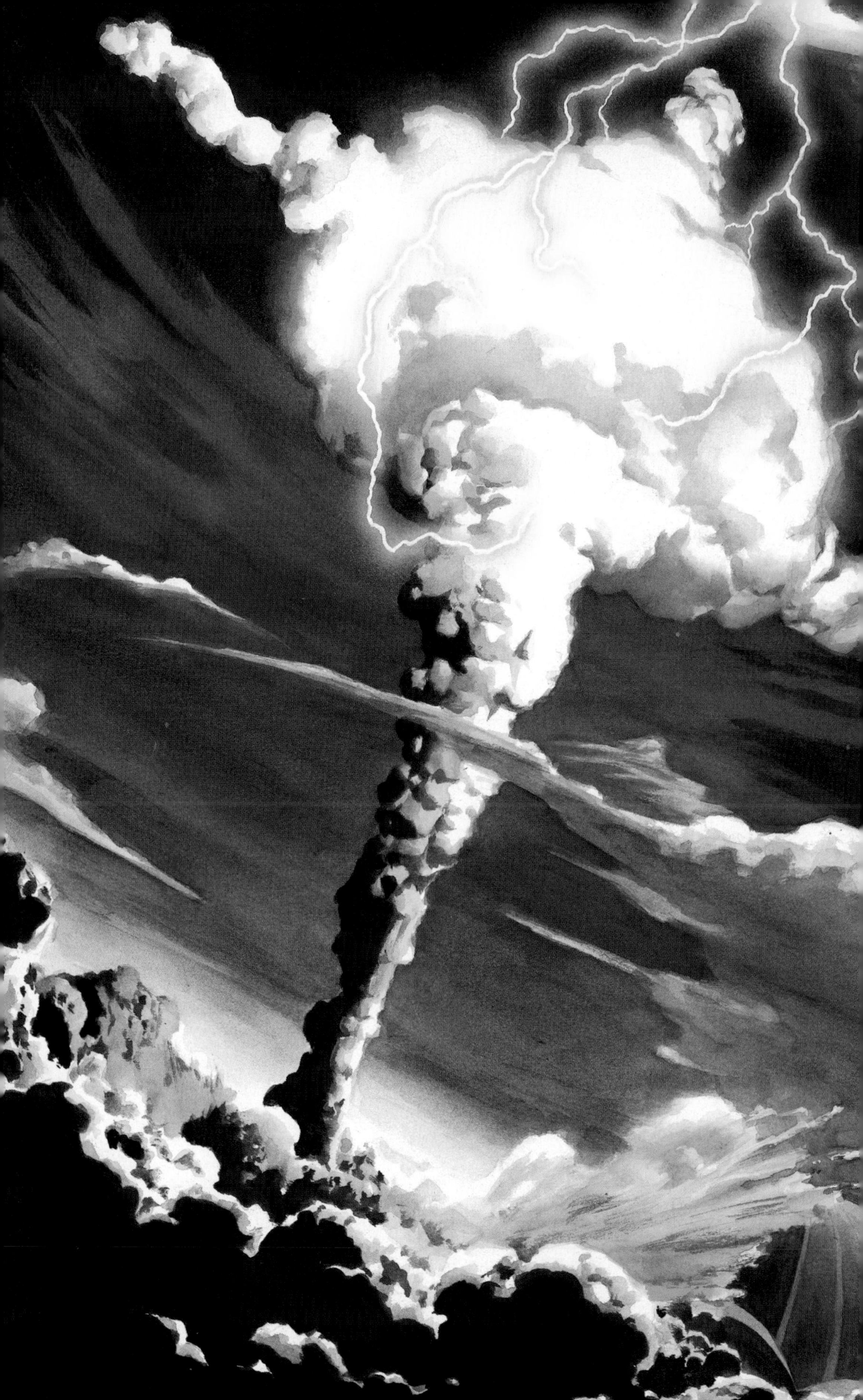

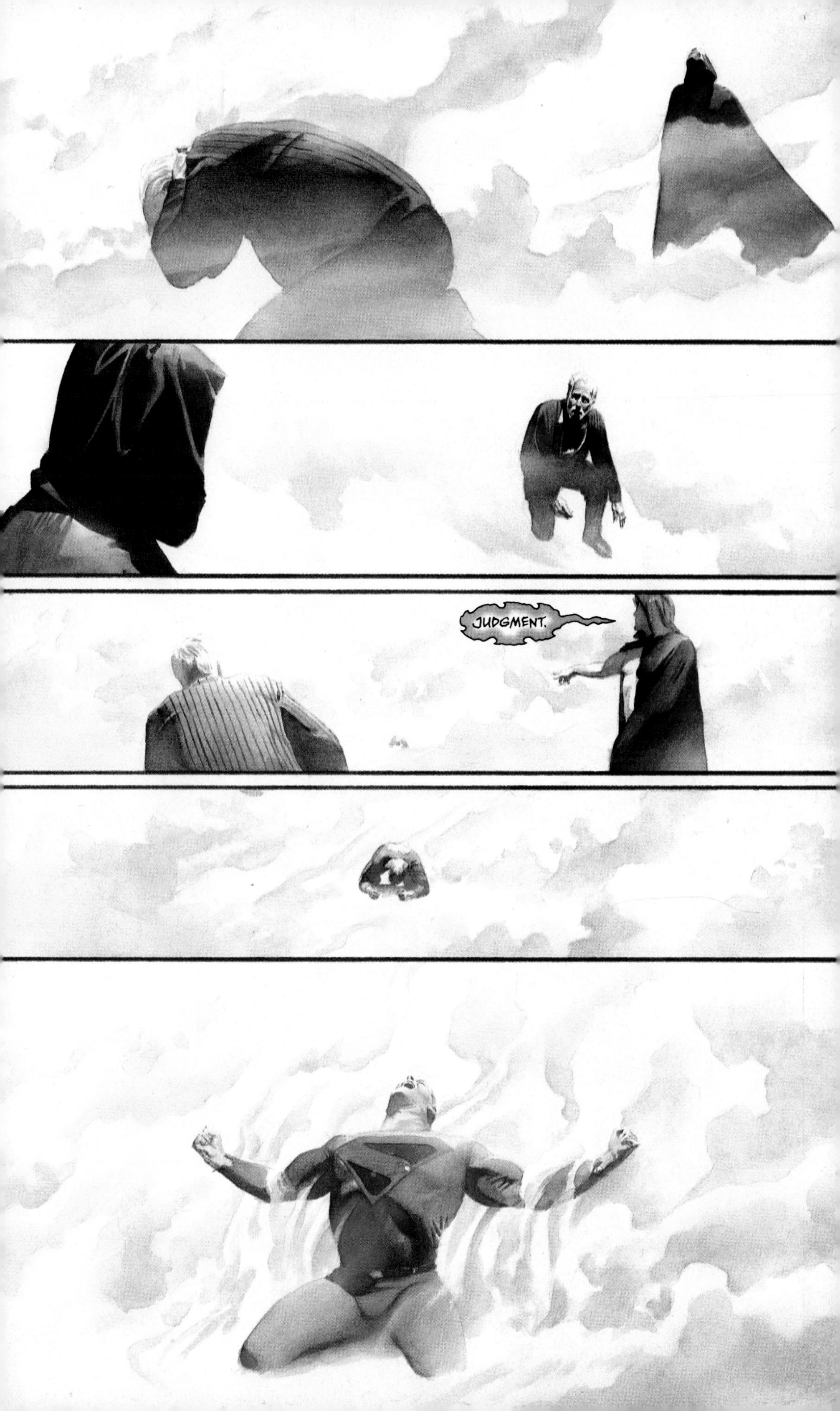
JUDGMENT.

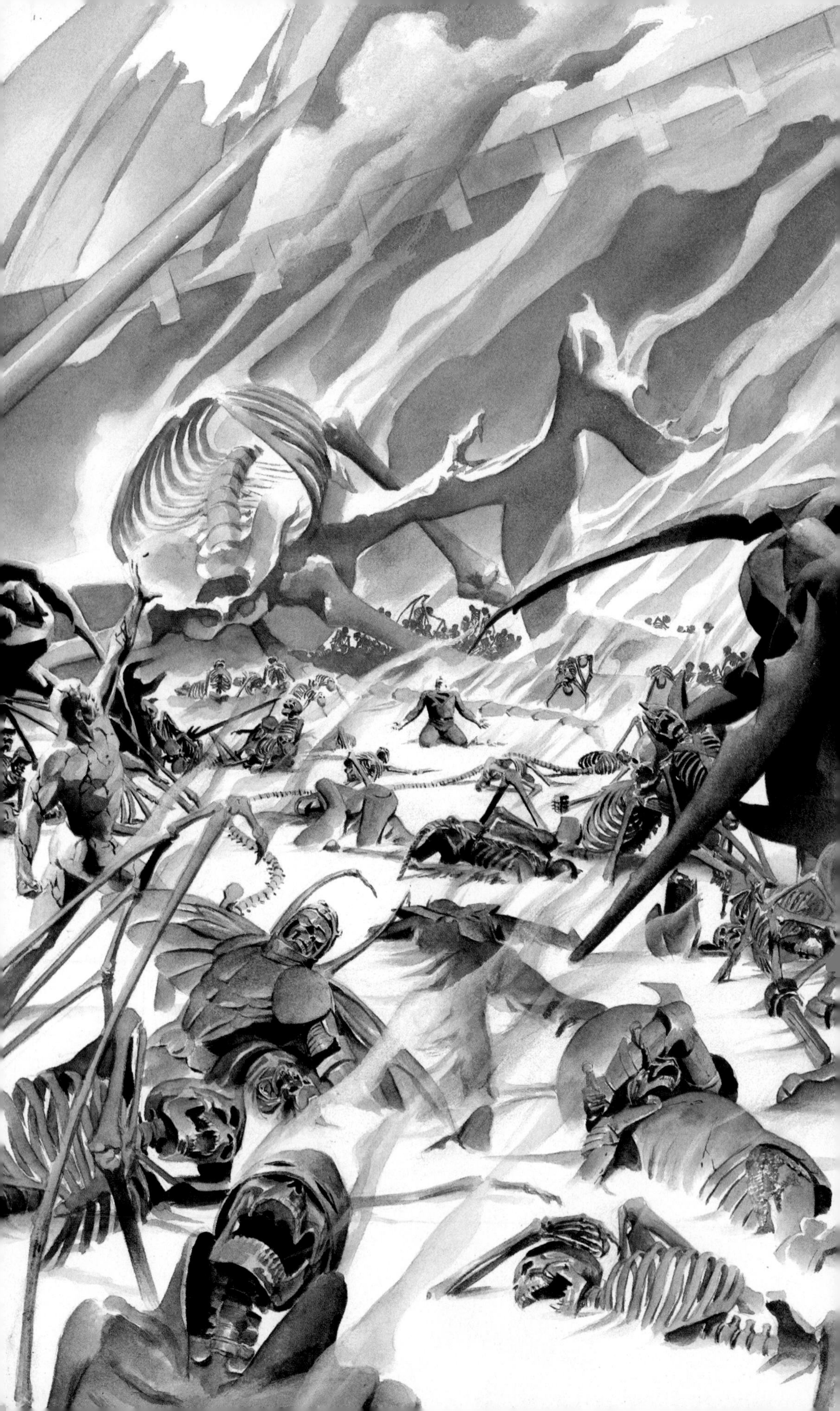

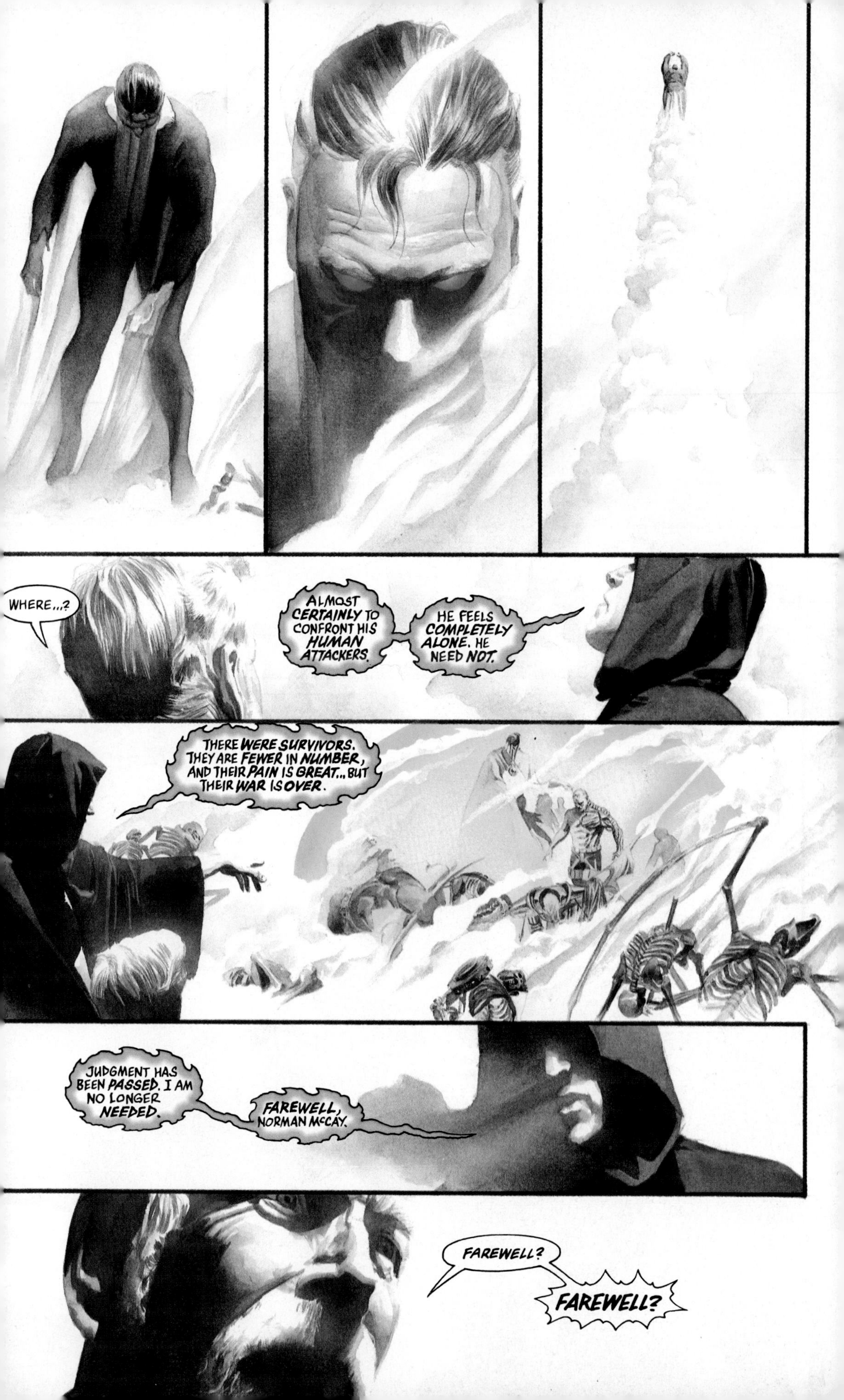
WHERE...?
ALMOST CERTAINLY TO CONFRONT HIS HUMAN ATTACKERS.
HE FEELS COMPLETELY ALONE. HE NEED NOT.
THERE WERE SURVIVORS. THEY ARE FEWER IN NUMBER, AND THEIR PAIN IS GREAT... BUT THEIR WAR IS OVER.
JUDGMENT HAS BEEN PASSED. I AM NO LONGER NEEDED.
FAREWELL, NORMAN McCAY.
FAREWELL?
FAREWELL?

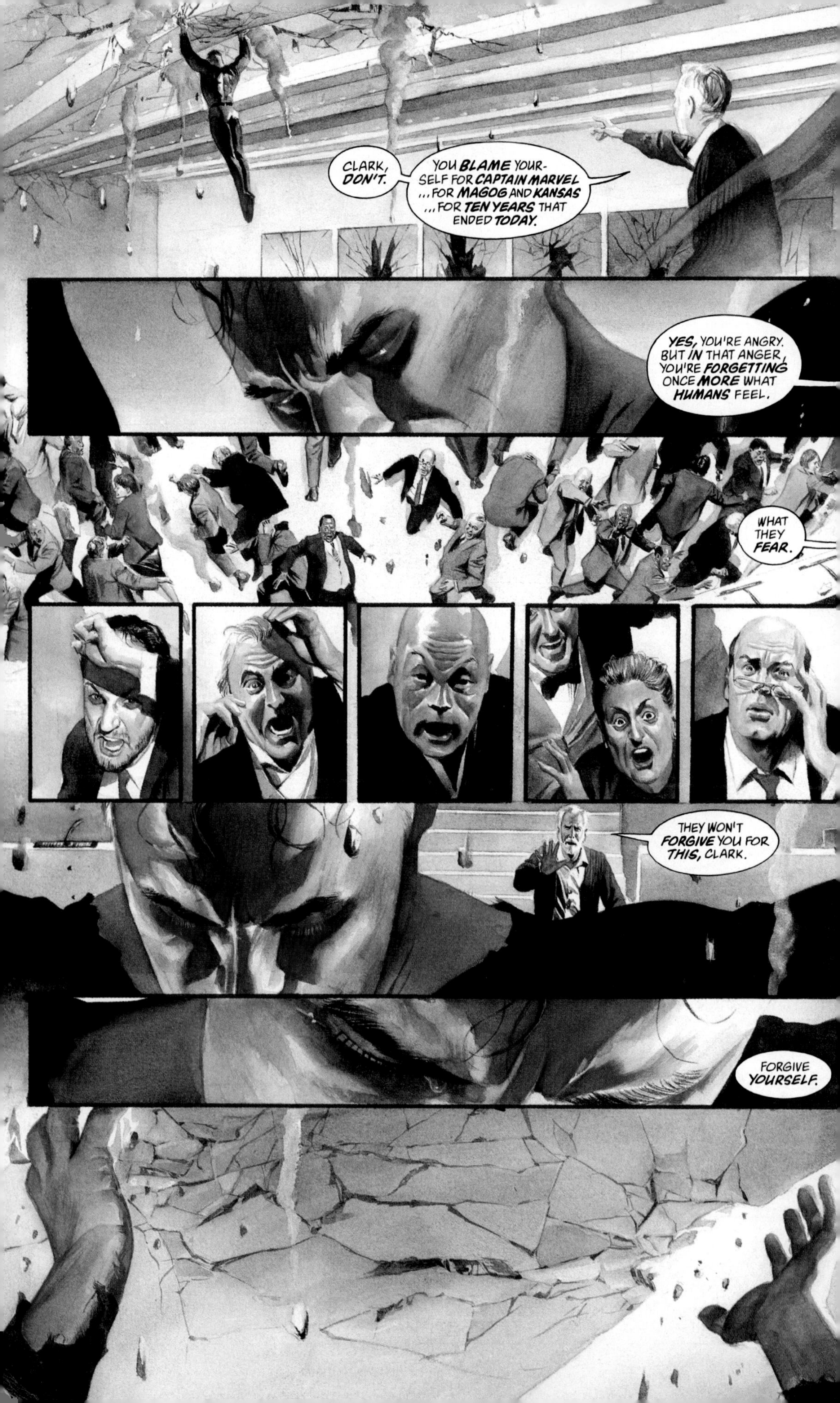
CLARK, DON'T.
YOU BLAME YOURSELF FOR CAPTAIN MARVEL ...FOR MAGOG AND KANSAS ...FOR TEN YEARS THAT ENDED TODAY.
YES, YOU'RE ANGRY. BUT IN THAT ANGER, YOU'RE FORGETTING ONCE MORE WHAT HUMANS FEEL.
WHAT THEY FEAR.
THEY WON'T FORGIVE YOU FOR THIS, CLARK.
FORGIVE YOURSELF.

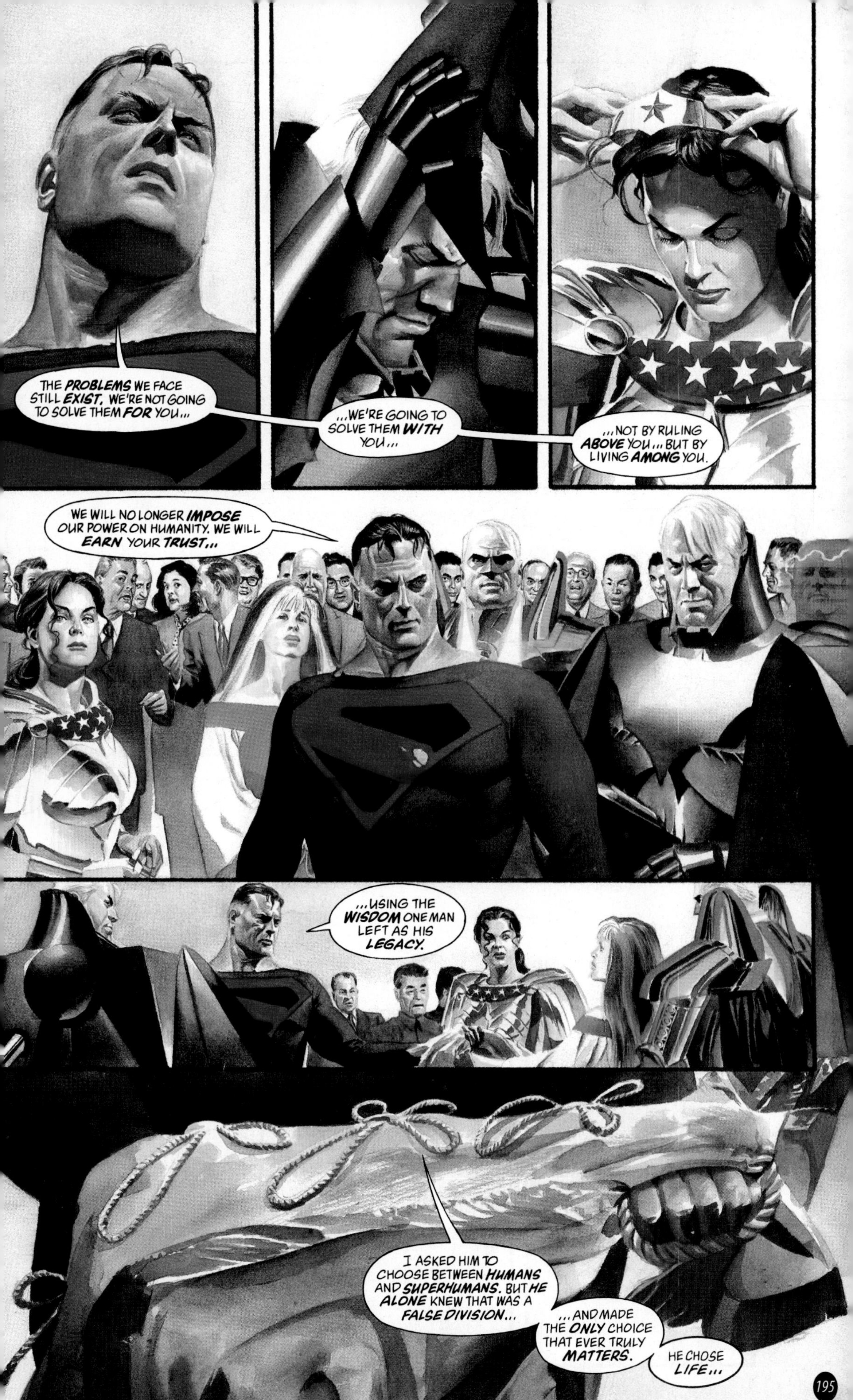
THE PROBLEMS WE FACE STILL EXIST. WE'RE NOT GOING TO SOLVE THEM FOR YOU...
...WE'RE GOING TO SOLVE THEM WITH YOU...
...NOT BY RULING ABOVE YOU... BUT BY LIVING AMONG YOU.
WE WILL NO LONGER IMPOSE OUR POWER ON HUMANITY. WE WILL EARN YOUR TRUST...
...USING THE WISDOM ONE MAN LEFT AS HIS LEGACY.
I ASKED HIM TO CHOOSE BETWEEN HUMANS AND SUPERHUMANS. BUT HE ALONE KNEW THAT WAS A FALSE DIVISION...
...AND MADE THE ONLY CHOICE THAT EVER TRULY MATTERS.
HE CHOSE LIFE...

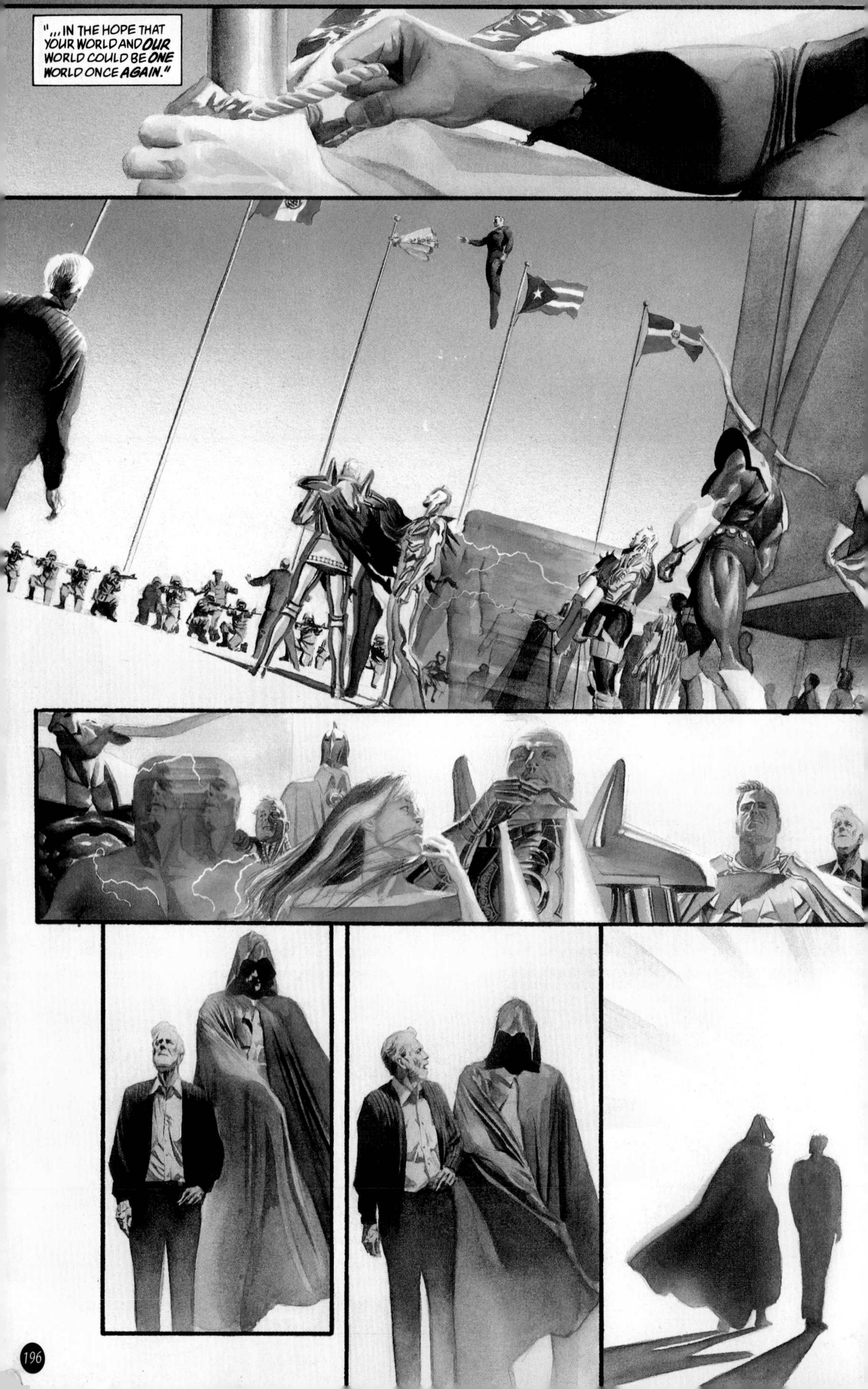
"...IN THE HOPE THAT YOUR WORLD AND OUR WORLD COULD BE ONE WORLD ONCE AGAIN."

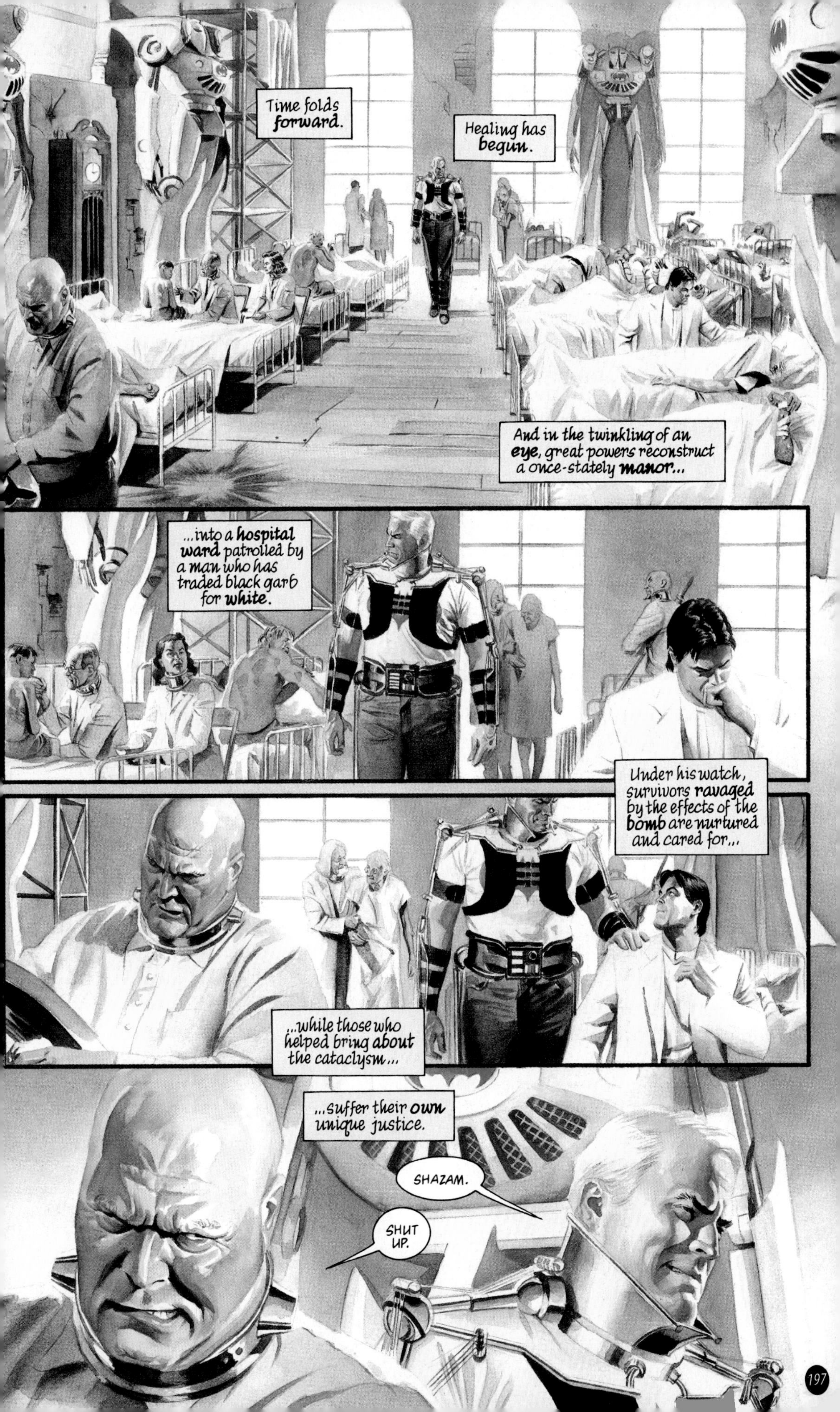
Time folds forward.
Healing has begun.
And in the twinkling of an eye, great powers reconstruct a once-stately manor...
...into a hospital ward patrolled by a man who has traded black garb for white.
Under his watch, survivors ravaged by the effects of the bomb are nurtured and cared for...
...while those who helped bring about the cataclysm...
...suffer their own unique justice.
SHAZAM.
SHUT UP.

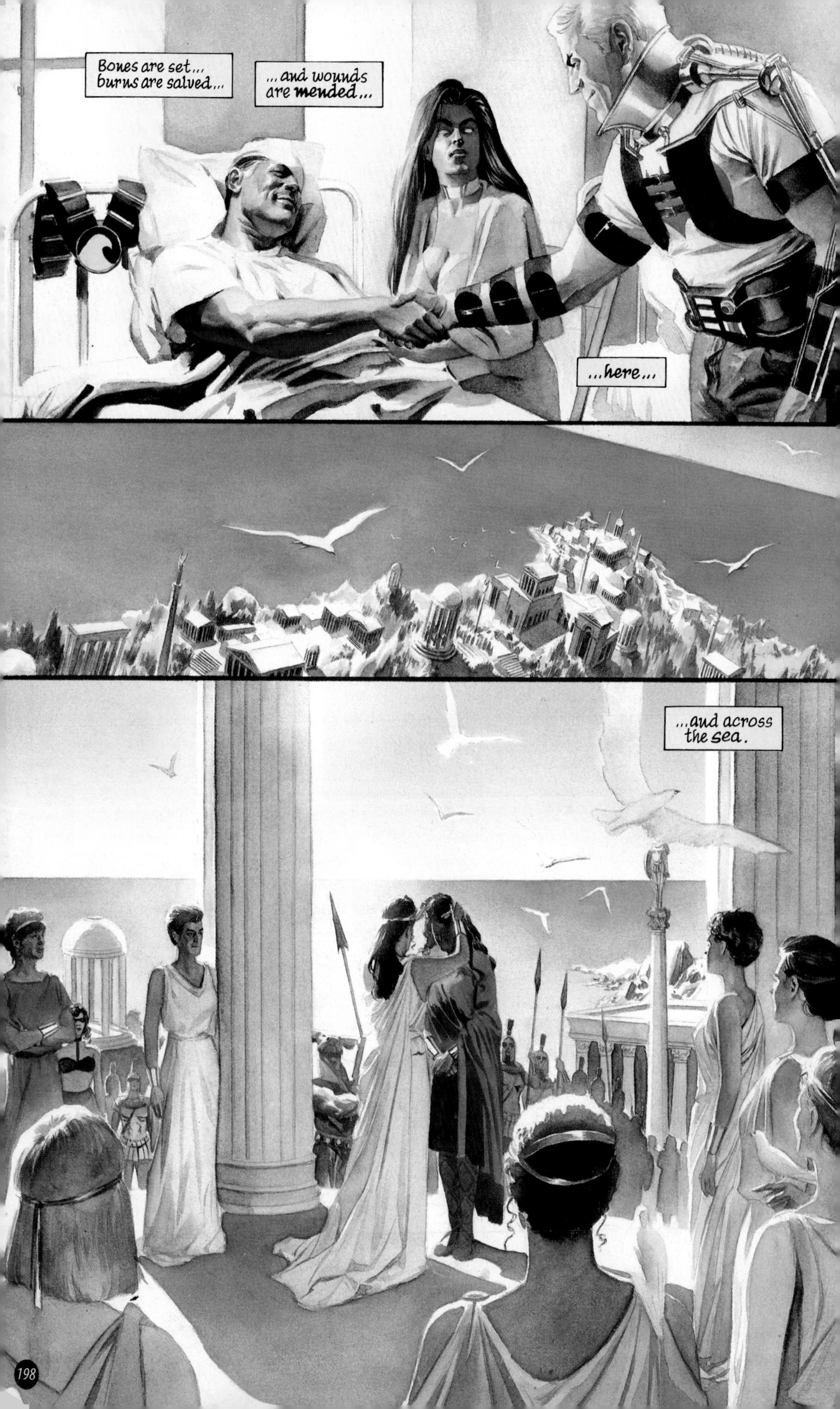

Bones are set... burns are salved...
...and wounds are **mended**...
...*here*...
...and across the *sea*.

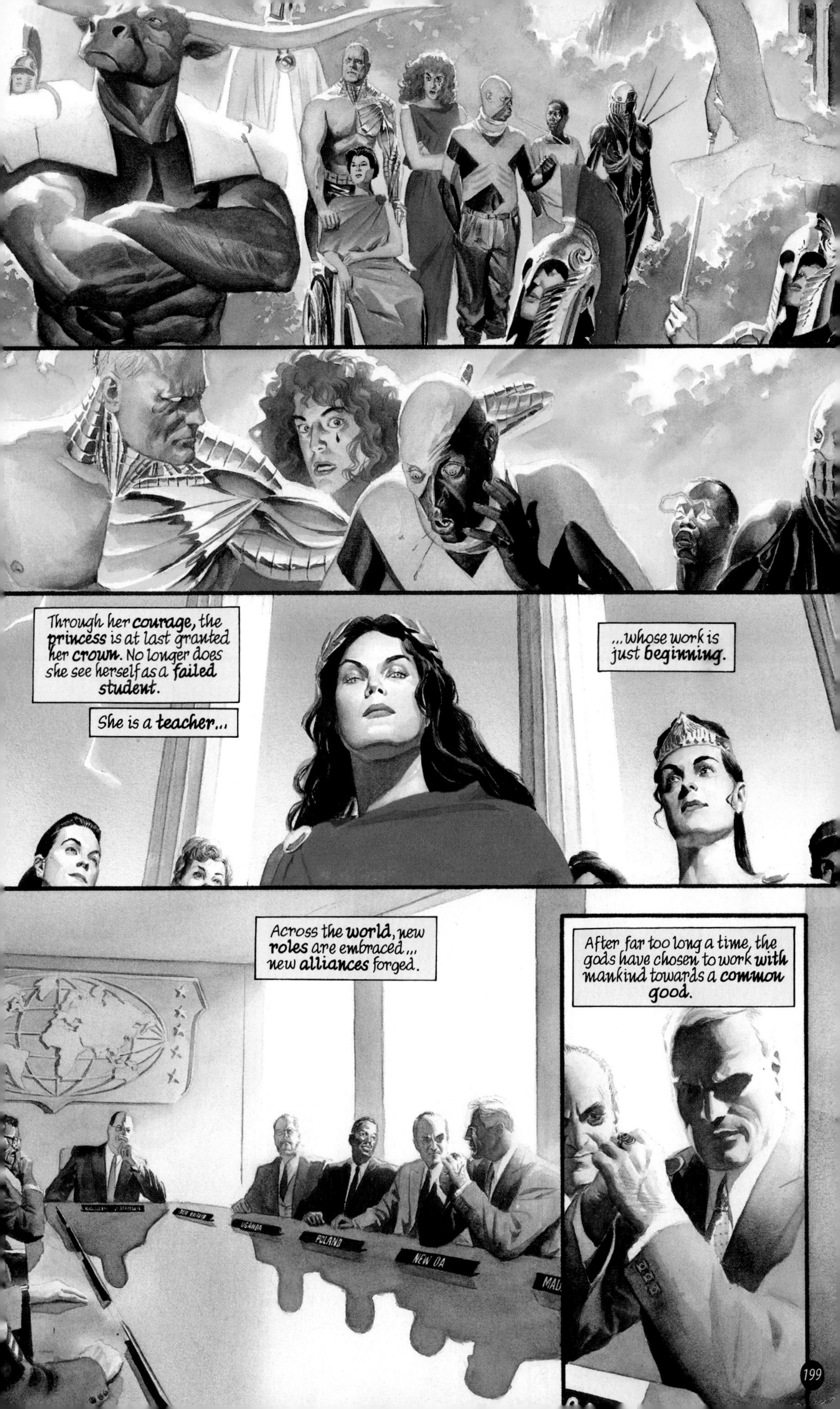

Through her courage, the princess is at last granted her crown. No longer does she see herself as a failed student.
She is a teacher...
...whose work is just beginning.
Across the world, new roles are embraced... new alliances forged.
UGANDA
POLAND
After far too long a time, the gods have chosen to work with mankind towards a common good.

Only **one** works alone.

QUITE A **MEMORIAL**.

AS IT **SHOULD** BE.

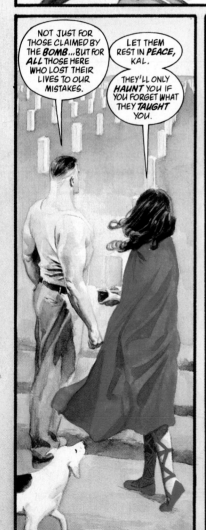

NOT JUST FOR THOSE CLAIMED BY THE **BOMB**... BUT FOR **ALL** THOSE HERE WHO LOST THEIR LIVES TO OUR MISTAKES.

LET THEM REST IN **PEACE**, KAL.

THEY'LL ONLY **HAUNT** YOU IF YOU FORGET WHAT THEY **TAUGHT** YOU.

SPEAKING OF **WHICH**...

WHAT'S **THIS**?

A **GIFT**.

A LITTLE SOMETHING TO HELP YOU SEE MORE **CLEARLY**.

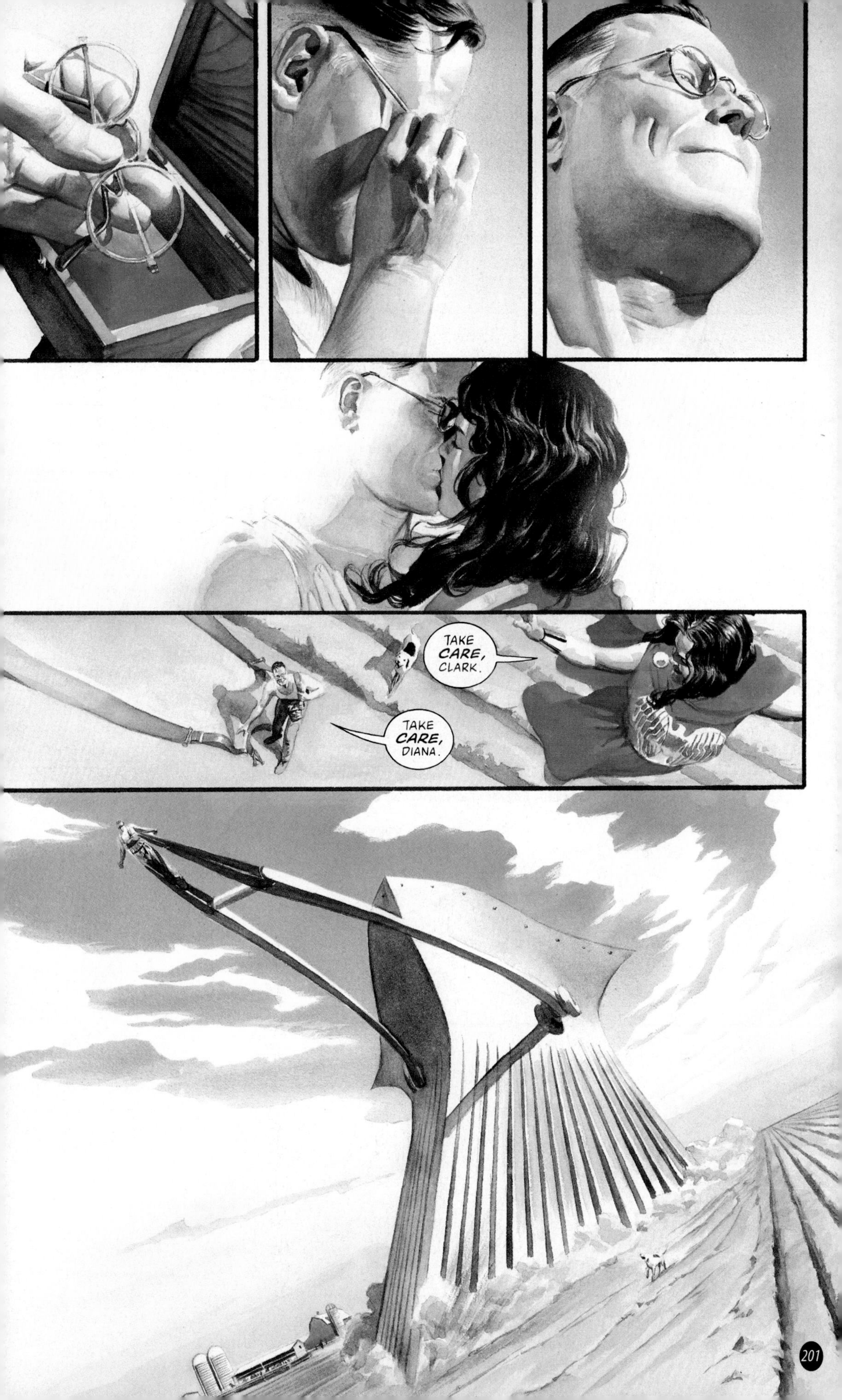
TAKE CARE, CLARK.
TAKE CARE, DIANA.

ALL THE *SINS* HAVE BEEN *EXPOSED,* SPECTRE. TELL ME, IN THE *END...* WHO DO YOU *PUNISH?*

WHO IS *RESPONSIBLE* FOR WHAT HAS HAPPENED?

NO ONE NEED SUFFER ANY *FURTHER* FOR THE TRAGEDIES WE HAVE *WITNESSED,* NORMAN McCAY. DO NOT *MOCK* ME.

I'M *NOT.* I'M MERELY *WONDERING...*

WHEN YOU FIRST APPEARED *BEFORE* ME, YOU SAID YOU NEEDED A *HUMAN SOUL* TO BE YOUR *ANCHOR...* AND YET...

...YOU YOURSELF WERE ONCE AN ORDINARY MAN. TELL ME... WHAT WOULD *HIS* PERSPECTIVE HAVE BEEN?

AN EXCELLENT *QUESTION.*

BE *WELL,* NORMAN McCAY. YOU HAVE WATCHED THE TITANS WALK THE *EARTH...* AND YOU HAVE KEPT *STRIDE.*

PERHAPS YOU ARE MORE LIKE THEM THAN YOU *REALIZE.*

YOU *EXIST...* TO GIVE *HOPE.*

202

ONE YEAR LATER..

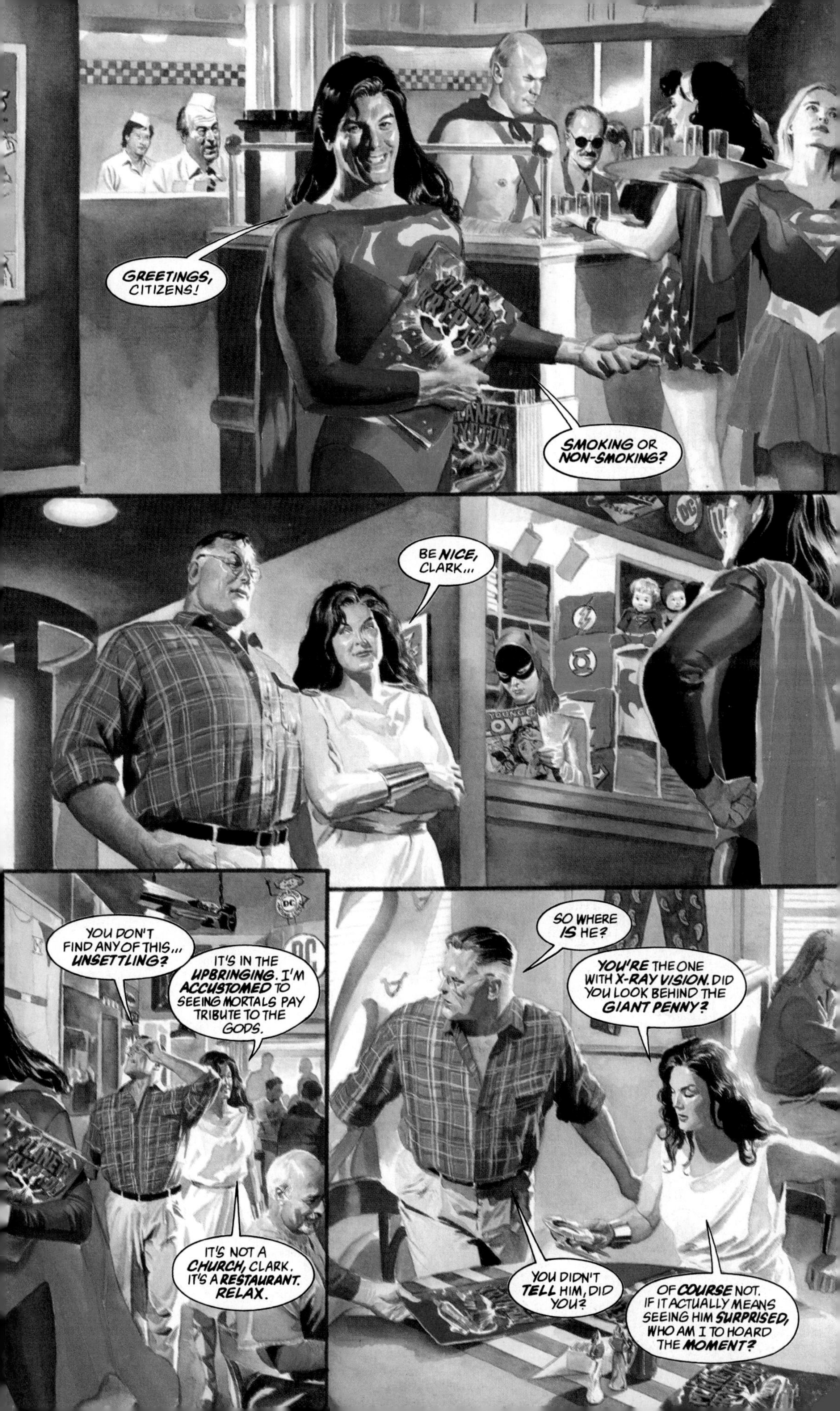
GREETINGS, CITIZENS!
SMOKING OR NON-SMOKING?
BE NICE, CLARK...
YOU DON'T FIND ANY OF THIS... UNSETTLING?
IT'S IN THE UPBRINGING. I'M ACCUSTOMED TO SEEING MORTALS PAY TRIBUTE TO THE GODS.
IT'S NOT A CHURCH, CLARK. IT'S A RESTAURANT. RELAX.
SO WHERE IS HE?
YOU'RE THE ONE WITH X-RAY VISION. DID YOU LOOK BEHIND THE GIANT PENNY?
YOU DIDN'T TELL HIM, DID YOU?
OF COURSE NOT. IF IT ACTUALLY MEANS SEEING HIM SURPRISED, WHO AM I TO HOARD THE MOMENT?

IT'S AWFULLY *CROWDED*. YOU'RE SURE WE WON'T BE *RECOGNIZED*?

HARDLY *LIKELY*. IN THE FIRST PLACE, YOU WROTE THE *BOOK* ON *SECRET IDEN-TITIES*...

KRYPTONITE

...AND IN THE *SECOND* PLACE, AMIDST ALL *THIS* TAWDRY BRIC-A-BRAC, I DOUBT THEY'D TAKE *NOTICE* OF US IF WE WERE FIGHTING THE *LEGION OF DOOM* IN *FULL COSTUME*.

CLARK. DIANA.

THERE YOU ARE. YOU SNUCK *UP* ON ME.

ME. HOW DO YOU *DO* THAT?

IT'S GOOD TO SEE YOU UNDER BRIGHTER CIRCUMSTANCES, BRUCE. HOW ARE THE *BOYS*?

DICK'S HEADED FOR A FULL RECOVERY. IB'N...*WELL*...

...DICK'S *DAUGHTER* IS...*COUNSELLING* HIM. MAYBE HE'LL TURN AROUND *YET*...IF HE CAN SHED THE LESSONS OF THE *LEAGUE OF ASSASSINS*.

THAT'S WHAT *HAPPENS* WHEN YOU'RE RAISED BY AN ISOLATED SOCIETY OF *ZEALOTS*. YOU END UP A LITTLE *BRAIN-WASHED*.

YOU *DON'T SAY*.

MAY I BRING YOU SOMETHING TO *DRINK*?

WATER'S FINE.

MILK.

COFFEE.

AND KEEP IT *COMING*.

206

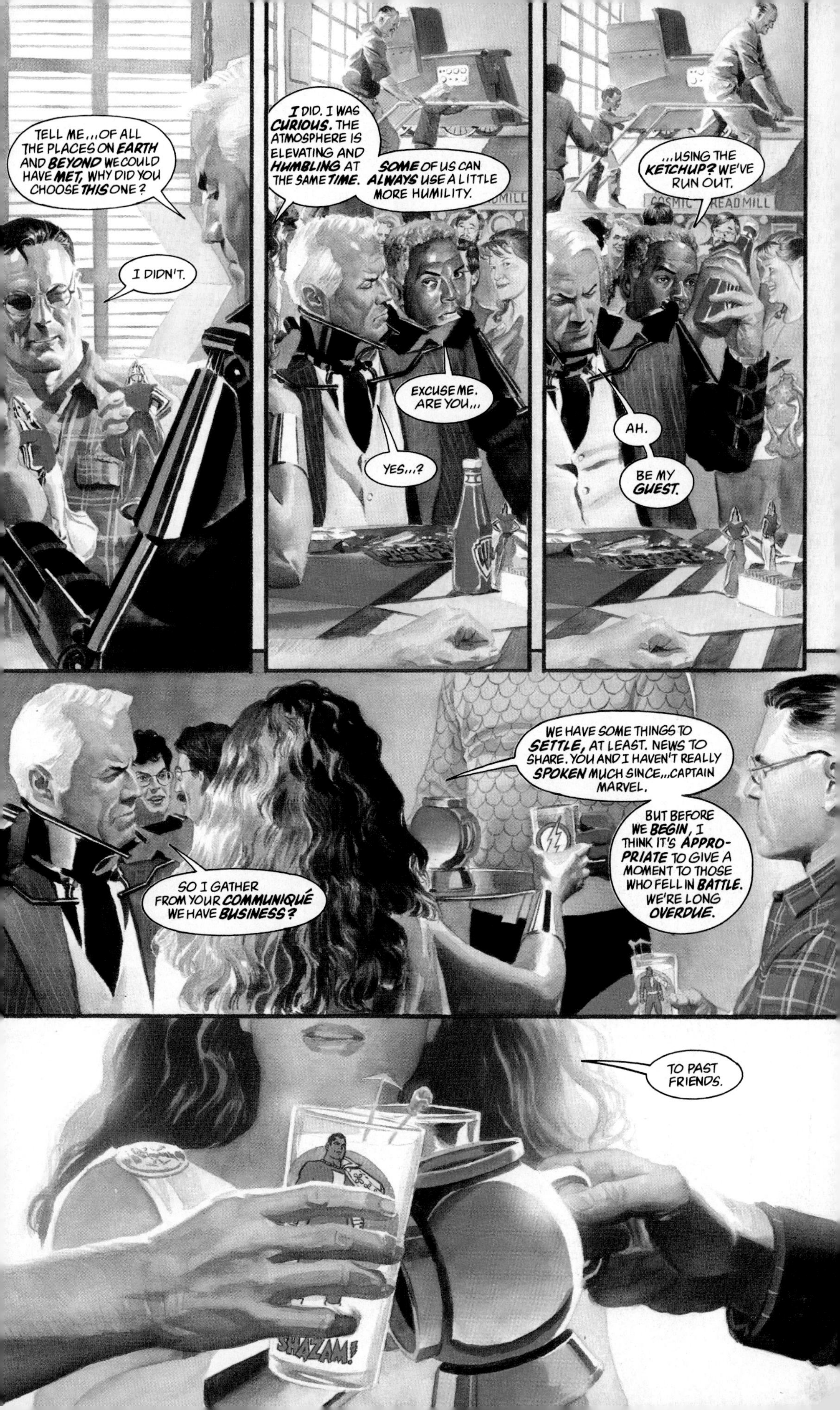
TELL ME...OF ALL THE PLACES ON EARTH AND BEYOND WE COULD HAVE MET, WHY DID YOU CHOOSE THIS ONE?
I DIDN'T.
I DID. I WAS CURIOUS. THE ATMOSPHERE IS ELEVATING AND HUMBLING AT THE SAME TIME.
SOME OF US CAN ALWAYS USE A LITTLE MORE HUMILITY.
EXCUSE ME. ARE YOU...
YES...?
...USING THE KETCHUP? WE'VE RUN OUT.
COSMIC TREADMILL
AH.
BE MY GUEST.
SO I GATHER FROM YOUR COMMUNIQUÉ WE HAVE BUSINESS?
WE HAVE SOME THINGS TO SETTLE, AT LEAST. NEWS TO SHARE. YOU AND I HAVEN'T REALLY SPOKEN MUCH SINCE...CAPTAIN MARVEL.
BUT BEFORE WE BEGIN, I THINK IT'S APPROPRIATE TO GIVE A MOMENT TO THOSE WHO FELL IN BATTLE. WE'RE LONG OVERDUE.
TO PAST FRIENDS.
SHAZAM!

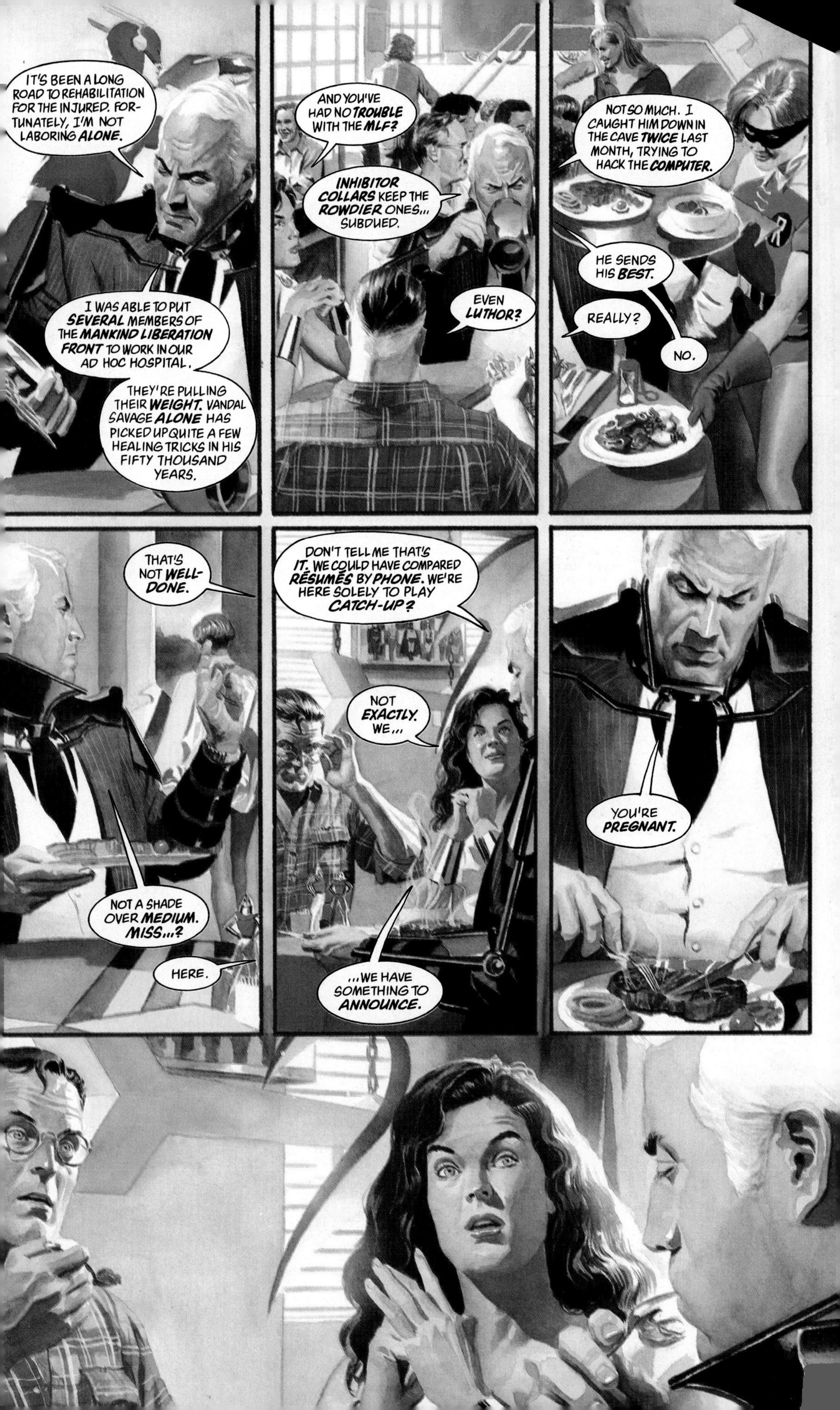
IT'S BEEN A LONG ROAD TO REHABILITATION FOR THE INJURED. FORTUNATELY, I'M NOT LABORING ALONE.
I WAS ABLE TO PUT SEVERAL MEMBERS OF THE MANKIND LIBERATION FRONT TO WORK IN OUR AD HOC HOSPITAL.
THEY'RE PULLING THEIR WEIGHT. VANDAL SAVAGE ALONE HAS PICKED UP QUITE A FEW HEALING TRICKS IN HIS FIFTY THOUSAND YEARS.
AND YOU'VE HAD NO TROUBLE WITH THE MLF?
INHIBITOR COLLARS KEEP THE ROWDIER ONES... SUBDUED.
EVEN LUTHOR?
NOT SO MUCH. I CAUGHT HIM DOWN IN THE CAVE TWICE LAST MONTH, TRYING TO HACK THE COMPUTER.
HE SENDS HIS BEST.
REALLY?
NO.
THAT'S NOT WELL-DONE.
NOT A SHADE OVER MEDIUM. MISS...?
HERE.
DON'T TELL ME THAT'S IT. WE COULD HAVE COMPARED RÉSUMÉS BY PHONE. WE'RE HERE SOLELY TO PLAY CATCH-UP?
NOT EXACTLY. WE...
...WE HAVE SOMETHING TO ANNOUNCE.
YOU'RE PREGNANT.

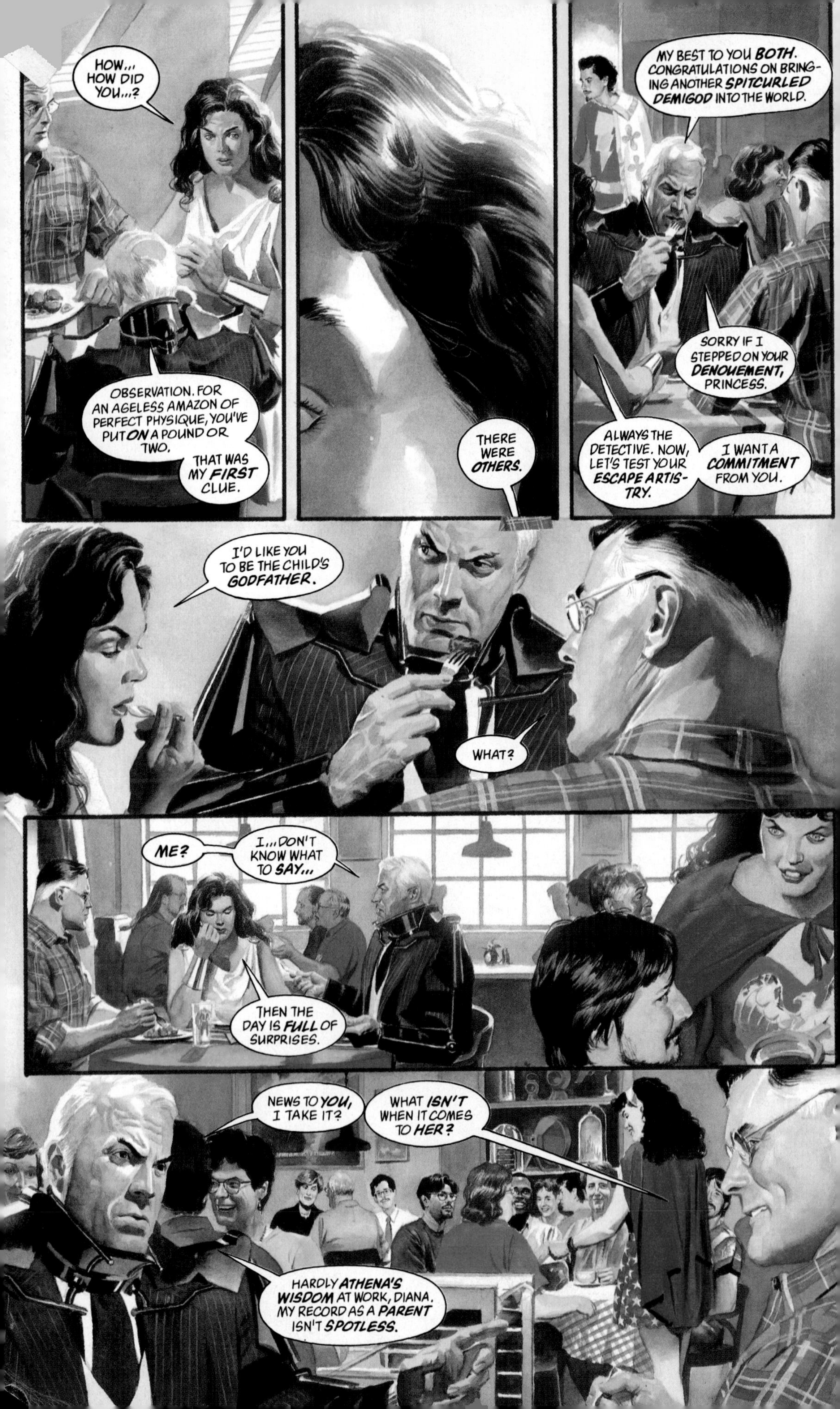
HOW... HOW DID YOU...?
OBSERVATION. FOR AN AGELESS AMAZON OF PERFECT PHYSIQUE, YOU'VE PUT ON A POUND OR TWO.
THAT WAS MY FIRST CLUE.
THERE WERE OTHERS.
MY BEST TO YOU BOTH. CONGRATULATIONS ON BRINGING ANOTHER SPITCURLED DEMIGOD INTO THE WORLD.
SORRY IF I STEPPED ON YOUR DENOUEMENT, PRINCESS.
ALWAYS THE DETECTIVE. NOW, LET'S TEST YOUR ESCAPE ARTISTRY.
I WANT A COMMITMENT FROM YOU.
I'D LIKE YOU TO BE THE CHILD'S GODFATHER.
WHAT?
ME?
I... DON'T KNOW WHAT TO SAY...
THEN THE DAY IS FULL OF SURPRISES.
NEWS TO YOU, I TAKE IT?
WHAT ISN'T WHEN IT COMES TO HER?
HARDLY ATHENA'S WISDOM AT WORK, DIANA. MY RECORD AS A PARENT ISN'T SPOTLESS.

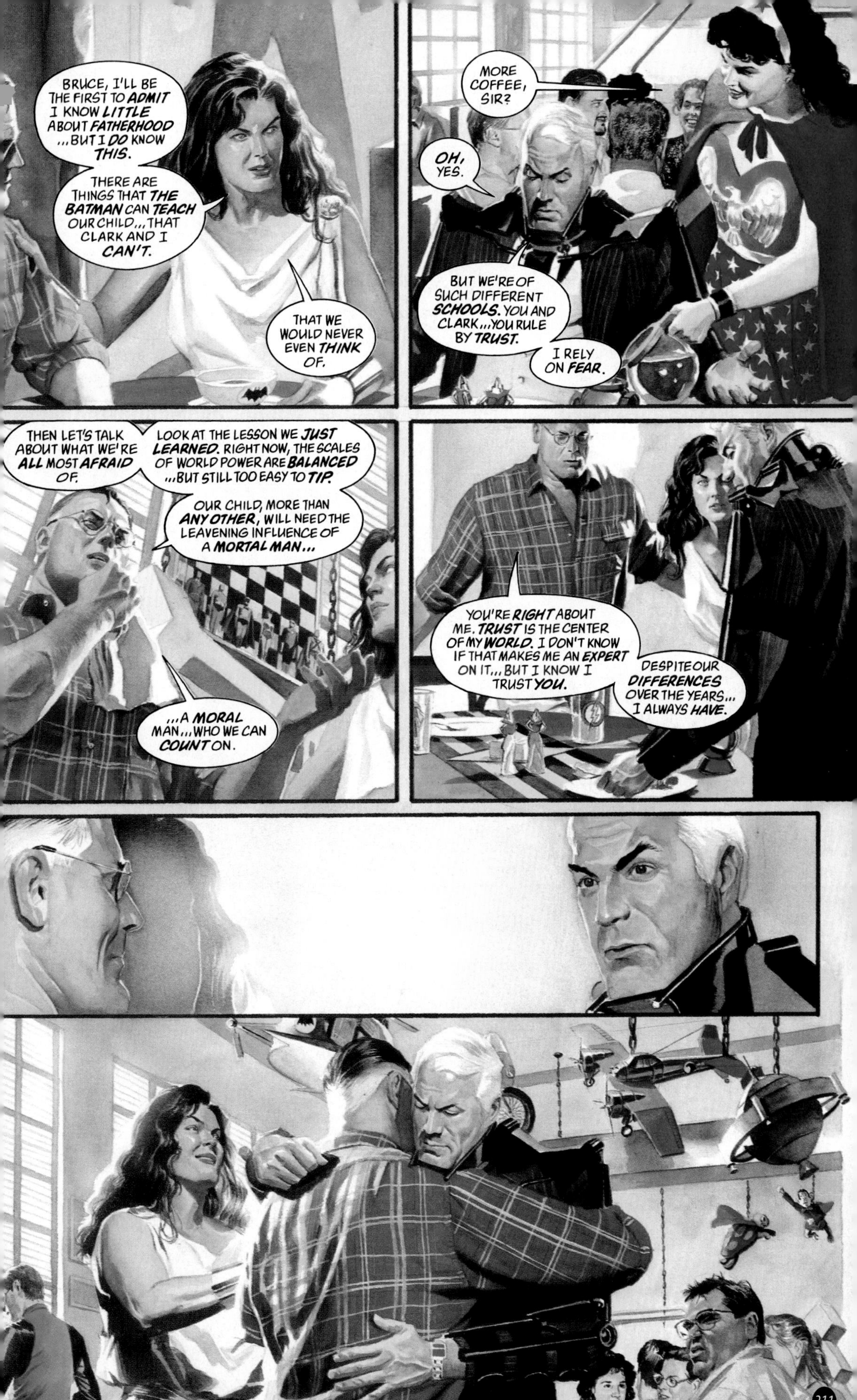

BRUCE, I'LL BE THE FIRST TO ADMIT I KNOW LITTLE ABOUT FATHERHOOD ...BUT I DO KNOW THIS.
THERE ARE THINGS THAT THE BATMAN CAN TEACH OUR CHILD... THAT CLARK AND I CAN'T.
THAT WE WOULD NEVER EVEN THINK OF.
MORE COFFEE, SIR?
OH, YES.
BUT WE'RE OF SUCH DIFFERENT SCHOOLS. YOU AND CLARK... YOU RULE BY TRUST.
I RELY ON FEAR.
THEN LET'S TALK ABOUT WHAT WE'RE ALL MOST AFRAID OF.
LOOK AT THE LESSON WE JUST LEARNED. RIGHT NOW, THE SCALES OF WORLD POWER ARE BALANCED ...BUT STILL TOO EASY TO TIP.
OUR CHILD, MORE THAN ANY OTHER, WILL NEED THE LEAVENING INFLUENCE OF A MORTAL MAN...
...A MORAL MAN... WHO WE CAN COUNT ON.
YOU'RE RIGHT ABOUT ME. TRUST IS THE CENTER OF MY WORLD. I DON'T KNOW IF THAT MAKES ME AN EXPERT ON IT... BUT I KNOW I TRUST YOU.
DESPITE OUR DIFFERENCES OVER THE YEARS... I ALWAYS HAVE.

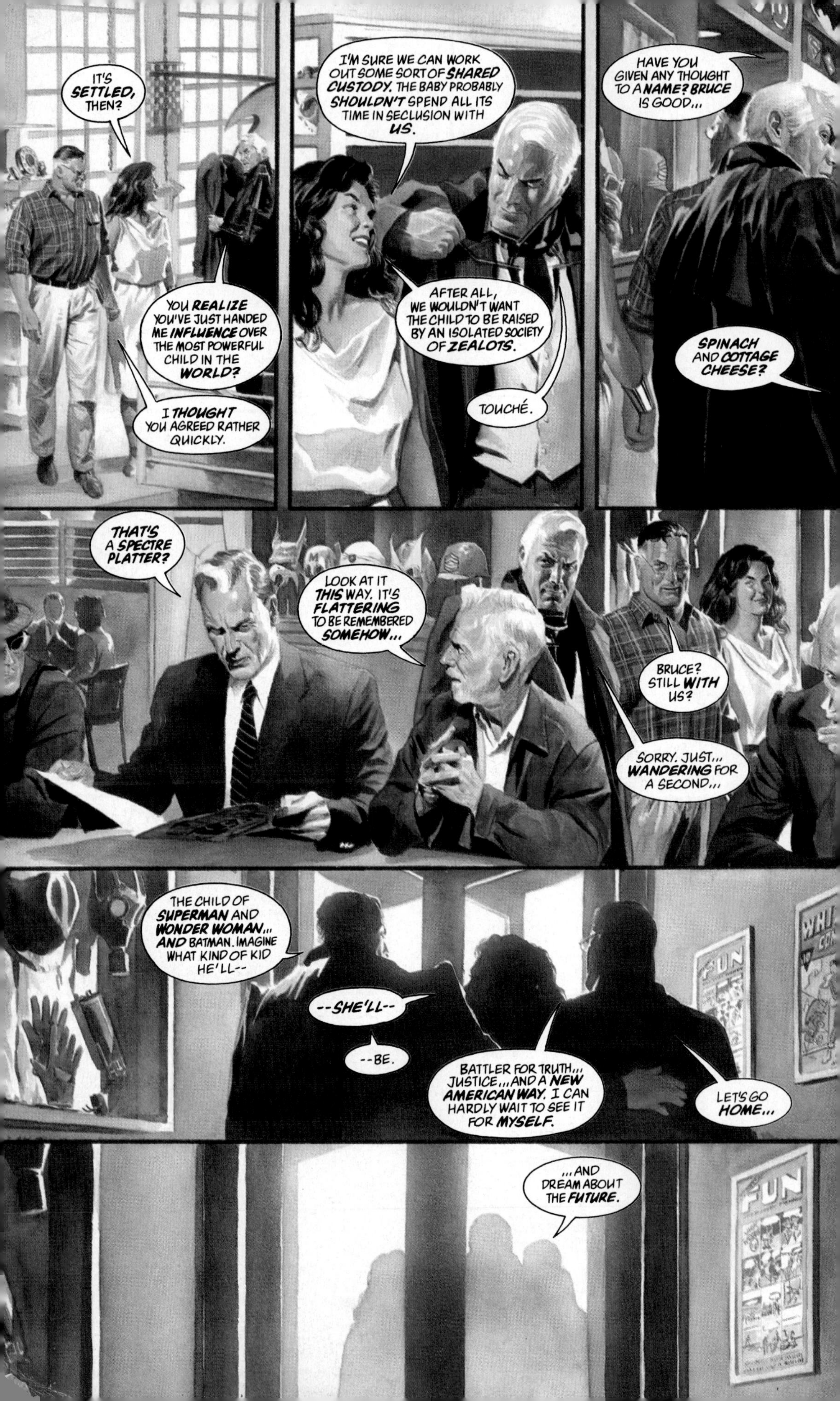
IT'S SETTLED, THEN?
I'M SURE WE CAN WORK OUT SOME SORT OF SHARED CUSTODY. THE BABY PROBABLY SHOULDN'T SPEND ALL ITS TIME IN SECLUSION WITH US.
HAVE YOU GIVEN ANY THOUGHT TO A NAME? BRUCE IS GOOD...
YOU REALIZE YOU'VE JUST HANDED ME INFLUENCE OVER THE MOST POWERFUL CHILD IN THE WORLD?
I THOUGHT YOU AGREED RATHER QUICKLY.
AFTER ALL, WE WOULDN'T WANT THE CHILD TO BE RAISED BY AN ISOLATED SOCIETY OF ZEALOTS.
TOUCHÉ.
SPINACH AND COTTAGE CHEESE?
THAT'S A SPECTRE PLATTER?
LOOK AT IT THIS WAY. IT'S FLATTERING TO BE REMEMBERED SOMEHOW...
BRUCE? STILL WITH US?
SORRY. JUST... WANDERING FOR A SECOND...
THE CHILD OF SUPERMAN AND WONDER WOMAN... AND BATMAN. IMAGINE WHAT KIND OF KID HE'LL--
--SHE'LL--
--BE.
BATTLER FOR TRUTH... JUSTICE... AND A NEW AMERICAN WAY. I CAN HARDLY WAIT TO SEE IT FOR MYSELF.
LET'S GO HOME...
...AND DREAM ABOUT THE FUTURE.

APOCRYPHA

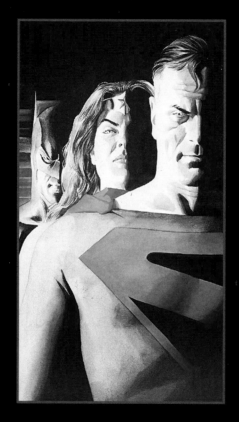

THE SPECTRE

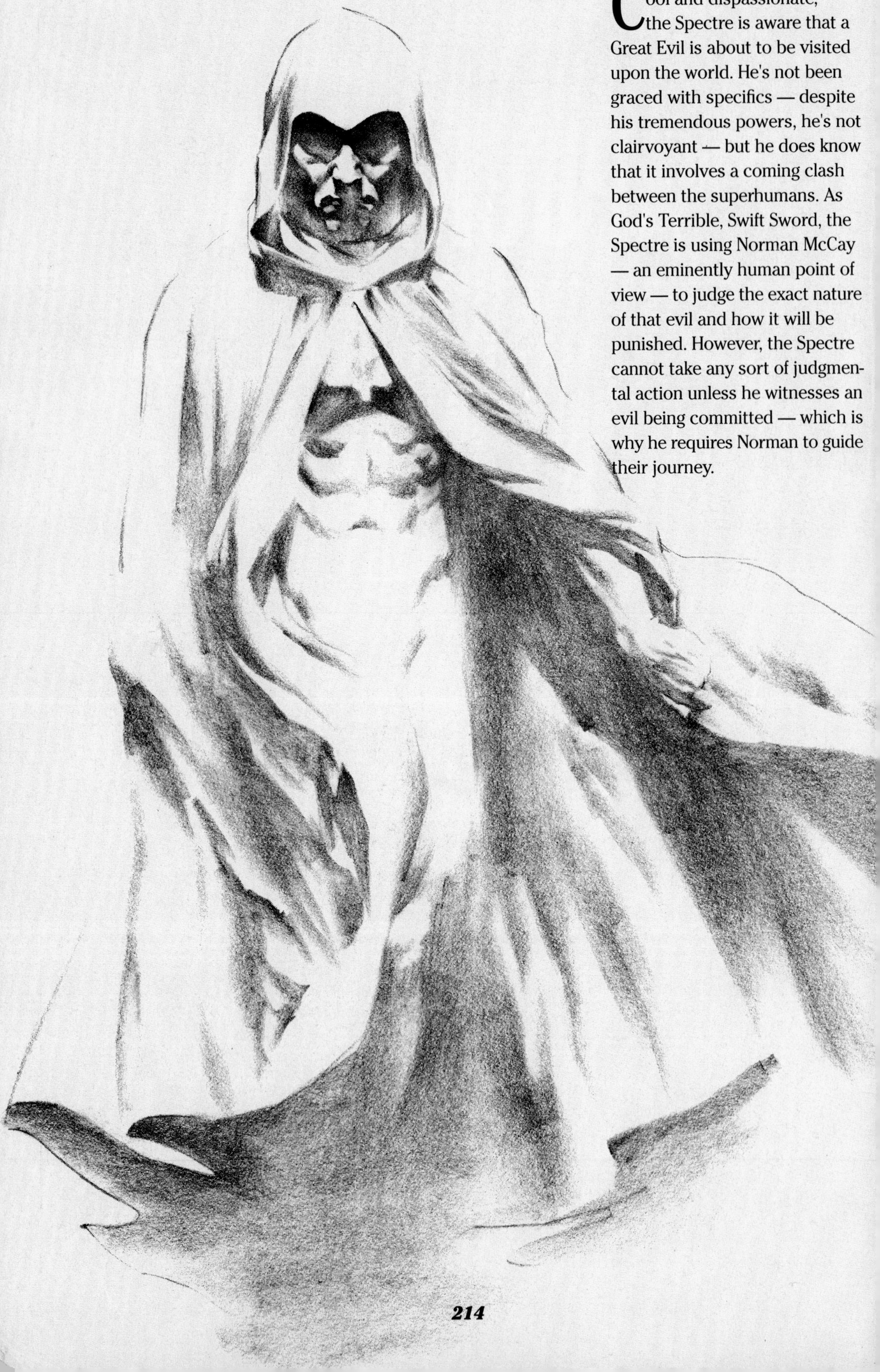

Cool and dispassionate, the Spectre is aware that a Great Evil is about to be visited upon the world. He's not been graced with specifics — despite his tremendous powers, he's not clairvoyant — but he does know that it involves a coming clash between the superhumans. As God's Terrible, Swift Sword, the Spectre is using Norman McCay — an eminently human point of view — to judge the exact nature of that evil and how it will be punished. However, the Spectre cannot take any sort of judgmental action unless he witnesses an evil being committed — which is why he requires Norman to guide their journey.

NORMAN McCAY

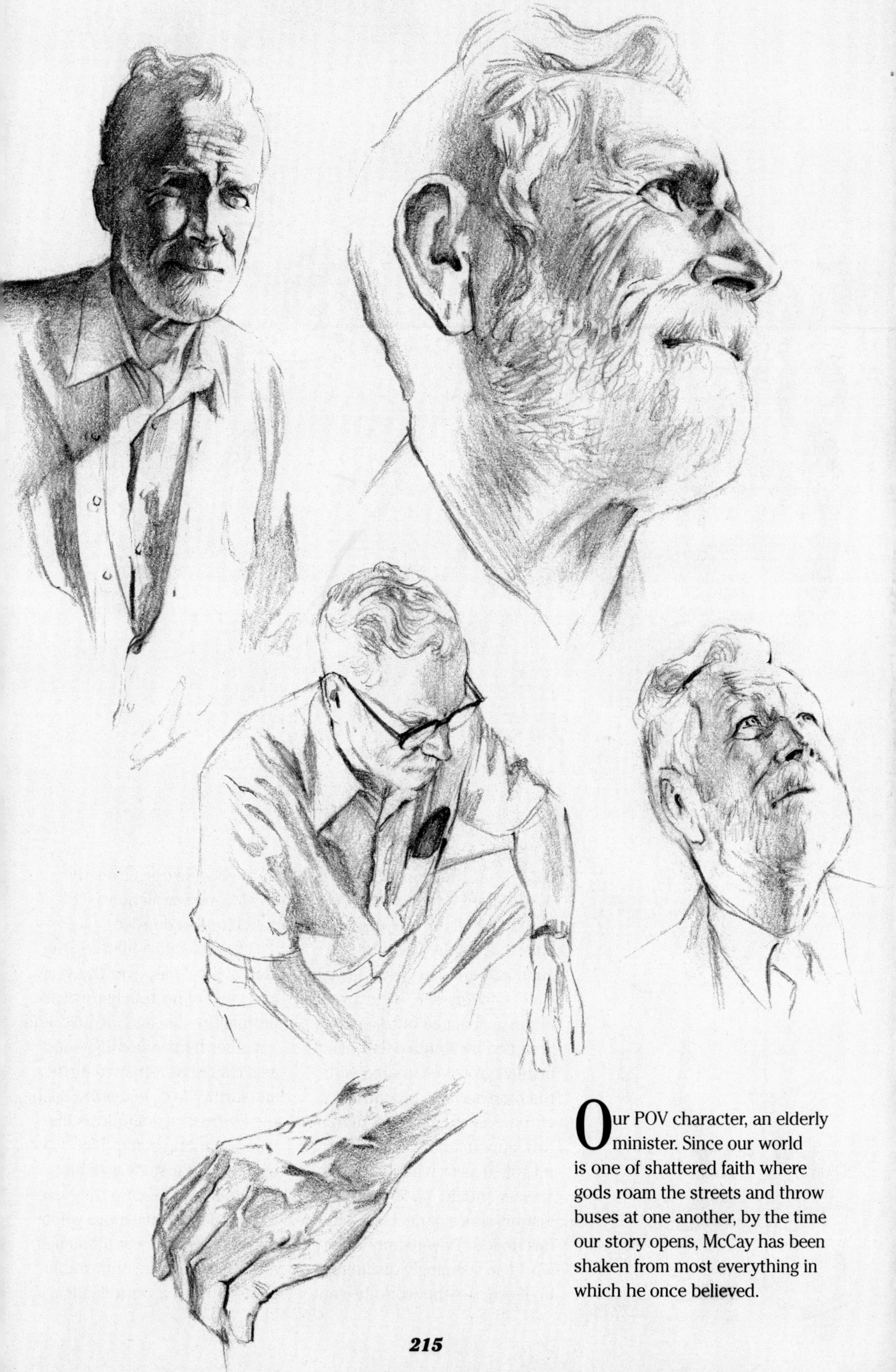

Our POV character, an elderly minister. Since our world is one of shattered faith where gods roam the streets and throw buses at one another, by the time our story opens, McCay has been shaken from most everything in which he once believed.

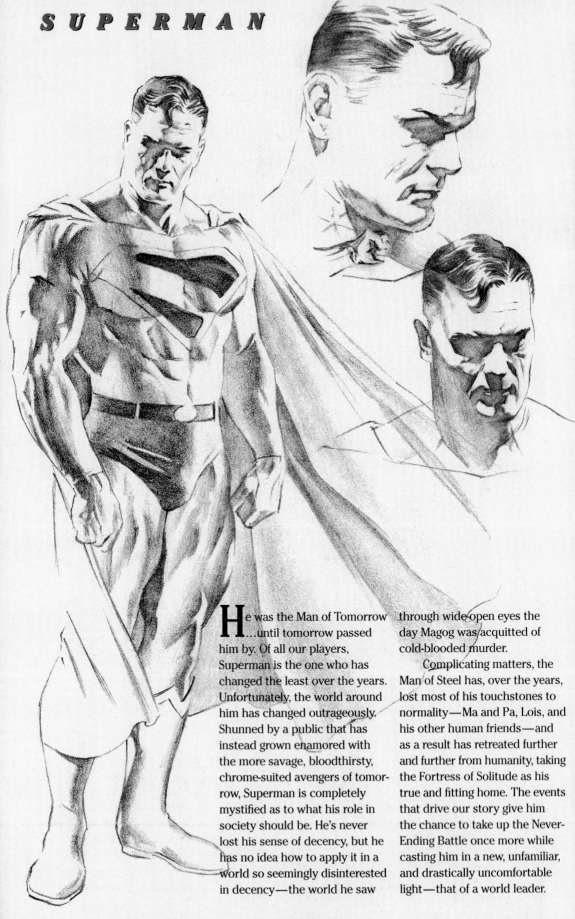

SUPERMAN

He was the Man of Tomorrow ...until tomorrow passed him by. Of all our players, Superman is the one who has changed the least over the years. Unfortunately, the world around him has changed outrageously. Shunned by a public that has instead grown enamored with the more savage, bloodthirsty, chrome-suited avengers of tomorrow, Superman is completely mystified as to what his role in society should be. He's never lost his sense of decency, but he has no idea how to apply it in a world so seemingly disinterested in decency—the world he saw through wide-open eyes the day Magog was acquitted of cold-blooded murder.

Complicating matters, the Man of Steel has, over the years, lost most of his touchstones to normality—Ma and Pa, Lois, and his other human friends—and as a result has retreated further and further from humanity, taking the Fortress of Solitude as his true and fitting home. The events that drive our story give him the chance to take up the Never-Ending Battle once more while casting him in a new, unfamiliar, and drastically uncomfortable light—that of a world leader.

She is much the same character she has always been—but she is coping (not well) with the realization that she has not well served her gods-given mission as an ambassador and teacher of peace but as an Amazon warrior. As our crisis builds, she will naturally seek deliverance through military strategy and final combat.

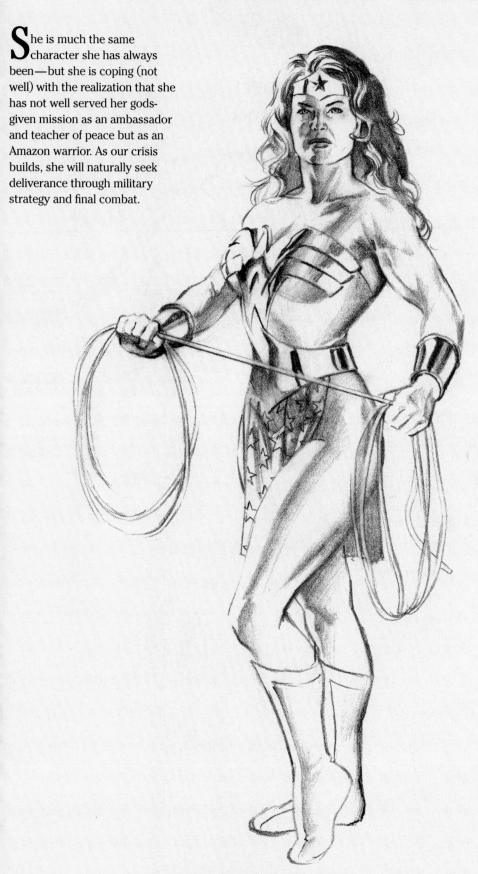

CAPTAIN MARVEL

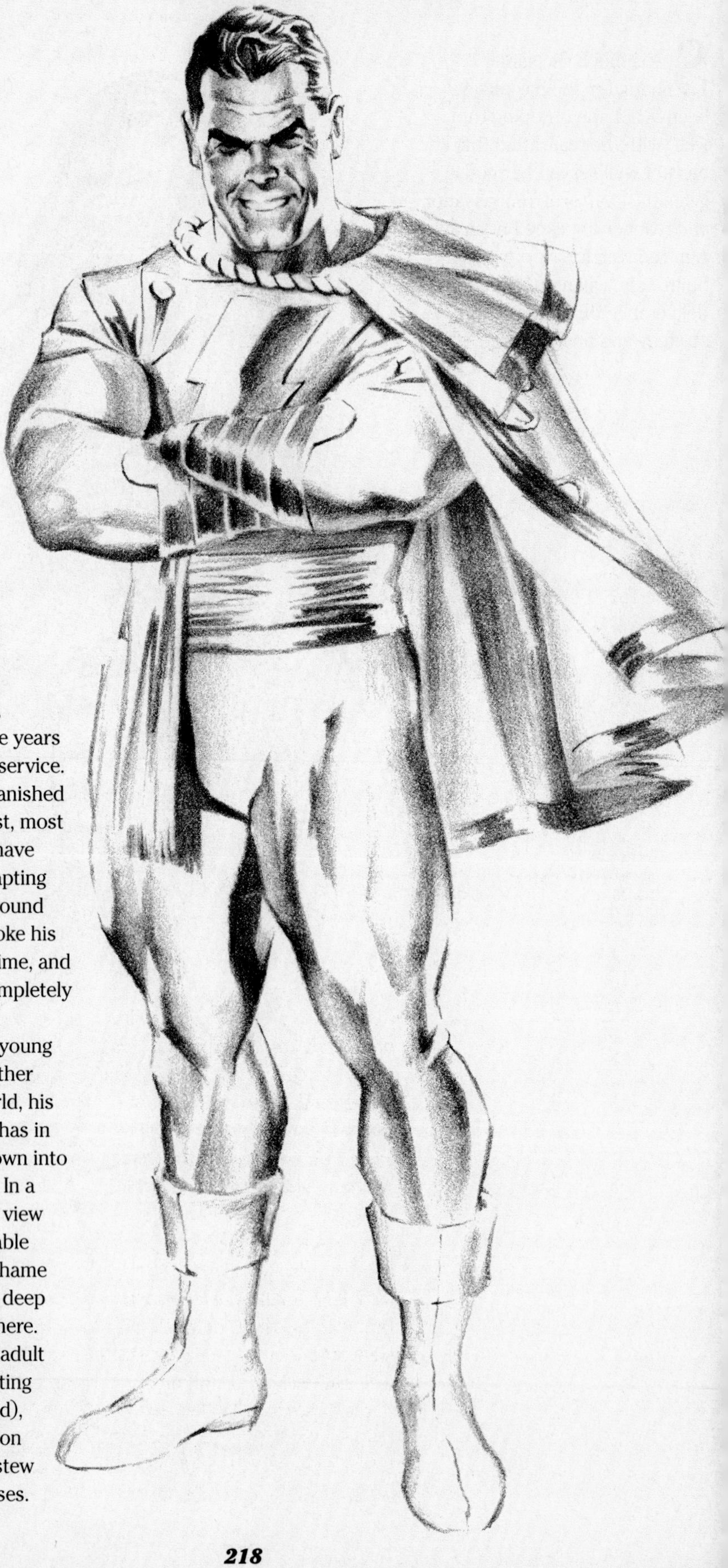

Like most of his peers, Captain Marvel chose years ago to retire from public service. In point of fact, Marvel vanished early; as one of the purest, most noble heroes, he would have had the hardest time adapting to the grim new world around him. One day, Marvel spoke his magic word for the last time, and Billy Batson's life was completely his own again.

Unfortunately, given young Billy's immaturity and rather naive outlook on the world, his attitude towards Marvel has in the intervening years grown into something quite twisted. In a society that has come to view super-heroes as undesirable monsters, Billy's secret shame is that he has one hiding deep down inside him somewhere. By the time we meet the adult Billy (grown into the spitting image of the Marvel of old), he'll be a leading champion of human rights…and a stew of schizophrenic psychoses.

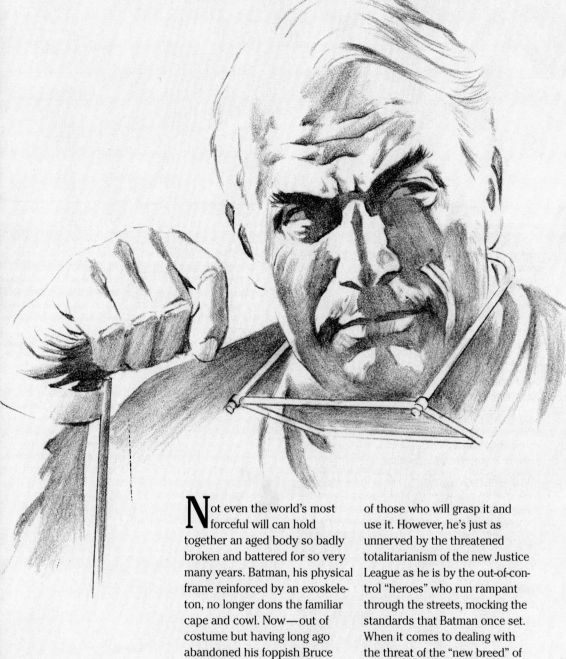

Not even the world's most forceful will can hold together an aged body so badly broken and battered for so very many years. Batman, his physical frame reinforced by an exoskeleton, no longer dons the familiar cape and cowl. Now—out of costume but having long ago abandoned his foppish Bruce Wayne persona—he holes up night and day in his Batcave, remotely monitoring his robotic Bat-Knights, using them (with tremendous success) to maintain order in Gotham City. Batman —the aristocrat—believes (as billionaires are wont to do) that a measure of power and rule rightfully belongs in the hands of those who will grasp it and use it. However, he's just as unnerved by the threatened totalitarianism of the new Justice League as he is by the out-of-control "heroes" who run rampant through the streets, mocking the standards that Batman once set. When it comes to dealing with the threat of the "new breed" of heroes, Batman—as always— has his own ideas. Like Luthor, he's convinced that a steady, concentrated, methodical approach to the problem will win him the world…but unlike Luthor, Batman is spurred on instead to fast, hard-strike action by the reemergence of the League.

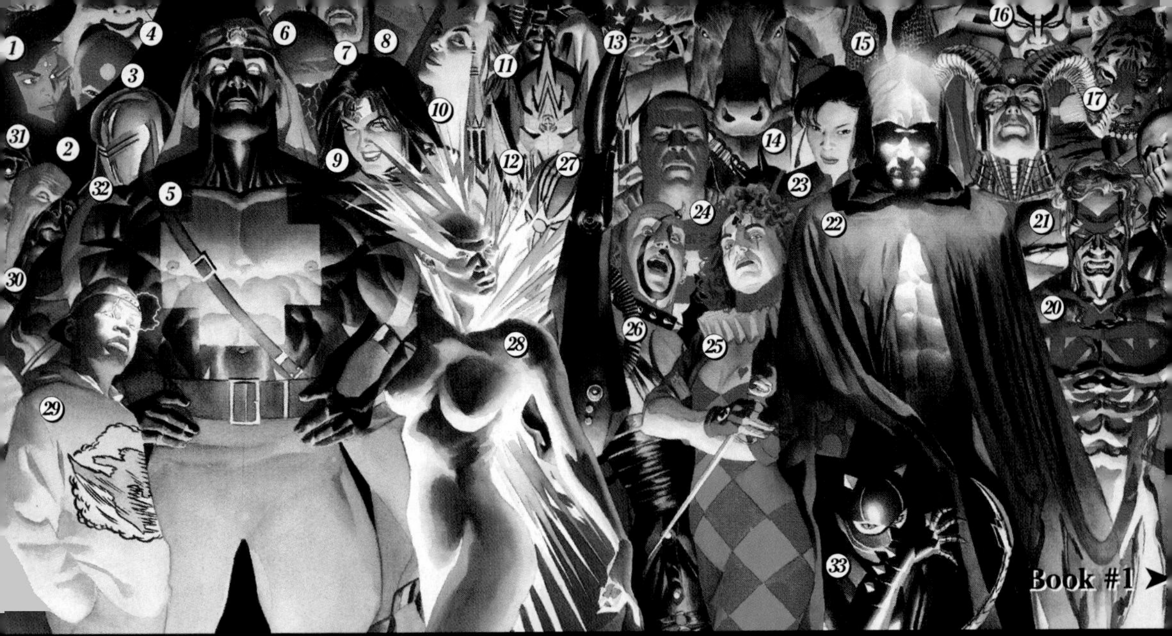
Book #1

1. Original Red Tornado - *Ma Hunkel armored with more than a pot for a helmet*
2. Hawkman - *combining the spirit of the old with the otherworldly flesh of the new*
3. Lady Marvel - *formerly Mary Marvel, caretaker of the Power of Shazam*
4. King Marvel - *formerly Captain Marvel Jr., caretaker of the Power of Shazam*
5. Aleea Strange - *half-human, half-alien daughter of Adam Strange and Alanna Strange*
6. Human Bomb - *still the same combustible hero of old*
7. Midnight - *a spirit manifesting itself as a living smoke cloud*
8. The Whiz - *son of Lady and King Marvel, and natural inheritor of the Power of Shazam*
9. Captain Comet - *Silver Age icon and one-time epitome of human perfection*
10. Bulletman II - *modern steel-coated human bullet*
11. Brainiac's Daughter-*the living computer's human progeny, and ancestor of Brainiac 5*
12. Bulletgirl II - *modern steel-coated human bullet*
13. Robotman III - *Victor Stone, formerly Cyborg, now an organism made of liquid metal*
14. Starman VIII - *formerly Star Boy, from the 30th Century*
15. Golden Guardian III - *second body cloned from the original Golden Age shield-bearer, the Guardian*
16. Powerman - *robot minion of Superman*
17. Hourman III - *current inheritor of the mantle with none of the time limits implied by the name*
18. Sandman IV - *formerly Sandy the Golden Boy, for whom the sands of time have stood still*
19. Red Tornado III - *fire-haired, wind-manipulating successor to the throne*
20. Living Doll - *daughter of Doll Man and Doll Girl*
21. Tornado - *re-formed spirit of the Tornado Champion*
22. Avia - *Big Barda and Mister Miracle's mega-rod-bearing daughter*
23. Atlas - *legendary demigod figure*
24. Atom-Smasher - *formerly Nuklon, godson of the original Atom*
25. Donna Troy - *formerly Wonder Girl, Troia, and Darkstar, now an Amazonian champion*
26. The Ray II - *son of the original, and Lord of Light*
27. Wonder Woman - *former Amazonian princess and now Superman's second-in-command*
28. Red Robin - *formerly Nightwing, Dick Grayson, the original Robin, is following in his mentor's footsteps again*
29. Norman McCay - *a preacher and the Spectre's human anchor*
30. Red Arrow - *formerly Speedy, the Arsenal, now following more closely th methods of his mentor, Green Arrow.*
31. Superman - *reluctant leader of the superhumans and still the greatest hero of any age*
32. Aquaman II - *formerly Aqualad, now inheritor of his mentor's mantle*
33. Power Woman - *formerly Powe Girl, and still a major superhuman wrecking machine*
34. The Flash - *emanating from the Speed Force, the future Flash may hold all the spirits of the previous incarnations*
35. The Green Lantern - *merging his lantern into himself, he is the most powerful champion of that name*

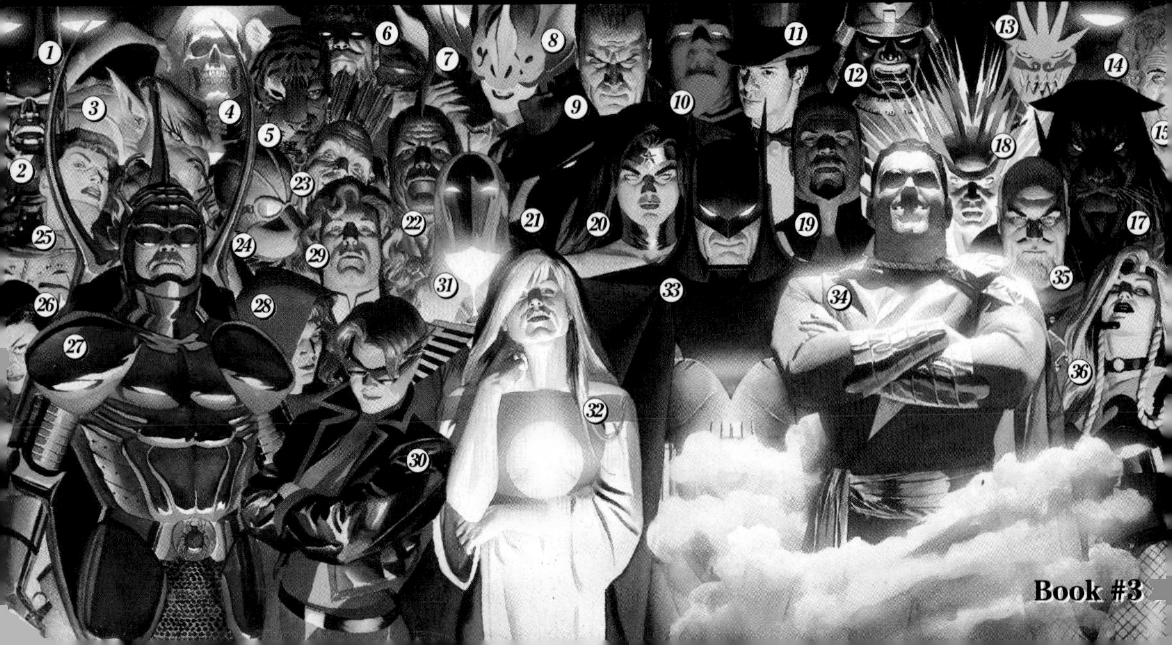
Book #3

Book #2

EVOLUTION

The Development of the Orion Pages

Make no mistake. This is not, in its strictest sense, "director's cut" material. These aren't rediscovered "missing pages" that somehow got lost behind Alex's filing cabinet one Tuesday. They do, however, comprise a sequence Alex had envisioned painting from very early on: Orion on Apokolips, having usurped his father Darkseid's throne. Alex never lost the desire to paint this image, not even after (striking though it might be) we could find no room for it within the strict page count of the original monthly series. The elbow room of an expanded collected edition, however, gave Alex the opportunity to indulge himself—and you. But what to make of this after-the-fact sequence? We didn't even know where to put it within the narrative until using Orion suggested Orion's brother-of-sorts, Mr. Miracle, Super-Escape Artist. How could we use him? Well…who better to design an inescapable gulag? Would Superman think of that? Not necessarily…but Orion would suggest it if Superman were to come to Apokolips asking to use the planet as a prison, a dumping ground. Still, the Last Son of Krypton would never suggest uprooting natives from their homeworld. However, given where we were in the story just before gulag construction began, Superman would absolutely consult with Orion, the ultimate Dog of War. In fact, their conversation would allow us a chance to touch upon something missing from our original series: Superman's inability to comprehend the dark potential of his own power…

Mark Waid

An example of one of the many photo references used by the artist.

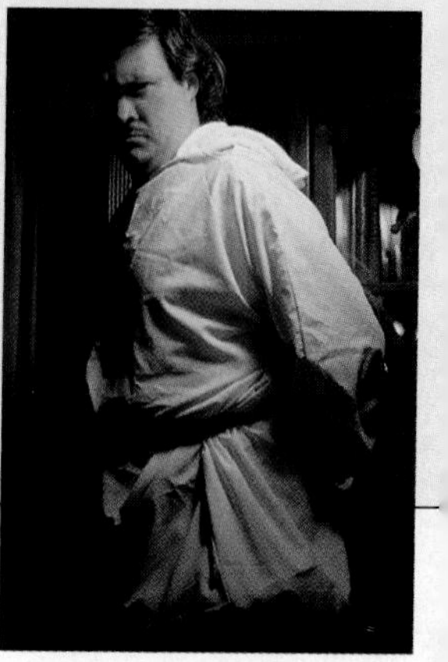

KINGDOM COME/New Orion Sequence/Ms. Page 2

PAGE TWO

PANEL ONE: LOOKING PAST ORION TOWARDS SUPERMAN. BIG PANEL, LOTS OF ROOM FOR CONTRAST BETWEEN THE BRIGHT, COLORFUL, SHINING MAN OF STEEL AND THE DISMAL ROOM AROUND HIM. IN FACT, DOES IT WORK TO HAVE ANOTHER "WINDOW" BEHIND SUPERMAN SO WE CAN CONTRAST HIM TO MORE OF THE OUTSIDE TERRAIN?

1 SUPERMAN: Far be it for ME to argue with the LORD of APOKOLIPS.

2 SUPERMAN: I'm IMPRESSED. Age has CALMED your legendary TEMPER. You seem fully in CONTROL.

PANEL TWO: OUR FIRST FULL SHOT OF ORION.

3 SUPER/off: You're more like Darkseid than EVER, Orion.

PANEL THREE: ORION, SUPERMAN. SUPERMAN LOOKS OUT THE WINDOW.

4 ORION: So it was written to BE. Our story has ALWAYS been a generational one.

5 ORION: It is said that MANY men eventually become their fathers.

6 SUPERMAN: I wouldn't KNOW.

7 SUPERMAN: I'd heard you'd finally...USURPED Darkseid's throne. I was curious to see what you'd ACCOMPLISHED in his STEAD.

PANEL FOUR: SUPERMAN, SLIGHTLY PAINED, LOOKS OUT OVER THE RUINS OF APOKOLIPS.

8 SUPERMAN: Not MUCH.

9 SUPERMAN: Frankly, Orion, of all the old allies I have ENCOUNTERED, YOU disappoint me the MOST.

10 SUPERMAN: You're a GOD. You have the power to CHANGE your world.

11 ORION/off: Or to DESTROY it.

PANEL FIVE: LOOKING PAST ORION AS HE STARES INTENTLY TOWARDS SUPERMAN, WHO CONTINUES TO LOOK OUT THE WINDOW.

12 ORION: You would be SURPRISED, I fear, at how easily ONE can lead to the OTHER.

Each page of *Kingdom Come* went through various stages of production and development. The first stage (not pictured here) was the preliminary outline. This summarized an entire sequence from the story. Consulting with the editors, Dan Raspler and Peter Tomasi, Mark then wrote a detailed script which paced the story by breaking down the contents of

Pencil Artwork
(actual size: 11 1/8" x 17 1/2")

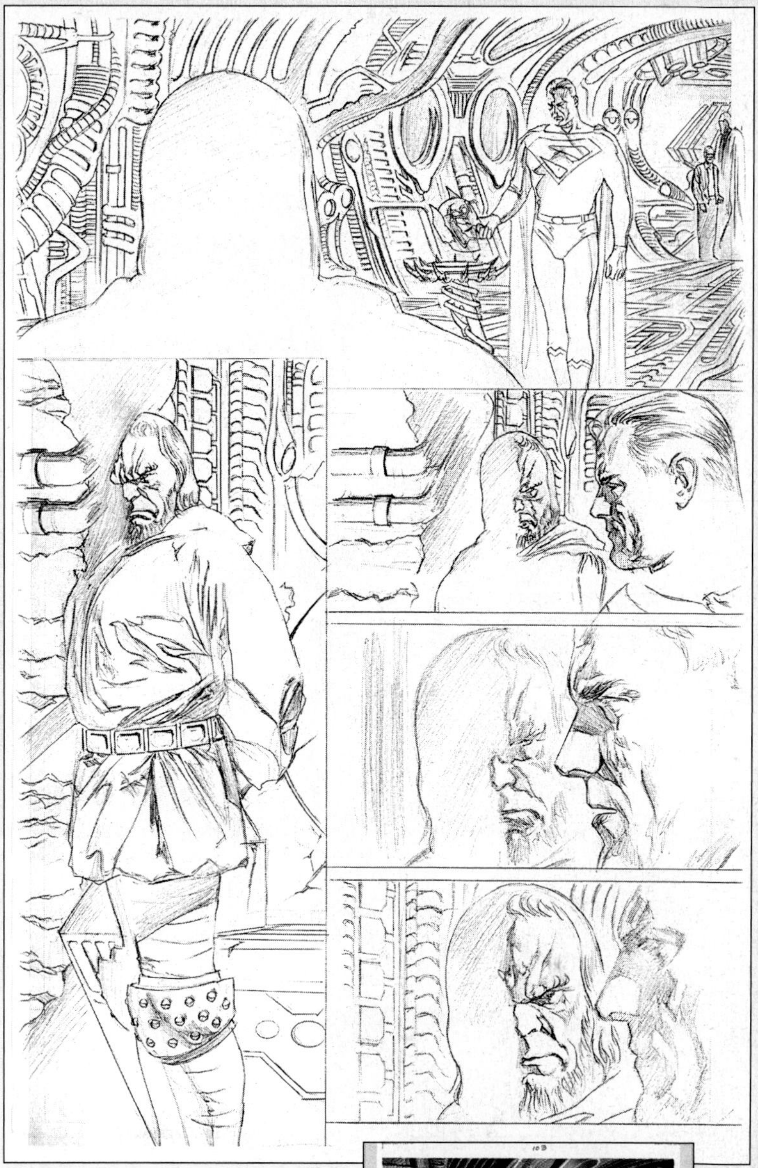

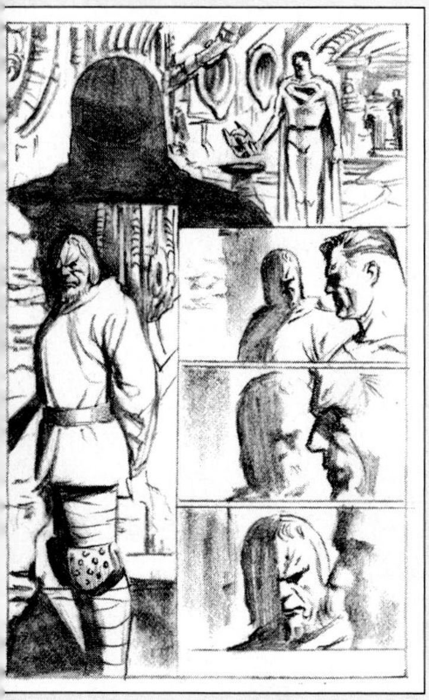

Thumbnail Rough
(actual size: 3 1/8" x 4 15/16")

each page. The dialogue as well as the setup for each and every panel were presented in text for Alex to then visually represent.

Before producing full-size artwork, Alex drew small thumbnail roughs which allowed him to work out compositional problems. This provided an opportunity for all involved to check the pacing of the story prior to producing the actual finished art.

Once all notes, modifications, and approvals were received, the thumbnail images were transferred onto oversize boards that eventually became the finished artwork. Copies of the pencilled art were made in order for Peter Tomasi to map out the placement of the word balloons. (Note the differences between the script and the art, which necessitated a reorganization of the placement of the word balloons within the various panels.) The balloon placements were then sent to Todd Klein, the letterer, so he could create and letter the word balloons from the script. In most cases, lettering is done directly on the art board. For *Kingdom Come*, as with most painted books, the finished lettering was placed on an acetate overlay.

Alex then rendered the images with gouache paints. First, he did a monochromatic black & white stage to fully detail all the forms, and then he layered over the color transparently. Some opaque painting and airbrushed lighting effects were also used. The lettering and painted art were then combined and sent to the separator to produce the finished comic page.

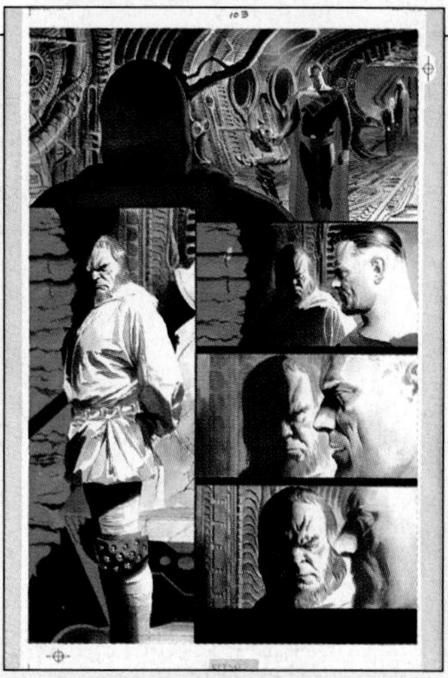

Finished Painted Art
(The finished version of this page can be found on page 103 of the Kingdom Come collection.)

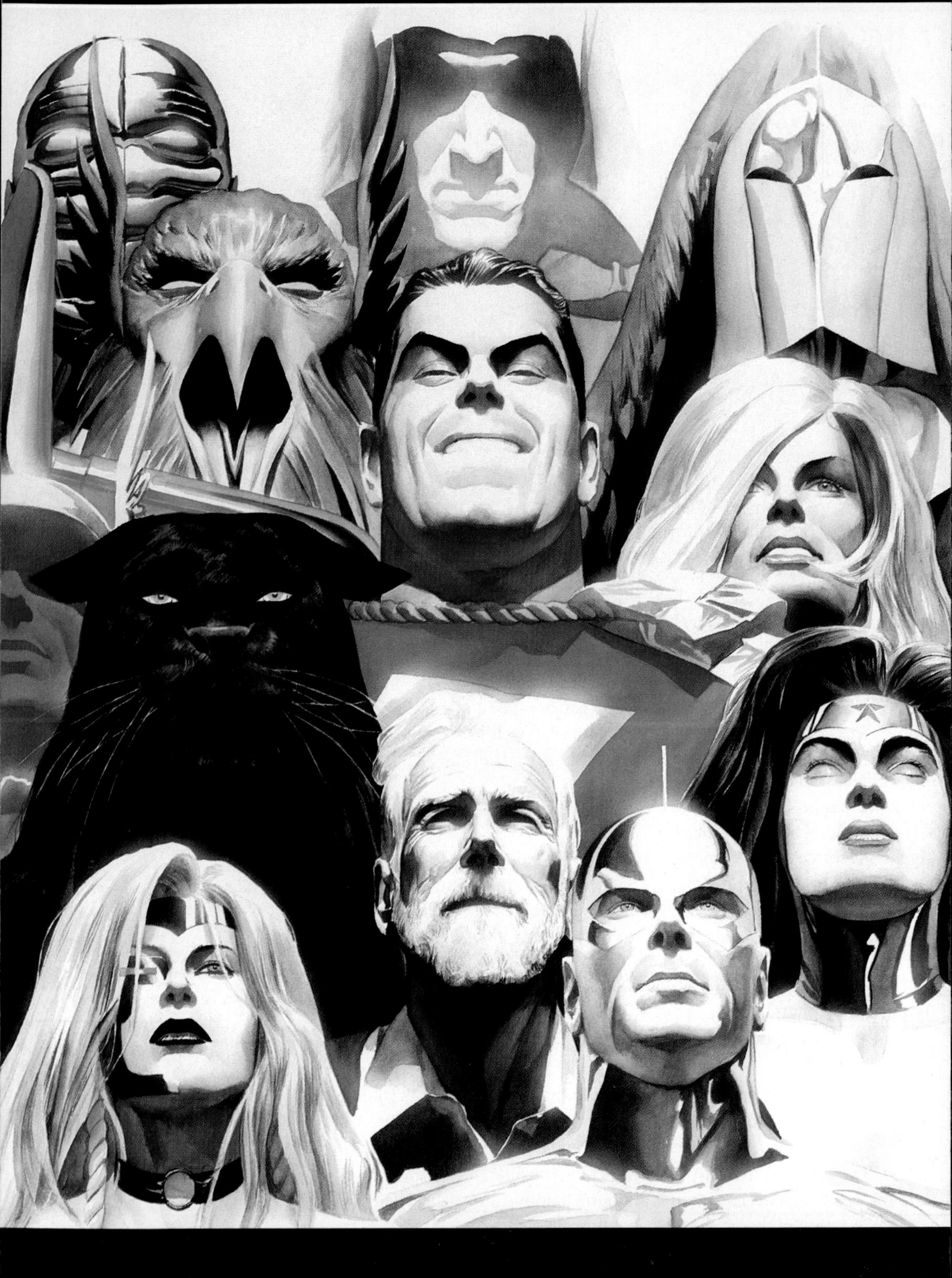

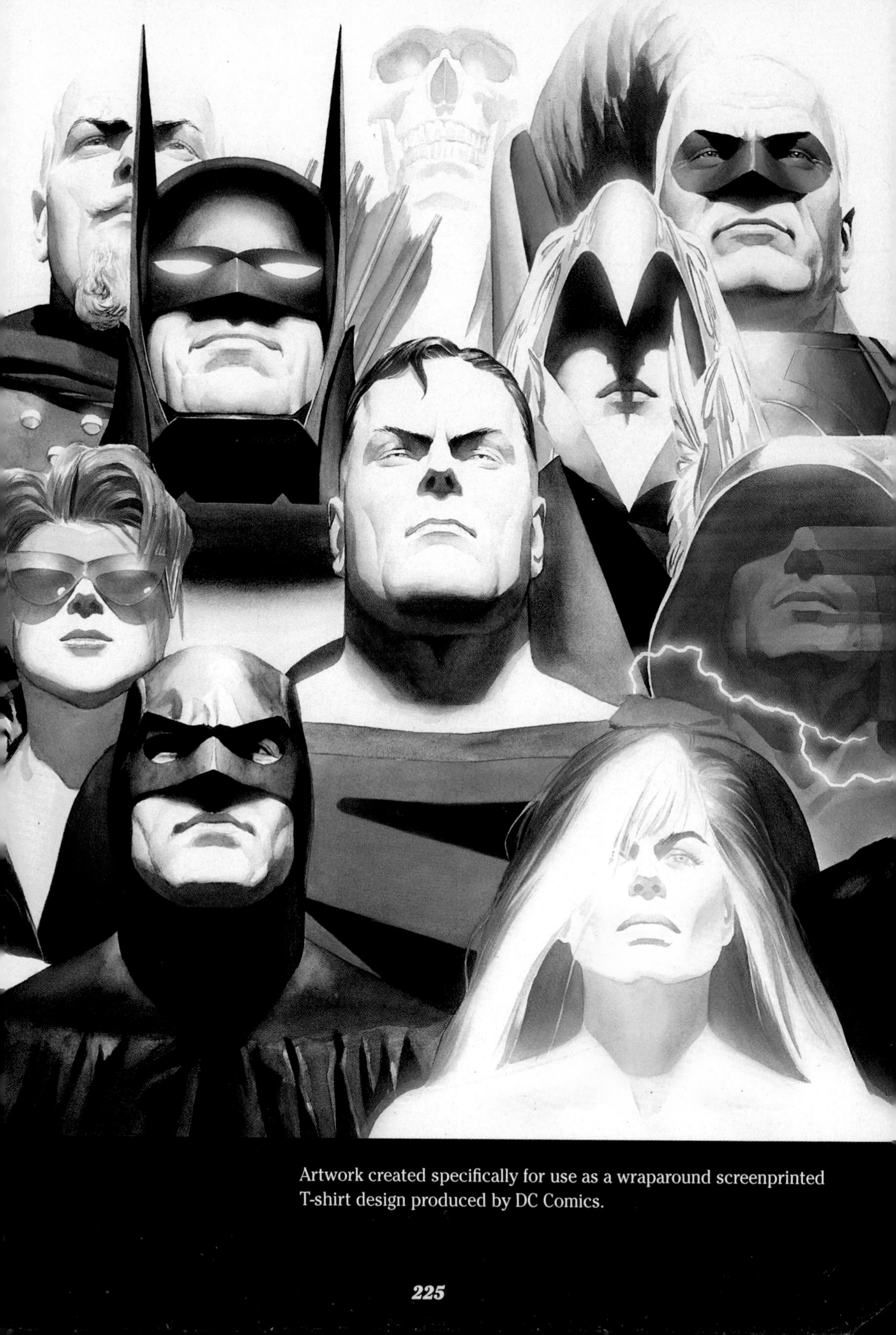

Artwork created specifically for use as a wraparound screenprinted T-shirt design produced by DC Comics.

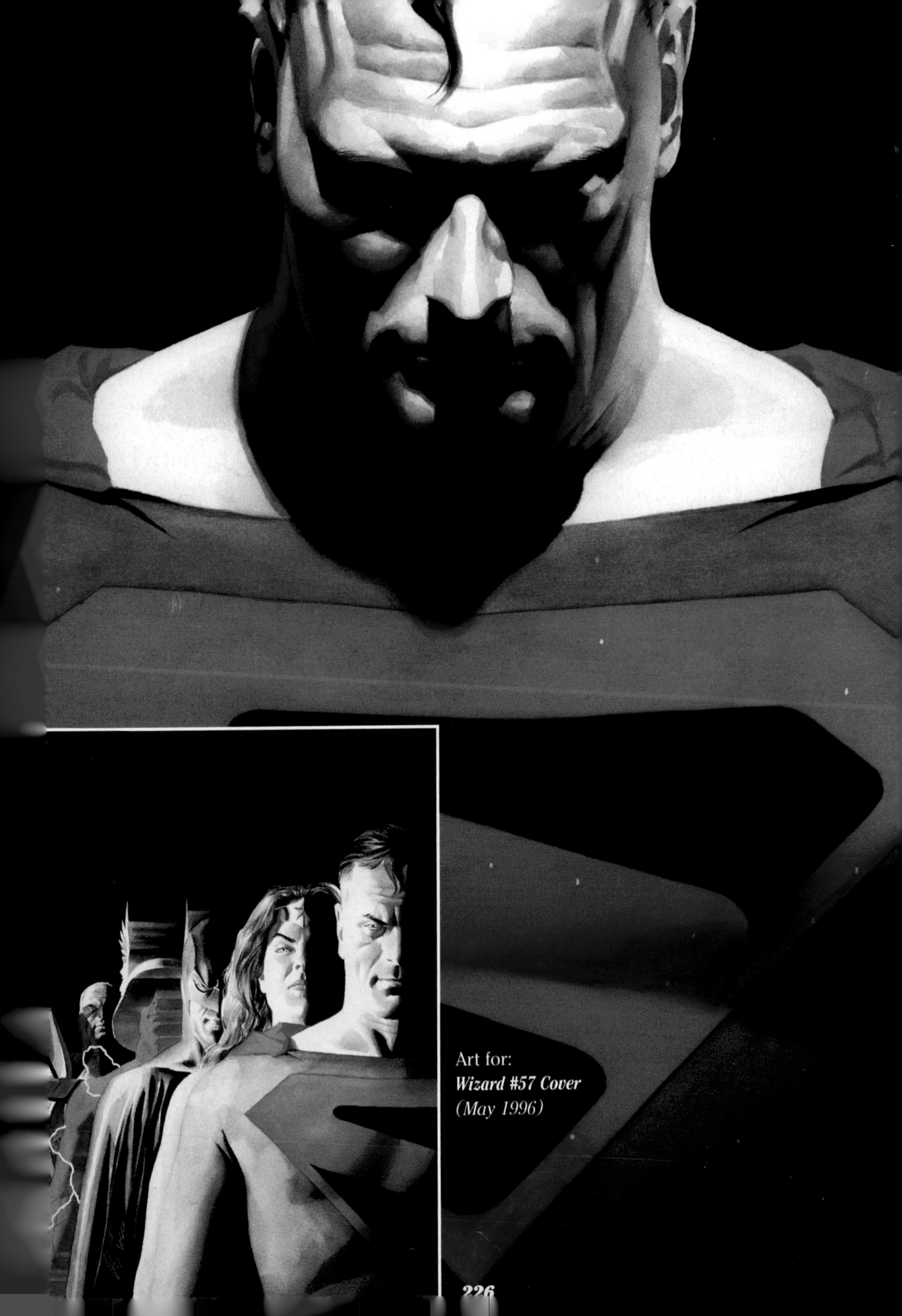

Art for:
Wizard #57 Cover
(May 1996)

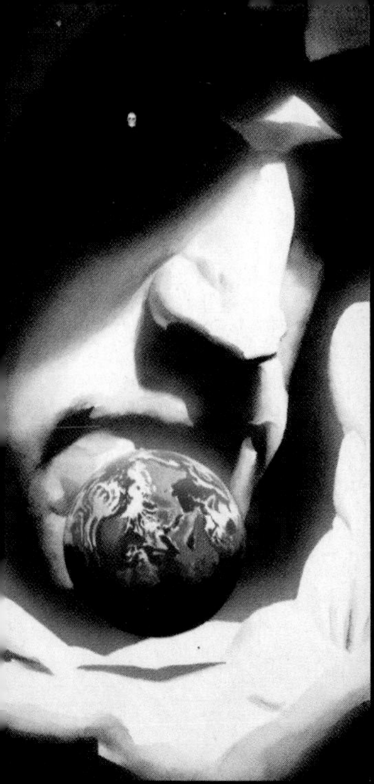
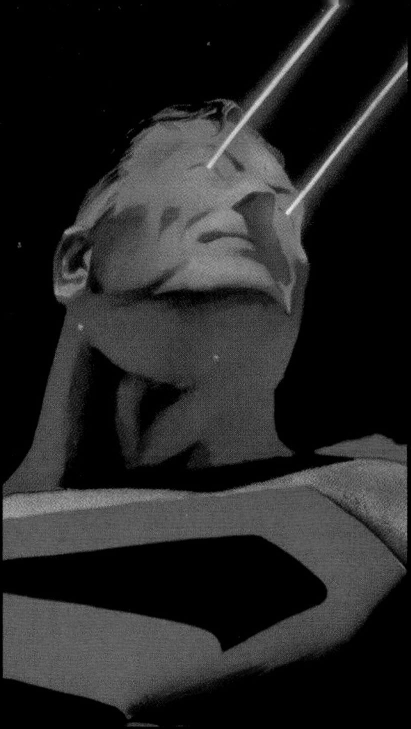
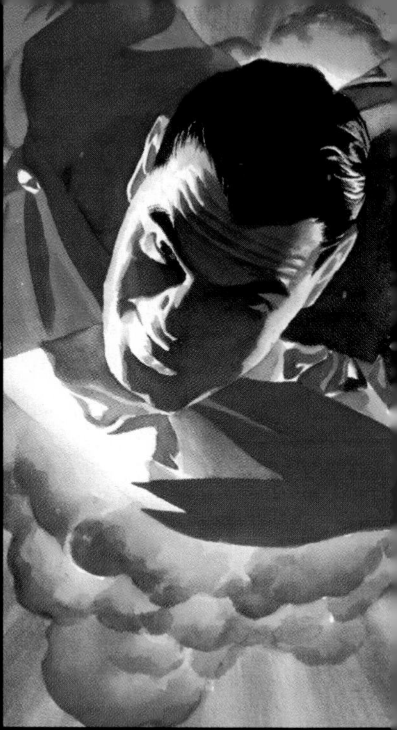

New artwork created for six bonus Creator Collection cards that were part of the *Kingdom Come* trading card set produced by Fleer/SkyBox. 12,000 boxes of these cards were produced for sale.

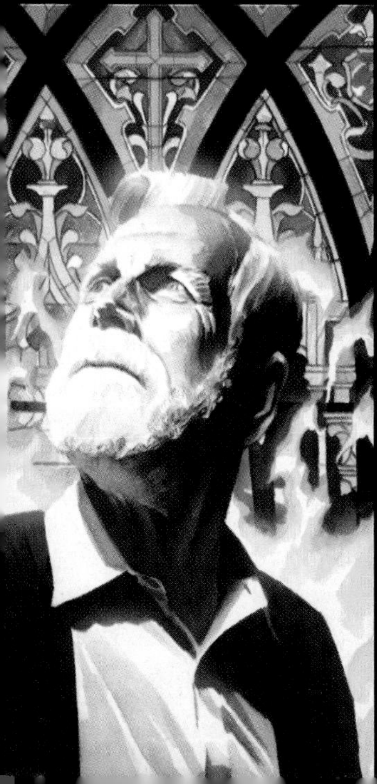
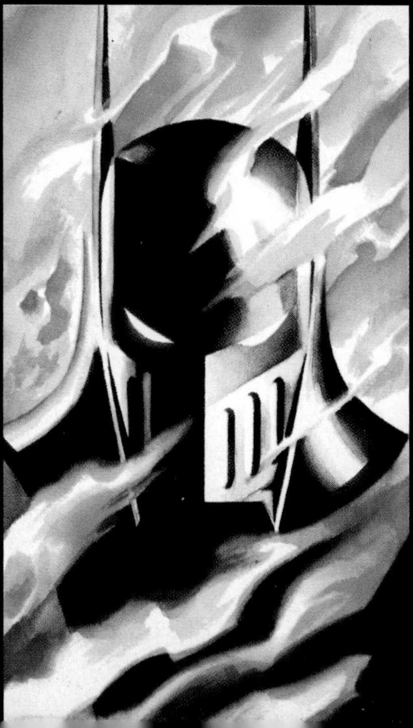
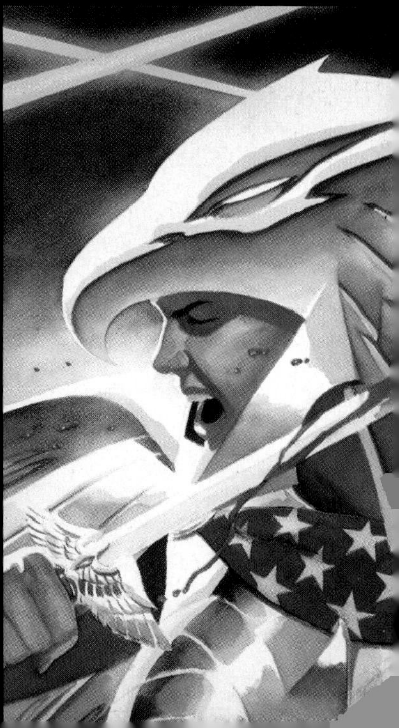

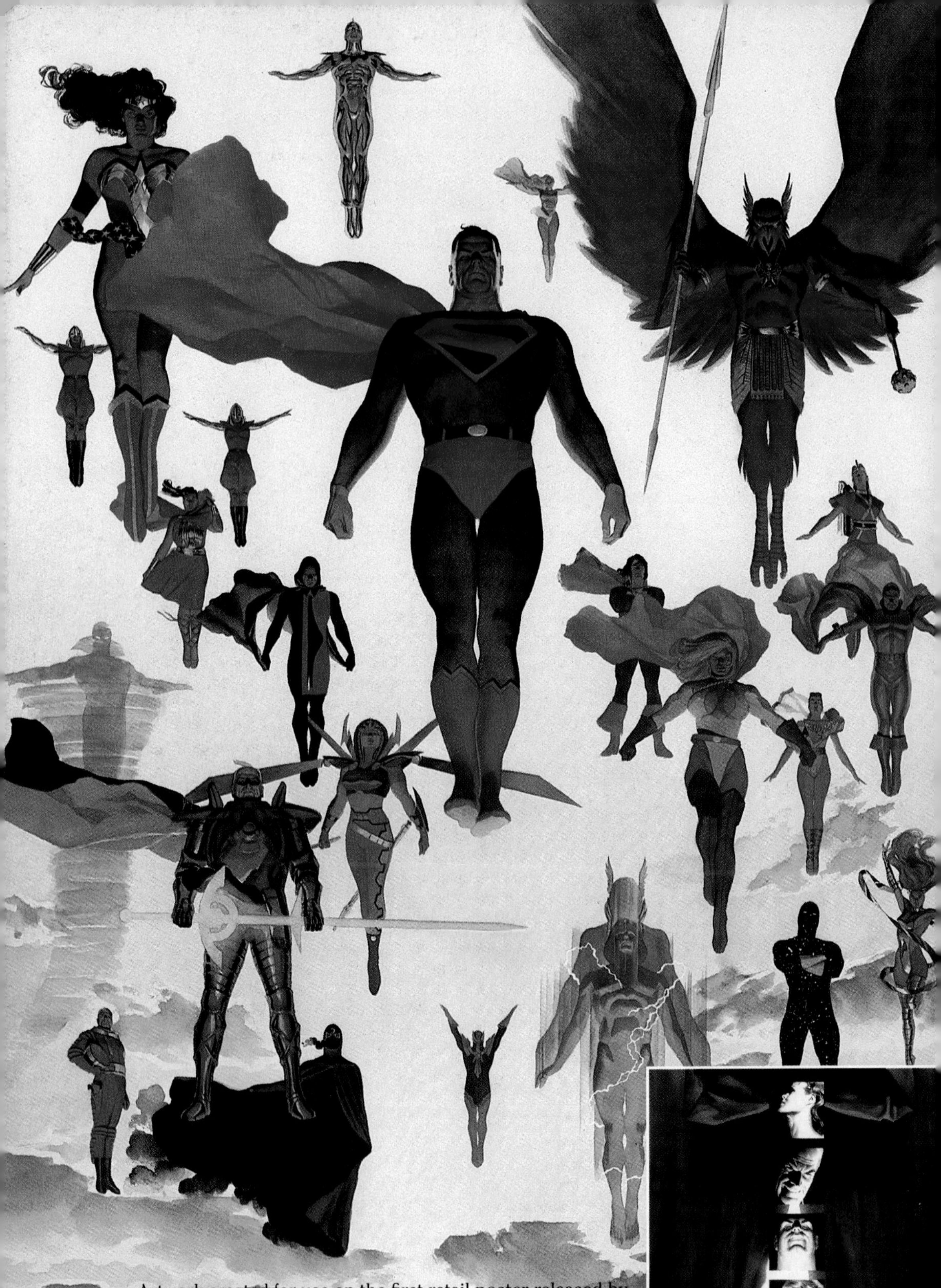

Artwork created for use on the first retail poster released by DC Comics. Poster measures *22"x 34"*. Second retail *Kingdom Come* poster (not shown) pictures the covers from the first three issues.

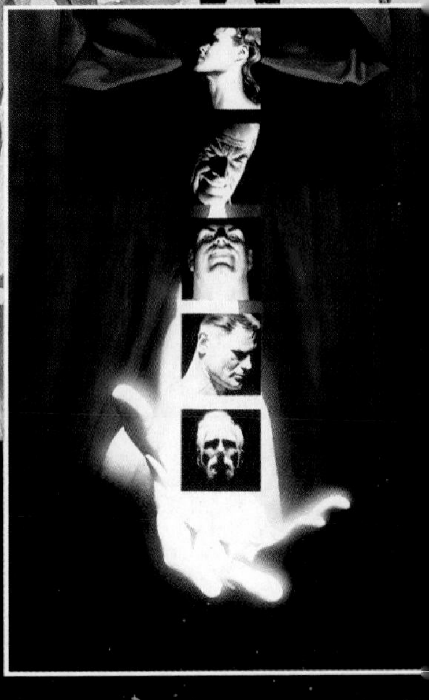

Artwork that was created for advance promotions for the series. Promotional poster issued by DC Comics measured *24"x 38"* and the text read *"The dreamer. The thunder. The bat. The eagle. The angel. Whose will be done? Kingdom Come."*

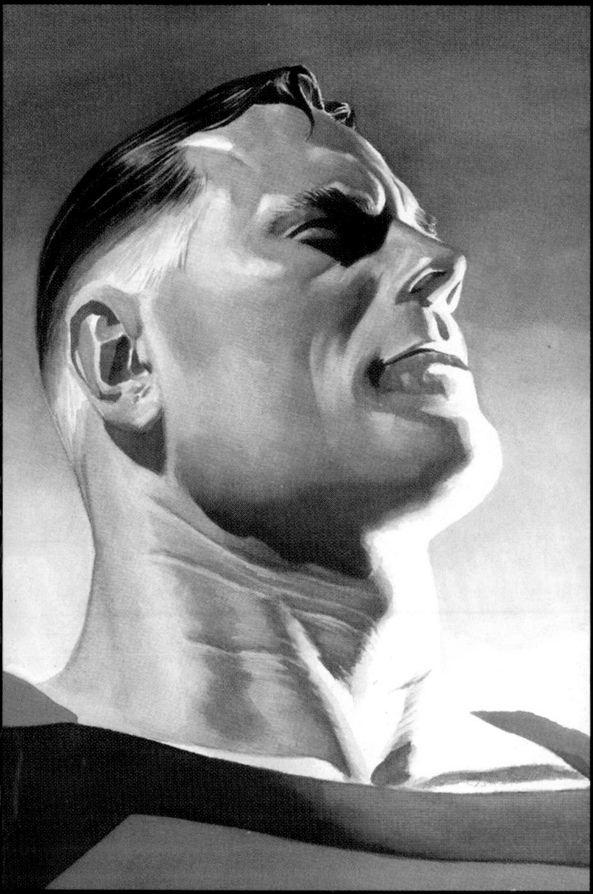

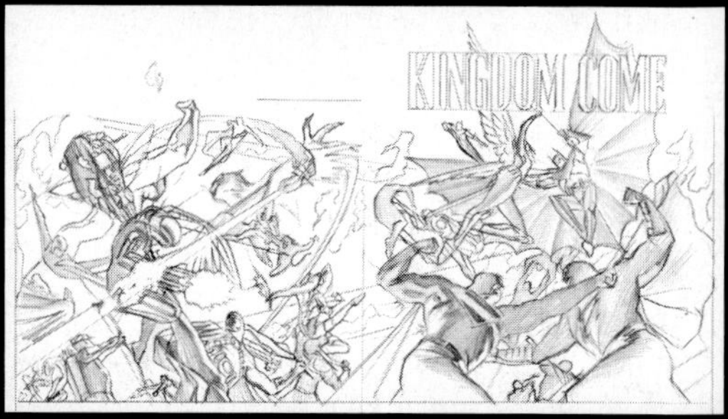
KINGDOM COME

Proposed cover rough for softcover edition of the *Kingdom Come* collection from DC Comics.

Color art from the cover of *Kingdom Come: Revelations* which was part of the *Deluxe Kingdom Come* limited-edition package produced by Graphitti Designs for DC Comics.

Final wraparound color artwork (without copy), of the Warner/Aspect *Kingdom Come* novelization by Elliot S. Maggin. Eight new pieces of art (four color and four black and white), were created for inclusion in this book as well as the cover pictured here.

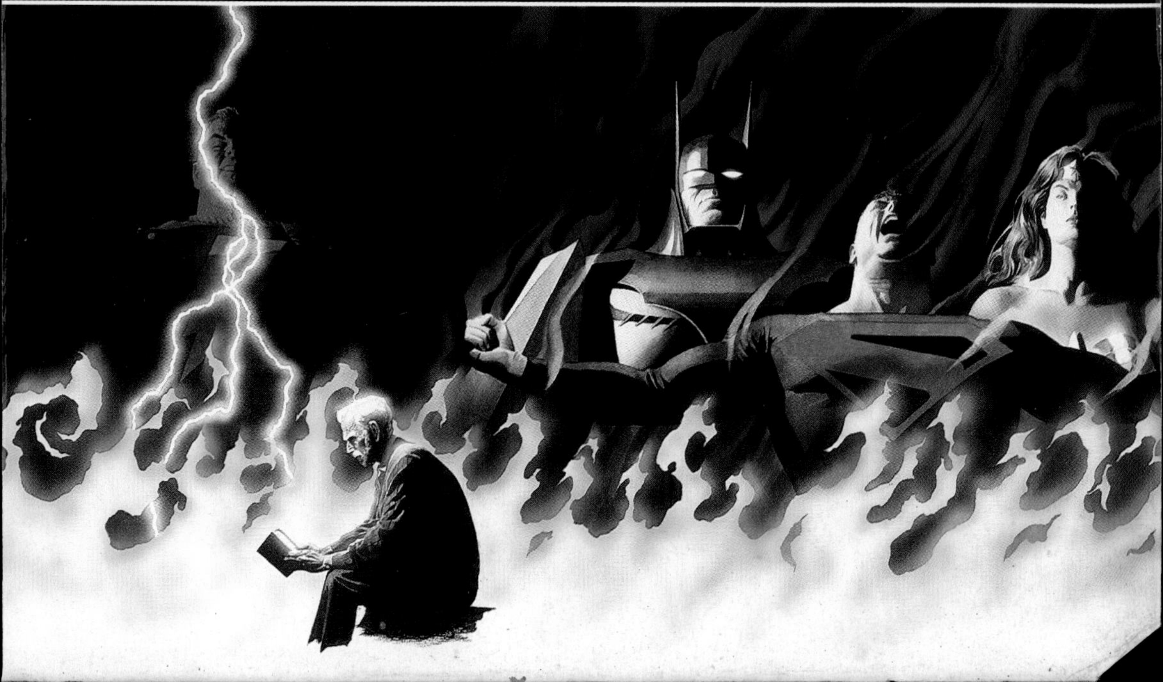

The two most important.

people responsible for

this project's existence

(and mine), are my folks,

Clark and Lynette. Clark

Norman Ross is certainly

the real-life basis for

Norman McCay and was

kind enough to model

for this project, helping

to make my tribute to

his profession and good

character possible.

Lynette Ross is the artist

who passed her gift on

to me. My very career is

a testament to her.

Alex Ross

FOR VANITY'S SAKE, I wish to show off my friends as to who played who with respect to the physical presence and personality they lent to my work. Their charity to model for me has been my greatest treasure.

Frank Kasy	Clark/Superman, Magog
Matt Paoletti	Bruce/Batman, John Jones
Lisa Beaderstadt	Diana/Wonder Woman, Big Barda
Sal Abbinanti	Bill/Captain Marvel
Ron Bogacki	Lex Luthor
Kenn Kooi	Red Robin/Ibn al Xu'ffasch
Jennifer van Winkle	Nightstar
Mark Braun	Ted/Blue Beetle
Kamilla Herr	Selina Kyle
Barry Crain	Edward Nigma
Jim Wisnewski	Vandal Savage, King
Mark Kolodny	Zatara II
Steve Darnall	Ralph Dibny
Jill Thompson	Joker's Daughter
Brian Azzarello	666
Tony Akins	Stars & Stripes, Condor
Scott Beaderstadt	Orion, Scott Free, Highfather, Zeus
Lindsay Ross	Captain Atom
Mike Spooner	Wesley Dodds

Karen Kooi   Holly Blessen   Sung Koo   Terry LaBan
Alex Wald   Ken Sanzel   Laura Strohl   Ruth Morrison
Aldrin Aw   Angel Medina   Maureen McTigue
Heidi MacDonald   David Vinson   Jason Liebig   Bob Kahan
Chantal d'Aulnis   Mike Carlin   Amy Schmetterling
Rob Simpson   Steve Korté   Scott Sonneborn   Scott Nybakken
Rich Markow   Nick Bertozzi   Laurie Kerr   Maura Healy

...and to the many others who unbeknownst to them found their way onto these pages.

ACKNOWLEDGMENTS

I've said this before, but it bears repeating: without the ideas and advice of Brian Augustyn, Tom Peyer, and Len Strazewski, the end result of the last three years' effort would not be *Kingdom Come*, but rather a handful of ill-sorted puzzle pieces that I would still be unsuccessfully trying to force-fit together.

Thanks are also due Dan Raspler and his assistant, Peter Tomasi, both of whom spent many a late night working editorial miracles, and to letterer Todd Klein, who graced us with work above and beyond the excellence of which he is routinely capable.

The two men, however, who will never know how much I owe them are Elliot S. Maggin and Christopher Reeve, who twice upon a time taught me who Superman really was…and who he could be. Together, they gave me one of the best friends I have ever had.

Mark Waid

My thanks also to Dan and Pete for their toil and sweat and for making my job all the easier with their great efficiency and frequent communication.

I am indebted to Sung Koo, James Robinson, Steve Darnall and Ruth Morrison for creative input.

The artists who lightened my load for character and prop design include David Williams, Tony Akins, Barry Crain, Dave Johnson, John Olimb, Aldrin Aw and Andrew Kudelka.

Costume props were provided by Lemen Yuen and David Williams. German and Japanese text was translated by Jennifer van Winkle and Alex Wald.

Thanks to Ken and Laura Sanzel of Four Color Images for enhancing the credibility of *Kingdom Come* and my work by mounting a successful gallery show of the artwork.

Thanks to Gethesmane Church for posing as itself.

Alex Ross